Imperial to International

Sheng Kung Hui: Historical Studies of Anglican Christianity in China

The Anglican (and Episcopal) tradition has been present in China for almost two hundred years. The purpose of this series is to publish scholarly, well-researched and authoritative volumes on the history of the Sheng Kung Hui ('Holy Catholic Church'), with an emphasis on its life and work in Chinese society. Sponsored by the Hong Kong Sheng Kung Hui, separate volumes in this series will include studies of particular people and institutions, as well as studies of the broader intellectual and social significance of Anglican involvement in Chinese history.

Series Editor: Philip L. Wickeri

Imperial to International

A History of St John's Cathedral, Hong Kong

Stuart Wolfendale

With a Foreword by Paul Kwong,
Archbishop of the Hong Kong Sheng Kung Hui

香港大學出版社
HONG KONG UNIVERSITY PRESS

Hong Kong University Press
The University of Hong Kong
Pokfulam Road
Hong Kong
www.hkupress.org

ISBN 978-988-8139-87-3 (*Hardback*)

British Library Cataloguing-in-Publication Data
A catalogue record for this book is available from the British Library.

10 9 8 7 6 5 4 3 2 1

Printed and bound by Paramount Printing Co., Ltd. in Hong Kong, China

To the memory of Francis Batson

Contents

Series Introduction

Sheng Kung Hui: Historical Studies of Anglican Christianity in China

The Anglican (and Episcopal) tradition has been present in China for almost two hundred years. The purpose of the series 'Sheng Kung Hui: Historical Studies of Anglican Christianity in China' is to publish scholarly, well-researched and authoritative volumes on the history of the Church as a contribution to the intellectual, cultural and religious history of modern China. With an in-depth focus on one particular denominational tradition, the series will present an interdisciplinary perspective that will also contribute to the history of Christianity in China. The emphasis throughout is on the life and work of the Church in society. Individual volumes are written for an educated audience and a general readership, with some titles more academic, and others of more general interest.

The spirit of Anglicanism is expressed by the Chinese term Chung Hua Sheng Kung Hui, meaning the 'Holy Catholic Church of China', the national church that was founded in Shanghai in 1912, and the first non-Roman church body in China. Anglicans stand between Protestants and Catholics in their approach to Christian tradition and church order, but are usually regarded as part of the Protestant movement in China. Since the nineteenth century, the Sheng Kung Hui has been involved in a wide range of education, medical and social welfare work, alongside efforts to spread the Christian message and establish the Church. In the first decades of the twentieth century, Chinese Sheng Kung Hui leaders began taking the lead. The Sheng Kung Hui has also played an important role in cultural exchange between China and the West, in Hong Kong and in Greater China.

Co-published by the Hong Kong University Press and the Hong Kong Sheng Kung Hui (Anglican Church), the first volume in the series is *Imperial to International: A History of St John's Cathedral, Hong Kong*. Subsequent volumes will include biographical studies, institutional histories, women's histories, a collection of essays and a general social and intellectual history of Chinese Anglicanism. It is hoped that the series will encourage further dialogue on the place of religion, particularly Christianity, in the history of modern China.

Philip L. Wickeri
Series Editor

List of Illustrations

Foreword

With a history of more than 160 years, St John's Cathedral is one of the oldest churches in Hong Kong and the oldest neo-Gothic cathedral in East Asia. During all this time, St John's has not only been a centre of Anglican activity in the territory, but a church for all peoples, a cathedral church for Hong Kong. St John's is deeply rooted in Anglican tradition, but at the same time part of the life of this important city. In the heart of the Central district, St John's Cathedral has been a site of Christian worship, a place for individual prayer and meditation, as well as a venue for public events and cultural activities. It is a church to which all are welcomed regardless of their beliefs. Hong Kong is an international city, and we like to think that St John's Cathedral is a spiritual centre for the community as a whole, open to the city and the wider world.

The book that now lies before you is the first full history of the Cathedral Church of St. John the Evangelist, to use the formal name of our church. It is also the first volume in our new series, 'Sheng Kung Hui: Historical Studies of Anglican Christianity in China', co-published by Hong Kong University Press and the Hong Kong Sheng Kung Hui (Anglican Church).

A few years ago, Andrew Chan, then Dean of the cathedral, and I asked Stuart Wolfendale to consider writing this history, and he committed himself to this task. As a member of St John's and a well-known journalist attuned to Hong Kong history, Stuart was the perfect choice. He has written a lively and engaging narrative, one that allows us to see the development of St John's from a colonial cathedral to an international church. He puts the history of the cathedral in the context of Hong Kong social history, especially in its first decades. In tracing the history of the cathedral as a building, a community and part of the fabric of life in this cosmopolitan city, he offers us many fascinating stories of people and events that have shaped the cathedral history.

This is not a story of the 'glorious past', but one that reveals the strengths and weaknesses of a community in historical perspective. In Wolfendale's view, the cathedral is a living community, rooted in the past but looking to the future. The building up of any church or religious institution is the product of the dedication and faithfulness of men and women, clergy and laity, who have also made their share of mistakes. This is not an 'official' history of the cathedral, and there has been no suggestion from any quarter to shape the history in a particular way or adhere to a theological perspective. I have never liked official church histories, for they always seem either very dull or not very real. There are controversial parts of any history, including this one, and I am sure that aspects of the narrative will raise eyebrows in some quarters. I hope this means that the book will provoke further discussion of our past, for this will help to influence our present and future.

As Wolfendale notes in his introduction, this is not a complete or comprehensive history of the cathedral, but a thoroughly researched study. Sadly, many cathedral records have been lost, especially those from the nineteenth century and the war years (1941–1945), and these are irreplaceable. Nevertheless, Wolfendale has unearthed reports, letters, minutes, photographs and other archival records that I did not know even existed. *Imperial to International* is therefore as full a history of the cathedral as we are likely to see for some time, and indeed, it may be seen as a model for future cathedral histories in this part of the world.

A cathedral church is the seat or the 'throne' of the diocesan bishop, an important episcopal *insignia*, and thus a 'mother church' (*matrix ecclesia*) dedicated to the worship of God. St John's Cathedral has been the seat of Hong Kong Anglican bishops since the arrival of Bishop George Smith, my predecessor and the founding bishop of what was from 1849 onward the Diocese of Victoria. Initially, the diocese included all of China and Japan, which made it the largest diocese of any church in the world. For the next one hundred years, the diocese was gradually reduced in size, and in 1951, we became the Diocese of Hong Kong and Macao. In 1998, the new Anglican Province of Hong Kong was inaugurated. St John's Cathedral then became not only the cathedral of the Diocese of Hong Kong Island, but the cathedral for the Province as well. This book centres on the history of the cathedral church, but it is also an important part of the larger history of Anglicanism in China as well.

Throughout our history, the cathedral has been served by outstanding clergy and lay leaders. In the mid-19th century, chaplains were appointed by the British Colonial Office, but subsequently they were named by the Bishop, in consultation with the Church of England Trust. Alfred Swann was appointed the first Dean of the cathedral in 1927. Most of the early clergy were English, but in the twentieth century, there were Eurasian and Chinese chaplains, as well as clergy from other parts of the world. Some cathedral clergy went on to distinguish themselves in church careers outside of Hong Kong. Leonard Wilson and H. W. (Harry) Baines became bishops of Singapore, and subsequently Birmingham and Wellington respectively. Barry Till and Michael Goulder had distinguished academic careers in England. Timothy Beaumont later became a politician and Liberal Peer, Lord Beaumont of Whitely. In 2005, Andrew Chan was installed as the first Chinese dean of the cathedral, a position he left in 2010 to become Bishop of Western Kowloon. Our new dean, installed last October, is Canon Matthias Der.

The clergy can never be the Church by themselves. This book shows how important the laity were for the development of St John's Cathedral. From its inception, the idea of building a cathedral in Hong Kong was a lay initiative. The laity have been the core of all cathedral committees, and they have lent their material and spiritual support to the life of the church and the wider community. Many of the laity used their expertise to help build up the cathedral, in tasks as varied as architectural advice, financial oversight, and the sharing of musical gifts. The laity pioneered in the mission and outreach work of the cathedral. The Street Sleepers Society in the 1920s, support for the Taipo Orphanage in the 1930s and the St James' Settlement beginning in the 1950s, as well as assistance with the Michaelmas Fair and support for Domestic Helpers—all these were lay initiatives. The names of many prominent figures in Hong Kong history, with distinguished careers in government, business and the financial sector will also be found in this book. Together with the countless numbers of women and men who have supported the cathedral through their prayers and contributions, laity and clergy working together have transformed St John's Cathedral from a colonial institution to the international community it has now become.

I heartily recommend this book to readers in Hong Kong, mainland China and overseas. It offers a perspective on Hong Kong history through the life of one institution, St John's Cathedral. Hong Kong is very much a secular city, but as this book shows, it has also been a society deeply influenced by people of faith and by religious communities and individuals. I hope this book will encourage readers to visit the cathedral for a quiet moment, a service of worship or a musical performance, for these have all been part of our history.

Paul Kwong
Archbishop of the Hong Kong Sheng Kung Hui
Lent 2013

Introduction

Up to this point, the Cathedral Church of St John the Evangelist has been served in print by a hardback handbook, *The Story of St John's Cathedral*, published by FormAsia and briskly written by journalist Stephen Vines, and by a softback, *St John's Cathedral Hong Kong: A Short History and Guide*, by Doreen King. Vines writes a concise account of the historical milestones, and King's particular contribution is an informed and expert summary of the fabric and furnishings upon which this book has gratefully drawn. *Imperial to International* moves on from both of them.

Any great and antique place of Christian worship in Asia which has survived and continues to breathe its faith is a phenomenon which deserves to be recorded. Anglican cathedrals in Asia are particularly rare phenomena which merit close attention. St John's in Hong Kong commands the particular attention which this book gives it, not just for its near pristine Victorian Gothic form set in a twenty-first-century Chinese city but for its testimony to the survival of organised Christian worship in Hong Kong from an era which we can barely recognise into an era we hardly dare make prediction for. This book looks not only at its architecture but at the development of its status, its liturgy, its ministry and charity, its social impact and, above all, the souls who populated it through its first one hundred and fifty years.

In September 2009, the Most Reverend Dr. Paul Kwong, Archbishop of the Hong Kong Sheng Kung Hui, whose seat St John's is, and then Dean the Very Reverend Andrew Chan asked me to write a thoroughgoing story of the church. Initially the dean conjured with the idea of an 'extended King'. The archbishop took it further and into hardback. He saw a spiritual and political history as well as one of structure and contents.

Archbishop Kwong added that he would like it to be 'readable' too. He was not looking for a work of microscopic academic propriety which set off ruthlessly along donnish tangents and performed feats of bar-bending to bring them back to the plot. He wanted people to put the book down and look forward to picking it up again. I have regarded this as one of the most important charges of my commission.

The commission was a generous one. It allowed the writer his own interpretation of events, which steers away from excessive idealism or hagiography towards a more realistic account. A consequence is that my views expressed are not necessarily those of the cathedral or of the Hong Kong Sheng Kung Hui. This book does not pretend to be an utterly complete history. It is a chronological medley of the important strains that ran through the life of St John's. It is not split into topic areas, which would have reduced it to a collection of essays and a great deal of repetition. It is a story during which, for certain topics, the narrative slows a bit, harks back and looks forward before resuming its pace. It remains, above all, a narrative.

As a story, there are parts which are missing. Records have vanished or were never properly kept in the first place. In a Christian congregation in which there was familiarity and trust, matters more to do with mission and spirit and less with law and cash were handled by word of mouth or unofficial jottings. The Japanese Occupation accounts for some of the shortfall and for the fact that, after the economic devastations of their stay in Hong Kong, paper of any sort became attractive as cooking fuel. Over a century and a half, there will have been remarkable instances of enterprise, enmity and charity of which we will know nothing.

There are also tantalising and quite unpredictable clues to structure and behaviour at the cathedral that can only be found in references in other subject areas. An aside remark in Church Missionary Society (CMS) correspondence or between church schoolteachers or government servants or Freemasons can throw a thin but fascinating beam on something that may have been going on in St John's. The history of the cathedral is a subject about which there will always be something new to be found. I am aware, for example, that the 'disestablishment' of the bishopric from 1874 and the Second World War and its immediate aftermath are periods on which more detail may exist but distantly and in the shade.

This book is not an exposure of what was previously unknown. It is an attempt to gather together and put into order material which has already been uncovered to some degree and from sources which are already familiar to many.

The Hong Kong Public Records Office (PRO), relocated in a Kwun Tong public housing estate to test the ardour of true scholars, is where all the official records of St John's Cathedral are kept up to 1965. These include the minutes of trustees meetings and their correspondence, minutes of some committees and guilds, an uneven spread of birth, marriage and death registers, *Church Notes* magazine and a few references to chapels of ease. Diocesan records at the PRO include the bishops' 'scrapbooks'—interesting if indeed scrappy correspondences and diary entries of bishops up to and including Gilbert Baker.

These records seem to have been a primary source for G. B. Endacott and D. E. She's *The Diocese of Victoria, Hong Kong: A Hundred Years of Church History, 1849–1949*. This work includes a helpful narrative account of the major constitutional events in the cathedral's life up to the Second World War. The records also informed Colonel R. F. Johnston, a Cathedral Council member who typed up a manuscript history of St John's in 1937, when the volumes were still in the church. This document was uncovered in the cathedral's own record office along with more recent official records.

Whereas the PRO records are open to the public with the permission of the Dean of St John's, the more recent records, dating from 1963, are kept in the cathedral office and can only be viewed by appointment. These include all council minutes and Annual Church Meeting reports, the latter being published in *St John's Review*. Within this more contemporary material are folded occasional fading gems of correspondence or memoranda from earlier decades which await rearrangement. It was from one such paper, a letter to Bishop Hall, pressed between dull accounts folders, that I learned that Dean Wilson, later the legendary wartime Bishop of Singapore, was less than universally liked among his parishioners.

There are more documents of interest in a series of basement rooms in Bishop's House, Lower Albert Road. A wealth of diocesan material has collected there over the years, initially, perhaps, because the occupying Japanese and the foragers who came after them did not intrude there, and pre-war documents were allowed to survive. This space is a prime example of where material telling the history of the diocese in other parts may well come to have a bearing on St John's. Its cataloguing was not quite in time for this book.

The fascinating and unimaginably painstaking card index of local people compiled by Carl T. Smith, historian of Hong Kong Christianity, and kept in the misnamed Central Public Library in Causeway Bay, often helped to flesh out names penned in the well-drilled Victorian handwriting of the minute books. Attendances at trustees meetings were recorded using only initials for Christian names. The minutes themselves followed the tradition of the passive voice and collectivity in decisions. Many of those listed left no trace of an opinion, let alone an identity, and could disappear either to 'home' or the graveyard without even getting onto the jury list either. In many cases, Carl Smith's monitoring of the courts and the obituaries gives these early church stalwarts a skein of identity.

The newspapers were available too at the Hong Kong University Libraries along with Colonial Records Office documents. The latter have already been well mined to discover the details of the cathedral's construction and financing and the colonial government's involvement. I have simply attempted to put the accounts in order and sieve the sensible from the implausible.

Newspapers I have resorted to for reportage on events that took place in and around St John's which the cathedral itself has left no record of. Sometimes the press could not be bothered with it, or an edition has been lost. I have included accounts of church services where they are particularly significant, moving or unusual and not just because references exist; otherwise, the book would become a catalogue of orders of service.

Structure and fabric receives attention where it matters, but this is not a handbook of architectural minutia which goes into detail over every roof repair and exterior wash. Nor does it trace the replacement of every altar frontal. That would not be the sort of book you would want to pick up again.

Attention has been paid to the people, long forgotten, who wore out the rattan in the rosewood pews and whose voices were absorbed by the silence of the stone and brick. Many hours have been spent with *Church Notes* and its successor, *St John's Review*, as well as electronic copies of *The Outpost*, the magazine of the Victoria Diocesan Association, trying to hear these people. The church itself is an impressive building in its quality, simplicity and neatness of design, but the overarching fascination to it is how its congregations of foreigners survived and even flourished to support it in this far-from-Christian land.

The story is not an entirely comfortable one to tell. The extraordinary geographical position which the newly founded church was placed in 1849 created a dichotomy in its purpose which was never completely resolved. It began as a colonial parish church for Hong Kong's expatriate British. Within a year, it also became the seat of a diocesan bishop with a missionary purpose for the whole of China. St John's could not opt to move between the roles when it suited it. They existed as 'parallel universes', as one dean described it, sometimes touching, even overlapping, but most often, keeping a distance.

As a colonial cathedral playing the role of imperial parish, St John's was always very grand and civic in its function. It was the state church of the colony. All the events of empire were celebrated there, and the national services held in the churches of London were duplicated as best they could be. The cathedral would be packed with Westerners and Chinese, and services in both languages might take place during the great day. Yet on an ordinary Sunday, for the first hundred years of its life at least, rarely was a Chinese to be seen at matins, and services would be dutifully, if sometimes thinly, attended by the white administrators and merchants of the colonial establishment to whom responsibility for St John's survival ultimately fell.

Their priorities and those of the missionary bishops, who either fancied the cathedral might do more towards China mission or put it at the back of their minds, were hard to reconcile. At the very least, St John's congregation believed the bishop should be more often at home as a bishop of Hong Kong. The bishops themselves—all CMS men up to the time of R. O. Hall—stated quite bluntly that their main responsibility was to spread the Word in China. This led to the existence of two Anglican churches in China, the English and the Chinese, each with its own structure. Even when China was removed from the equation in 1950, the distinction lived on within the Hong Kong rump until 1974.

A truth at once uncomfortable but honest to arrive at is that St John's Cathedral was never effectively a diocesan cathedral. It was the 'cathedral', the seat of the city's bishop, but it was rarely a focus or a resource for the parishes within that diocese. It was, however, a very effective civic church, a focus of thanksgiving or remembrance for the whole city, even as the leading lights within that city shifted from Western to Chinese faces and the faiths of the establishment became less and less often Christian.

There were moments when the parallel universes overlapped, and they were inspiring. Examples are the ordination of Lo Sam Yuen, the first Chinese to be made a deacon in Hong Kong, and the consecration of Bishop Mok Shao Tsang in 1935, prior to him becoming Bishop of Canton.

Yet, for the most part, the order of the day was linguistic and racial distinction, not of an antipathetic sort but one easily resorted to by two cultures which were happy to view themselves as mutually exclusive. Up to 1941, at least, St John's was, for the most part, a church of the British and their sympathisers. The inevitable detachment of that once exclusive, colonial congregation from the mission work of its bishops among the Chinese has left a legacy in the organic relationship between the cathedral and the Chinese parishes, even though the diocesan pattern and the constitution of St John's have altered beyond recognition.

On the face of it, it would seem difficult to write a sympathetic history of a Christian organisation which operated in a world of colonial exclusivity. Yet writing history is neither about delving for sentiment nor arriving at judgement. That, as sensible Christians know, lies elsewhere. There is no purpose in bringing the haughty libertarianism of the twenty-first century to bear upon men and women who believed in all sincerity that they were trying to live their very best by the precepts of God, king and country.

I have tried to write about St John's in the light of the social conditioning by which the cathedral's succeeding generations lived. When I describe certain situations in which behaviour has been somewhat archaic, I hope I will be excused if my tongue is sticking through my cheek a little. Otherwise, I have seen people of a different age going about God's business with a period purpose and admire them for it.

If I have felt any annoyances at the material, it has been with some expatriate church people of the more immediate past who persisted in a suburban, Little Englander parochialism which kept China at bay as effectively as a 'members only' recreation club. One eminent historian in Hong Kong told me that he only liked to write about people who are 'good 'n' dead'. In the case of the St John's story, I could not afford myself that luxury. For those who I refer to who are good 'n' living and don't like what they read, may they forgive me as they are commanded.

The narrative proper stops around 1998. That is the point by which the last significant structural alteration within the cathedral compound was completed. Most of the current outreach ministries had been set up. All the present daughter churches had been established. The clergy structure and the council and committee structures were all very much what we have in 2011. At the diocesan level, the Province of the Hong Kong Sheng Kung Hui had just been created. The remains of the colonial period were about to end.

The diocese had its first Chinese bishop. The cathedral was yet to see Andrew Chan as its first dean. Yet, by this point, it is already moving towards a multinational purpose which will reinforce its civic importance to Hong Kong as an international finance centre and, in a sense, compensate for the historical imbalances which prevented it from being a purely diocesan centre.

Chapter 1
Genesis, 1841–1850

On the afternoon of Thursday, 11 March 1847, in Hong Kong Harbour, a piratical craft, with all the appearance of a mandarin boat, fired upon a Chiu Chow (Chaozhou) vessel. It was an ambush. The lead pirate was known to the Chiu Chow ship's master as a man to whom he had sold salt. The imposter craft carried twelve-pounder guns of European mounting, according to a report on the incident in the *Friend of China*.[1]

A few column inches along, the paper gloatingly noted that, since Hong Kong had so thoroughly usurped Macau as an enclave in the six years since the Union flag had been hoisted at Possession Point, the Portuguese colony was 'ruined and insupportable'. It was rumoured that France or the United States was considering buying it.

On that same day, at the centre of this typically confused Hong Kong canvas of lawlessness and a risk being well run, the governor, Sir John Davis, was laying the foundation stone of the colonial Church of St John the Evangelist, halfway up 'Maritime Hill' in the City of Victoria. The first Colonial Chaplain, Vincent J. Stanton, made an address based on Matthew 12:6: 'I tell you something greater than the temple is here'. He was, hopefully, out of earshot of the bogus mandarin's twelve-pounders.

We cannot see the foundation stone anymore. We do not even know exactly where it is, short of it being somewhere under the nave. Records tell us what it says down there under the concrete:[2]

> The cornerstone of this church, dedicated to St John the Evangelist and destined for the worship of Almighty God, was laid by Lord J F Davis, Baronet, a legate of the British Queen in China and bedecked with proconsular dignity on the fifth day of the Ides of March in the tenth year of the reign of Queen Victoria AD 1847.

Though Davis was a baronet and so merely 'Sir John', he gained an unwarranted peerage in translation from the Latin. Also odd is the use of the 'Ides of March', which was the fifteenth of the month in the Roman calendar, marking a full moon. How one can have a 'fifth day' of it and line it up as the eleventh is an early puzzle of St John's.

It had taken seven years just to achieve this stone-laying although events were to pick up speed from here on. Yet, though fundraising had been criticised as dilatory, and discussion over costings and architecture had taken up years and thousands of sea miles in a time before the telegraph, there is little trace of any doubt amongst the traders, military, clergy and officials who lived there that there should and would be a church of the Anglican rite built on that island.

Scepticism about the future of Hong Kong seemed to be much the preserve of officials in Britain. Palmerston's complaint that Hong Kong was a barren rock with barely a house upon is set to be quoted in perpetuity. His successor, Lord Aberdeen, saw Hong Kong as too expensive and potentially a political embarrassment in dealings with China itself and other European powers.[3]

People on the ground in China perceived the advantage of Hong Kong more keenly. Captain Charles Elliott, who had replaced the late and floundering Lord Napier as superintendent of trade in China and succeeded in first acquiring the island under the briefly observed Convention of Chuenpi (Chuanbi), was obviously a fervent advocate of it. He in turn was replaced by London for his presumptions in the absence of clear direction. He had exceeded himself in bagging a doubtful outpost and restoring to the Chinese the ostensibly more attractive but in fact most perilous island of Chusan (Zhoushan) outside Ningpo (Ningbo). An East India Company factory had been set up there. It was briefly but uncomfortably occupied by British troops in 1840, and the home government thought more fondly of it than it did of Hong Kong.

His successor, Sir Henry Pottinger, who became Hong Kong's first governor, carried with him officials' doubt about Hong Kong but came to share Elliot's enthusiasm for its strategic and financial possibilities. In this, at least, he was in harmony with the British traders who were desperate for a haven from which to pursue the trading of opium along the China coast.

The die was cast over Hong Kong as early as the spring of 1839 and the onset of the First Opium War between Britain and China. Macau had never seriously pretended that it could defend itself against an attack from the Chinese rear or organised disobedience by Celestial subjects living within, so when the unusually upright and passionate Commissioner Lin Zexu in Canton (Guangzhou) ordered the Portuguese governor, Pinto, to expel the entire British community, the governor did as he was told.

The British all took to their ships and sailed off to wallow for weeks in the calm if pent-up safety of Hong Kong Harbour. As they lay there, reinforcing their dwindling provisions from nearby villages, cramped in their hulls, slippery from the humidity but not quite as unwell as they might have been on the mosquito-ridden land, the seed of a project was planted in some men's minds, and it germinated with alacrity.

The opium business, which was the fulcrum at the time of the British imperial trading system, had fallen into rougher hands after the Qing forbad its import in 1796, and the monopoly of the relatively gentlemanly East India Company ended in 1834. The Chinese government and its officials, who ran the stringent factory system which penned up Europeans in Canton, were used to dealing with the company's sense of collective responsibility. The Honourable Company had directed business from its mansion on Portuguese soil. It was the small adjacent building, housing their printing press, which was bought as a mortuary chapel in 1830, passed into the care of the British consul in Canton in 1859, along with the Protestant cemetery, and became what is now the Anglican Morrison Chapel.

The company's control was wound down and then replaced by a large unorganised body of independent traders. These more free-wheeling traders were an increasing aggravation. Business became perpetual conflict, a running war with Chinese authority. The hapless and poorly Lord Napier, appointed superintendent of trade with extraterritorial jurisdiction in 1834, was supposed to resolve this but lacked the knowledge, finesse and stamina. The decidedly unaristocratic Elliot had all of those if not much direction. He delivered not a resolution, which would never be happily arrived at, but at least a safe harbour.

The British free traders, like W. Jardine, the Matheson Brothers and W. S. Davidson, needed a safe haven of their own, and there was no British-held territory between India and Australia. The deep, completely sheltered anchorage, free from danger and unpleasant surprises, in which the British lay homeless and at anchor that spring, must have recommended itself mightily. The traders were the men that mattered, their business being the very purpose for the civil servants, the sailors and the soldiers in China. What they needed they were likely to get. If there can be any doubt about what the men who mattered wanted, for this world and the next, it is helpful to look to the very beginning of the yet-unnamed and unfounded colonial church.

Even before a flagpole had been stabbed into the hard soil of Western, a circular memorandum was issued in spring 1840, to the 'British and foreign community residing in China'. It spoke of a 'very prevalent wish amongst those residing at and acquainted with Hong Kong' that a church should be erected 'in the event of it becoming a British Settlement' so that 'Divine Service could be performed according to the Rites, Ceremonies and Doctrines of the Church of England'.[4] The notice declared that a provisional committee had been formed to raise private subscriptions.

Sir Henry Pottinger, as administrator of the new acquisition, responded to the committee. He undertook that Her Majesty's government would match the amount raised privately. He promised that a colonial chaplain would be appointed and said that he had already earmarked a site on 'Marine Magistrate's Hill'. All this was of course contingent on the island becoming a permanent British colony. The provisional committee announced themselves as George Cooper (Chaplain of HMS *Blenheim*), Alexander Matheson, M. Leslie, I. Pearse (commander of HM Sloop *Cruizer*), Crawford Kerr and Captain John Mylius of the 26th Foot.[5]

Placed between the chaplain, the soldier and the sailor were three influential representatives of the British merchant class in those parts at that time. Their foresight for Hong Kong was firming up.

The *Friend of China* of July 1842 reported its belief that 5,000 to 6,000 dollars had already been raised and that the list was being sent up to the British expeditionary force fighting the Chinese in the north. It also said that Lancelot Dent, *taipan* of one of the most princely of *hongs*, although in Singapore on his way home, had transmitted five hundred dollars, so much did he approve of the venture.

References to the subscriptions committee are scanty in its early period. By October 1842, the *Friend of China* was wondering whether it existed anymore and accusing it of 'supiness' if it did. Little is recorded from it until July 1844, when Governor Sir John Davis came up with an amended and more specific funding proposal. Her Majesty's government had confirmed it would provide double the amount of voluntary subscriptions raised up to a maximum, on its part, of 6,000 pounds. After that, the subscribers were on their own. The three civilians, Matheson, Leslie and Kerr, clearly remained from the original subscription committee. They were joined by fifteen others, including the Reverend Vincent J. Stanton, occupier of the newly minted post of colonial chaplain, who acted as committee secretary.

As far as they were concerned it was the government that had been dragging its feet. It had not been until September 1843, after the ratification of the Treaty of Nanking formally secured the colony, that the governor, Pottinger, had told the secretary of state, Lord Stanley, that a new church was wanted.[6] The committee deeply regretted that 'so long a time of action has passed' and thankfully welcomed the offer made by His Excellency. At an early date they hoped to 'behold a building rising in our midst, commodious, substantial and, in every respect, suitable.' Despite the alterations, pinching of pennies, the occasional stiletto between the shoulder blades and a long wait, this is close to what they got.

Their subscription list, thus far, was an impressive one. It had two hundred seventy-five entries. Pottinger himself had given $150 and John Davis, his successor, had matched that. The earliest merchant settlers vied for spiritual as well as social prominence. Jardine Matheson gave $500 and was matched by Launcelot Dent's donation signalled *en route* to Singapore. W. T. Gemmell and Co., opium traders recently moved down from Canton, gave $400, Lindsay and Co. $200 and M. Leslie $100. Cockerell and Company, one of the largest firms in the East India trade, pledged $500, but there seems some doubt as to whether they paid up.

There were scores of $10 and $5 donations from individuals. 'A Friend' gave a whole $200, and Mr. J. McGregor may have changed his mind about his $100 because it seems to be scored through. The officers aboard the *Peteiro* gave $82.50. Given the transience of their profession and that their chances of worshipping in a cathedral for which sod had not yet been broken were small, their generosity was large.[7]

By 24 April 1846, Stanton could report to the government that 2,726 pounds had been pledged and 1,379 pounds collected although 120 pounds had been lost because some pledgers could not cope with the delay in beginning the building. They had died, or some had simply left.[8] They may have felt firm in their obligation to worship in dignity, but the merchants of Hong Kong were not entirely sanguine about the future of the colony. In fact, in the early years, they were having a hard time of it, or at least that is how they liked to present themselves to the home government and Parliament.

Thirty-one firms memorialised Colonial Secretary Lord Stanley on the serious decline of the European commerce in Hong Kong, on 13 August 1845. A deputation consisting of A. Matheson, G. T. Braine, Gilbert Smith and Crawford Kerr presented a second memorial on 29 August 1845. Three of those men, Matheson, Kerr and Smith, sat on the church subscriptions committee. 'Hong Kong has no trade at all and is a mere place of residence of government and its officers with a few British merchants and a very poor population,' it read.

The Times of 6 April 1846 sympathised with them. 'Hong Kong has quite lost its caste as a place of commercial operations. Many of the merchants have already abandoned the Island.' *The Economist,* suitably primed, declared on 8 August 1846, 'HK is now nothing more than a depot for a few opium smugglers, soldiers, officers and men-of-wars' men.'

Commentary in the colony itself could be equally gloomy for its spiritual and temporal future. In its 1 August 1846 edition, the *Friend of China* was characteristically sarcastic:

> If the British Government has made Hongkong the seat of a Bishopric—as was announced in the late monthly papers—there is no idea among the Magnates of Saint James that the colony is falling into insignificance, and that it has lost the commercial character, which it was rapidly acquiring, when the ill-advised measures of the Governor blasted the vigorous shoot, which promised to flourish in the youthful colony.

Later, as head of Jardine Matheson and a member of Parliament, Alexander Matheson was to tell the House of Commons in May 1847 that, had they not already invested so much money in land and buildings, most English firms would have left Hong Kong years earlier.[9]

Missionary, sinologist and Hong Kong government official Ernest J. Eitel, writing in his history *Europe in China*, thought that this represented merely the disappointment 'aroused by an unusually prolonged period of depression consequent upon a previous unnatural inflation ... Hong Kong itself stood smiling like Patience on a monument bearing the bold legend "Resurgam".'[10] Eitel may be right, but even if the words of Matheson were not a petulant push for political favour over tariff changes, the point was that these men had taken careful calculation, considerable faith and made those investments.

This was now being tested. A telling testimony to their deeper certainties was their committee and that subscription list, begun even before the beginning and being held to in the hardest of times.

The British were bent on building a colonial church in Hong Kong. It would only become a cathedral the year after it was completed, but that status was already being talked about by the Church in England, and Hong Kong had a sense of it as early as 1844, when the church's design was being discussed, or rather, disputed. The British Empire was not at its height in this period, but it was arguably at its most vigorous. It may have swapped backwaters or given up redundant coaling stations, but it did not walk out on Crown Colonies or desert Anglican cathedrals. Opening the book on St John's was, for the hardier of the merchants, administrators and clergy, a statement of resolve.

The other constituency with a strong interest in a proper church was the British military which garrisoned the island or passed through to combat in China. St John's was at its inception a garrison church as well as a diocesan cathedral, and it was to remain so with gently decreasing intensity for another century. In truth, the most immediate need of the troops was proper or, to the point, disease-free accommodation. They eventually got this from 1845 onwards, when Major General D'Aguilar began the Murray Barracks, directly opposite the site for the church. In the meantime, European and Indian soldiers died from malaria, typhoid, dengue and dysentery in numbers which Qing troops could only have dreamed of inflicting.

Captain Mylius, who was on the original provisional subscriptions committee, served in the 26th Regiment of Foot which, at one point, could only field 110 weakened soldiers out of a complement of 900. The 55th were so in danger of 'dissolving away' that they were simply sent home in 1844. The 98th, which had arrived in 1841, were in a terrible state. In 1845, 167 men were dead and 200 invalided. The garrison overall had 858 dead or sick out of a total force of 1,600.[11]

The very first church constructed for this needy army was a wooden hut with calico windows, built in 1841 by Reverend Edward Spencer Phelps, Chaplain in HMS *Bellisle*, and Captain Thomas Maitland Edwards of the long-suffering 98th Regiment. Family connections in the colony sometimes ran long. Cathedral Council member Colonel H. L. Dowbiggin, in letter to *St John's Review* in October 1948, recalls that Edwards was his great-uncle and assistant adjutant general to the China command. He died in Hong Kong on 13 November 1844, aged 35, doubtless of the plague that wracked his regiment. There is no clear account of where the wooden hut was put up. It is likely that it was near the present cathedral, and it is equally likely that it was at Stanley. There was a fort there from the earliest times, and a later Senior Chaplain of St John's, Vyvian Copley-Moyle, was quite clear in his view, written in an article in the 1927, that Stanley was where the wooden church was built.[12]

About a year or so later, a much larger 'mat-shed' church was constructed on what was to become Murray Parade Ground and is now the Cheung Kong Centre, and other bits and pieces of roadway and overpass that lie between the tramway and St John's north wall.[13] The mat-shed was a bamboo frame covered with woven rattan and palm mats. It provided shade and some shelter from the weather, but it decayed quickly and was hopeless as a home for any permanent fittings. This makeshift church was an unhappy match to the mat-shed barrack rooms where the soldiers slept in soft, wet, ramshackle conditions. These structures provided easy passage for the mosquitoes which were the unrealised cause of the sickness.

Two years after St John's was opened in 1849, the mat-shed barracks were gone and a new bricks-and-mortar complex spread down the hill over what is now the Citicorp Building, China Bank Building and Murray Road car park sites. The church and the army were to stand close together commanding the city centre, in complement and paradox, and in a fashion that only a colony could conjure.

The Church of England itself had views on its position in Hong Kong and China as a whole and, as usual, they were diffuse. In the early 1840s, Anglicanism was still pondering on what mission it could achieve in this massive and incoherent zone. A Baptist chapel was opened early in Hong Kong, and William Boone, an American Episcopalian Bishop, headed a diocese that had already been established at Shanghai. From London, George Smith and Thomas McClatchie were sent out by the evangelical Church Missionary Society (CMS) to the China Treaty Ports to examine which would be suitable for missionary purposes. It is mildly ironic that, seven years later, Smith would be appointed to Hong Kong as first Bishop of Victoria because, at this point, he thought very little of the place as a potential nurturer of Christian mission.

In his account of the trip published in his *Travels*, he makes unfavourable comparisons:[14]

> While in the northern cities on the mainland of China daily intercourse may be held without restraint with the more respectable

classes of native society, and a foreigner everywhere meets an intelligent and friendly population, at HK on the other hand, missionaries may labour for years without being brought into personal communication with any Chinese except such as are generally speaking of the lowest character and unlikely to exert a moral influence on their countrymen.

His perception of the problem from the Christian standpoint is quite accurate. 'Two other serious disadvantages to Hong Kong, however, are the frequent spectacle of European irreligion and the invidious regulations of the police,' he says. 'Scenes frequently occur in the public streets and in the interior of houses, which are calculated to place the countrymen of Missionaries in an unfavourable aspect before the native mind.' Observing that the Chinese were treated as a 'degraded race', he concludes that, until a more liberal policy was adopted towards 'Chinese fellow-subjects', immigration of a more respectable class of Chinese would be looked for in vain.

It was going to be even beyond the end of Smith's bishopric in 1867 before the colonial government felt secure enough to let up on the curfews, floggings and other regulations in place to hold down a volatile and transient population. At the time and in many ways forever after, the future Bishop Smith was preoccupied with the CMS remit to take the mission to the Chinese. The Church of England in its role as the established Church was mandated to minister throughout the empire to those British 'countrymen of missionaries' who were making such an exhibition of themselves indoors and outdoors.

It was the officials and subjects of Her Majesty residing in the colonies for whom a church would be built and a colonial chaplain appointed by her government. The Hong Kong administration, heeding the call of the provisional subscription committee and assessing the development of the island, applied for a chaplain to the Bishop of London, who handled these affairs overseas where there was not a diocese.[15]

The choice of the Reverend Vincent J. Stanton could not have been more appropriate. His determination to serve in China had been irrepressible. In 1836, in his second year at St John's College Cambridge, studying divinity, he went to the CMS in London and offered himself specifically for China. He was below the recruiting age limit, so they sent him back to university. Stanton had money of his own, though, and shortly afterwards, he made his way to Macau under his own steam. He began by doing what most freelancing students do to earn money on foreign soil: he tutored the children of the wealthy; in this case, British merchants. It was here in 1840 that he fell victim to an intense bout of hostility between the British and the Chinese.

In June of that year, the British laid down a quite effective blockade of the Chinese coast in reaction to Imperial Commissioner Lin Zexu's intensifying campaign against the opium trade. The Chinese authorities put a price on the head of British soldiers but could not really get at them. In decrepit Macau, which was becoming overrun with Chinese soldiers and agents, foreign civilians were more accessible. In this situation, Stanton was incautious. He went bathing with fellow missionary David Abeel in Macau Bay. He went a little ahead of Abeel, who could not find Stanton when he arrived. With pessimism, the bay was dredged for his body, but it was eventually learned that he been abducted on the shore by agents of Lin Zexu and imprisoned in Canton.

Protracted negotiations were going on over two hundred British and other Europeans captured from the vessel *Kite* near Ningpo, who had been kept, initially, in chains and cages. Stanton was released by the Chinese to Captain Charles Elliot, as a sign of good faith. The imperial official Qishan, with whom Elliot negotiated most closely, is said to have visited Stanton in prison on 10 December 1840. He walked in on the young man deeply immersed in his Bible and was so impressed by his piety that he took him to his residence as a guest for a few days before handing him over.[16] If Stanton himself was kept in chains,[17] they must have been lightly applied.

He returned to England. One might think that, after three months in a Qing jail, his interest in China might have been thoroughly lost. Missionaries of that period were made of redoubtable stuff. He was ordained by Charles Bloomfield, Bishop of London, in June 1842. He served a mere eight months as a curate at St Peter's, Mile End, Stepney, and with delighted haste, accepted the offer of the new colonial chaplaincy of Hong Kong in January 1843. In March, he married Lucy Head, daughter of a prominent missionary and herself a teacher dedicated to Christian education. In June, now fully packed, he set off on the six-month voyage round the Cape of Good Hope, back to China.

He had already been raising funds in England with the clear prospect in mind of putting up a church and a school in Hong Kong. The church was '… to be of a large size, on a more expensive plan than those already operating in England', he explained in a submission for aid to the Society for the Promotion of Christian Knowledge (SPCK). Already, in 1843, Stanton could foresee St John's cathedral status. He also asked for assistance towards 'schools for Chinese children, conducted by English and Chinese teachers'.[18]

He may have had a series of schools in mind, but the one he succeeded in starting became known as St Paul's College and has been associated with St John's in varying degrees of intimacy ever since. It is worth mention at this early point because it was actually open and with students before the St John's foundation stone was laid. The school was originally intended to train young Chinese catechists to go out and convert their brethren. As such, it was not the concern of the subscriptions committee, the governor or the secretary of state. The SPCK gave 250 pounds in response to Stanton's request. He raised or personally donated much of what was needed to build the beginnings of St Paul's College, which is now Bishop's House, on its promontory at the corner of Glenealy and Lower Albert Road.

In a letter from retirement in England to the diocese's second Bishop, Charles Alford, he explained that the college was founded by 1,000 pounds from family and friends and gifts of library books and of furniture.[19] There lingered a barely restrained resentment against the first Bishop, George Smith, who went into Hong Kong in 1850, as Stanton was on the way out, sick. Armed with 5,000 pounds in donations specifically for the school, he took over and expanded the building. The reputation for foundation shifted from Stanton to the bishop and his benefactors. It is the date of Smith's foundation, 1851, that you can see still carved into the boundary wall on Lower Albert Road.

When Vincent Stanton first arrived in Hong Kong, he and his wife lived in Morrison Hill, where their son Vincent Henry was born, a novel birthplace for a future dean of Trinity College Cambridge. The subscription committee was in place and Stanton joined it as secretary, bringing a single-minded and now clerical vigour to the effort.

Military Anglicans were worshipping in a soggy mat-shed. Not all the civilian congregation was necessarily with them. By April 1848, provision for Divine Service had been made in the Cover Hall of the Supreme Court Building, according to a notice in the *Friend of China*. This placed them opposite the old Hong Kong Club building at the junction of D'Aguilar Street and Queen's Road Central.

In 1847, Stanton sent a progress report to his SPCK benefactors on both school and church.

> I have the gratification to inform you that a large portion of the
> house is now ready for occupation. I have the prospect of com-
> mencing early in the summer ... The Church is in progress ... On
> 11 next month, we hope the foundation stone will be laid. The
> grants of Her Majesty's Government and your Society together
> with the subscriptions are equal to all the anticipated expenses.[20]

The Reverend Stanton's powers of anticipation failed him at this
point, as had everybody else's. The funds available would not be equal
to the cost overruns, changed plans and false assumptions which were
to dog the management of the project. The process was a mudbath of
misapprehension, confusion and some politicking, which clerks and
clerics splashed around in for the best part of seven years. It is a
testimony to the powers of dogged determination, artful compromises
and doubtless blind faith that it all eventually worked out in stone
and brick and on balance sheet.

Coming to grips with a coherent and safely costed set of plans
proved a slippery business. In March 1845, not a sod of soil had been
broken. Governor Davis was explaining to the secretary of state that
A. T. Gordon, the surveyor-general, was on long on leave, the office
was understaffed and producing plans for the church was beyond its
capability. By August he was more confident that his deputy, Charles
St George Cleverly, a power in the early story of the cathedral, should
be able to handle it.[21]

Cleverly appears as a man of determination, intellect and technical skill, with probably a generous dose of political guile. Born in
Kilworth County Cork in 1819 but not thought to be native Irish,
he was the grandson of a Thames shipbuilder. He was probably most
famous for the construction of Government House, Hong Kong,
which was neither as complex nor as sturdy as the cathedral. For
further posterity, he got a street named after him in Sheung Wan
(Central) district and a son, Osmund, who was private secretary to
British Prime Ministers Stanley Baldwin and Neville Chamberlain.
He retired to homes in South Kensington and Worcestershire, where
he died in 1897.[22] While it would go too far to describe Cleverly as the
architect of St John's, he was the adapter, pilot and project manager
who got the building up.

In the six years between 1844 and 1851, a series of crises was
kicked up over plans for the church and their costs. A dust of mystery
has settled over the muddle, but the one item that comes out of it

upon which the church was built is the plan presented and then implemented by Charles Cleverly.

In all, three plans for the church are referred to in the correspondence between Hong Kong and London.[23] The first plan was the Hardwick design in the pointed or Gothic style. This is presumed to be Philip Hardwick, a distinguished London practitioner, whose work is associated with railway stations, warehouses, some parish churches and one Church of Ireland cathedral. He appears to have produced a plan for a Hong Kong church through the offices of the Bishop of London sometime around 1844. Indeed the governor, Davis, was quite closely concerned with it. He wrote to Lord Grey on 25 August 1845, telling him about the plan and that it had originally been 'procured by my brother Major Davis of the 52nd from Mr. Hardwick the Architect'.

This plan would doubtless have been splendid had it resulted in its entirety. Unfortunately, nothing of the original drawings survives and, according to Doreen King, author of St John's Cathedral Hong Kong: A Short History and Guide, Hardwick's biographer can find no reference to them in the architect's papers. However, the influence of these ethereal drawings floats through the story. Doreen King, in her history of the church's fabric and fittings, says that a revision of a design was ordered by A. T. Gordon, the surveyor-general, before he left Hong Kong. This Gordon design, King believes, was likely drawn up from Hardwick's by an office draftsman called George Strachan, who disappears off the scene in 1844, probably, like modestly placed young Europeans of the time and place, on to more lucrative business or down a drink and opium sinkhole in the Lower Bazaar.

Before Strachan left, John Pope, a civil engineer, joined the office. He was a nephew of Sir William Cubbitt, the prominent builder, and was much thought of. The Friend of China goes as far as to say that he was 'without doubt the greatest genius the Surveyor-General's department in Hong Kong ever knew' and attributes the design of the church to him. It was more than usually wise at the time not to believe everything one read in the newspapers. There is no evidence to support Pope as the creative genius. He worked as an assistant to Cleverly. We have one letter from him to the trustees in August 1844,[24] telling them that he would supervise the project if they wanted him to, since the government was a principal subscriber, but they still needed the services of an architect. Pope died aged 27, of a plague, in December 1847.

Gordon himself disappeared at the same time as Strachan but for more accountable reasons. He went on leave for two years, as civil servants did in the age of long home voyages, and returned only very briefly in 1846, before giving up his office altogether. This long leave, more than anything else, did much to harm Gordon's reputation in this story. He was not there to prevent his own modifications being modified further in ways he did not like, nor could he halt the run of doubts that were being cast over his ability to make accurate estimates, doubts which Charles Cleverly did nothing to dispel and not a little to support.

While Gordon was away, Cleverly's design came into being. Professionally, it was a fair and necessary response to criticism from the Colonial Office that Gordon's estimates were too expensive. Although there was an attempt to resuscitate the original Hardwick design, that too was now pushed aside in a drive for economy and simplicity. Both the Hardwick design and the Gordon modifications were considered stylistically too tricky for local Chinese workers to execute.

A letter from Sir John Davis to the colonial secretary, Lord Stanley, as long into the process as 24 February 1846, illustrates the time, distances and lapses of attention from which a project like this could suffer in those days. He thought it 'desirable to draw your Lordship's attention once more to the great want of a fitting place of worship'. He reminded Stanley that 'the servants of the Government and other English inhabitants have for more than three years assembled in a sort of a shed'. He wrote of the need for a 'modern' church. Enclosing Cleverly's design to Stanley's successor, William Gladstone, three months later, he described it as being in 'the plainest Norman style'. Davis was mistaken in his architecture. The church was not to be Norman but Gothic in the Early English style.

For this design being more faithfully kept to, we may have a soldier to thank. Major Edward Aldrich, commanding officer of the Royal Engineers, who had much to do with the building of Murray Barracks and who was thanked with shoddy treatment, wrote to Major Caine, acting as colonial secretary, later in 1846, having looked over the estimates and drawings. He had crossed out the word 'Norman' and replaced it with 'Old English'. He knew more than just the terms.[25]

'The roof will be more in keeping with general style if trusses are ornamented with painted arches in the intervals on a Queen Post Truss instead of in a Norman style on a King Post Truss.' Here

was a couth and knowledgeable engineer. Yet, he and the rest predictably underestimated the skill and adaptability of the Chinese
masons and craftsmen to skilfully imitate the finer points of English
medieval architecture.

Both the relationship between the estimated and the actual costs
of the plan and the equation between the government's contribution
and those of private subscribers disintegrated as the building of St
John's proceeded. By August 1845, the Colonial Office was losing
patience with the staffing shortages in the surveyor-general's department. On the 20th, Davis was ordered to send thorough plans. The
governor had not received that instruction before he wrote to London
on 26 August, asking to be supplied with the original Hardwick design
in the possession of the Bishop of London. Cleverly had urged him to
take recourse in Hardwick's design because, understaffed and Gordon
on long leave, he did not relish the work that would be needed to alter
Gordon's version.

Why it was still not in the possession of the surveyor-general is
not clear. If they never had the Hardwick design in the first place,
then what was Gordon's design based upon? At the bottom of this
lies the difficulty in believing that Gordon or anyone in a colonial
surveyor's office would have had the skill and application to come up
from scratch with a building of the authenticity and accuracy in style
and structure which St John's turned out to have.

In the meantime, on 24 October, Davis came to grips with Lord
Stanley's overlooked missal of August. Patching up misconceptions from dispatches which crossed under sail-powered mail was
commonplace before the telegraph was laid. Doing as London was
bidding him, he enclosed the 1844 Gordon design, which Cleverly
did not want to deal with, hurriedly priced at 11,000 pounds but
without working drawings or detailed estimates. This was all too
vague for London.

A new secretary of state, William Ewart Gladstone, acted with
characteristic firmness and wrote straight to the Treasury, asking for
approval to proceed with the Hardwick design because Gordon's was
too expensive and uncertain. Gladstone, said the clerk, 'needs a quick
reply'. He got one. A month later, he was telling Davis not to proceed
with the Gordon plan. Hardwick's original was now enclosed, and he
was to work out an estimate for that.

On 22 May 1846, Davis reported to Gladstone that Hardwick's
design turned out to be almost identical to material from Hong Kong

that he had already reported to Lord Stanley. If everything that had been done in Hong Kong had been based on drawings that were Hardwick's in the first place, this should not have been surprising. To pull out of this *cul-de-sac*, Cleverly and his team seemed to have buckled down to his own adaptation. Cleverly made a series of modifications to the Gordon design, but the one that was most telling in both structure and economy was his reduction of the chancel from three bays to barely one. A single-storey structure containing vestries skirted around its side, but the chancel proper now just had room for the high altar. The church had become, effectively, T-shaped.

His main aim was to produce a cheaper church and one that would fall within the scope of the government's original promise to provide a maximum 6,000 pounds as two-thirds of the total cost. He came in with a design at a pre-contract estimated cost of 6,600 pounds. Almost inevitably, this turned out to be a work of fiction.

The governor wrote to Gladstone telling him that, though he would level the ground for the church, he needed confirmation of approval of the proportion the government should pay. Cleverly's estimates of 6,619 pounds 12 shillings 4 pence for the main building and 1,686 pounds 9 shillings 8 pence for the tower, along with Colonial Chaplain Stanton's optimistic accounts of the subscription campaign, were enclosed for Gladstone. Gordon had returned to the colony from leave just in time to put his signature, in no service to his reputation, above Cleverly's on both the estimate and the plans. Gordon foresaw the need for St John's to be a cathedral church. He took the opportunity to object to the truncated chancel but to no avail.

Five months later, on 8 October, the secretary of state replied to the governor that a promise to cover two-thirds of the cost of the church had been made in March 1844, the estimates complied with the costings of 1844, and therefore work could commence. This did not include approval for the tower. The government never intended to approve a tower, a point over which Davis, Cleverly, Stanton and the fundraisers charged on with fervent disregard.

As early as November 1846, alarm bells were being sounded over the estimates. Major Aldrich, in his capacity as superintendent engineer, told Colonial Secretary Caine that they were too low in some specific respects. Carpenters and plasterers in particular had not been fully accounted for, and their costs estimates needed raising by 20 per cent. In response, Gordon, in his last official gasp, raised the whole estimate to 6,959 pounds from 6,600 pounds, making further allowance for timber costs in unkind anticipation of defective workmanship by Chinese carpenters.

Work could be postponed no longer. Davis passed an ordinance on 11 March 1847, fixing the government's contribution to 4,600 pounds. Responsibility for the site was handed to a board of trustees. Building the church was handed to Cleverly, and the inadequacy of the estimates was instantly revealed. All the tenders for the project were described by Cleverly to Caine as 'extravagantly high'. In fact, it was the estimates that had been scrimpingly low. Even the lowest tender for the whole job would have exceeded the estimates by 3,000 pounds.

Cleverly was resourceful. Building was proceeded with in piece-meal contracts. He was buying time rather than economy. The trustees were taking one step at a time even though they knew that, whatever happened, they had somehow to go the whole way. The work was divided into six contracts. The initial site works had gone to Ah Wei in August 1846.[26] For reasons unknown, he failed to complete the job, and it had to be finished under a new contract, with Ah Sing and Ah Chi in May 1847. The substantial contract involving $16,000 for the walls and roof went to Lei Ah Tung, as did the third contract for plastering and flooring. Hau Ah Lok took on the work of cutting the approaches. Wong Ah Fo put in the seating and the pulpits, and Ah Ming completed the controversial tower, last of all in 1850.[27]

Charles Cleverly must have suspected that the November 1846 estimates would not hold. As early as May 1847, he was already laying the grounds for disappointment at a trustees meeting. He told them the estimates were too low and that costs would overrun.[28] But Chaplain Stanton was in a more buoyant mood. He could affirm that donations stood at 1,963 pounds and 400 pounds more would come. He wanted more stonework introduced in the light of this prosperity. He also foresaw the need to extend the chancel for a future bishop and the church's inevitable cathedral status. He urged this even though he knew it would affect the acoustics and that the congregation would hear the east-end celebration of the Communion service less distinctly.

One might imagine the ire rising in Cleverly over this insupportable wishfulness. With the backing of one equally cautious trustee, Colonel Philipson, he persuaded the trustees that the delay alone was impossible to accommodate and heartily concurred in the acoustic values of a short chancel. It must have been an annoying meeting for Cleverly. A rambling and heated discussion disguised as a 'general conversation' took place over trustees poking their noses into the building site and giving orders as well as interfering with payments agreed by the surveyor-general and the colonial secretary.

The trustees agreed to organised site visits and to engage an English foreman at $60 per month. That same day, they decided on an aesthetic improvement which is enjoyed to this day: wooden shutters on the windows. It was only 900 pounds and a two-month delay which prevented them from ordering stone and not wooden window jambs.[29]

In an April 1848 meeting, Cleverly, who had now been surveyor-general since November 1846, decided to reveal to the existing trustees the extent of the pickle they were in. They were, he told them, underfunded by 1,041 pounds 17 shillings and 4 pence. The Roman cement for exterior plastering had been seriously underestimated, and the stairs in the turret could not be put in for five times the sum allowed. This was entirely the fault of his predecessors, he said, and there was some restrained mockery of the unnamed Gordon. The trustees, though they had not existed as a body at the time, most surely would have realised as individuals that the estimates were something of a guess and deliberately on the low side to ignite progress, said Cleverly. Not wishing to appear as imperceptive individuals, they quickly and unanimously absolved Cleverly of any blame.

A strategy of justification began, which was to run until 1851 and to the final payments. Cleverly, in a spurious take on accountability, said that he had not informed the trustees earlier because the inadequacy was public knowledge anyway. Had not the Aldrich report made that clear, and he had done his best to stay within bounds by running piecemeal contracts? Of course, Governor Davis had been forced to approve the building work because building season had to be caught.

These arguments were to take different shape and direction depending on who they were put to. Gordon would remain the whipping boy, but one strain of truth runs through what turned out to be a difficult argument with the Colonial Office. These pioneering colonialists, businessmen and officials, soldiers and clergy were adamant in their intention of seeing a church of the national religion standing in their colony as quickly as possible. None of them could have known with any certainty what quantities, quality and time would be involved in building a large Gothic Revival church using a workforce to which it meant nothing in a setting and climate for which it had never been conceived. If it took an overly optimistic estimate to get the foundation stone laid and a string of moving excuses to get it topped out, then so be it.

A new governor, Bonham, party to none of that, yet stoically in the middle, asked a new colonies minister, Lord Grey, if he could help in all this. The trustees had told Bonham that the job had to be finished while the scaffolding was up, a forceful persuader in the building trade. Bonham asked Grey for 694 pounds to finish off the tower; the remainder of the shortfall, 347 pounds, could be raised by subscription, in keeping with the two-thirds principle.

Mentioning the tower was a strategic error. Grey declined the request. No more public money than was promised on 2 February 1847 could be spent. The tower was unnecessary. If the CMS-trained clergy were adept in taking the Gospel out to China, the lay trustees were practised at playing hardball back to London. They asked the colonial secretary to tell the secretary of state that it was the poor subscribers who did not know that the estimates were too low, not the trustees, who had not even been created at the time. At a stroke, this public who had been so knowledgeable had ceased to exist. The now-departed Davis had his colours repainted. His laying of the foundation stone suddenly became less to do with the weather. It had implied to everybody else that there was enough to proceed on, said the trustees. They topped off their plea by playing the patriot card. An unfinished tower would damage the image of the British.

Grey still saw 'no reason for altering my earlier decision' which, in ministerial language, means that he could not be bothered to argue. By then, St John's had opened with funding still a hole in its confidence and a stop to its progress.

The trustees were tenacious. Throughout 1850, they pressed their point on the home government. The obstacle to their relief was that the amount the government had agreed on and contributed had been set into the legislation which had established the church, Ordinance 2 of 1847. At the time 2,300 pounds had been contributed by subscribers, and so the government gave 4,600 pounds. In fact the church was costing 8,736 pounds, of which the government should have paid 5,824 pounds under the two-thirds arrangement.

By 19 August, 863 pounds remained outstanding. Colonial Secretary Caine, repaying the trustees with some of the abruptness for which he was known when he was chief magistrate, told them to lop off the costs outstanding on the tower which would never be met. That left 165 pounds which he would refer to London and the discretion of the minister. Grey still stood firm until Bonham, though tactfully agreeing with his position, pointed out to him that the trustees had in fact settled the outstanding debts and were personally 455 pounds out of pocket. Did not the circumstances suggest a payment? This must have touched the gentleman in Lord Grey. The irksome trustees had behaved like gentlemen themselves. It was not right in law, he said, but they should be reimbursed. They had not established any legal claim, but the consecration of the church could not be delayed because, under ecclesiastical law, no church can be consecrated whilst it lies under outstanding debt.

In the end, the total cost of the church was 8,673 pounds, 371 pounds over the original 8,302 pounds—including the tower—which went with the Cleverly design. Just under half, 4,136 pounds, was paid for by subscription. This set a precedent in the relationship between Church and state up to 1892 for regarding government contribution to major works as fifty per cent and not two-thirds.

One payment that does not seem to have been made was the alleged promise of a 460-pound commission to Charles Cleverly for architectural services. It seemed a doubtful arrangement for a civil servant and trustee. An attempt was made to include it in the request for funds to London. It is easy to see how that was dismissed out of hand as Bonham's problem by the Colonial Office. There is no record of Bonham or anyone else taking it on.[30]

Cleverly was a politician and an opportunist. He had the traits for survival in an unstable environment, unforgiving of the slow witted. Amongst them, and most clearly to his credit, were determination and skill which delivered a physically sound, well-planned and aesthetically accurate Gothic Revival cathedral on the coast of South China. At the beginning of the twenty-first century, it serves its Anglican congregation as fittingly as it did in the middle of the nineteenth. Although it is unlikely that a building in that style would be begun from scratch now, its arches and turrets, its tower and stained glass are looked upon by passers-by more as regal old friends than as colonial oddities. As Jan Morris said in her book *Hong Kong: Xianggang*, what had 'once seemed so alien an intrusion now looked almost venerably organic'.

Charles Cleverly leaves us a clear account of what the church was built of, and the materials are summarised in the St John's Cathedral Conservation Report of 2007.[31] The foundations are of dressed granite on limestone and sand, and the plinth, the platform between ground level and the finished floor surface, is of 'wrought granite'.

The nave is of paved granite, and under the seating and in the vestry it was overlaid by timber flooring of China board over Manila joists. The aisle and side aisle are Chinese marble on eight-inch thick concrete. The Roman cement, which Surveyor Gordon is supposed to have sadly underestimated, covers granite steps, the pillars inside the church and was on the mullions in the former east window. The former high altar at the east end has marble steps.

The walls are of Canton grey brick which were covered with one layer of Roman cement with joint marks to imitate ashlar stone blocks. This imitation, as we shall see, is the one minor misfeasance in St John's display of the neo-Gothic. The church's doors have moulded panels and are studded, bolt style, in Manila wood. Granite blocks at two-foot intervals hold the doors and windows by iron bolts leaded into them. Mouldings are cut in brickwork and finished with plaster coats.

The roof was a double layer of red tiles lined with softwood pine, which was to prove a running banquet for termites and was to be twice replaced. The underside plywood lining is currently an interesting mid-tone blue, but the original specifications called for varnish. The roof supports were queen post trusses with a curved brace springing from a stone wall bracket. The only decoration is a red and yellow dogtooth design of the brace infill. From correspondence,[32] we know that more elaborate designs for the roof were discussed. Economy may have snuffed them out, but the plainness of this beautiful feature bears faithful witness to its medieval origin, and there may have been a resolve to stick with it. Its impact on those who look up at it for the first time justifies that.

Out of the criss-crossing of plans, the turmoil of costings and the husbandry of Cleverly, St John the Evangelist grew to be an almost textbook example of Early Victorian Gothic. It would have passed the scrutiny of the pickiest of its proponents such as Augustus Pugin, a Catholic convert, who gave form to the belief that classicism had helped suck the life out of religion and that a return to a medieval style would restore the values of a more passionate religious age.

It is true that the Gothic Revival in church architecture in English cities was for a while closely associated with the Anglo-Catholic movement which was gaining traction at the time. Yet evangelical revivalism in the Church of England was a power which coincided with it, and by mid-century both wings of the church took the Gothic to heart. Gothic's vaunting, buttressed romanticism struck a chord with the Victorians. Although the origins of St John's plans back in England may have lain with High Church sympathisers, their adoption in Hong Kong did not necessarily represent similar sympathies amongst the merchants and military there. Quite the contrary, a more Protestant and less sacramental approach to worship seems to have been the preference amongst the English colonial population then and for some time after.

Given its timing, St John's is an early and seminal expression of the form based on Early English Gothic. Its sculptural sense, details like the bar tracery in the windows, the lancet arches, the ribbed course lines and the roof's queen post trusses, make it a thorough example of the Early Revival.

Pugin himself laid down some strict rules about what was genuine Gothic, important among which is that the original construction material must be frankly expressed and not disguised. St John's fell down on this point with the lines cut in the cement covering the bricks on the walls, faking stone blocks. The cement could be excused as moisture control for damp weather conditions. Adapting to climate was a central tenet of the Gothic school, and Cleverly did just that with the church. He installed prominent shutters and ventilators. 'Ventilation in the ceiling is made in the bosses, passes into the roof and exits through circular openings in transepts' is how he describes it. He raised the seating six inches above the floor ventilation, a thoughtful move for humans in the climate, but did not appreciate the paradise he was building for rodents.

He built only a short tower with typhoons in mind. English church towers of the type and period can be much loftier. A previous design of Philip Hardwick, Holy Trinity, Bolton, built in 1837, in wet but not so windy Lancashire and an optimistically enormous parish church in a Victorian boom town, attests to this.

The shortened chancel of 1849 was a cost expediency, lamented by Gordon and Stanton, among others perhaps, but turned into something of a virtue. It was a novelty, almost a T-shaped church, and it was dealt with skilfully. Around the back of this briefest of chancels was a projecting, semi-circular vestry or 'half ambulatory', as the architects describe it. It was flat roofed, kept to a small scale and considered unusual. The shift in scale from the main building was dramatic.

The design gives the impression of an easy symmetry, but this is an illusion. There are departures from it. The most significant is the

double-height extension of the north transept over the original baptistery, which is now the quiet chapel. This skillion roof structure is
recessed slightly behind the transept's main north gable so it escapes
too much attention. Originally, the north and south transepts also had
entrances on their east side, both sides of the 'half ambulatory'. For the
general coming from Flagstaff House and his officers from their Mess
a little lower down the hill, this would have been most convenient.

These arrangements were all to be done away with only twenty
years later, when the chancel was extended. Yet from the very opening,
chaplain, trustees and congregation would face challenges from the
structure and its installations and to their own tempers and charity as
the cathedral broke itself in.

Since 11 March 1849 was two years exactly from the foundation
stone laying and was to fall on a Sunday, it was resolved to declare St
John's more or less complete and hold the first Divine Service that
day. It is fair to imagine a few ragged edges to the event. There would
have been walls not quite painted, trim to be finished off and bamboo
scaffolding still lodged in corners and most prominently around the
porch. The tower was not completed and would not be for another
year. Negotiating entry through the west door may have been hazard-
ous to clean uniforms and civilian finery.

The records do not go to lengths about the proceedings.[33] The
newspapers seem not to have bothered with it. Quite simply, the
Reverend Stanton conducted a morning service with the Reverend
N. L. Onslow, the Chaplain from HMS *Hastings*, and in the afternoon—presumably evensong—he was accompanied by the Reverend
A. Studman, the Military Chaplain. We have to remember that this
was not a service of consecration. That could not come for another
three years, until the debts were settled. Happy and populated though
it would have been as an event, it was more akin to what the hotel
business calls a 'soft opening'.

As with all first runs, discoveries were made. A row of seats was
afterwards taken out of each transept. They were too packed. Bamboo
blinds had to be found for the doors. If these were against the sun,
they may also have been to keep out mosquitoes.[34] Years later, in 1868,
bamboo sun screens were extended as awnings over all the entrances
so that 'chairs' could be put down under them and occupants pro-
tected from the sun as they got in and out.

Shortly before the service, the colonial chaplain made another discovery, along with the other trustees and some of the press. The coat

of arms of Sir John Davis and Sir George Bonham had been moulded above the north and the south sides of the porch. There was objection to this.[35] 'Disgraceful appendages' is how the *Hong Kong Register* described them in its edition of 15 October 1850. Interestingly, the press reserved particular venom for Davis, levelling accusations of self-promotion and private enterprise. He was long gone by then, but it was a measure of his unpopularity in the colony even though, through his persistence in the building of St John's, he probably deserved the memorial. It was too late to chisel them off and there they remain.

A summary look at St John's in 1850 shows us what can be fairly described as Cleverly's plan now brought to its conclusion. Moving from west to east stands a five-bay nave with aisles, transepts and one bay of chancel, creating the near T-shape. Behind the high altar is the half ambulatory, a single-storey canted bay acting as a vestry.

At the west end is a porch inside a tower, a tower built more with bluff than with funds, for which the trustees were staring down London until it blinked and paid, which London did in 1851. Original designs for the tower were altered. An 1845 drawing of the west elevation shows that battlements were planned. They never appeared. Another fortress theme, the slit lancet window, was disapproved of. 'This little window is bad' a no-nonsense critic has scrawled next to it. The round one has replaced it. The stained glass in there may be the only original glass left in the building. Round windows in the tower and on each of the transept gables are a last-minute exception to generally pointed windows and openings. The aisle and lower transept windows are all lancets with a Y tracery supporting a small round window at the junction. The corner turrets of the tower kept their pointed 'archer-slits'.

The interior lining of the porch is timber framed with a hard plaster ceiling. There is manhole in it. If necessary, a rope could be dropped from the bell tower, down through the gallery and through the hole so that a bell could be rung from ground level. Inside the tower, directly above the porch, is the west gallery looking out over the nave and, beneath, a timber-panelled tympanum over the door. You get up to the gallery by a tight little staircase in the tower's north turret. A stair was never put in the south turret, so it is definitely difficult one-way traffic, in and out. The uses the gallery has been put to are obscure and intermittent. There was once an organ up there. From time to time choirs have taken themselves up to sing. Currently, it is repository for amplifying equipment.

Eastwards, at the end of the nave, stood the pulpit, up against the main 'pier' pillar where the nave meets the south transept. It was regarded as an integral part of the structure and included in the plans. Drawings for it still exist. It was of surprising elegance. A graceful curving balustraded staircase led up to the pulpit itself. The octagonal desk was decorated with lancet arches to match the windows, but the surprise was in the backdrop and the canopy (or sounding board) with *fleur-de-lis* crenulations, which look distinctly Tudor. It must have been an interesting delicacy in a stronger and simpler setting.[36] The reading desk, of which we have no pictures, was directly opposite on the north side, and this may have been the undoing of both of them. According to some conventions, they were wrong way round. When that was righted, the Tudor gem did not survive the move.

This readjustment of the fittings was one of several that the trustees had to cope with in the coming twenty years. None was more sensitive and persistent than the manoeuvring of the seating. St John's pews are a generous delight to the worshipper. Made of teak and rosewood, the benches have individual seats with arms and rattan insets. They have the depth and width which would allow an officer with his sword or a lady in broad crinolines to sit in comfort in the tropical climate. The space between the benches allows you to thrust yourself onto your knees rather than slide down as is customary in tighter layouts. On the lightly clad congregations of the twenty-first century, this space is almost extravagant.

Some of the pews are original, and you can tell them by the slightly more elaborate carving at the arm joints. The ones with arms were for renting, and those without, in the aisles, were free. In the planning stage, it was decided, thoughtfully, that these seats for the poorer classes should have backs to them.

The seats in Cleverly's plan ran right through the crossing of the nave and the transepts. In each transept there were originally eight rows of pews, until the opening service demonstrated that this was at least one row too many. Finding enough of these pews, placing the people in them and keeping them there contentedly was a repeated strain on the nerves of the trustees and, of all their tasks, the most thankless. There were times in the years up to 1873 when disputes over 'sittings' were so relentless and acrimonious that they must have wondered why they took on the office at all.

Chapter 2
Imperial Parish, 1850–1873

It is surprising for such a prominent detail but why the cathedral was named after St John the Evangelist is unclear. This is a nugget of fact waiting to be dug up. It has been suggested that it was to honour Sir John Davis, the governor, who did enough to bring about the church's existence, but he was so widely excoriated as to make this unlikely. The answer could be more covert. St John the Evangelist, with St John the Baptist, is considered a co-patron saint by the Freemasons. A significant number of British merchants, clergy and officials in Hong Kong were, in those days as in this, Freemasons. There may have been a natural inclination to the apostle when time came to title the church.

The government of St John's was established by Ordinance No. 2 of 1847. For a brief year after its opening, it stood as a church. Ordinance No. 3 of 1850 elevated it to the status of a cathedral upon the creation of the Diocese of Victoria and transferred certain powers held by the colonial chaplain to the bishop.

St John's as a cathedral in 1850 was governed like none in England. It had no dean and chapter of canons. Its governing body was a small group of laymen. Its chief and sole clergyman was a chaplain on a government stipend. It was structured to operate as a colonial church ministering principally to the British population along with any overseas Episcopalians, occasional Presbyterians and local Chinese converts who chose to attend.

There were six lay trustees, four appointed by the government and two by an annual meeting of the subscribers and seatholders. The 1850 ordinance made the bishop chairman of the trustees, with authority to depute the chairing of the regular meetings to the colonial chaplain. Given the lengthy absences and other business of the bishops, this became a *de facto* situation. The trustees were required to meet quarterly. The Annual General Meeting of Subscribers and Seatholders could not propose actions but just approve them so usually no one, except the trustees, bothered to attend.

The trustees were responsible for the finance, the fabric and the general management of lay affairs, including the rented seating or 'sittings'. The chaplain concerned himself with matters spiritual and pastoral, including the liturgy and the ordering of services. The bishop could request special services such as confirmations and ordinations to be held at particular times. Because the bishop had ecclesiastical control over the chaplain and the cathedral was his seat, it was unlikely that any radical liturgical changes could have been made without his consent. In the first two episcopacies of Bishop Smith and Bishop Alford, it would have been difficult to oppose any service proposals that were the bishop's will.

But then the government had controls over the chaplain too when they wanted to exert them, for the chaplain was paid by the government. The governor could and did require special services to be held for matters with bearing on the community. Overlapping authorities provided potential for friction though constitutional disputes involving the cathedral are not a pressing feature of the first two episcopacies, very likely because the bishops were so rarely in town. In those early days there were more practical teething troubles.

Trustees noted as attending a meeting of 31 May 1847 included Cleverly, Lieutenant-Colonel Philpots, a royal engineer representing the military; W. T. Mercer, colonial treasurer at the precocious age of 25; and Wilkinson Dent of Dent and Co., elected by the subscribers. Dent was succeeded at the annual meeting in April 1849 by another Dent and Co. merchant, C. J. Braine, who was a passionate collector of ferns and had one he found in Hong Kong named after him. T. R. Neave also joined as an elected trustee.[1]

As well as providing four trustees for the cathedral and the chaplain's pay, the government was responsible for contributing funds for its repair and maintenance. Precisely for which purposes and up to what point was not defined in law. The government's say in what happened at St John's could be a loud one in those early days. Its voice was raised surprisingly rarely, but its influence could be felt in odd ways. From time to time, a governor might choose the hymns for Sunday if it suited him.

A bishopric was created for Hong Kong in February 1849. George Smith was consecrated as its first bishop, with Letters Patent[2] on 29

May, and he arrived in his new diocese on 27 March 1850.[3] What had been, for the briefest of periods, a colonial parish church now became the seat of a bishop whose diocesan authority reached, conceptually at least, from Hong Kong Island to Japan and whose objective was to spread the Gospel there in hegemony with the imperial purpose.

The idea of the Church of England expanding among the pagans in tandem with the empire did not sit comfortably with Liberal politicians in mid-Victorian Parliaments back home or those who saw the established Church as a facility for England and the English. Funds for it to do this were not being voted. Others, prominent among them Charles Blomfield, Bishop of London, who had ordained Victor Stanton, believed that the state had deserted its religious obligations and that the expansion of Anglican Christianity in the British Empire could not be left to missionary societies. It must be episcopally rooted. A bishop had to be planted in every territory.

A meeting of clergy was held in London on 27 April 1841.[4] The Archbishop of Canterbury, William Howley, was present and vocal. Bishops, he said, exerted authority and moral influence. Dissent had spread in the North American colonies for the lack of them. The Roman Catholics threatened to reap a harvest in the British Empire. Blomfield pressed that the country's huge expansion made the Church of England a missionary church. Greater integration of the two would present a united front throughout the empire.

Blomfield proposed a fund administered by a committee of English bishops to complement funds raised by colonists. The committee would confer with government ministers on the creation of new bishops, and the bishops would be issued by the Crown with Letters Patent to secure their legal status. The pressure group was a powerful one in both Commons and Lords. The Colonial Bishops Act was passed in 1841, creating the Colonial Bishoprics Fund. Both colonial and missionary Anglicanism was to come under episcopal control.

You needed private donations to make this work, of course, and it did catch the imaginations of the wealthy. Angela Burdett-Coutts, for example, gave 35,000 pounds for dioceses in South Australia and the Cape and 50,000 pounds for British Columbia. Hong Kong found a brother and sister as benefactors, J. C. Sharpe of Gosling and Sharpe's Bank, and Lady Elizabeth Smart, wife of Admiral Sir Robert Smart, ultimately commander-in-chief, Mediterranean Fleet. They donated 10,000 pounds, 5,000 pounds of which was intended for St Paul's College.

A pastoral appeal in England brought 6,000 pounds to the Hong Kong fund, 2,000 pounds came from the Society for the Propagation of the Gospel (SPG) and an equal sum from the SPCK. This total satisfied Her Majesty's government that sufficient funds existed for a bishop to function without embarrassment or turning cap in hand to them. The Bishopric of Victoria could be created.[5]

This plan for the Church as a missionary church to the Chinese, and colonial bishops as missionary bishops covering imperial distances, was a plan which St John's, conceived as a parish church for the colonial English, had to sit up to. It was a dual role which created demands on the cathedral that were sometime risen to, sometimes just met but never fully accommodated.

Bishop Smith arrived in Hong Kong on 27 March 1850. The *Friend of China*, using an adjective all of its own making, gushed over the bishop in the tones of a celebrities magazine. 'Mr. Smith's appearance and preaching are familiar to many of us—a young man having a particularly "youthy" look, with which his soft and dulcet tones are in perfect harmony.' Mr. John Wright, a post office clerk who kept a rather interesting diary, confided to it on 30 March 1850,[6] that he was less taken with the bishop's appearance: 'His Lordship the Bishop of Victoria landed at 8.15 a.m. in HMS *Hastings'* barge. He is a tall thin pale looking man.'

The colonial chaplain received him at home, in the college on the promontory above Glenealy. It had been cut into the hillside and embanked with solid granite. It is known today as Bishop's House though the building was St Paul's College right up to the Second World War. Bishops lived there in their role as college warden, of which Smith became the first.

Present at his reception were teachers and students, including thirty-four boarders.[7] The teaching staff were to have a chequered history. J. Summers, the Precentor, was cast into a Macau gaol in June 1858, for showing insufficient respect to the Corpus Christi procession and was sprung by a Royal Navy raiding party. Tutor E. T. Moncrieff and his wife died in the Siege of Cawnpore in 1857.

Stanton handed staff, students and authority over the college to the bishop before leaving Hong Kong for good, a sick man, 'never to see its pleasant rooms and balconies again,' as he lamented. Stanton's role in the foundation of St Paul's was diminished by Smith's immediate expansion of it. He got to work applying the earmarked 5,000 pounds from Sharpe and Lady Smart, which included building a terrace of houses on the upper slope.

'The income from that is what you are enjoying,' noted Stanton in a later, somewhat rueful letter to the second Bishop, Alford.[8] In it he claims that his founding struggle for the college was being forgotten, as it was until later historians such as G. B. Endacott disinterred it. Stanton's son, Vincent Henry, when Dean of Trinity, wrote to Bishop Alford about his father with a rarely recorded note of criticism on Bishop Smith. '[His] weakness was that he was too much absorbed in that which was more immediately concerned with himself.'

On Easter Day 1850, Bishop Smith preached his first sermon in the cathedral. John Wright, clearly not a fan, says of it, 'At Church in the morning the Bishop preached—did not think much of his sermon.'[9] The bishop administered Holy Communion to seventy people, 'merchants, government officials and naval and military officers'.[10] That can be pictured as a thin gathering in the nave of St John's. However, in June of that year, Governor Bonham was telling Lord Grey in connection with quite another matter that 'the whole Protestant community in this Colony does not exceed, exclusive of the Troops, two hundred in number.' Some of those Protestants would have been Dissenters disinclined to attend an Anglican service. Not all of those present will have received Communion. To have garnered nearly half of that community together, including leading lights, was a significant showing.

Smith's presences there were to be intermittent. Essential to his role in expanding the Church of England's mission in China and Japan was that he should be a travelling bishop. His Letters Patent covered all the domains of the emperor of China and ships within one hundred miles of his coast. All persons in Holy Orders therein were placed under his jurisdiction. He was a body corporate and a perpetual corporation. He was Lord Bishop of Victoria. The cathedral was his seat, he had episcopal oversight over the clergy and he could—and did—appoint canons and archdeacons though those canons would have no part of its government.

This is not to say that the bishop was at all timid or indifferent in exercising his authority over the cathedral. On 5 June 1855, the *Hong Kong Register* published a notice of 'a day of fast' for the disasters of the Crimean War.

> Given out at the cathedral on Sunday last. That Wednesday the 13th to be a day of public fast and humiliation on account of the war, and of prayer for the restoration of peace.

National fast days were popular among Protestant Victorians and the Queen herself, who declared these days to make atonement at times of crisis. Bishop Smith and the Reverend James Legge at Union Church announced Her Majesty's penance to Hong Kong. The government was furious. This was a declaration that should have been executive, not episcopal, said the governor and, anyway, it applied only to England and Ireland. Smith insisted that government employees be allowed to down tools and come to the cathedral, even that Irish Catholic troops of the 59th Regiment could go to their church. Many did, including all the senior officials who usually attended church, except Bonham. Most European businesses closed for the day. Ships could not leave port for want of paperwork.

In the service itself, the bishop pointedly omitted any references to Britain's allies, 'the infidel French nation', as he was heard to describe them by Sir John Bowring. The governor suspected that the Roman Catholics cooperated in the fast day because they mistakenly believed it was officially sanctioned. A Colonial Office note described Smith as 'factious'.[11]

Of the fourteen years Bishop Smith was in the diocese, he spent a total of six in Hong Kong itself. Apart from China, he visited Japan, Australia, India and Ceylon. His energy and courage were remarkable. Whilst delivering an episcopal charge at a service at Holy Trinity, Shanghai, the building itself came under fire. He was greatly taken by Hong Xiuquan and the Taiping Rebellion. He saw it as a tremendous opportunity for a sudden rush of Christianity across China and wrote to the Archbishop of Canterbury at excited length with his observations.

For many Christians, most particularly men of missionary spirit like Bishop Smith, the empire was at once a great opportunity for them and a cause of arrogance and abuse which offended Christian principle. In May 1857, he explained to an audience at Exeter Hall, London (where the Strand Palace Hotel now stands) what drove him in his dilemma and articulates the resolution of it for many colonial Anglicans.[12]

> We are impelled forward in spite of ourselves … it might be appalling unless every new accession of territory is made an opportunity of advancing the Redeemer's kingdom … every new addition to the territory of Britain is laid as a humble additional contributions at the foot of the Redeemer's cross.

Victor Stanton, far from travelling, had been absorbed by religious and education work within Hong Kong. The contrast was one

St John's was going to have to accommodate throughout most of its future. It was the seat of bishops who were forever far off on horseback and riverboats getting to the Chinese. It was the responsibility of chaplains who stayed at home and ministered to a congregation that moved around by chair and rickshaw getting to business.

Stanton left in 1850 because of illness. Most chaplains, deans and bishops retired prematurely from maladies well into the twentieth century. Stanton himself, though in fluctuating health, became Incumbent of Southgate in Middlesex, followed by the chargeship of the Parishes of Halesworth and Chediston. He survived until 1891, outliving Bishop Smith by twenty years.

Many sick clergy also had similar good fortune. Hong Kong's climate and its viruses were potential killers. Europeans who tried to weather them or withdrew too late often died. Those who took doctor's orders, read the signs or got out while youth was on their side, survived to reminisce and pester new men going out with outdated advice.

It was Stanton's successor, Samuel Watson Steedman, who was present for the consecration of St John the Evangelist on 19 September 1852. The cathedral has no surviving records of this service. We have what we know from the correspondent of the *Friend of China* edition of 23 September. A service order sixteen pages long was left in each pew. The trustees and the registrar read a paper, standing near the Communion table, 'the purport of which was difficult in the distance to obtain'.

The bishop, followed by Steedman, the Colonial Chaplain, and Reverends Carroll, Harrison, Brown and Odell, walked from the east end to west door and back again repeating alternately verses of Psalm 24. The bishop then sat on the north side of the communion table and received the deed of conveyance and read it to congregation. The chaplain read the first sentence of the consecration and then commenced the usual service of the day. The formal ceremony was concluded. The correspondent went on to observe:

> The Bishop preached on 2 Chronicles 7–12. He exhorted his listeners to make offerings of a suitable value. As it was not shown that there was any great want of funds, the appeal was not responded to we apprehend with general liberality.
>
> Hale men of the 59th regiment were in attendance and being provided with hymn books, assisted in better harmony than the churchgoers of Victoria are in the habit of hearing, a defect which, now the church is out of debt, we trust will soon be remedied.

Details of St John's early colonial chaplains are sparse, and their impact on the cathedral is difficult to assess. The minutes and correspondence of the trustees, the narrative backbone of intelligence on the cathedral itself in the earlier years, are lost between 1850 and 1858. Samuel Watson Steedman took up his post in 1852. The ill-fated E. T. Moncrieff from St Paul's was acting chaplain in the interim. Steedman had been military chaplain in Hong Kong and had officiated at the opening of 'the British church' as it was called, in Canton in 1849.

If Steedman's tenure was brief, Reverend William Baxter came and went after him in a blink. Baxter, it turns out, was in debt in England, where he had been charged by petition to the House of Commons. This gave rise for a letter on the matter from Major Caine, as acting governor, dated 21 August 1854, to Lord Grey, the secretary for the colonies. Bishop Smith suspended Baxter's licence, pending investigations. This must have curtailed his use to St John's, and then he was gone.[13]

James John Irwin, who held the position for over a decade from 1855, we are a little more informed on, at least about his domestic life. He married twice and had four children by two wives. His first wife, May, who bore him a son, died in July 1857, which may explain the leave of absence he took in the October of that year. It lasted till February 1859. In May 1865, now with his second wife, Emma, who had given him two children, he took leave again to return in December 1867, when he appears to have been immediately replaced by William Beach.[14]

Irwin was a friend of Robert Lechler, a vigorously eccentric pioneer of the Basel Mission, who worked in China for fifty-two years and took Irwin in a missionary-cum-shooting party up the Pearl River to Sham Chun (Shenzhen). It was an interesting group, including Thomas Stringer, a CMS missionary; Ernest Eitel, linguist and historian; and one Captain Drummond of the 99th Foot. There recording this was Jonathan Fry, a young Englishman from CMS, who was teaching at St Paul's College and doing his best to immerse himself in Chinese language and culture. Unfortunately, all he could note of Irwin in this account was that he slept on deck at night.[15]

For whoever held it, the colonial chaplaincy was no sinecure. Ministering alone to a fluid, opinionated parish, trying to teach and to take the Gospel to the locals as well as being responsible for a large and developing cathedral church bore with it considerable strains. One of the most testing tasks was to mediate among the trustees, usually men of confidence, authority and attitudes under pressure from other colonialists who were bent at once on maintaining Christian virtues and social status.

An issue delivered to them even before the building was completed was the putting up of memorials. The procession of coloured windows, tablets and plaques that the cathedral was to collect over ninety years became inexorable. Only invasion halted it. Even at the beginning, the trustees sought restraint, but it was difficult to exercise. By the time of their removal by the Japanese during their occupation, they had become an elaborate, cluttered, often poignant mural of clues to the past of both church and city.

The first application was quite grand. At a meeting of 1 May 1848, the family of Lord Napier, the late superintendent of trade, asked that a memorial be erected in the grounds of St John's.[16] This memorial already existed. It had been bought in England years before, fallen into pieces after a fire and become an unlovely wreck. The trustees baulked at accepting the shambles. However, rejecting it would have been letting the imperial side down. They agreed to repair and erect it. Whether it ever stood in its entirety is questionable. Certainly an inscribed part of it got to the church wall, telling us that Napier had been 'sacrificed to zeal with which he endeavoured to discharge the arduous duties of the time'. Also approved was a plaque erected by the ship's company to William Hardy, captain of HMS *Scout*, who had been killed in a pirate attack. Rather ungraciously, it would appear, the Reverend Stanton asks that the sailors be charged for the inscription. By the late 1860s, a charge for erecting a tablet, at a starting point of $100—for Thomas Boulder, bosun of HMS *Perseus*, lost fighting the Great Fire of 1857—to $250 to P&O for the loss of a ship, was becoming as predictable as a funeral fee.[17]

The same meeting welcomed the gift of encaustic tiles from Herbert Minton of Staffordshire. These innovative, delicate and colourful pieces can still be seen in the quiet chapel, which they first adorned when it was the baptistery, and in a part of the sanctuary. What cannot be seen is decorative crosses that had been cut into the building's buttresses. Objection on grounds unknown, perhaps excessive Romanism, was made to them, and they were filled in.

The cathedral's walls were quick to remember those who had perished in the early days before they were built. A sizeable tablet stood to all those men of the early regiments, the 11th, 18th, 20th,

75th, 98th, the Ceylon Rifles and in some cases their entire families who died from plague and are buried at Stanley. From it you learn, with pathos, that in 1844, Mary Anne was a popular name.

The sea is not forgotten. There was a tablet to the warmingly named vessels of the India and China trade which had disappeared beneath the waves in the ten years previous, sixteen in all, including *Mischief, Coquette, Mavis, Caroline* and *The Anna Elisa*. Some of them perhaps were named after the women who would be standing on paths up the Peak straining to see the Lye Mun Gap for ships that would never return.[18]

A sign of where not so much the sympathies as the assumptions of the cathedral community lay at that time was the erection of a memorial tablet in 1851, to the extravagantly named Augustus Frederick Hippolyto Da Costa, a 27-year-old captain of the Royal Engineers, who was 'wantonly attacked and murdered by Chinese pirates while walking by the seaside' accompanied by Lieutenant Dwyer of the Ceylon Rifles, who was also despatched.

This was briefly a *cause célèbre* in Hong Kong, not all the foreign community's sympathy lying with Da Costa. The alleged killers were a pirate, Chui Apo, and men in Wong Ma Kok Village near Stanley Fort. The pair were beaten, trussed and thrown into the sea. Villagers gave a convincing account of two young European men, arrogant with alcohol after a long lunch, abusing and molesting a girl. When Chui Apo asked them to stop, they fought.

Police identified the village, and Chui fled to his pirate fleet, which was decimated by the navy. He hid in China for two years before being arrested by Manchu officials and taken away from Canton by a British ship.

The plaque went up even before a verdict. The judge agreed that the soldiers were provocative but gave Chui life transportation. A huge controversy raged, including on the point that he should have been tried by Chinese court. Chui preferred, he said, to die. He hanged himself in his cell. Da Costa remained on the cathedral walls described as 'esteemed for … his upright character' for ninety more years.[19]

Naturally, some memorials were put up by families who could afford it. One such with great loss to assuage was the family of Fitzroy Delamere Foster, who died on Her Majesty's Brig *Bittern* in 1857, on 'the Canton River' from causes unspecified. He was 16, most likely a junior midshipman. George Urmson, a 37-year-old merchant who had been in Hong Kong for sixteen years, was trying to get home to Frodsham, Cheshire, in 1860. He did not make it. He died at sea before he got to Penang. Somebody missed him enough to want us to remember.

Other tablets went up by public subscription. One of them—'a faint expression of universal regret at lamented death'—is to Lieutenant Colonel Richard Tomkins RA and Lieutenant James R. Lugg RA, who were blown up by a dynamite stock whilst fighting the Great Fire of 1857. Another is to the crew of the P&O steamship *Corea*, lost in a typhoon in June 1865. This so touched the public heart that the governor, McDonnell, used his authority over the cathedral to require a memorial service.

More onerous for the trustees than the control of memorial plaques and tablets was the ordering of worshippers in their rightful seats. Encouraged by England's Church Buildings Act of 1818, the better seating in a church was often rented out to individuals, firms or families on an annual basis, as a means of raising funds. The welcome revenue was called 'pew rent'. In the case of St John's Cathedral, seats were allocated by the trustees not only according to availability but to the perceived station of the applicant in society. As well as sitting uncomfortably with the spirit of the Gospels, this was a system sufficiently subjective to prove inflammatory amongst rank-conscious Victorians, unless operated with unfailing deftness. Such was the pressure on early cathedral seating that it was sometimes not.

Of the 640 seats available in the completed church, 250 went to the military. One-third of the total was reserved for 'the poor', that is to say they were free, and the balance was for rent. The original pick of the rented seats or 'sittings' was made by the principal subscribers before the military took their apportionment but after free seats had been allocated to the governor and the military commanders. On 13 December 1848, choice was taken in order of the amounts subscribed, and gentlemen who had subscribed equal sums balloted for first their order of choice.[20]

It is no surprise that the front row pews in the nave and seats immediately behind went to names like Dent, Matheson, Bell, Lindsay and Halliday. Of individuals, Mr. Braine, our ferns collector, had fourteenth choice. Messrs. Parker, Cleverly, Mercer and Johnson, all serving or future trustees, had between eighteenth and twenty-second pick, and Major Caine, formerly chief magistrate and later colonial secretary but never a trustee, was twenty-third.

The trustees' correspondence still carries details of the military allocation by seat numbers but, such have the changes been in seating layouts since then, they do not signify very much and the cathedral gave up numbering seats a long time ago. There are still occasional hooks at pew ends, where the rent account book would have been discreetly hung.

Pew rents were set at $5 per sitting, per annum, in 1849. This was not the Hong Kong dollar that we know today. It was the Mexican silver dollar, a persisting legacy of the Spanish imperial trading network. The Mexican dollar enjoyed wide confidence in East Asia into to the twentieth century.

There was a hunger for seating and a need for revenue from sittings in a church not yet grown into the role it had been cast in. In a meeting of the trustees on 14 May 1858, there is a lengthy, faded record of their discomfort over how the cathedral was built to a scale which was meant to accommodate the military, the government and the Christian populace but had been left to the 'seatholders and stakeholders'—the original subscribers—to maintain. The cathedral needed official, regular financial support, they agreed as one.

St John's never did get precisely that. Indeed, the prospect of it receded over the century and had vanished entirely by the end of it. Sittings were to remain a major revenue source. It is unreasonable perhaps to have expected the congregation to be so ahead of its time, or the trustees so self-sacrificing of scarce income, as to abolish pew rents. Indeed, over time, when needs became urgent, up went the rents.

For example, the trustees held their quarterly meeting on 12 May 1859. Present in the vestry were George Cleverly, Francis Firth, George Lyall, M. Leslie, Thomas Walker and Henry Kingsmill, heavyweights of the early cathedral. This was not always the chosen venue. Sometimes they met in St Paul's College. Once they met in the rooms of the Asiatic Society. On some occasions the venue is not referred to. On this occasion, the accounts, audited by Hugh Bolder Gibb, showed a balance in favour of $155.45.

Francis Firth, who was with the Hong Kong and Shanghai Bank, actually proposed dropping the pew rent from $7 to $6. The argument for this generosity must have been interesting but is not discernible. He did not find a seconder. On the contrary, they put it up to $8.

There was pressure on space, and this was aggravated when fixtures and fittings were moved around and added to as the cathedral discovered how to operate better. On 4 August 1858, Cleverly, as surveyor-general, was authorised to take down the 'Singing Gallery' in the south transept and put 'fittings' in the vacant spaces. Victorians hated a decorative vacuum. At a meeting on 13 June 1860, after obvious delay, he was further pressed to take down this gallery and put in seats at floor level, where it had been.

We do not know what this gallery looked like or what sort of singing went on in it. We might presume it held a choir, but references to a choir are few up to this point. We can be quite sure, though, that it was in the south transept. A trustees meeting of 14 July records pretty prompt complaints from seatholders in that transept saying they had been moved to inconvenient places because of the addition of the seating.

At the time, the trustees were also trying to plan for a new organ up in the west gallery. There must have been seats up there, because they were having to be moved, and a ruckus was building. The trustees decided on firmness.

> Resolved that rows of seating in the West be immediately … added to the number of pews in the North transept and those sitting in the East {of the South transept} … be written to asking that, for the sake of providing sufficient accommodation for the choir, to suspend any further complaints until the organ gallery is completed.

Here there is a clear reference to a choir, in its infant state, and that it is destined for a place in the east. Where precisely the choir was seated is not exactly clear. One clue lies in a resolution of the trustees at their meeting of 2 November 1865. It was resolved that seats and cushions for the choir should be provided on the north side of the chancel, similar to those on the south side. This was seven years before the completion of the extension. In the shortened version of St John's, there barely was a chancel. It must have been a tight squeeze or a small choir.

Apart from costs and congestion, a significant pressure on sittings and the temper of the trustees was precedence. A 31 March 1866 meeting considered the request of Vice Admiral Sir George King, the naval commander-in-chief, for a row of sittings for him and his staff. The trustees were aware that there was disgruntlement in the Senior Service that the general officer commanding, then Major General Sir Philip Guy, had better seating and that some 'adjustment' needed to be made. No equivalent seating was available in either transept.

There was nothing for it but to squeeze another row at the front of the south side of the nave.

A four-foot depth was needed for a pew, but only two feet could be shaved off the area taken up by the altar. Trustee Wilberforce Wilson came up with an idea. Wilson was an assistant surveyor-general who was to succeed Cleverly that year. Three years later, he was to set up Wilson and Salway and build St Peter's, St Joseph's, Hong Kong Pier and Godown, and the German Club in Wyndham Street. This proposal was more modest. Shift all the pews starting from the west end back one inch and by the time you had reached the front, the clearing would be achieved. To avoid perceptions of demotion, the seat numbers behind the new naval row would remain the same.

Such simplicity took no account of the perception of one Albert Emile Vaucher, Broker and Merchant, formerly of Canton and now of Balls Court. Mr. Vaucher and his wife worshipped in seats 36 and 37 of row 6. Now they perceived that they were worshipping in what was really the seventh row, probably about eighteen inches further back from the pulpit from where they had been. That precise space was now taken up by seats 29 and 30, rented by Captain H. G. Thomsett RN (retd.), the harbour master.

Vaucher believed that the seats he had rented went with the very square of granite they stood on proximity to the pulpit being as much to do with rank as spiritual uplift. On 2 June 1866, the trustees were persuaded to write to Thomsett asking him to swap seats. They picked the wrong sailor. Thomsett was a sea dog in an already wounded frame of mind over sittings. Twice the trustees had given him the promise of a sitting and then broken it because, Thomsett suspected, somebody more important than him had come along. Finally installed in seats, he was less likely to move of his own volition than was Lion Rock.

There was a testy correspondence, head-tossing and the stagey turning of backs and, worse, a scene in the nave in which Mrs. Vaucher confronted Thomsett. Mrs. Vaucher was alone, either because Sunday recreation was more attractive to her husband or he thought that Thomsett would not hit a woman. The trustees, at a loss, asked the Attorney General to mediate, which goes to show how much of an officials' church St John's was.

But not sufficiently for this. The governor himself replied with a refusal. 'The aisle is not a suitable place for disputes ... a little common sense and forbearance ...' was the command of Sir Richard McDonnell. He was not obeyed. The matter was sent to legal counsel in London. Opinion along the lines of 'parishioners have the right to be seated according to their rank or station' came back. Somehow, this told against Captain Thomsett, which must have heated his sense of social grievance. Vaucher was restored to his seats.

The row was acclaimed as 'The Great Pew Debate', or words to that effect, although less had been said about a much more exalted and aggressive struggle coming out of the same furniture move. It erupted from James Whittal, a junior partner in Jardine Matheson who, on 27 April 1866, vigorously objected to the *hong* being shunted out of rows 3 and 4 by the army. He was furious for the standing of his firm, at the lack of notice and the indignity of being told by 'a sexton' to leave the seats.[21]

Francis Parry, trustee and lawyer in the firm of Birley and Co., replied in a direct fashion, laying out the regulations and powers of the trustees, which fanned flames and incurred dissent from some of his fellow trustees. Whittal waded into the division, questioning the very right of the trustees to tell subscribers where to sit. Jardines would not move. The fuss got bigger. The heads of the trustees were clearly singing over sittings. The suggestion was made that Jardines and the general sort it out between them.[22]

General Guy swept away the problem at a stroke. He was not very concerned. Jardines could have the seats they insisted on, and his entourage would shuffle elsewhere. In a statement of marked ungraciousness, Whittal said that he got what he wanted not by the general's consent but as of right. Whittal was clearly a tempestuous man. He left China in 1878, and started his own business based on London and Colombo. He was a director of the Chartered Bank until his death in 1894, upon which the *China Mail* wrote of him:

> He had a kindly disposition … a splendid specimen of what the British merchant can be … shrewd and honest with a kindly thought and word for all with whom he was brought into contact.[23]

His recorded contacts with the Church in Hong Kong were short on the 'kindly'. In 1872, he fell into a rash dispute with trustee F. W. Mitchell after termites had been found in the nave roof, claiming that Mitchell, in exchange for a donation he solicited from Whittal, guaranteed that the roof would last ten years. The accusation was made in the Legislative Council where both sat, Mitchell being the postmaster general. Mitchell denied in the chamber even having solicited a donation. Discomfited, Whittal had to back down and donated iron railings for the chancel, in penance.[24] These have not survived. Temperamental to the end, his will records that he cut off his son Percy 'with only a shilling'.[25]

Behind the unseemly squabbles around seating that had been disturbed lay the nineteenth century's argument in favour of the pew rent system. In a society that drew its certainties from the justness of rank and seniority, assurances were needed for calm within the church. On Sunday mornings there should be no rushes for favoured places, ill feelings over pre-emptions, squabbles over good seats being saved for latecomers or, most commonly, a false sense of proprietorship over perfectly free seats sat in repeatedly. The allocation of rented pews put all these concerns away, so that concentration before the service could be on devotions and snatches of socialising, *sotto voce*.

The trustees attempted flexibility and sympathy in the management of the system. By April 1866, Lindsay and Company had gone out of business. They had been $500 subscribers to St John's foundation. Now their seats were to be redistributed like the property of a deceased. At their meeting of 13 April, trustee Cecil C. Smith, then registrar general and one of the first three administrative cadets recruited to the new Hong Kong Colonial Service, proposed that a Mr. Linstead, who had occupied one of their seats for nine years as a company representative, be allowed to keep it instead of being cast onto the waiting list. After a little juggling with the wording, the motion was passed.

The largest and most costly item the trustees had to juggle with was the organ and, given its size, it was to be the most delicate. In fact there have been five organs installed during the history of St John's. Two were pipe organs, although they were moved about or modified and, since 1949, there have been three electronic instruments. The installation of the first organ was understandably the most protracted, coming all the way from England with an organist preceding it and, relatively speaking, the most expensive.

Consideration was given to raising money for an organ in January 1850. The trustees held back from this until the bishop arrived and in the hope that subscriptions to the tower appeal might cover the organ. That hope proved a forlorn one, and time drifted on until 5 May 1858, when there was a special meeting of the trustees to discuss the project. Present were the bishop, Henry Kingsmill, John Day, Thomas Walker and a Lieutenant Sewell, who may have been of the Royal Scots, stationed in Hong Kong at the time. The bishop was probably present, acting as chairman in the absence on leave of James Irwin and out of undoubted interest too.

Up to now, singing had been accompanied by a harmonium. It was decided to obtain a proper instrument from England at a cost of no more than 425 pounds. With what wisdom this sum was arrived at is not known, but clearly some homework had been done. They knew that they wanted an instrument with 25 stops and 1,124 pipes. They also knew that they would need an organ fund for raising the money. They had $1,400 earmarked already and were optimistic of subscriptions from European residents. Mr. Day was charged with forwarding the money to England.

The bishop was requested to contact Sir Frederick Gore-Moseley, professor of music at Oxford University, and ask him to find an organist and choirmaster for 200 pounds a year. One hundred pounds was to be spent on his passage round the Cape.

In an August 1924 edition of the cathedral's magazine, *Church Notes*, an article delving into the records has Henry Kingsmill writing to Gore-Moseley, countermanding this request for an organist, leaving the other trustees furious.[26] There is no obvious wording to this effect, and there was no clear reason for him to do this. What he did do was to alter the travel arrangements for the newly appointed organist, Mr. C. F. A. Sangster. An extra 50 pounds was voted to bring him overland so that he would be ready and waiting for the organ's arrival. In the event, he could have sailed twice round the world and still have been there before it.

By May the organ fund was overdrawn by $625. This was offset by $200 raised through collections by the Reverend W. R. Beach. Mr. Beach was to become colonial chaplain in December 1868, after returning from missionary work in Tientsin (Tianjin). However, in 1858, he was announced in the *Government Gazette* as being acting colonial chaplain, replacing the Reverend Harry Robinson, who had also been acting thus. Beach was demonstrating the enthusiastic energy for structural improvement that was to mark his later term.

By November, frustration was registering over delay in the organ. Bishop Smith said he had written in 'strong terms' to builder Bryceson and Sons, a highly respected but smaller, fast-growing organ builder in London, whose order book had probably bitten off more than it could chew. The bishop formed an enforcing subcommittee of himself and G. C. Leslie to deal with the unfortunate builder.[27]

The two must not have been quite tough enough. The organ had still not arrived by the trustees quarterly meeting of 9 May 1860. Mr. Sangster had long since arrived and had to be paid 100 pounds for doing nothing. He would not have been personally idle though. He came with legal qualifications too, and for much of his time as organist he was also a clerk to the courts and in the registrar general's office. The 100-pound payment was a rare moment of generosity towards Sangster. The trustees were to prove ever after grudging over giving him money. A striking example was their initial refusal of half pay while he applied for long leave in 1869, for the first time in nine years. Only when he suggested finding a substitute organist for half his pay would they pay him the other half.[28]

Present at the fully attended quarterly meeting were the main players in the organ drama: W. T. Mercer, the colonial secretary; Henry Kingsmill, Acting Attorney General; Charles Cleverly, surveyor general still; and Thomas L. Walker, architect and surveyor and deputy to Cleverly. The two elected members were James J. Mackenzie, a partner in Dent & Co., and George Lyall, a merchant of Lyall, Still and Co. and agent for the Hong Kong Steam Packet Company. Lyall had the distinction of buying what was effectively Government House in Spring Garden Lane, Wan Chai, when it was vacated by Sir George Bonham. In what was becoming the spirit of Hong Kong, he cleared the site and built godowns and a coal depot.

Discussion that day postponed talk of the organ and focussed on the 'circumstances of the last meeting', which remain mysterious, except that we know it involved the chaplain, the bishop and the colonial treasurer. The minutes themselves admit to a 'heated discussion'. There was no resolution. The 'question' was dropped. On 28 May, at a special meeting with Beach in the chair, calmer heads discussed Kingsmill's proposal to alter the western gallery and put the organ up there.

Henry Kingsmill was a barrister who had just worked his way up to the post of Attorney General. One senses a certain sunniness and imagination under what would have been the starched cotton and heavy frock coats of his position. Before he left the colony in 1877, he is recorded as living in a house called 'As You Like It' on Albany Hill Road.[29] Kingsmill said that the organ could be low enough off the gallery floor for the pipes to clear the roof. Thomas Walker countered with a motion that it be put on a platform in the south transept. Not having a head for heights, Beach, Walker and Lyall outvoted Kingsmill and Mercer in favour of that.

At the next meeting, on 4 June, Kingsmill rallied with objection that the south transept windows are always open in summer. Perhaps disingenuously, he suggested a move to the north transept. Lyall objected immediately, pointing out that that was where the typhoons come. Mercer slipped in with a motion that it should go back to the west end, and this is carried unanimously. Walker must have swapped sides between meetings. He pulled out a plan for a western gallery extension, showing how to alter the west door to preserve the symmetry of the cathedral and how the height of the gallery above the west door must be altered some feet to give the organ pipes clearance.

Thomas Walker's plan did not survive. Although we can be sure that the organ did spend time in the western gallery, we can only imagine what shape this outward extension took. If you stand in the east and look back at the gallery, everything is in perfect symmetrical order. There is no evidence it was tinkered with. Perhaps this is tribute to the care the trustees took to restore the site when the short-lived installation came to an end. It was taken down, eventually, in 1872.

By the end of the month, the trustees were paying off Messrs. Jeffrey Livingstone, freighter, and the organ account with Brycesons, the builder, was being settled. By Christmas the organ had arrived. Only a casting vote by Reverend Beach got the impecunious trustees to approve $20 to Quarter Master Sergeant Margate, recruited by Kingsmill, to put up the organ. The harmonium was bought by the navy, possibly for the dockyard.[30] There was so little in the trustees' purse that they had to be tight with the strings. They had an annual cash flow of only around $600, which was manageable if nothing untoward cropped up, but the costs of installing the instrument and paying the organist were overpowering and called for another appeal for subscriptions.

The placement of the organ made great vibrations through seating arrangements and the positioning of other fixtures. The unforgiving climate and technical ignorance made the instrument a rolling curse on costs. Even the church coolies wanted more pay because they had to pump the bellows. They got a dollar. Mr. Sangster ran up $15 costs for buying music and was paid with a grinding of teeth and the admonition that he must get trustees' approval before he bought any more.[31]

By June 1864, it was broken. Sangster had spent $180 on *ad hoc* repairs to the pipes and bellows. Agents and solicitors J. J. Mackenzie in London were told to arrange repair with Brycesons—and substitute a trumpet stop for a *posaune*, according to a hasty insertion in the minutes. Mackenzie was to make a deal to bring out a skilled builder who knew his stops, for a total of $325 including passage, freight and insurance, second class return. The report back was alarming. Such a package would cost 415 pounds. The trustees were not ready to bite that bullet. They cast about for local solutions. An encouragingly musical-sounding Mr. Montabelli was considered but regarded as not up to it.

By November 1865, the trustees were desperate to bring out from 'home' a competent organ builder, repair it and remove it to the 'north end'. We have no plans for what was intended there, but it seems likely the organ was placed at the east of the transept and into the area now called the quiet chapel. Gone were Mr. Lyall's sensitivities to typhoons. Indeed, gone was Mr. Lyall, but not from this earth or even yet Hong Kong. He was to die in 1890, in Wellington, Somerset, the birthplace of Bishop Smith.[32] Thomas Walker on the other hand passed away only six months after he had sketched out the organ's future in the west gallery. Whatever happened up there cannot have been satisfactory, but a measure of consolation was that the gallery would be space for more free seats.

The 1865 trustees were W. A. Alexander, Wilberforce Wilson, Cecil C. Smith, Francis Parry, Robert Walker and J. Simpson. Unfortunately, Alexander and Smith had not been at the November meeting, they had not received notice of the proposals and did not approve of the resolutions. At the December meeting they forced a further resolution that 'no meeting shall be called unless the main business is clearly defined in a circular from the secretary four days in advance'. So it remains to this day.

Trustee Alexander suggested, sagely perhaps, that organ alterations should wait until the projected chancel extension was built, but he was voted down 4 to 2. The original proposals were carried by the same margin. 'H. E. Governor's approval was laid before the meeting.' The governor's approval was an interesting condition to an internal alteration, particularly since there is no record of him paying for any of it. At this point, Bishop Smith has gone, the see is vacant and the colonial chaplain is on leave. Perhaps the trustees looked for sanction from some higher authority. The trustees decided on another appeal for money. At this point Wilberforce Wilson suggested to unanimous and relieved approval that work on the west gallery at least should be delayed until the results of the appeal were known. It seems likely that the fitting of seats up there was never gone through with.

There were predictable tensions with the organ builders Brycesons, who were considered responsible for a defective organ. Brycesons, however, did not consider themselves responsible for its reaction to destructive humidity it could not be designed for. R. B. Parr, a former trustee and acting for them in London, had a 'most unsatisfactory interview' with the company in February 1867. They despatched to Hong Kong an organ builder, an unfortunate Mr. Stuckey, who died so early on the way out that Mr. Parr was told to try and negotiate a full refund of his ticket from P&O. It became a Mr. Fletcher from Brycesons who, having survived his passage, was called on to account for repair costs at the trustees meeting of 5 November. This was followed by a 'long discussion'—minutes' code for disagreement—on the way money was being spent.

The trustees showed their irritation by being disapproving of a $100 payment made to the hapless Mr. Sangster by Francis Parry, acting as treasurer, he having simply circulated his intention to the trustees. Wilberforce Smith went as far as to call it 'irregular and illegal'. Parry was deeply upset, calling the language 'very unparliamentary'. Smith appealed to Bishop Alford, who had now arrived in the diocese and was in the chair in the absence, still, of any chaplain. Allowing just one of those words and not the other, His Lordship ruled with obtuse diplomacy that, 'in abstract', Parry's action was irregular.

A row followed over the settling of the organ account with Brycesons. They claimed that 191 pounds was outstanding. The trustees denied there was a penny. Disagreement was so protracted that a settlement of 29 pounds 10 shillings was not reached until April 1871. The original estimates for this work, arrived at on 1 January 1866, were $1,750 for repairs to the organ, $100 for its removal, and $700 for alterations to the north-east corner. The bill from Mr. Fletcher of Brycesons in 1867 turned out to be 200 pounds for 'materials', 230 pounds for Mr. Fletcher himself, whose work on the organ was acclaimed by Mr. Sangster, 10 pounds for coolies and 10 pounds for 'travel'. The trustees at this point were 328 pounds short of meeting the bill, plus the fare for the deceased Mr. Stuckey, which they seemed unlikely to get back. Chow Ah Tuck was the contractor who moved the instrument, and it was reopened at a choral service of celebration on Sunday, 23

February 1868, to a setting by Tallis. Chaplain Beach preached, and they sang the 'Hallelujah Chorus' whilst a collection was made for the organ fund. The local *Musical Express* magazine described the organ as 'decidedly the best this side of Suez'.[33]

In that long-ago 1866 meeting which sanctioned the moving of the organ, approval was given to the extension of a more mute fixture which had just as much impact. *Punkahs* had been installed in part of the cathedral the previous year. Languidly inefficient though they were, it is difficult to imagine the discomfort that the stoically formal and heavily dressed European congregation must have suffered before them. Now they were to be extended throughout the building. The *punkahs* were made of fabric, 540 square feet of it costing $1,081, and stretched out on iron frames costing $393. A 'special collection' was made for them. W. L. Pattenden, a trustee and an original Cathedral Council member, in his farewell speech in the cathedral hall in March 1930, recalled how they were operated. Boys, real, small boys, sat in the gutter outside the church building, pulling the ropes that swung the *punkahs*, and an adult 'boy' wandered round giving them a kick if they slowed down or nodded off.[34]

No sooner had the new *punkahs* been put in than pulley wheels were stolen in 'sight and sound' of the church coolies, who seemingly made no effort to catch the thieves. There were usually two coolies on staff at this stage. The Number 1 Boy was paid $8 a month and the other, $6. Fire them both was the initial temper of the trustees. However, following a motion by Mr. Simpson, in a calmer mood, they fired the older coolie as more culpable and as a warning to the younger one, who probably got his job.

Where to keep the coolies was a question that occurred around this time. Although they were expected to live around the premises, they were not supposed to live in them, so it was quite a surprise when one clergyman discovered bedbugs in the vestry. Clearly, the men had been dossing down in this solid structure instead of under flimsy outside awnings. So, they built them a coolie house for $400. That was not of bricks and mortar either, more of wood and fillings, but better than before and what they might expect elsewhere. The location was in the area of what is now the Li Hall kitchen and lavatories extension.

If the organ and the coolies' house represented extremes in alteration, other substantial changes to the look of St John's were made in the twenty years before its lengthening. Important, a little mysterious and with a moment of farce was the repositioning of the pulpit. In February 1862, both the bishop and the governor asked the trustees to consider moving it from 'its present position at the first and most eastern pillar on the south side of the nave'. The objection was not only that, liturgically, it was on the wrong side. Officiating clergy were having difficulty being heard in all parts of the cathedral, they said. Those in the most forward nave pews had the preacher talking away from them, and in the south transept they only saw the back of him.

Bishop Smith seems to have become as involved as he could in this. He formed a subcommittee of himself and Cleverly. Then he went to Foochow (Fuzhou). Cleverly and the influential Mr. Alexander also absented themselves. Those left behind conducted 'sundry experiments' in placing the lectern where the pulpit now was. They were concerned that no move could be made without the consent of the affected seatholders. Sittings would be lost and 'injury done' to some of the best of them by putting the pulpit further away. By the same measure, humbler folk in once ordinary seats would suddenly find themselves shot up in the order of things by it coming nearer.

Then came a moment of farce. There was, in some quarters, profound objection to the canopy, also known as a sounding board, which hung over the pulpit. The practical purpose of these features was to prevent the sound from the preacher drifting upwards, by deflecting it outwards to the congregation. They were often decorated, as this one was, rather elegantly, and may have offended more Puritan temperaments by seeming too regal or 'popish'.

There was a gathering on 11 February 1862, in the home of the Reverend Lewins, attended among others by Reverend Pitkins and Lieutenant Howarth of HM Gunboat *Weazel*. Given the company, we must assume that drink was not taken but emotions became heated nonetheless. Reverend Lewins declared to Howarth, 'I would give you $25 if these (sounding boards) were taken down.' That would also include the back panel to the pulpit.

Howarth took him in earnest. The foolish fellow went to St John's with men from the aptly named *Weazel* and dismantled and took away the boards. At the inevitable inquiry held by the more bemused than angry trustees, Howarth was required to reinstate the sounding boards at his own expense. Lewins said he did not expect to be taken seriously although he had told the gullible Howarth that he was 'chairman of the trustees' and that 'the church coolies will assist without any trouble'. In that, he spoke the truth. When a party of uniformed Europeans entered the church giving orders, they prudently cooperated.[35]

Yet, as soon as Howarth had put the boards back up, they were taken down again. The trustees agreed by circular letter of 7 March to take down the boards, and they were removed later in the month. There was clearly inherent opposition to them. Howarth of the gunboat had just jumped the gun. The trustees convened again on 24 March 1862, with the chaplain, one presumes Mr. Irwin, in the chair. No direct reference to the removal of the pulpit to the north side is made here. All that is observed is a detail, that the preacher would be more audible if the pulpit was lowered 'one or two feet' and placed against the north-east or the south-east pier.

What was actually resolved was teasing for pinpointing the pulpit. The reading desk should be relocated, they said. The only point in doing that would be to take it to the south side, and by convention the pulpit would be opposite it. The bishop's throne was to be moved to the south side of the choir, 'the usual and proper situation'. Bishop Smith approved these measures with his customary signature, on 8 April and with the stipulation that the throne must be on the opposite side of the church to the pulpit. This and other adjustments were to be made as soon as funds were made available by the colonial government. The government had discretion over what of the cathedral projects it funded, and it was choosy in this. We cannot be sure if they came through with this money and whether the moves were made as completely as resolved. From a meeting of 25 April 1867, five years on, there is a motion ordering, or pleading perhaps, that arrangements of the bishop's throne be carried out. An amendment to it, which was carried, stated 'that simply a chair should be made at present'.

It has been said that a pulpit move was not made until a time in the twentieth century. Photographic evidence seems to refute that. A photograph of the nave, looking east, taken around 1896, shows what appears to be a raised pulpit, without canopy or backboard, on the north side, in the same position as the pulpit of the present day. The strong suggestion is that the move was made after spring 1862, and certainly before 1896.

The other adjustments sanctioned by the bishop were to move the sedilia, the three-seat arrangement for officiant, deacon and subdeacon, and the clergy stalls to the west of the choir. That is close to where they are presently positioned, yet how all this furniture could have been moved about with any distinction in such a tiny chancel as that of the shorter St John's is a testimony to ingenuity. Included too was a decision that the 'present vestry should be made into the Bishop's robing room'. The step is a measure of the authority that Bishop Smith had established over his cathedral despite his many absences. Never afterwards is there a reference to any room being in the possession of the bishop. Indeed, only eleven years on there would even be the question raised as to whether the bishop had any right to so much as enter St John's without being invited by the chaplain.

In its earliest years, St John's had just one permanent clergyman serving it, the colonial chaplain. The chaplain was to carry on largely singlehanded until the first assistant was brought in in 1899. He might be assisted or deputized for by CMS clergy, ministering or teaching in Hong Kong or in transit to China, or by services chaplains.

In 1851, the clergy consisted of Bishop Smith, Chaplain Victor Stanton, E. T. Moncrieff, the St Paul's schoolmaster who deputised for Stanton and acted as domestic chaplain to the bishop, and M. C. Odell, 'junior tutor' at St Paul's. Odell, and C. R. Carroll, licensed to St John's in March 1853, acted for the second Chaplain, Steedman. The Reverends Robinson, Beach, John Wilson and Charles F. Warren, who was made priest at the cathedral in December 1867, stood in during the lengthy absences of Irwin.

John Piper, ordained as a priest in St John's in 1869, has been claimed by the CMS as Beach's 'successor', as colonial chaplain proper, for covering eight months of the interregnum between Beach and the fifth incumbent, Richard Hayward Kidd. That status has never been acknowledged, and his name does not appear on the roll by the west door of the cathedral. Thomas Talbot succeeded him until Kidd's appointment. Thomas Springer's name does not appear on the board either, he who was one of the Rechler mission and shooting party to the Mainland which Irwin joined. CMS records merrily claim for him three years as colonial chaplain, but it is difficult to see how, entirely unsung, he could have squeezed those into the sequence.

Apart from men like Warren, who was licensed for work in Hong Kong, it became a policy that all men who were to be ordained as clergy for missionary work in the vast diocese should be ordained in St John's. This gave the cathedral some founding connection with the missionary effort led by its bishops, who called it their seat.

In those first decades of its life, though, it was rare for it to be involved in the ordination and despatch of Chinese missionaries into the field. There were few it could engage with, because the conversion of locals was slow and patchy. The cathedral's attention was held by the city and its mostly British inhabitants. A confirmation service held at the cathedral on 25 January 1863 included 32 Europeans and 18 Chinese. Another service on 13 December yielded 9 Europeans and 6 Chinese. In fairness, the total numbers here are not too different from those of adult baptism and confirmation services in the cathedral at the beginning of the twenty-first century, and the ratio of Chinese to Europeans for the time seems encouragingly high. Yet the total number of Chinese confirmations recorded during the episcopacy of Bishop Alford, 1867–72, was 3 out of a total of 70.

In the shade of disappointment, the year 1863 stands out as a bright moment. On Monday, 21 December, catechist Lo Sam Yuen was made a deacon in an ordination service at St John's. Bishop Smith was joyful over this. Lo was the first Chinese to be ordained in Hong Kong and only one of two deacons Smith had admitted in his time in China. In a report to the CMS made on 1 January 1863, he wrote that it was 'with much satisfaction and thankfulness that I have admitted your excellent native catechist Lo Sam Yuen to deacon's orders'. He said that his knowledge of his character both in Hong Kong and the Australian goldfields fully justified admitting him.[36]

Smith had good reason to declare his certainties. He had suffered considerable hurt from another catechist, Chan Tai Kwong, whom he had taken up in London and actually presented to the archbishop, who had given him books. Back in Hong Kong, Chan, empowered by quick wits and English, quit St Paul's College and became involved in a large opium monopoly. This fell apart and, accused of bribing the colonial secretary, he fled Hong Kong. Though he prospered again later, it marked the end of his connection with the Church.

Lo's progress was a shining vindication. The ceremony took place in what Smith describes as 'the nave of our beautiful structure'. Forty English residents were present in the cathedral, including the wives of the acting governor and the Attorney General. Also present were two hundred Chinese 'among them the more influential portion of the native population', the bishop reported to the CMS.[37] This included the pupils of St Paul's and the newly formed Diocesan Native Female Training School plus several native interpreters and writers in the public offices. This did not include the businessmen and secret society leaders of the Lower Bazaar, whose influence in the city was most considerable in those jockeying times, but that would have been too much to hope for.

On Christmas Day, Bishop Smith preached in the cathedral on behalf of the CMS and in support of the 'native minister'. Lo was in his surplice and assisted in administering the elements in their own language to the Chinese portion of the communicants. Chinese converts numbered 25 out of the 75 communicants. A collection brought in $400. Lo never went on to be priested. He assisted CMS agents in the running of St Stephen's Church and looking after its congregation.[38] In 1863, the bishop ordained another deacon in Shanghai and achieved sixty Chinese conversions in the diocese. It was his twentieth year of mission in China. He had been 'humbled under … a sense of unprofitableness'. Now he saw 'streaks of hope lightning up the dark horizon … To God be all the glory.'[39]

Glorification in bricks and mortar, with considerable complications, was coming to St John's. Ten years on from Bishop Smith's streaks of hope, the chancel was to grow to its present length, bells were to be hoisted in the tower—and the nave roof was to be found rotten. Trustee Wilberforce Wilson, representing his architectural firm, Wilson and Salway, handed in his design for a chancel extension to the trustees meeting of 9 June 1868. No mention is made of submissions from elsewhere. W. Keswick and Thomas Pyke, another merchant from Birley and Company, were new seatholders' representatives, but attendance at this meeting cannot have been good. Francis Mitchell, postmaster-general, later auditor-general, was called away by the governor to an Executive Council meeting, so they adjourned inquorate.

The design of the cathedral with its abrupt chancel would obviously have proved a restriction on choir and clergy seating and liturgical movement. Yet reasoning for its extension remains obscure. More seats were needed for the military, was a principal reason given to government. There may have been a surge in garrison strength in the later 1860s. A sceptical Governor McDonnell observed that the church was never full as it was.

Trustee Edward Pollard, who arrived from New South Wales in 1847, began as a judge's clerk and rose to become a Queen's Counsel, was 'solicited' to draft a letter to the government asking them to share the costs by matching public contributions dollar for dollar, as it had turned out with the original cathedral. His words had some effect on the doubtful McDonnell. He in turn had an impact on the Earl of Kimberly, the colonial secretary to whom he wrote on 11 September 1872, '... the Colony should provide Church accommodation for the troops and it is partially on this ground that I think the vote of the Legislative Council to be justified.' The government came back with a specific pledge of $3,500 if the same amount could be raised to match it.[40]

Even more tellingly, the governor, now Sir Arthur Kennedy and not even an Anglican, concluded with a piece of philosophy which was to resonate through the relationship between St John's and the Crown even after the cathedral was 'disendowed'. 'In a Crown Colony,' he wrote, 'having so long as the Church of England is the State Church, she has peculiar claims on the State for aid in carrying out works of necessity ...'[41]

At the same time as Wilson's plans were being submitted, Francis Parry, a former trustee, was donating bells. One bell, cast as far back as 1845, was already up there.[42] Parry is notable for having fathered seven children between 1865 and 1873.[43] He was obviously at a stage in life when bells were ringing for him, and he offered three more to the cathedral, with ringing mechanism, if the trustees would pay for their installation. This was to cost them $329, but they agreed. On 2 January 1870, the second Sunday after Christmas, Parry's bells, cast by Messrs. Mears and Stainbeck of Whitechapel, were dedicated in the belfry and rang for the first time. They were to ring on until a shocking Christmas seventy-one years later. Alan Jephinson, a clerk in the naval yard, was granted a free sitting in exchange for ringing them.[44]

Chaplain Beach was a writer not shy of flourish, and he penned a prayer to what he called 'the festal chimes'. The last line was as sonorous as any bell.

> Grant that as the passing bell warns of a soul summoned home,
> we may have grace to think of our last hour and to prepare for
> the great account.

Mr. Beach was a man of some resource and sensitive to opportunity. To mark the visit of Alfred, Duke of Edinburgh, second son of Queen Victoria, to Hong Kong in 1869, he not only compiled and published an illustrated book from the visit which ran into two editions, but he also bagged the prince for the foundation stone laying of the cathedral extension.

Now in the keeping of Cornell University, the book *Visit of His Royal Highness, the Duke of Edinburgh … to Hongkong in 1869*, written at the behest of the governor, according to Beach, gushes with patriotic deference and hyperboles which not even the most ardent royalists could bring themselves to today. Yet it is a splendidly full account of the visit down to the sailing history and complement of HMS *Galatea* (officers 46, petty officers 65, seamen 305, boys 46 and marines 68) which brought Prince Alfred, and excruciating detail of a comedy 'A Wonderful Woman' staged for the prince by the Amateur Dramatic Club at the City Hall. Gratitude is owed equally to J. Thompson FRGS, who contributed invaluable photographs, including the one clear picture from outside the old east end of St John's with the foundation stone, freshly laid and standing off on a plinth, ready to receive the extension.

Prince Alfred squeezed in the stone laying hours before embarking for his departure on the afternoon of 16 November. It was quite a grand affair, as one would expect. At 10 a.m. the clergy, choir and an honour guard from the 75th Regiment lined up to meet him along with the Honourables J. G. Austin, W. Keswick, E. H. Pollard and Messrs. Mitchell, Moorsom and Pyke, the current trustees. The national anthem and Psalm 84 were sung. There were prayers and a reading by R. O. Callaghan, the Naval Chaplain.

The prince placed mortar on the stone with a silver trowel and an invocation of the Trinity. There followed a hymn, suffrages for the Queen and royal family and then Canon Beach made a speech. It is worth noting that Beach described himself in his book as the Reverend Canon Beach.

It would appear that, by 1868, Bishop Alford had created, as he was entitled to do, four canons of the Cathedral of St John the Evangelist: J. H. Gray, Archdeacon of Canton, T. McClachtie of Hankow (Hankou), C. H. Butcher of Shanghai, and Beach. All of them, bar Beach, were missionary clergy in China. If Prince Alfred could be described as a casual visitor, he might have thought he was officiating at an overseas version of an English cathedral. Beach occasionally styled himself 'The Reverend Canon' and 'canon residentiary', though resident in what is difficult to tell. You could hardly describe Battery Path and the coolies' house as a precinct.

Canonical government was an illusion. It was an aspiration which was to reappear with Bishops Hoare, Duppuy and Hall, based on hope but not the mechanics of St John's founding structure. In this Beach was, more modestly, an employee of the governor and under the ecclesiastical authority of a bishop. A prison chaplain would recognise the circumstances. Beach, though, had the added complexity of needing the cooperation of six laymen to conduct the secular business of his parish in an age before parochial church councils had been thought of. The relationships were fudged but they were to evolve. As with any evolution, this would not be without some pain.

Constitutional considerations did not distract Canon Beach from his liquid blueberry prose for the occasion or the placement of capital letters which put God and the Sovereign on almost an equal footing.

> It is our constant prayer that the most high God whose servants we are may be pleased long to keep and bless the Person and prosper the reign of our beloved Sovereign and that He may ever bestow His choicest gifts upon all the members of the Royal family.

It is not difficult to see why republicanism in Britain enjoyed such traction around this time.

Starting the job was still some way off. In January 1870, trustee Moorsom was finding fault with Mr. Wilson's plans, and it was not until April 1871 that they were resubmitted and steps were taken to begin the tendering process. Two days later, sanction from the 'Lieutenant Governor'—an unusual title for Hong Kong—was sought as formal authority to build.

No working drawings of chancel lengthening survive. It was completed towards the end of 1872. There were complaints of a delay, put down to bad work by the contractor, who cut some stones wrongly, although that was nothing compared to the time it took for the trustees to get the work started in the first place. The result, though, is a quiet but considerable architectural achievement.

As Peter Lovell points out in the first volume of his Conservation and Management Plan prepared for the trustees of St John's Cathedral in 2007, the 1873 additions all maintain the 1849–50 style of Gothic detail. The architect—conceivably Wilberforce Wilson of Wilson and Salway—did not fall into the temptation now all around him of moving into High Victorian Gothic. This new long church of 1873 was a 'transforming change in St John's Cathedral's perceived mass'. It moved from being what in England would have been recognised as a big parish church into the proportions which also define Ely, Canterbury and Salisbury Cathedrals as well as Westminster Abbey.

Success was achieved by simply repeating the bays and keeping the structure, the windows, the angles and other details exactly the same as the nave original, except for one point. The chancel ended up one bay longer than the nave itself. This is not entirely unknown in other churches, but it is highly unusual.

One structural feature of the new east end has fascinated subsequent generations. A narrow tunnel runs under the sanctuary from the clergy vestry to the choir vestry. Although servers at the Eucharist have said they found it useful for changing sides discreetly without cutting across the celebration, its purpose has never been clarion clear. One explanation is that, immediately before the service began, the chaplain, now robed, could have wanted to cross to the choir, lead them in prayer and then return to his vestry unseen.[45]

Outside, there was no expansion of ground levelling around the extension. The church was carried out on a deep base which simply fell away down a steep side. Development to its north over what was the Murray Parade Ground has filled in this effect, but contemporary illustrations show St John's standing out commandingly over the scene.

Indoors, there was some indecision. Should there be congregational seating in the new chancel? When you consider the argument that the trustees put to the government for chancel extension in the first place, it seems an extraordinary question, but Chaplain Kidd, who took office in 1871, after that pitch had been made, said he was against it. There was enough seating in the church already he said, echoing the previous governor's view; there was no money to provide it, and anyway, there were ecclesiastical objections to seating the laity that far up. This was August 1872, and the contractor was tapping his feet, waiting to lay the flooring. The trustees decided to agree with Kidd. Then, at an October meeting of the trustees, Kidd surprised them by changing his mind. He would have 64 seats in rows of 8.[46]

Richard Hayward Kidd, who was the son of a Rector of Potter Heigham in Norfolk and grandson of the classical scholar Thomas Kidd, arrived in Hong Kong in October 1871. He was to have a difficult personal life there. At this point his first son had just died, in March 1872, at 26 days old. Three years later his wife, Mary Maria, died at 38. Weeks later, he moved out of his Albany home, auctioning the furniture, and took leave in England. In July 1879, he died from dysentery at an address in Bonham Road, the only chaplain to die in office.[47] A notable feature of Kidd's incumbency was that he doubled as District Grand Chaplain for the Freemasons' lodges in Hong Kong. He was described in his obituary as 'an energetic and enthusiastic mason ever ready to advise an erring brother and assist him with his purse as far as he was able'. The link between the cathedral and free-masonry was made clear when the Masons were permitted to hold a service there on the Feast of St John 1875, in the hope that this would become an annual event.[48]

Perhaps Kidd's about-turn on seating was born of stress or pressure. He was to get more of it. Two trustees who had been absent from the meeting and disagreed with its decision forced a resolution, in October 1872, that no decision of a meeting could be reversed within six months without prior notice of intent to each trustee. They did not achieve a further reversal, but the point became moot. The roof was about to fall in, literally.[49] Lieutenant MacHardy of the Royal Engineers reported 'white ants', that is termites, in the roof of the nave. They had eaten their way into the soft wood. It would have to be replaced entirely by teak.

References to 'white ants' are unbroken through the cathedral's history. The first one crops up in May 1858, when arsenic and tar are purchased as the recommended measure against them. Over the years, enough arsenic must have been used around the cathedral's affected arboreal perimeter to knock out an army. Costs were one of the reasons that the pew rents at that time went up to $8. In 1872, the rents went up to $10, though the government was applied to and did contribute $5,000. The congregation—all of it—was forced to move into the new and hastily floored chancel for services while the nave roof was replaced. We hear nothing more of congregational seating in the chancel after the roof and order are restored.

The trustees were bracing themselves for another subscriptions exercise to find money for a new holy table, until unexpected help came from 'home'. A former worshipper at St John's, now back in England, Herbert Lawrence, raised funds from old China hands in Britain. In addition to the table, they sent out an altar cloth, litany stool, credence bracket, altar book desk, kneelers, service book with plain song chants, an alms basin and a brass eagle lectern. The P&O Line shipped everything out for free.[50] These were clearly shippers with conscience. They did it for St John's, frequently, decades hence.

Also to be born in mind was that the P&O's Hong Kong superintendent, Thomas Sutherland, was a partner of tycoon Douglas Lapraik, soon to be memorialised in coloured glass in St John's, and both were

Freemasons in the Zetland Lodge, along with many of the trustees, including Mercer, Kingsmill, Cleverly and Whittal of Jardines, who added his iron rails at this point. The charitable shipment would have come only naturally. Freemasonry was an almost ubiquitous brotherhood among the prominent merchants and professionals in Hong Kong from its introduction in 1846.

This last item on the shipping list, the lectern, is the one survivor of this largesse. The Lawrence donation is the first significant donation of accessories and fittings by parishioners. The cathedral came to recognise the usefulness in asking individual parishioners for items of pure function, beauty or both. With rare exceptions, like Sir Paul Chater, they could not alone provide fundamentals, but they were a resource for beautifying the church. As we shall see, future chaplains and deans would openly advertise 'wish lists' and wait for the pennies to drop.

The lengthening of the chancel and the altering of the east end of the church changed the destinations of stained glass memorial windows which were dedicated around that time. The original east end window consisted of three parallel lancets over the apse. At a trustees meeting of 24 January 1864, the officers of the Royal Regiment are thanked for donating two stained glass windows in memory of their men lost in the Arrow War. These windows are recorded as being installed in the north and south lancets. The centre lancet 'remains in its original state and irregular in appearance'. Henry Kingsmill and J. J. Mackenzie ask permission to put in a centre window that would harmonise. Then the wall changed and the window grew in size.

Into the new space went a memorial window to Douglas Lapraik. Lapraik, who had died in 1869, was a classic of the meteoric money legends which Hong Kong is made of. He began as a watchmaker's apprentice, created his own watchmaking business, branched out into shipping, started a steamship company and co-founded Hong Kong and Whampoa Dock Company. He founded the Hong Kong, Canton and Macau Steamboat Company and was on the Provisional Committee of the Hong Kong and Shanghai Bank. He was certainly a man big enough for an east window, and his grateful nephews, to whom he left everything, donated it at a cost of 600 pounds.

The window was made up of five grouped lancet lights supporting a rose panel. It was in Decorated Gothic style, giving a distinct thirteenth-to fourteenth-century look. Its themes were the Crucifixion, the Ascension and Old Testament stories. A much later Cathedral Council member and stalwart, A. S. Abbott, recalled it in a fundraising booklet for the new hall in 1955, in which he wrote with barely muted dislike:

> It showed the crucifixion involving centurions on horseback. Elijah was in a whirlwind ascent. Samson was burning Philistine's corn and Adam and Eve were staring at an apple.
>
> At the apex a green scroll read, 'That the abundance of Thy goodness may be known.'[51]

The Royal Regiment's windows would have been moved, because they are recorded as having been fitted into the north aisle. Henry Kingsmill must have waited long enough for his generous intentions to be deflected to the north transept. There, in 1868, was erected a window, by William Morris, to the memory of his wife, Frances. It featured women of the Old Testament. It was to share the site with a window to D. F. Stewart, a colonial secretary and former director of education who had clashed with Bishop Smith on the subject. Its theme was Christ and 'suffer the children'.

The south transept was not to remain bare. In 1872, former students of St Paul's College collected $480 to raise a window there to the memory of Bishop George Smith. The bishop had resigned, a sick man, in 1865, and gone back to England. He had remained an 'active supporter' of the CMS from whence he came, and he died in 1871.[52]

He was succeeded by Charles Richard Alford, a vigorous evangelical, dedicated to mission who carried 'the rather unusual combination of decided Protestantism with a vigilant guardianship of the rightful position of a Bishop', according to a CMS report.[53] His brief episcopacy was to be dogged from the beginning by a proposal to split his diocese. His successor was to arrive in 1872, reduced in authority.

St John's Cathedral, though, was now greater in splendour and more established in its city. That it was the heart of civic worship was readily recognised even by society's enemies. In 1858, there was an alleged if unpromising plot to tunnel under the cathedral and blow it up when the governor and the colony's worthies were present. Reverend James Legge speaks of it in a lecture on the beginnings of Hong Kong, which he gave in November 1872 at City Hall.[54] Governor Bowring, reporting to Lord Lytton at the Colonial Office, mentions it as one of several attacks on the authorities listed in a paper found on 'an emissary' apprehended in Jardines' stables.[55] The conspirators were alleged to have originated in Shun Tak, present-day Shunde.

Fear of covert hostile action by ill-disposed Chinese was not entirely paranoia. The attempt to poison the European population through their bread supply on 15 January 1857 was very real and shook the foreigners. Four hundred people, including the governor's wife, were affected, and some made quite poorly, but no one actually died. So rattled were they that a service of thanksgiving for their deliverance was held in St John's on 18 January. The day before, the *Friend of China* had urged its readers to 'be on the lookout'.

The cathedral was never blown up. Apart from an occasional sneaky robbery and Japanese shelling, no assault was ever made on it. Yet, though St John's was physically intact, it was about to have its relationships with bishop and government thoroughly shaken out.

Chapter 3
Quiescence and Struggle, 1873–1906

The decades following the completion of the chancel extension were, for St John's and its clergy, involved in defining boundaries. Mostly this was to do with the extents of authority within the church, but a boundary which defied precise description was one of the smallest of all, the extent of the cathedral compound and who the land belonged to.

On 6 February 1867, the trustees actually approved 50 pounds for the purchase of 'large and small' gates for the compound, to be ordered from England. There is no indication this was ever carried through though it does suggest that the cathedral thought the compound was its to lock up if it wanted to.[1]

The point of principle first arose where money was concerned. In November 1867, Gepthard and Company asked the trustees if they could enclose a tiny piece of the compound which abutted their offices, for a consideration. Wilberforce Wilson was feeling robust on the issue and said that the 1847 ordinance vested the land in the cathedral. Trustees Mitchell and Smith were doubtful. Where was the deed of covenant?

Where indeed, said the government, and refused permission. A deputation from the trustees, led by William Keswick, went to Governor McDonald in June of that year, asking him to give them title or otherwise define the powers of the trustees in the compound. That may have been too vexatious at the time. They came away empty-handed. Attorney General Julian Pauncefote is on record in the trustees' minutes of 1871, saying 'no grant even of the ground on which the cathedral stands has ever been made by the government'.

Undeterred and looking for some sort of security, in 1872 the trustees returned to the notion of setting up gates to the compound. Kennedy, now governor and an Irishman not worried about standing on ceremony, said he would come down and inspect the site himself. It is not certain that he took the walk, but the compound was certainly not enclosed. Mr. Ford, the government gardener was, however, kindly sent to set out shrubs.[2]

Ambiguity on this issue was very difficult to shake. In those days the retaining wall at the north of the compound, topped by a balustrade not more than waist-high on most adults, looked down over a vertical drop onto Murray Parade Ground. In 1879, it collapsed under two sailors.[3] The implication of responsibility by the cathedral suggests they were merely sitting on it rather than coming at it with the force of a brawl. They seem to have survived the drop.

The trustees approached the colonial secretary, who agreed to repair the wall though not to liability for it. There was a price. The surveyor general declared that the roadway through the compound was 'a public thoroughfare as great a convenience as any other in city'. The trustees accepted this and a right of way was conceded. Their concerns were still with fabric. The east wall was in bad repair. Edmund Sharp, sometime Crown solicitor and founder of Johnston, Stokes and Master, the prominent Hong Kong firm, gave $500 to its repair, if the first, not the greatest of his largesse to the cathedral. The government, continuing to perplex in this matter, refused a contribution.

No granting deed to or article of conveyance of the compound may have been identified in the first forty years of St John's, but the intention of the law was made clear, in statute, after the Church Body was created in 1892. A plan of the compound was deposited in the Land Office on 29 April 1892. The St John's Cathedral Church Ordinance of 1899, which consolidated the property-owning authority of the trustees, is clear on the position of the compound in section 6(1).

> Saint John's Cathedral Church and the precincts thereof (a plan of which, signed by the Director of Public Works and sealed with the seal of the Colony, was deposited at the Land Office on the 29th day of April, 1892) together with all buildings, rights, easements and appurtenances thereunto belonging, and together with all the estate, right, title and interest of the Church Body as heretofore constituted *shall vest in the trustees in fee simple* for the sole and express purpose of a church and to the intent that divine worship and the services usual in the Church of England shall be therein performed and carried on in accordance with the rites and ceremonies of the said Church.

This was reiterated in the Church of England Trust Ordinance of 1930, out of which the cathedral finds its modern constitution, and included in all consolidating ordinances over subsequent years.

According to Colonel R. F. Johnston's informal history manuscript of 1936, the plan deposited in the Land Office was rediscovered after having been mislaid for many years. Johnston tells us that it described the compound as a rectangle, between four boundary stones, conveyed to the trustees, subject to a public right of way from the north-west stone for 273 feet to Garden Road. The maintenance of this was the responsibility of the government, he says. Sad to say, this defining piece of paper disappeared for a second time, during the Japanese Occupation. Disappearing twice, it pushed its luck too far. It has never been recovered.[4]

As the years went on there were frequent references to the untidy state of the compound. Rectifying or even beautifying the place all depended on whether there was someone in the cathedral at the time with enough passion, or in the government with sufficient willingness. One such year was 1894. The government took steps to beautify the area, and the Public Works Department gave permission for the trustees to put up gas standard lights on it. In 1898, there was a planting of Formosan ferns, evergreens, two-feet high with pentagonal tripinnate fronds, the two lowest pinnae pointing downwards.

In 1903, letters were sent by the then Church Body to the Public Works Department, claiming government's responsibility for the appearance of the area and for the retaining wall over the parade ground. The government accepted its responsibility for maintaining the roadway but would be pinned down on nothing else.

In 1918, some improvements were made from private contributions from a Mr. Tutcher and Phoebe May, daughter of the governor. One of them was to actually thin out trees around the cathedral. Foliage was denser in the cathedral compound by this point, so much so that it was said that visitors had searched for the building while being within a few yards of it.

The cathedral choir has known no bounds in the church's story. At the very beginning, we have difficulty seeing it at all. In 2010, St John's was home to seven choirs. The choir has shrunk or expanded for reasons of finance, liturgy, war and personalities. It has been one of the strongest centres of fellowship in St John's, a font of rivalries, a musical educator and creator of excellence which presented the cathedral to the wider non-Christian, non-British populace. Its origins are somewhat obscure. At times it dwindled almost to nothing. At others it had such a large opinion on affairs, it posed interesting challenges to both clergy and trustees.

The existence of a choir is referred to in the trustees' minutes of 1858, when the need for more lady members is voiced. These would have been British ladies. It would be some time before Chinese ladies were heard.

We do not know exactly who fitted into the elusive 'Singing Gallery' that was removed in 1860, but there is a clear need to find room for singers in the south transept furniture reorganisation of that summer. Four years later, Mr. Sangster, the organist and choirmaster, was asking for $45 for improved choir seating. He was very lucky to get that, because shortly afterwards he was refused hassocks for his choir members.

It is worth remembering how much this popular, long-serving and-suffering musician was ignored by the trustees. Not only did they refuse him hassocks and cause difficulty over his paid leave, they refused him an assistant and a free sitting, they rejected applications for tuning fees and cost for the repair of rain damage to the pipes, and they denied him metal organ stops instead of wooden ones.[5] G. B. Endacott puts this down to an indifference to all matters musical on the part of the trustees, but it could also be an irritated suspicion on the part of merchants and lawyers of anyone whose principal talent and passion was for music over money.

In 1873, the choir sang at the inauguration of the new chancel, of which we know very little else, and in 1875 there was a fundraising musical event for them. There may have been a question of attendance dogging its future. It was suggested that the choir be paid or disbanded. It was decided to pay choirboys.

They were still in very short supply in 1898. 'Will not parents lend their children to the Lord?' cried the chaplain, Cobbold, in his *Church Notes*[6] message at Easter. 'The advantages to the boy are great.' Perhaps there were not that many European boys available for borrowing. Children of better-off families would be packed off early to England for education, where the advantages were even greater. The younger boys of the cathedral choir were likely to have come from the less well off, senior clerical, technical and 'overseer' class of the white population, where opportunities for betterment were fewer.

The 1897 Christmas services were 'bright and hearty', we are told, but extra singing help was needed on Christmas Day.[7] There became a long tradition of that help coming from servicemen in the garrison. In 1899, there was an innovation which may well have deterred the parents of some choirboys and turned lending to the Lord expensive. For the first time, offerings were taken from the choir during services.

Around the turn of the century, the choir seems to have been in the ascendant, as the empire was showing the first signs of decline. To 'acknowledge the signal mark of the providence of God without delay', there was a service of thanksgiving for the entry of the Allied Relief Force into Peking (Beijing), to quash the Boxers. The choir practised specially after evensong on Sunday to sound at their best for this the following day. At 10.45 a.m. on that Monday morning, the church was 'almost full', and the introit hymn was 'Now Thank We All Our God'. Readings were Isaiah 10:1–5 and Romans 11:9–21. Anthems included 'Why Do the Nations' by Handel, and 'Oh Give Thanks'. Bishop Hoare preached on 'Behold God is my Salvation' and 'Vengeance is Mine' and, after the blessing, the choir, forty-four strong, sang the 'Halleluiah Chorus' by Handel. Alex Marsh was a soloist, and A. G. Ward, Sangster's successor, was on the organ.[8]

To improve quality and incentives amongst this growing band, choral scholarships were initiated and a scholarship fund was set up. With opportunity came stringency. Rules on discipline were established. Victorian children did not always only speak when spoken to. It seems that behaviour in the church and the vestry was poor.

The choir was ready to emerge as a force. In 1900, an agreement between the Church Body and a choir committee recognised the choir as a body in itself. There was to be a choir fund, for which the honorary treasurer would keep accounts distinct from those of the cathedral. Generally, income was from the Sunday collection, organ recitals, musical services—to weddings and funerals—and donations. Expenditures included the payment of choirboys, the purchasing of music, the scholarships, clothing and advertising. If the choir were putting on a performance, they clearly marketed themselves.

At its first annual meeting, the choir flexed its muscles, a little petulantly perhaps. Members said they felt unappreciated and unrecognised. Sufficiently strong was this feeling that they managed to nominate one of their members, W. Armstrong, to a seat on the Church Body, which had succeeded the previous committee of largely government-nominated trustees.[9] The choir's influence grew apace. In 1901, in the search for a new assistant chaplain, the choir was able to insist on a man with a baritone voice. This gave rise to Bishop Hoare's agreement to use the single, cost-saving password 'trombone' in a telegram if he found such a priest when he was on leave in England.[10]

Death swung its scythe through the ranks from time to time. Indeed, losses in the choir are some of the most frequently recorded in the cathedral. In 1899, for example, Francis W. Stokes, described as a stalwart of the choir, died, leaving a native Ceylonese wife without support. There was a whip-round for donations so she could be sent back to Ceylon, where she could work as a nurse in 'Native hospitals'.[11] In 1901, on 14 September, a choirboy, 'little Stanley Ford', was taken by the Lord on permanent loan. He was buried in Happy Valley, where he lies still. Nothing quite so final happened to leading choirboy, T. Martin, in the autumn of 1915. Only his voice broke. Then his dad, a sidesman, died. All *Church Notes* managed to say about that was that it hoped Martin junior could come back as a tenor or a bass.

The service marking the coronation of Edward VII on 9 August 1902 was apparently a *tour de force*. The choir was out in strength and with supporters. The complement of choristers is written in *Church Notes* as: Mrs. Hagan and Seth; Misses Hance, Chunyut, Leykum, Abrahan and Seth; Messrs. G. P. Lammert, (a soloist) A. Cunningham, A. Russell, W. J. Terrill, F. G. Whittick, J. Jenkins, J. Moorhouse, G. H. Rigby, J. Hays, H. Hughes, J. S. Mcnab, H. Arthur, W. V. Thompson, Master Gunner Thurloe and, from Union Church, Mr. W. Coster, Mrs. Muidie and Miss Ramsey. The choirboys were E. and W. Hagan, H. and B. Shortman, H. and F. Flood and E. Hickinsdon. Instrumental support came from Sergeant Hunt, Corporals Glanville, Bolstridge and Warner; Bandsman Morris and Drummers Evans, Wilmott Curl of the 22nd Battalion of the Royal Welch Fusiliers.

On Ascension Day 1903, a strong turnout from the choir nearly outnumbered the congregation. Mr. Sangster, who had retired in 1895, died. One of his more successful moments in a long career had been in 1883, when the first ailing organ in the north transept was declared 'past service'. With a budget of 2,000 pounds, he was commissioned by the trustees to order a new one from Walker and Sons on his leave trip to London. The government refused any help, an appeal for $12,000 was launched and a now mysterious 'Snowdrop Society' gave $246. The organ box was installed by C. E. Palmer, the architect and partner in the prominent firm Palmer and Turner,[12] and Mr.

Burdekin from the builders in what is now the St Michael's chapel. The organ console sat where the present bishop's throne does. The organ pipes were set out, less than decorously, on platforms without any casing. A trustee suggested the old organ should be raffled. This was thought 'undecorous'. It was sold to Union Church. The final cost was 1,346 pounds, and it would not be very long before this new one was broken.

Colonel R. F. Johnston, a council member, diligently composed a cheery manuscript account of St John's history up to 1937, now held in St John's Cathedral. The fading typescript on yellowing pages in a red folder, frayed by its passage down the decades, was meant to be helpful to anyone who might want to write a full history of the cathedral for the colony's centenary. By 1941, folk found themselves otherwise occupied, and its usefulness was postponed. Johnston, who was not cavalier with his conclusions, asserts that A. G. Ward, Sangster's successor from 1897, failed to match him and was squeezed out by the choir. This is difficult to believe. Ward lasted eight years. Evidently, much was achieved under him, including the beginnings of a diocesan choir festival. He left in 1905, because he was offered an interesting job in Japan, and died in that post a year later.[13]

Denman Fuller, the third organist, was a Fellow of the Royal College of Organists, previously in charge of a large choir in Bournemouth. He played impressive voluntaries after evensong and produced a bound book of anthems. Almost immediately, battle was joined with the Church Body. He demanded a higher salary and control over the music in services. Coupling a merely difficult request with an outrageous one worked for him. He got his raise but not musical control, which stayed with the clergy.

Choir numbers were hovering at just over thirty around this time. A choir festival was held on 15 March 1907 at 9 p.m., a helpful hour before which people could eat their dinner. Its lateness had unforeseen consequences. There was 'irreverent behaviour' during the performances, not through excess of wine with dinner but noise from visitors leaving before the end.

Featuring Walmsley's 'Magnificat', Mendelssohn's 'Hear My Prayer', Handel's 'Organ Concerto no. 9' and Stanford's 'Last Post', it must have been an irreverent success. It was repeated on the 19th, and takings were donated to the cathedral's electric lighting fund.

The following year, 1908, saw two performances of selections from the 'Messiah' in aid of the same cause. The Good Friday performance brought the largest number of people into St John's ever seen there. The collection was a paltry $297. An anonymous donor, 'ashamed and angry 'at the news, gave $50.

Not all takings were so depressing. At Easter 1915, a first performance in St John's of Louis Spohr's oratorio, 'Last Judgement', earned a record $650, which went to the wartime Prince of Wales Fund. At the time, Spohr was mentioned in the same breath as Beethoven. This oratorio was very popular and features repeatedly in the repertoire. By 1919, the choir was fifty strong, which was viewed as a matter of importance in the chief Anglican Church. Indeed, the colonial secretary and trustee Claud Severn was a soloist in Stanier's 'Crucifixion' and you could not, in those days, get more important than that.[14]

Still, the choir of the early twentieth century was a distant image from the one you would see in the early twenty-first. 'Bunny' Abbott described it in his 1955 fundraising publication.[15] There were no girls, only ladies. In 1909, Mr. White, deputy organist, was saying 'no' to Diocesan schoolgirls for the choir. Get ladies with good soprano voices, was his direction.

The ladies did not robe. They did not process with the men. This led to odd sights at evensongs of low attendance, when clergy would process behind one choirman.

Furthermore, ladies kept their hats on throughout, and very large hats they were. Abbott described one lady member nicknamed 'Bassa Profunda'. Her hat had a veil and it was only lifted for actual singing.

There was one moment, in 1913, when the choir expressed a characteristic anger over a proposal from a Church Body member, whose name in this connection seems to have been expunged, to make services more appealing. Cathedral income was, as ever, parlous, and as a means of making services more attractive to the untapped agnostic public outside or loosen the purse strings of those within, he suggested in a Church Body discussion that the singing should be more 'congregational'. By this he meant that more of the music should be familiar hymns to tunes that vulgar, flat voices could sing with gusto.

Nothing seems to alarm a choir more than being deprived of the complex fretworks of difficult settings and acrobatic anthems. Forced to sing 'Praise My Soul the King of Heaven' to John Goss's 'Lauda Anima', their eyes glaze over and they plan lunch. The reaction on this occasion was a defence of choral standards so furious that nothing more was heard of it.

If the choir expanded in its numbers and activity, the vast, mostly empty, Diocese of Victoria was shrunk geographically and altered constitutionally between 1872 and the First World War. This had little bearing on the life of St John's. The cathedral was not much involved with farther-flung missionary work in China. That was run by the CMS which, in turn, had little to do with the English diocese. However, when the status of the Bishop of Victoria began to alter in the flux of events, the cathedral was pulled in.

Bishops were not easily accepted by everyone, even some who were members of an episcopal church. This was especially so with missionaries who saw themselves as purists, doing specialist grass-roots work and resented being under the aristocratic authority of a diocesan bishop. This implication of spiritual superiority caused an offence to bishops so abiding that Bishop R. O. Hall can be found inveighing against the vocational autonomy of missionaries as late as the 1930s.[16]

It is not as though Bishop Hall was shy of taking the gospel into the furthest crannies of ignorance and disbelief. None of his predecessors were, either. All the Hong Kong bishops had immaculate missionary credentials and, until Hall, who came out of the Christian Student Movement, all were originally CMS men. However, once they put on the mitre, they took on themselves the wider authority and responsibilities of episcopacy which the founders of colonial bishoprics believed were so essential to the correct dissemination of the Reformed Church in the empire. They earned thereby the powerful suspicions of the missionary societies.

The CMS did not see the Victoria Colonial Bishopric supplying their needs well. After Bishop Smith left in 1864, they pushed for a purely missionary bishopric in China, independent of the colonial one. Bishop Charles Alford, his successor, sometime incumbent of Holy Trinity Islington and later principal of Highbury Theological College, was a firm supporter of the CMS but also of his own authority. He came to Hong Kong at a point when the missionary bishopric idea had been approved by the Archbishop of Canterbury, but no practical arrangements for it had been made. On arrival, Alford, who had not demurred in London, dug in his heels and opposed any erosion of his territory or authority.

The CMS wanted the new bishop to take over all purely missionary work in China. Bishop Alford wished to maintain a missionary role for his diocese and responsibility for all Europeans in China. The

Archbishop of Canterbury saw it neither way. Not quite Solomon-like, he split the issue in two. He divided China along the 28th parallel—which would have bemused the Guangxu emperor, had he understood it. All Church of England work to the north was put under the newly consecrated Bishop John Russell in Ningpo, and that to the south of it, under the Bishop of Victoria.

When he heard of this, Bishop Alford was visiting England, where his wife had returned in 1868, her health unable to cope with Hong Kong's climate. Finding this erosion of his commission difficult to accept, and unwilling to face the administrative complexities, he resigned, *in absentia*, in February 1872.[17]

Although he was rarely in Hong Kong, his relationship with the cathedral was significant. Alford pushed for the chancel extension, and his vigorous fundraising, much of it in England, aided the building of St Peter's, the 'Seamen's Church'. This was the second English-speaking church in Hong Kong and, as its life progressed, it grew so dependent on the cathedral for support, it became, in fact, its daughter.

Even before Alford had resigned, and the two years and eleven months of interregnum until the installation of John Shaw Burdon began, episcopal authority had been further eroded. This was not the doing of anyone in Hong Kong but the result of a dispute within in the Church in far-off South Africa and the obduracy of the mathematically precise Bishop of Natal, J. W. Colenso, who insisted that the calculations surrounding the Pentateuch were hopelessly wrong.

The outraged church authorities there were fundamentalists uninterested in the transience of accuracy, and sought his removal. The ensuing fight went to the Judicial Committee of the Privy Council, which in 1865, found in Colenso's favour. However, the Privy Council pulled a rabbit out of the hat. It discovered that colonial bishops were not what they seemed to be. This was to have an impact on Bishop Burdon and on what he had assumed was his cathedral.

John Burdon was Glaswegian and a missionary who had been ordained in Shanghai, been chaplain to the British Mission in Peking and had travelled and preached with great courage through Taiping rebel territory. He arrived in Hong Kong after what he described as a 'pleasant voyage' on 4 December 1874, to find Bishop's House in 'a wretched condition'.[18]

When he presented himself at the west door of St John's on Sunday morning, 13 December, he would have appeared as a stout man, but the coolies did not find him a problem carrying him in his chair, it seems. There were four episcopal chair carriers in uniforms of bright red, and they moved along at quite a lick.

The bishop was received by the clergy, the registrar, the choir, even the verger, with all the respect and ceremony[19] accorded to his two predecessors but, in his authority, he was travelling lighter than they did.

The bishop read the Antecommunion. The choir chanted the Nicene Creed with a moment of fame for choirboy Master Iburg, who sang a solo. Burdon preached to Romans 1:16. He took the opportunity to strike a familiar chord. His first and foremost dedication was to missionary work, he said. It would be a mistake to believe that the bishopric had been founded purely for the English residents of Hong Kong and the Treaty Ports. To grind the point home to an audience which might not have been loving what it was hearing, he told them—with what reads like an airy scoff—that this congregation of his fellow countrymen was hardly enough to warrant a bishop. There was a touch of hubris in this. Some were about to question whether he was a bishop at all.

Officiating as readers of the prayers and the lessons that day were the Reverend W. H. Baynes and the Reverend A. Hutchinson.

It is interesting that both these men were to have a falling-out with Burdon, Hutchinson over the correct Chinese form of address for God, a dispute known as 'the Terms Question', and Baynes over the bishop's very authority in Hong Kong. What that settled on came next. The chaplain, Canon Beach, read the Letter of Commendation of the Bishop from the Archbishop of Canterbury. It was not what that letter said but what it was not, which was Baynes's bone of contention. It was not Letters Patent.

The 1865 Colenso judgement had revealed that colonial bishops were being appointed by Letters Patent to colonies, like Hong Kong, which had their own legislatures. This act was *ultra vires*, according to their Lordships, and contradictory to the authority of those assemblies. Appointment by the Crown had to cease and be replaced with appointment by the Archbishop of Canterbury. To the current observer, this may seem as inconsequential as it was sensible. To the Victorian mind, especially one stratified by life in the colonies, it was as important as it was alarming.

In the records room at Bishop's House Hong Kong, the Letters Patent appointing the bishop as Lord Bishop of the Diocese of

Victoria survive. Although he lived on until 1898, he never went back to collect them. It is a large document in excellent condition still, and clear and demanding across the top of it in a banner of scroll, are the words 'Victoria, By Grace of God ...'

You are looking at something rare, an issuance of the Royal Prerogative, a command of the monarch, in theory at least, beyond even the sanction of Parliament. It bestows upon a bishop authority which is quasi-secular and lordly in its extent. He may take actions in the interest of the spiritual realm which cannot be contradicted by the temporal power.

Since the appointment of Bishop Smith, the episcopal authority over the colonial chaplain in Hong Kong had been accepted, or at least never been challenged, by the governor even though the chaplain was his secular employee. Colonial bishops were a new thing, and the arrangement was unusual, but the Letters Patent could not be disregarded. Yet now they had been swept away. A Letter of Warrant from Queen Victoria dated 1 November 1873, just as grand as her original Letters Patent, states with equal unequivocality 'that we have revoked and terminated the Letters Patent of 11 May 1849 and 14 January 1867 ... and every clause, article and thing therein.' That left the bishop with purely a Letter of Commendation from the archbishop and, for standing a man in equivalent authority to a governor in his own colony, that simply did not cut it.

Burdon ran into trouble almost immediately from W. H. Baynes, who was Chaplain to the Mission to Seamen and therefore the direct employee of a British-based society. Baynes claimed the colonial bishop, without royal sanction, no longer had any authority over him. Burdon was 'merely a private person with no jurisdiction indeed with no connection to any clergyman of the Church of England except that of friendly feeling'.[20]

The bishop complained to the archbishop, who probably moved in the matter. In May 1875, the foreign secretary, Lord Derby, wrote to the British consuls, the Admiralty wrote to naval chaplains and the secretary of state, Lord Carnarvon, wrote to the administrator in Hong Kong—John Gardiner Austin, in Sir Arthur Kennedy's absence—all saying that recognitions and courtesies would remain as before and that it should be business as usual with the new bishop.[21]

The Archbishop of Canterbury said in a letter of 28 September 1874, 'Our endeavour ought to be as far as possible to place the bishop in the exact position of his predecessor.'[22] Neither this endeavour nor the directions of the home government solved a problem peculiar to St John's Cathedral. The Hong Kong Attorney General stated that 'the Bishop of Victoria is now not so styled within the meaning of Ordinance 3 of 1850'. So, could a bishop give instructions to a colonial chaplain? On whose authority did the bishop use the cathedral?

On 16 September 1875, the trustees arrived at a resolution and moved that the bishop consider St John's as his cathedral and maintain his throne there and that none of that should affect the rights of the colonial chaplain under law. This reflected more goodwill than precise thought, but nonetheless it was conveyed to the government for approval. To do this, Cecil C. Smith, honorary secretary of the trustees, sent it to himself because he was also colonial secretary. As such he sent it to John Austin who, as we saw, was the officer administering the government.

Austin took great offence. The trustees, he said, had no right even to draft this resolution. The colonial chaplain, as a servant of the governor, had control over services and the access of a bishop without need of a trustees' resolution. The trustees did not take that lying down. They replied that they were representatives of the subscribers and seatholders and therefore they had some say in the overall order of things. Furthermore, the colonial chaplain had been in the chair and agreed with them. Again, Smith sent this to himself, who sent it to Austin on 4 October. Austin huffed off that claim in a one-line reply. The chaplain, Richard Kidd, now demonstrated a flair for diplomacy which must have been valuable balm in these disputative times. He had dinner with Austin. A form of words was worked out. The resolution was acceptable if it said that it was arrived at in concert with the colonial chaplain 'by virtue of the power conferred on him by Ordinance 3 of 1850 section 6'. Cecil C. Smith, exhausted by his split identity, reunited himself by resigning as a trustee.[23]

This was an elegant courtesy but useless as a solution to the dichotomy. The episcopate, in effect, had been disestablished. St John's, by contrast, remained a colonial chaplaincy under the authority of the governor. The bishop's position in 'his' cathedral was an anomaly.

There is a story told, even now, that the bishop—likely Burdon—was physically denied access to the church, that a door was slammed in his face. This is possibly a legend mingling the sense of unease at the time, growing to mild paranoia on the part of the bishop, who wrote lengthy letters of affront and complaint to the Reverend H. Wright of the CMS. The particular responses he received from the

Reverend Hutchison drove him to epic epistles of objection. The local press treated him in 'a low and scurrilous manner'. The 'extraordinary conduct' of Dr. Eitel 'caused me bitter pain for weeks and has cast a cloud over me'.[24]

A feeling of exclusion from his rightful dignity hung over Bishop Burdon's time. He may have been resilient in the missionary field, but when it came to being unloved as a bishop, he seems to have had thin skin. He wrote in hurt tones to Governor Sir George Bowen in 1883:

> The local government considers the previous ordinance with reference to the Bishop's status null and void ... I think this was a mistake. It is a slight on the office. I am not seen as a bishop at all. There have been unseemly attempts on the part of chaplains to decline allegiance to me. If changes are to be made in the management of the cathedral, it is a fitting time to remedy this mistake. It feels like an anomaly going in as an assistant and not a chief.

His tone becomes more dismissive, then fatalistic:

> I have done more English work in the cathedral than any of my predecessors yet, personally, I have no desire to take services in St John's. On Sundays, I am occupied with Chinese services, lecturing, preparing books and training native missionaries. No change is likely to be made in my position. The retirement of the present chaplain is a remote contingency.[25]

The retirement of the Reverend William Jennings, appointed after the sadly deceased Kidd in 1879, came about in June of 1891. It was not too late for Bishop Burdon to see. He held office up to 1895. Jennings was 30 years old on his appointment, a scholar held in high regard who translated the *Shi King* and Confucian analects. He moved on to become Rector of Breedon in Berkshire and is described as an 'exciting' translator of Chinese poetry for his 'unique' 1891 translation of 'Fortuitous Concourse'.[26]

The letter suggests that relations between chaplain and bishop were strained. It was the departure of Jennings that the 'changes to the management of the Cathedral', alluded to by the Bishop, were waiting for. Jennings was to be the last colonial chaplain. Once the terms of that appointment had been ended, the trustees and the government could embark on a process that was, to many, obvious, urgent and yet risky. St John's was to be disendowed. Financially, it was to be cut off from the Crown and totter on its own two feet. For the congregation, this was to prove stimulating. For episcopal authority, it meant that the battle lines were being withdrawn.

The existing government of the church had worked itself into a simple structure given to wooliness where finances were concerned. The chaplain was provided by the Colonial Office. The Hong Kong government assisted on non-recurrent expenditure items, largely where it chose, which always left room for private effort.

The seatholders meeting was held every April, passed the accounts and elected two trustees and an auditor. Four trustees were appointed by the government, and so predictable did the proceeding tend to be that only the trustees showed up. A notable exception to this was the time Nathaniel Ede attended in 1880, to represent the congregation in passing a testimonial to the bishop for being such a good stand-in chaplain after Richard Kidd's death.

References to individual parishioners are rare, so let us pluck Ede from the flow for a moment. Records tell us he was a seatholder who worked for Union Insurance, died at the ripe age of 80 in Hampshire in 1915, leaving $375,000. He had an interesting temperament. He got a Chinese three months in prison by complaining against him for cutting down a tree he was fond of. Defence of the environment could be brisk in those days. He also owned an Amati violin.[27] He helped make the not-very-serious suggestion that Bishop Burdon might like to continue as chaplain permanently. The meeting's warm disposal towards Burdon does hint that his difficulties may have grown with the arrival of Jennings.

The trustees looked after the fabric and administration of St John's and had between $500 and $600 a year for general maintenance. The chaplain ordered the services, and the congregation remained largely mute. The arrangement might have appeared neat if uninspired, but the problem was that the church was never properly endowed.

The government contributed to fabric costs on a loose fifty-fifty basis. Assistance was vicarious and on merit as the government saw it. In 1872, they contributed to the roof replacement, but in 1884 not a cent was given towards the second organ. The trustees tried to live within their means, which were mostly pew rents topped up by occasional fees.

As early as 1873, the home government had suggested making a fixed annual contribution and leaving overall responsibility to the trustees. That proved too much to stomach for what was, after all, a volunteer body, and it was dropped.

The situation was untenable, not least because of the struggle over control of the chaplain and because Hong Kong was, by now, being treated by the Colonial Office as a special case. All the other Treaty Port churches had been cut loose. In 1882, it was decided to do the same with St John's. The trustees petitioned against it but in vain. In January 1886, they found themselves discussing a draft ordinance.[28]

At the April annual meeting of 1891, the process was begun, or rather it would have been if more than nine seatholders and subscribers had attended. At a special meeting called for November to gain more consensus, eighteen showed up, and the form of a new 'Church Body' was decided on to include the bishop, a senior chaplain and six elected trustees.

This took form in Hong Kong Ordinance No. 11 of 1892, to provide for the due performance of divine worship and other services in accordance with the rites of the Church of England at St John's Cathedral Church at Victoria in this colony and elsewhere, to incorporate a Church Body, to vest the said cathedral in such body, and for other purposes in connection therewith.

Thus began the blueprint for the cathedral to look after itself. The chaplain had control of services 'subject to the control of the said Bishop for the time being', said the legislation. This was still vague enough to create a new line of tension between the bishop, now fully included in the Church Body, and the other members. Indeed, even before the ordinance was passed, a circular sent around the seatholders and subscribers proposed that services, rites and rituals should be clearly put in the hands of the chaplain. There was a vote of 40 to 34 in favour of that. An exasperated Bishop Burdon finally found the moment to make his stand. He stated plainly to the new Church Body that, if the condition was changed, he would resign from it. That was a disconnection far too difficult to digest, and the clause went unaltered. The bishop was re-established in the cathedral.

There was nothing inevitable in this. The authority of the bishop within St John's is far more evident than it would be in an English cathedral where episcopal involvement in management is more distant. Closer engagement would be traditionally guarded against by a highly independent dean and chapter. The sense of that was strong amongst the seatholders who voted on the circular. Yet, in 1898, there was no dean and chapter, just one clergyman and a committee of volunteers, low on funds. They had just been cut off from a royal parent. To deny the episcopal one, at this point, may have courted an isolation too sudden and too strong.

The Church Body was in charge of the fabric. It could fill any vacancies on itself and appoint chaplains and lay employees. In addition to electing the trustees, the subscribers and seatholders could approve or veto proposals but not initiate or amend. This left possibilities for fireworks, which occasionally went off in comparison to the torpor of earlier years. The new ordinance continued the old trustee responsibility for the arrangement of sittings and the keeping of registers. Any changes to the regulations or Church Body would be notified to the colonial secretary and gazetted. As for the role of the government, firm commitment was confined to maintaining the public road through the compound.

G. B. Endacott describes the new system as a 'diarchy'. The mutual independence of the Church Body and the subscribers and seat-holders may not have been as marked as that term implies, but the liberties disendowment brought, along with its uncertainties, made the seatholders more perky about their oversight than before. This showed occasionally in the teething stages of the new constitution.

They began by appointing the six lay members to the Church Body annually. In 1897, as part of an overall redraft of the regulations to the ordinance, and with puzzling pre-emption, the chief justice and a trustee, Sir John Carrington, made the terms of office for life or until the holder left the colony. The next annual church meeting was mightily displeased by this turn of events. It demanded the restoration of annual renewal. As a demonstration of intent, five of the six members resigned on the spot and stood for re-election and, making the point that this was no hollow procedure, two of them were not returned. For five more years, which is how long it took to put the regulations back where they were, all six members regularly resigned *en bloc* at the annual meeting.[29]

Ecumenism did not come in tandem with democracy. At the 1900 annual meeting, the Church Body came up with a new form of quali-fication for its members. They should be 'communicants with the Church of England' it said, to allow for Presbyterians to join. This is an interesting provision. The Scottish element in the European population was a significant one. The Presbyterian Church was the established church in Scotland. The congregation at St John's would have been sufficiently 'low church' to be accommodating. However, though the bishop may be put in his place from time to time, acknowledgement of the apostolic succession was not dispensable. At the meeting, 'there was much debate' and, in the end, the proposal was voted down and the Church Body asked to come back with the words 'communicants of the Church of England'.[30]

There was a certain independence being asserted even if it did draw the occasional hard line. The governor, the service chiefs and the senior police had their free seats taken away from them. The governor had to wait to be allotted one for the memorial service for Edward VII. The royal coat of arms, carved into the end of the first row on the south side of the nave, was purely window dressing for the governor after the Second World War and long after the abolition of pew rents. The Church Body could now complain loudly to the military about the damage the soldiers did to the seats.[31]

There was a growing sensitivity too to being seen as still an outstation of the government. In 1892, Attorney General W. M. Goodman refused to be appointed as a trustee because there would be, 'too many officials'. It was a worthy aspiration but not an easy one to meet. If we look at the members of the Church Body elected in 1897 as baldly listed, C. Ford, T. Jackson, F. A. Cooper, Captain H. B. Lethebridge, R. M. Rumsey, Sir Thomas Jackson of the Hong Kong Bank and Ernest Osborne of the Wharf and Godown Company were the only ones who were not members of the Executive or Legislative Councils or office holders.

No matter how much some in the cathedral may have wanted to at least strike a balance in the involvement of Crown officials on the Church Body and in later years the council, their personal loyalties to the established Church were, to a degree, inevitable and their presence in its counsels, in practice, desirable. Their knowledge, authority and connections made them invaluable to the survival of the cathedral in Hong Kong. Neither must it be forgotten that the cathedral itself, disendowed though it was, never shook off a sense of obligation as the Church of England far off, ministering to the subjects of His Majesty overseas and therefore deserving of government's help and favour.

The new Church Body tested the limitations of its power not only with the bishop but on the chaplain too. With Jennings gone to become rector of Grasmere, it met in January 1892, to appoint the first 'senior chaplain'. This title dispensed with the word 'colonial' and aspired to the notion of junior chaplains, who came rather later. They engaged the Reverend Rowland Francis Cobbold and appealed for donations and subscriptions to maintain him. He was appointed on a three-year contract and stayed in the post until 1902.

The Church Body took him to task twice at meetings in 1897. On the first occasion, Cobbold's churchmanship may have been rising a little too 'high' for the congregation's taste. They criticised the number of candlesticks on the altar. Defending his control over liturgical matters but wishing to settle the issue, he said that this was not a point that could be discussed within the meeting but could be taken outside.[32] Their second complaint was procedurally correct. They said that the chaplain had acted injudiciously in appealing for gifts for the chancel, without consulting the Church Body. Cobbold may have been impetuous in doing that. He had firm views on the standards of appearance in a church and lamented the absence of respectable accessories.

'We furnish our homes luxuriously ... the house of God goes uncared for,' he observed scathingly in the newly created *Church Notes* in 1897. *Church Notes* was a publication giving notices of events and a usually quite lengthy letter from the chaplain. It was an early attempt at communications, which was supposed to be supported by subscriptions that were notable for being overdue. It was wound up as too costly and was replaced by *St John's Review* in 1924, which took advertising.

It was here that Cobbold began his lengthy 'wish list' of improvements which got him in trouble with the Church Body and which were to launch a decade of additions and embellishments to the interior. The east end was cold and bare and the sanctuary was too small, he thought. The altar frontals and hangings were old and unsightly, he observed. Coolies nailed the frontals to the altar to stop them slipping off. The chaplain himself offered repositioned altar rails to make the sanctuary larger, if the congregation would do something to beautify the altar. Cobbold expanded on his theme. A reredos was needed at the east wall. The sanctuary floor was of 'rough granite and Cantonese marble' and needed a carpet. A new chalice was sought, the current one being 'beautiful but awkward'.

Outside the sanctuary there was a need for a new pulpit, a new reading desk, even new offertory bags. Most important of all was the call for new choir stalls. The scruffiness of the compound had not avoided his meticulous eye. It needed to be more like a garden, he thought, and it needed a flagstaff.

The response was sympathetic. The governor, Sir William Robinson, promised a pulpit and a brass desk. The pulpit survives. Captain and Mrs. Woodstock gave a silver paten. Alms bags were donated. Mrs. Ritchie gave red brocade as a dossal for the altar backcloth. T. Pratt and Sons gave a red silk frontal. Even a flagstaff was promised. The chaplain began the 'Sanctuary Fund', which was later graduated to a general improvements fund.

Mr. and Mrs. Hancock gave a prayer desk, a litany desk and a Bible. Captain C. B. N. Dodd gave a carved credence. A chalice was presented by the Peak Church, a chapel-of-ease to the cathedral on Peak Road. An anonymous donor had suddenly given it a chalice, trumping the use of funds just raised for that purpose. The communicants decided to buy one for St John's instead. Of the heavier of Cobbold's wishes, F. Danby, the honorary architect, drew up plans for the choir stalls which were of oak, procured from the hulk of HMS *Victor Emmanuel*, a former hospital and receiving ship in the harbour which was being sold.[33] The new pulpit from the governor was being constructed by C. E. Palmer of Palmer and Turner. This firm grew out of Wilson and Salway, which we have seen (Chapter 2) built St Stephen's Church and were, likely, the architects of the St John's chancel extension.

No matter how skilled Palmer was, the pulpit could not be inaugurated until the *punkahs* had been taken down for the winter. The *punkahs* did not let you see the preacher easily. If you were seated near a side aisle you got to see nothing at all. These devices were a blight upon sight, sound and lighting and were to remain so for some years to come.

The extension of the sanctuary was completed after Easter 1898, although Cobbold was still waiting for designs for a proposed chancel screen. The congregation had been generous. Subscribers to the Sanctuary Fund in 1899 included Governor Blake, and Messrs. Jackson, Gascoigne, Chater, Pollock, Mody, Babington, Chatham, Rumsey and Cox. The governor's pier has been lost to reclamation, but a garden in his name survives. The rest of the list reads like a Hong Kong street map.[34]

In early 1899, the fund stood at $1,079 before becoming a general fund, yet donations and installations continued to come to St John's as it passed into the Edwardian period. The two sons of Bishop Alford donated the cost of a bishop's throne which was designed by H. W. Bird and built in stunning detail by local artisans.[35] Only the basic chair survives and is used now by the bishop for confirmations and ordinations. It is modest evidence of the elaborate and glorious rosewood surround and canopy in which it was once set and to which a few photographs are left as testimony. This was a fitting that was truly cathedralesque.

J. A. Barton gave a font cover. There is more to that than meets the simple term. This was an enormously heavy wooden lid in the form of a four-foot tower in the Gothic style, which had to be raised and lowered onto the font by means of chains and a pulley. The Victorians were fond of this feature. It is with mixed feelings that one reports it was lost during the Japanese Occupation. The font it covered is an eight-sided stone Gothic basin supported by columns on a plinth. It was donated by the lawyer Edmund Sharp, who had equipped the baptistery with it and two windows in memory of his wife, Lucille, just a little earlier, in 1890. The baptistery, originally floored with the Minton tiles, had been enlarged after the chancel lengthening. It existed as an open extension to the north transept and quite a handsome sight, letting a lot more light into that quarter than is now the case. In the 1930s, the font was moved to the north door and the baptistery was turned into a choir ladies' changing room, walling it off from the transept. This was an act of organisational attrition not yet quite recovered from.

Edmund Sharp, who was the Crown solicitor, a trustee, founder of a major solicitors firm and persistent benefactor to the church, died in 1897 but should not be let go without noting one of his forward views. On death, he wrote in his last testament, 'I am much averse to the present fashion of wearing black as mourning. Young people could wear grey and silver, which I want for my mourning cards.' [36]

Even more doubtful a gift than the Gothic font lid was from the Hong Kong Bank chairman's wife, Mrs. (later Lady) Jackson, in 1898. She made arrangements for the glass in eleven clerestory windows above the chancel to be replaced by coloured pieces. Stained glass applied without restraint can be a dark, leaden business. Mr. Cobbold probably found it difficult to say no to a lady of such station. Dean Swann, arriving years later, had not a moment's hesitation in having them taken out and replaced by plain glass, to 'let in God's good light'.[37]

More elaborate stained glass made its way into St John's in this period. A memorial window to Elizabeth Frances Higgin and Emma Gertrude Ireland, two nurses who died of the plague nursing victims in a government hospital, was erected in July 1899, in the north transept. Bubonic plague had struck Hong Kong in May 1894. It mainly affected the Chinese lower classes. Totally 2,500 died, and 80,000 people left the colony. The government introduced house-to-house searches for infected persons and quarantine on a hospital ship, measures which were widely resented by the Chinese community. The two nurses, working so close to the threat, were of the few Europeans who died.[38]

Designed by Kate Coughtree of a Hong Kong family and executed by Heaton Butler and Bayne of London, the window's upper portion featured one woman looking up to Jesus and the other giving a cup to a dying man. Over them, an angel bore a martyr's leaf and the words 'Inasmuch as you did it to one of these …' In the lower portion an angel carried a crown and another scroll saying, 'I will give thee a crown of life … I will give them an everlasting life.'[39]

The window was lost during the Second World War. Ultimately, all the stained glass was, including a moving memorial to the Hong Kong inter-port cricket team, all but two of whom drowned, along with 114 others, when their ship, the *Bokhara*, was sunk in a typhoon on 10 October 1892, returning from Shanghai. Most of them were officers and non-commissioned officers from the garrison, and three civilians. That window had two lights, one featuring St Paul at his shipwreck and the other of St Peter walking on the water. The attached brass plaque stated, 'No other cathedral in the world contains a memorial to members of a cricket team and we trust that no occasion will arise for one to be erected.'[40]

The loss of the *Bokhara* caused much grief in European Hong Kong. There was a memorial service held in the cathedral attended by the governor, Sir William Des Voeux. Des Voeux complained that the date set for it was not to his convenience. This was the first year of disendowment, and the bishop must have taken at least a slight pleasure in reminding His Excellency that 'government grants to the Cathedral now having been withdrawn, the control of services now rests with the clergy'.[41]

Congregational life at St John's involved increasing incidences of services such as memorials, thanksgivings and celebrations. The cathedral's role in the diocese as the centre of ceremonial and commemoration of great moments became firmly established. Chinese members of the community showed up in numbers for events like that, either to join the European congregation or to hold a separate service in Chinese. Even though St John's had been formally disendowed, its role as the state church in the colony grew.

No grander example of this function was the Thanksgiving Service for Queen Victoria's Diamond Jubilee in 1897. Eight hundred seats were filled. The entire establishment of the colony was present. The Hong Kong Volunteers lined the nave. The Union Flag and the Royal Standard were suspended from the beams; the Standard horizontally, the Irish harp sagging a bit, from evidence of a grainy photograph in a collection at the cathedral. Otherwise, it was an event of 'heartiness and impressiveness' according to *Church Notes*. Reverend G. R. Vallings, the Garrison Chaplain, intoned the prayers. The Reverend W. Bannister, secretary of the South China CMS, read the lessons. Bannister, a selfless man and knowledgeable of his field, was to be made an honorary canon of St John's and created Archdeacon of Hong Kong when the office was revived for him by Bishop Hoare in 1902. The chaplain, Cobbold, preached on 1 Samuel 10:4. 'God save the King.' There was no bishop present. It had been six months since Burdon left, and the vacancy continued.

In the afternoon, there was a 'very large congregation' of Chinese Christians belonging to the Church of England and other Protestant missions. They used part of the 1662 Accession Service, translated, and a choir of 130 young people sang hymns in Chinese. The Reverend Kwong Yat Shau of the CMS gave an address in Cantonese, concluding with a sentiment which carried an interesting distinction. 'We, who are not her subjects and yet are at one with them in the bond of a common faith, thank God today for the life and reign of the Queen of England.' Mr. Li Shing Yau of the Basel Mission spoke in Hakka on the text 'Wait on the Lord and keep his way' and demonstrated a similar dichotomy. 'Would that the rulers of our own Empire might speedily know this secret,' he implored, wistfully, one imagines.

When the queen died, a celebration service for the coronation of Edward VII had to be hurriedly altered to prayers of intercession for his recovery from acute appendicitis, which carried a high fatality rate in those days. Cobbold described the event as part of the 'golden chain of sympathy which unites empire and home'. There was an afternoon service in Chinese, at which the prayers were led by a newly ordained deacon, Mok Shau Tsang, rather small in stature but muscular in spirit, who was to leave a deep impression on the Chinese Church over forty years as Archdeacon and Bishop of Canton. *Church Notes* observed that 'there was a large attendance of Chinese Christians with, as usual, the sexes being separated'.

The cathedral was generous to the Germans, having no presentiment of what was to come. In 1910, it gave itself over to the German community and sailors of the German Navy's China station for an afternoon service at Christmas. In 1913, there was a celebration of Kaiser Wilhelm II's own jubilee in the cathedral, attended by Prince Henry of Prussia, who was passing through Hong Kong, as well as the governor and the general officer commanding.[42]

A touching and unusual military ceremony took place in St John's on 12 October 1902. A body called the Hong Kong Regiment laid up its colours there. This was not the local Hong Kong Defence Force, later 'the Volunteers', but a regiment of Indian Muslims raised in the Punjab and north-west frontier by the War Office in 1891 specifically for overseas service. Their purpose must have been done. They were trooped in Happy Valley in front of the governor, Sir Henry Blake, and then marched to the cathedral. Subadar Major Sadar Khan, Commander of the Indian Empire (CIE), led the native officers and presented the colours for laying up. The regiment returned to India on 23 October and was disbanded. The colours of this brief and almost-forgotten regiment were later highlighted by Dean Swann in a glass case and subsequently lost.[43]

Governor Blake's daughter provided a shining example of what would have been a society wedding in Hong Kong 1903. Olive Blake married Captain M. V. P. Arbuthnot of the Scots Guards, who was *aide-de-camp* to her father. It was a picture-book ceremony for a textbook match. The choir was out in force. The couple were married by the bishop in his convocation robes. The best man was Major the Honourable H. W. Trefusis. Mr. S. T. Dunn of the Botanical Department, but likely not the upper-middle class, was brought in to decorate the church.

In September of the following year, the chaplain, now Frederick Franch Johnson, made a stern observation in *Church Notes*: 'We do not often refer in these pages to any society that is not of an avowedly religious character.' There was, he wrote, an exception in the case of the St John's Ambulance. This was the first year in which the brigade was allowed to hold its annual service in the cathedral. It does so still. Once a year, their band approaches playing British marching tunes, and scores of Hong Kong Chinese men and women, in starchily immaculate British-style uniforms and caps, move amongst each other, briskly exchanging salutes with swagger stick clamped under arm, before filing in to give thanks. That over half of them may be Taoists matters not a fig.

Johnson may have been tough on who got mentioned in *Church Notes*, but it turned out that no such restraints were applied to who used St John's. In the best tradition of the Church of England, anyone not known to impugn it publicly could go in it. The cathedral became a centre in the community for public groups which sought God's blessing on their endeavours, be they judges, Freemasons, national groups, orders of chivalry or nurses. More specifically, Chinese Christians grew to appreciate St John's significance as a place of worship on the greater church and state occasions. Even as the diocese altered its shape and texture, Chinese Christians came to St John's for special events even though they would rarely be seen there on more ordinary occasions.

But then, neither would a majority of their European counterparts. In a colony where life could be fast and stays were often brief, it was a struggle to maintain physical attendances, let alone spiritual commitment amongst the colonial British. This also meant that it was harder to sustain income. As Cobbold observed wryly, 'Losing the habit of attendance in a way relieves them of the duty and responsibility of support.' He tried hard to establish new opportunities for fellowship amongst the congregation. He set up a parochial guild of the sort that flourished in English churches. He believed guilds would 'restore the church to its former noble influence'. He began a guild committee for district visiting, a repeated theme through the cathedral's early twentieth-century ministry, imitating Anglican pastoral work in a typical parish. Cobbold attempted to set up a branch of the Brotherhood of St Andrew, an Anglican network whose mission it is to evangelise men and boys. He was the beginning of the clerical push at St John's to introduce Holy Communion as more staple worship.

He strove to inform his flock of opportunities to come together. 'It is not generally known and not sufficiently appreciated that there is a bible reading fellowship for Men in St Paul's College on Tuesday evenings.' You can hear a stern deliberation in his phrasing which may have not have whipped everyone to his side, and he shared the Victorian belief that evangelisation was a muscular business with no place for women.[44] After one guild meeting, the chaplain records simply, 'fair attendance … one new member'. Communicant classes were thin, though, and references to the brotherhood disappear. He was working from a very small nucleus of committed men, and that may have shifted too from postings, leave trips and sickness, all of which were perpetual features of European society in the colony.

In 1898, the average attendance at the cathedral on a Sunday was calculated to be 328. The number of communicants for the Sundays of February 1897 was 38, 11, 18 and 6. For April it was 40, 6, 40 and 10. Holy Communion was at midday on the first and third Sundays at this period, which may explain the higher numbers. On the other Sundays it was at 7 a.m.[45] Still, figures were slim and the subject of veiled sarcasm in high places. At the annual meeting in 1905, 'the bishop said that services were thoroughly enjoyed by those who attended them'.[46] He meant that remark to have wide currency, because the cathedral's annual meetings were reported in great detail by the English press until after the Second World War.

Sixteen years later, the governor, Sir Reginald Stubbs, opening the cathedral's new hall, 'lamented that attendance at the cathedral shows that the congregation of the Church of England is not as enthusiastic as it might be'. Stubbs knew perfectly well that the *South China Morning Post* report would reach the Englishmen who were home and abed. Attendances were an issue, pointedly so for the clergy, at least on high days and holy days. 'Good Friday is not a day of careless holiday pursuits,' they were told by Cobbold. Easter is a day of obligation; those who are satisfied with a minimum number of communions are reminded of this,' he said, managing a double-headed lecture in one sentence.

Ascension Day was a particular source of disappointment. On one occasion, the choir nearly outnumbered the congregation. Ascension Day 1911 'was observed in a slightly better manner than in some previous years though there remains much room for improvement'. Not just in numbers, either. Cobbold was also looking for '... a little more decision in the utterance of the responses and the amens. At the early Celebrations it is sometimes impossible for the clergyman to hear even the slightest sound from the congregation.' Some people were still not standing for entrance procession, either.[47]

There were frequent adjustments to the times and substances of services in the early twentieth century. Sometimes the garrison's schedule had to be accommodated, often the social routine of the congregation had to be borne in mind—and this was a consideration that has never really gone away—and there was a growing attempt to encourage an interest in the sacraments and spread worship out from Sunday morning matins. There were certainly full schedules. On Good Friday 1898, there was a Garrison Parade Service at 8.30 a.m., Litany and Antecommunion at 10 a.m. and matins with sermon at 11 a.m. From 2 p.m. there was a 'special service with addresses' and evensong with sermon at 5.45 p.m.

In early 1900, a circular was sent round asking for views on what would be the most suitable hour for a daily service. Attendances at weekday services were generally low. There seem to have been no replies whatever to that, so matins was set to be daily at 9 a.m. On Sundays that year, Holy Communion was separated from matins, to avoid 'unseemly exits' and 'the tramping of feet'. This pairing then splitting of the services was to move in cycles over the coming years. By the Christmas Day service of 1910, Holy Communion was being held at 7.45 a.m. and 11 a.m., the latter with sermon. Indeed, people uneasy about overdoing sacramentalism were assured that, if perchance they missed the 11 a.m. matins, the 11.45 service would still carry with the full diet of Epistle, gospel and sermon.

Some of the preoccupying spiritual issues were very much of their time. For the three Rogation Days before Ascension in 1898, the topics for intercession were 'country, colony and church'. Prayers of humiliation cropped up again in 1900 for the Boer War. Cobbold thought they should 'avoid extremes of fanatic and cringing humiliation which is boasting'. This was thoughtful, yet the sincere terms with which Christian gentlemen could address war embarrass the eye today. He spoke of 'humble thanksgiving for the blessings of war which are already plain in evidence of the solidarity of empire'. That war could have blessings was still a digestible concept; 1914 and Wilfred Owen had not yet come.[48]

An aspect of the cathedral's spiritual life which was of growing significance was Sunday school. Parents may have been slow to show up at church sometimes, but they were keen that those children who were in Hong Kong with them were tutored in the basics of the faith. In 1899, there were fifty pupils. Unfortunately, a Sunday school room at an estimated $2,000 was one item on the chaplain's 'wish-list' which did not find favour with donors. Only two guarantees of $100 each were made. The idea was that the once large, free-standing and hideous memorial to Captain Bate should be removed to the Happy Valley Cemetery from the site where the war memorial cross now stands and the room be put up there.[49] Instead, the school had to meet where it could, including Bishop's House.

The school was also contributing to a backlog of young people waiting for confirmation. The vacancy in the See of Victoria between the departure of Bishop Burdon in 1897 and the arrival of Bishop Hoare lasted many months. Confirmation classes were being held in the hope that bishops from elsewhere in Asia might oblige if they passed through Hong Kong on their way to the Fourth Lambeth Conference. If not, then there would be a dispensation for the 'ready and desirous' to take Holy Communion. By February 1898, Cobbold was 'quite unable to account for the extraordinary delay in filling the See'.[50] Such was his frustration that he wrote a quite strident letter of complaint to the Archbishop of Canterbury, who was, after all, responsible for the situation. It was brave move for a man who might have had concerns over his own preferment.

It was not only children who were in the queue. When he finally arrived, Bishop Hoare confirmed three bandsmen of the Royal Welch Fusiliers and one 'other rank' of the Royal Engineers, on 8 December 1898. The following month he confirmed thirty-six civilians, of whom one, George Ng Fuk-shan, was Chinese. *Church Notes* must have thought this worthy of mention, since the cathedral had stopped distinguishing Chinese from Europeans in its confirmation records.

The Church Body was acutely aware that the more they committed themselves to the church and took an interest in the church's affairs, the more financial support was likely to be forthcoming. The bulk of income was from pew rents, raised to $18 in 1902, then subscriptions and donations and service offertories in almost equal portion although offertories showed the healthiest increases. In 1913, the Easter Day offering actually went directly into clergy pockets in line with Church of England practice, but it found its way back to general funds within a few years.

In 1898, Hon Treasurer A. P. McEwen, definitely a man who worried a bone, made an analysis of the service collections for the preceding year. Given in total, by type of coinage, there had been 1,923 one-dollar pieces given, 3,831 twenty-cent pieces, 6,579 ten-cent pieces, 2,864 five-cent pieces and 1,436 one-cent pieces. This averaged out at $0.24 per person. 'Bad money' found in the bag was up to 4 per cent.[51]

Repeatedly, the chaplain and trustees hammered home to the congregation that there was no endowment fund and no government safety net. The government had offered $600 per annum for services at gaol and hospitals plus $5 for the burial of a destitute. The Church

Body eventually beat them up to $1,200. Burial fees—a clergy perk—were set at 1st class, $10; 2nd class, $5; 3rd class, free. It remains a matter of speculation as to who qualified as a third-class corpse.

St John's got by but in a hand-to-mouth fashion. The treasurer's report stated that the 1908 financial position was 'distinctly bad'. Three years before had seen a 'high water mark'. It had been all 'downhill' since then due to financial depression, low trade levels and a very high exchange rate—that latter point inflicting serious cramp on clergy incomes too. There had also been the loss of some 'liberal subscribers' to homeward passages, which, as with the Sunday school, seriously affected numbers. Still, the report insisted, a rich colony should be able to find the $1,400 and the $1,200 shortfalls of the previous two years.

There really was not very much available to disperse amongst charities. Charitable activity was largely funded by individual money-raising events. Outreach of that kind was through some very generous loans of locations. For example, the grounds of Government House were made available for a November 1898 fete in support of the Sisters of Charity. Money raised went to hot breakfasts for starving children and night refuges for women—in London. There may have been cultural confusion over the meaning of the expression 'charity begins at home'. Hong Kong were conditions not beyond St John's imaginative reach. Quite imaginatively, Harvest Sunday, which was too far removed from the cycles of the waving wheat in English fields, was replaced by Hospital Sunday, at which offerings were made to the Alice Ho and the Nethersole Hospitals, both for poor Chinese, managed by the London Missionary Society.

Social concern was expressed by regular donations to a CMS institution, the Victoria Home and Orphanage. A report of 1903 by teachers Miss Hamper and Miss Bachelor describes it as having fifty-four residents, mostly girls and victims of the *mui tsai* system in which young girls whose parents could not support them were sold as 'little sisters' into domestic service. Six girls had left in that year, two had died and the home had moved to new premises in Kowloon City, which was described as 'semi-rural and beneficial in many ways'. In fact it was the rapid development of that neighbourhood in the 1920s which forced the school to move and amalgamate with Fairlea Chinese Girls' School and become today's Heep Yun School.

Another favourite recipient of support from the cathedral ladies was the Eyre Refuge in Causeway Bay, run by a Miss Eyre, to provide a safe and Christian refuge, principally for 'fallen' girls. Assisted by the redoubtable missionary lady Miss Pitt, the girls were busied with laundry, sewing and some reading. They ran classes for *mui tsai* who were brought by their mistresses. Some of these mistresses the ladies observed as soft, allowing their *mui tsai* to become vain and insubordinate and reject marriage. The refuge died with Miss Eyre.

Not all offertory monies were received in the cathedral itself. As an English-speaking church, St John's was not entirely alone. The Peak Church opened as a chapel of ease to it on 17 June 1883. For the absence of any tower and the arrangement of its bays, it was known by the nickname 'Jelly Mould'. The church was built to meet the needs of the growing number of prosperous Europeans who were making their homes on the Peak, to escape the heat of the lower levels. Many were Anglicans in business and government for whom the journey down to the cathedral was an unwelcome trial and a repeat of one they made six days a week. The Peak Tram was not opened until 1888, so, prior to that, worshippers would have had to make the trip there and back in a sedan chair.

The principal service was 8 a.m. Holy Communion on Sunday mornings. Surviving records from 1904 to 1934 show that attendance was modest, at between five and twenty on most Sundays. However, on Easter Day and Christmas Day, numbers would shoot up to between forty and eighty.[52] Usually the senior chaplain officiated at the service. Frederick Johnson, and then Vyvian Copley-Moyle from 1911, showed up almost without fail. With Dean Alfred Swann, the duty was more widely spread between him and his chaplains, Koop and Evans. This may show that life for the clergy was busier down the hill, and whoever officiated was the one who could slot in the trip the most easily. Evans, who lived in Lyttelton Road, made it less frequently than Koop on Tregunter Path. For a spell during the summer of 1906, the bishop was the celebrant every Sunday. These services were some of the last that Bishop Hoare was to perform before his sad drowning in a typhoon in September.

The Peak Church was used for baptisms and, in that restricted residential area, they were all European. The elite up there were not over-generous to the offertory plate. They gave between 50 cents and a dollar a head. If you look at the pavement on Peak Road opposite Stewart Terrace, you might try and imagine the 'Jelly Mould' standing there. There are no remains. The Peak Church's affairs were formally wound up at a Special General Meeting of Electors and the

Committee of Management on 29 September 1958, but it had ceased to be a place of worship in 1941. The building itself was demolished in 1945, by which time neglect and an incendiary bomb had turned it into a wreck.

If not many dollars came down to St John's from the Peak, none at all came from the other English-speaking church of the period, St Peter's West Point. The flow had to be in quite the other direction. The first mariners' church came into being in 1851, but little is known about it. The Sailors' Home and Mission to Seamen was built at West Point in 1861, and St Peter's Church, also known as the 'Seamen's Church', was built next door ten years later. The seed money was given in memory of Henry Davis Margesson of Macao and Hong Kong, who had drowned. Bishop Alford raised considerable funds, and Jardines made a substantial donation.

The *Hong Kong Daily Press* tells us that, at the foundation stone laying on 26 March 1871, a choir chanted Psalm 84, the bishop read 'two or three collects' and the Reverend Piper read from Hebrews 10. Our assertive friend James Whittal, representing Jardines, alarmingly 'descended into the pit' with the stone, joined by the bishop, chief justice, colonial secretary, Attorney General, United States consul and Douglas Lapraik and gave an opening speech.[53] The church turned out to be of stone and brick with a spire, a fifty-eight-foot-long nave and red and black brick window surrounds. Photographs suggest it was an acquired taste.

There were 200 seats, of which 50 were reserved for seamen. A chaplain was appointed, and the first service was held on 11 January 1872. Peace was disturbed in 1895, when the Mission to Seamen no longer considered it their duty to provide a chaplain. From 1900 to 1911, The Reverend J. H. France took charge, and the church prospered as an early example to St John's of what a priest could do working with a lay council, created in 1909. There were even plans for expansion.

They were misconceived. Wharfing patterns changed. The ever-fleeting population of sailors gravitated to the Eastern Praya. Attendance dropped precipitously and income with it. The Mission to Seamen withdrew their chaplain again in 1913, and the cathedral took up the cost of supplying one, which it could ill afford. St Peter's ended up hidden in an unrequited corner of Hong Kong up a very steep hill with no settled income. It had a band of dedicated laity, many of them Eurasians, attracted almost by its very helplessness.

With the Reverend N. V. Halward, the bishop's chaplain transferred to it, the flag was kept flying for a while, but it could not last.
Under the Church of England Trust Ordinance of 1930, St Peter's
became a chapel of ease of the cathedral which, in a way, was its
death knell. Its site became a trading point with the government for
the establishment of a new Kowloon church. Closure was suggested
in the cathedral treasurer's report of January 1932. It happened
barely months afterwards. It was used for a while after by the Street
Sleepers' Shelters Society. Its stained glass windows, though one had
been given by Sir Paul Chater, were politely declined by anyone else
and broken up.

Bishop Charles Hoare, who arrived in time to take the confirmations backlog in 1898 and was to preach his last sermons in the
towerless church on Peak Road, was a scholar of Trinity College
Cambridge and spent twenty-three years as a missionary in China
and a publisher of theology who wrote in Chinese. He was forty-
seven when he became bishop and retained an evangelical vigour. He
was installed after evensong at 3 p.m. on 12 November 1898, the
Reverend L. Lloyd as his chaplain and Sir John Carrington, chancel-
lor. He had insisted that it be along the lines of recent installation
at Newcastle, with 'less law and more worship'. In his sermon, he
promised that he would not neglect Hong Kong, and within days he
was off to Foochow.

Within Hong Kong, his shining achievement was the Chinese
Church Body Incorporation Ordinance of 1902, which recognised the
work of the Chinese-speaking branch of the Church and formalised
it. It was an early move towards an Anglican communion apart from
the Church of England, a first real attempt at Anglicanism without
its Englishness and an independent Church in China. Inevitably, the
English Church in Hong Kong continued. It effectively created two
churches within one diocese. They took seventy years to fuse.

Hoare took an assertive position on his power in the cathedral.
According to G. E. Endacott, he secured a decision from the Church
Body at a 1901 meeting to the effect that, because, like all clergy, the
chaplain was subject to episcopal control, the bishop had a voice in
regulating the services of the cathedral beyond a mere question of
legality. That is how the situation remained, but it did not necessarily
rest. The Church Body were uneasy over the accretion of episcopal
control it had allowed. It sought Sir John Carrington's interpretation
of the ordinance on the matter, and it did not like what it heard. He

said that changes to services could not be made without the bishop's consent. This was as a right, not an expediency.

The Church Body retorted with what they had wanted to hear. In March 1902, they wrote that the chaplain was subject to canonical obedience in a way he was not when colonial chaplain, but this did not give bishop the right to alter legal services, and the chaplain still had immediate and direct management of them.[54] Simply stating that did not reverse the situation.

This, it appears, had a direct bearing on Chaplain Cobbold's resignation that year. The chaplain had gone on leave to England and announced his resignation from there, for 'family reasons'. Then he returned, which other clergy, resigning similarly, did not find necessary to do. Writing in *Church Notes*, he explained why. He wanted to speak face to face to his parish and to supervise a handover. His reminiscences of his office were all about the sanctuary, the parochial guild and the choir and nothing of administration until the very last sentence when, suddenly, we read, '… I found that I had not practically such liberty in the management and direction of services as I think your chaplain ought to have'.[55]

Was this an afterthought, dwelling on the principle laid bare by the Church Body's disagreement with Carrington, or was it a practical problem he had struggled with, at odds with the bishop? Was he a sad bystander in the struggle, or had he been an active part in the Church Body's attempt to see the ordinance reinterpreted and now, thwarted, compelled to resign? Cobbold must have played his cards close to his chest. A further, powerful reason for leaving emerged only months after he had gone. He married Lillian Hoppe Parkes, daughter of Harry Parkes, minister to China and Japan and sister of Mrs. J. J. Keswick. He was made Rector of Beauchampton and later Bratton Fleming in Devon. He died in 1945.

Bishop Hoare died tragically sooner than that. On Saturday, 15 September 1906, he went on a seaborne preaching tour in a house-boat with four students, two sailors and a ship's boy, up the western New Territories, spending the nights on board and preaching during the day. 'Evangelical theology through ambulando,' he called it. On Monday, the 17th, they sailed for Sha Tan 6 a.m. on the Sham Chun River. They got stuck on an oyster bed for a while, got off it and anchored for the night. On the morning of the 18th, the bishop was intending to make for Tung Chung, but his crew told him a storm was coming, so they decided to head back to Hong Kong.

The strong and unheralded typhoon caught up with them in Deep Bay. The students and the bishop were last seen holding onto pieces of the superstructure. One boatman made it to shore to tell the tale.[56] The 1906 typhoon caused the most fatalities of all in Hong Kong's recorded history. It is estimated that 15,000 people died in it.

Memorial services for Bishop Hoare were held in the cathedral on 30 September, morning and evening. Archdeacon Banister presided, and J. H. France of St Peter's preached. Mrs. Hoare pluckily played the harmonium. An afternoon service in Chinese was conducted by the Reverend Mok Shau Tsang. Ironically, but with equal sadness, the harbourmaster, Lionel Barnes-Lewis, a member of the Church Body, the Legislative Council and president of the YMCA, died that day on dry land, in bed, of an unstated illness.

A memorial window to Bishop Hoare was installed in the south transept of the cathedral. It was by William Morris, featuring, in the upper portion, St John on Patmos writing the Revelations under the instruction of God's angel. In the centre light was the Lamb enthroned and the Book with seven Seals worshipped by the elders and surrounded by hosts of angels. At the base off the window were three scenes of Christ on the water. On the left He called James and John mending their nets, at the centre, He stilled the tempest and on the right, He walked on the water before the disciples in their boat.[57] The governor, Sir Frederick Lugard, unveiled the window in 1909. It met with unusual critical acclaim. Our earlier commentator A. S. Abbott rated it as the only window he liked.

The year 1907 reaped some of the older personalities from St John's formation. Mr. Sangster, the first organist, had died in 1902. Now A. G. Ward, the second one, succumbed in his new job in Japan, and a brass plate was put up to him in the north transept, along with another to the non-commissioned officers and men of the 1st Battalion Sherwood Foresters. Canon William Beach died in Reading, Berkshire, and Bishop Burdon died at Royston, Hertforshire. He had gone back to China at age 70 on missionary work and had only stopped after his wife died there in 1899. Major John Aldor Burdon of Nigeria and E. R. Burdon MA of Cambridge, his surviving sons, presented to the cathedral a solid silver alms dish, designed round Bishop Burdon's seal. It is still in use.

In the late Victorian and Edwardian years, the cathedral had struggled for administrative boundaries. Its 'quiescence', a word used by

G. B. Endacott in his history, was more a spiritual one. A colonial congregation was sitting at the peak of imperial assurance, looking straight ahead and not at the inevitable and imminent descent. The cataclysm of 1914 was not far away, but its social consequences and its blow to the minds of men would roll out gradually through to the cathedral over the coming thirty years.

Chapter 4
The Search for Substance, 1902–1927

When Frederick Franch Johnson stepped into the post as senior chaplain in 1902, he was already in office in St John's. He was the first man to have been appointed as an assistant chaplain. Up to this point, the colonial chaplains, followed by Cobbold, had ministered alone. They had been backed up intermittently by CMS missionaries, naval chaplains and ordained schoolmasters. Commitment to a full-time assistant chaplaincy found great difficulty in gaining a foothold on the craggy finances of the cathedral.

In 1896, Cobbold had wrung a commitment of $200 a month from the Church Body and went to find a chaplain while on leave in England. He cabled success to the Church Body and they cabled back that, on reflection, $200 was not enough. They got 'cold feet'. We have seen how simple and unadorned the cathedral's income was in those days. They had a genuine fear that they might ship a man all the way out and run out of the funds to keep him.[1]

Bishop Hoare, prior to his arrival in 1898, was very keen on having an assistant chaplain to handle the Peak Church, the Kowloon ministry and the Treaty Ports. The Church Body felt the pressure and found $250 a month to offer. Hoare picked Frederick Johnson, and he arrived in February 1899. His role in the Treaty Ports turned out to be imaginary, but he took services in Kowloon, where worship was held in the curiously transient setting of the navy's torpedo depot, before St Andrew's Church was built.

When Cobbold's initial three years as senior chaplain had been up in 1895, the Annual Church Meeting (ACM) renewed his appointment but only after the newly invigoured subscribers and seatholders had held a ballot. In 1901, when the Church Body offered Johnson the job, the ACM found a new if finicky reason to posture power. It claimed that Johnson was too young. It questioned the process of his appointment. It demanded that the Church Body minutes on the matter be read. This was objected to on the grounds of propriety, but they were nonetheless read as 'a matter of courtesy not a matter of right'.[2] The strutting did not stop. A resolution was passed condemning the Church Body for appointing Johnson without consulting the subscribers and seatholders. Fervour took them too far in that. The Church Body definitely did have the power to appoint under the ordinance, but the meeting had become very serious about its rights to oversee. Mr. Johnson's age was not the true concern. The issue was the power of appointment, not the appointee. He could stay.

Johnson's promotion meant that a new assistant was needed. Imagining they had coped with an assistant chaplain only by the skin of their teeth, vacillation returned to the Church Body. When Bishop Hoare sent his single-word cable 'trombone' from London saying he had found a musically inclined replacement, the Church Body reneged, saying they needed the money for an organ overhaul.

The foundation stone for a new church in Nathan Road, Kowloon, had been laid in December 1904. Funds for it were provided by Sir Paul Chater and land by the government. Eventually, the Church Body was persuaded that this new Kowloon vestry could share, with the cathedral, the costs of an assistant chaplain. His special preserve would be what was to become St Andrew's, but he would still be a cathedral chaplain with duties there too.

The Reverend A. J. Stevens was appointed. He was a Durham University graduate and well travelled after curacies in Birmingham and Gateshead and chaplaincies in Odessa and South Africa, where he had been acting chaplain to the forces. He was secretary to the British Syrian Mission. His wife was more cautious in her movements. She would not come with him to Hong Kong at first.[3] Steven's time was almost entirely taken up by Kowloon. St Andrew's was dedicated on 5 October 1906, by Archdeacon Banister, accompanied by the Reverends Stevens, Longridge and France. In the Early Gothic design with a fifty-five foot long nave, it seated three hundred people. These people no longer had to consider themselves cathedral parishioners. Mr. Stevens was now in complete control, according to the Church Body.[4]

Even so, Stevens was not allowed to forget who employed him. In 1907, he took a short holiday without notice. This annoyed the Church Body. They ruled that clergy must apply for an exeat before leaving Hong Kong. This tidy, boarding school rule must have lapsed. Church Council members of this era would find it hard to recall any occasion when they were asked to grant an exeat to a dean or a chaplain.

The Reverend Stevens left St Andrew's in February 1909, but his full-time work there had left St John's once more understaffed. In 1908, the Reverend A. B. Thornhill, a curate at St Philip's, Litherland, was appointed as a new assistant chaplain on a three-year contract year. Thornhill was married in the cathedral by the bishop to Ada Jones St Clair, daughter of Lieutenant Colonel T. Y. St Clair of the Royal Berkshire Regiment. Mrs. St Clair was working with Queen Alexandra's Royal Army Nursing Corps at Bowen Road Hospital. The honeymoon was spent in far-off and rural Tai Po. When his contract was up in 1911, Thornhill left.

Very shortly after, so did Chaplain Johnson. His health seems to have been unsteady during his time. In 1904, Johnson spent six weeks on a busman's holiday in China and Japan, staying exclusively with clergy. He is reported as 'feeling healthier than when he left'. In August 1911, he went to Sydney for treatment and rest, which was quite a jaunt, but had returned to Hong Kong still in 'conscionable pain'.[5] By November, it had become all too much and he resigned, leaving in March 1912. For one who was not well, he took a potentially jarring route home too, by train through Russia. He was mostly fortunate. 'It was quite interesting and comfortable as far as Moscow', he reported, 'but the slow train to Berlin was most uncomfortable.'

His successor, Vyvian Henry Copley-Moyle, asked for an appointment on permanent terms with a notice period, and this time there was not a peep of protest out of the seatholders and subscribers. Copley-Moyle was a man of interesting shades. When he retired fifteen years later, Bishop R. O. Hall described him in a letter to the Victoria Diocesan Association newsletter, *The Outpost*, as a man of 'strength and humility' and of 'faithful unflinching life'.[6] He had charm and a penchant for socialising, a flowery pen, a talent for self-promotion. Some of his fame was uncomfortable and called on that unflinching quality. P. S. Cassidy, stalwart of the cathedral, in his retiring speech to the Victoria Diocesan Association, recalled how Copley-Moyle had been the centre of controversy in 1913 by refusing to marry a high official whose wife had been divorced and being admired for his courage.[7] Ultimately, he had a desire to stay in office, eventually stronger than that of the Church Body, which prised him out of it very much against his will.

One of the legends that built up around him is that he soldiered on alone for much of his term. This is not strictly accurate. For slightly over three of his fifteen years, he was without an assistant chaplain although his longest spell, which may have founded the impression, was from his appointment to February 1915, when the Reverend H. T. H. Holman arrived. After Thornill had left, the Church Body decided, yet again, that they could not afford a chaplain. Now that Johnson was gone too, they were forced to offer $25 a Sunday for CMS clergy to take the services, which was something of a staffing low point.

In 1912, the Honourable Claud Severn, colonial secretary, sometime officer administering the government and Church Body member, offered to the Church Body 25 pounds a year for three years towards the salary of an assistant chaplain if nine others would do the same and he could select the man. Severn was a short man of otherwise considerable stature and energy, a choir soloist and clearly fond of a dramatic packaged solution. His colleagues did not want it. They raised the barrier to 300 pounds and refused to surrender appointing power.

By this point in its history, the finances of the cathedral were in a poor condition. The cost of the assistant chaplaincy had been considerable. St John's had given unstinting assistance to St Andrew's Kowloon—as it did to St Peter's West Point—and it had suffered a loss of seatholders living in Kowloon who were now attending St. Andrew's. Essentially, the income it could earn from parochial services and the offerings it could expect from its congregational base were simply not enough to meet its costs. It crucially lacked endowment and therefore investment income.

The financial crisis of this period is interlocked with the desperate need to afford assistant chaplains. They had to be resolved together, or St John's would have faced a certain if imponderable decline as an active church. The leadership at the time could see this. There were hapless attempts at solutions and doubtless a lot of prayer until a Good Samaritan was sent along the way, a surprising one, a little shocking perhaps, and unstinting as Samaritans usually are. In 1910, a Cathedral Endowment Fund was created, but the method of attracting an endowment was rather limp. Bishop Lander, Hoare's successor, was asked to write to 'several gentlemen in England', but the response was not overwhelmingly gentlemanly. Sir Thomas Jackson gave $500 and Sir William Goodman, $50.[8]

Bishop Lander, from Trinity College Cambridge and with Merseyside parochial experience, had been enthroned on 23 November 1907 in the cathedral at an evensong service. Archdeacon Banister and Chaplain Johnson took the principal parts of the enthronement. G. A. Bunbury and Sherwood Jones were his chaplains. A. J. Stevens and Michael Longridge, the Naval Chaplain, officiated at the evensong in two parts. The procession from the west door included both British and Chinese clergy, A. D. Stewart and Mr. Fong, the Church Body, Dr. Atkinson, Messrs. Hastings and Clarke, and 'Chinese Lay Representatives'.[9] Lander arrived committed to a merging of the English and Chinese churches and, in this, he was to be disappointed.

In 1913, a special meeting was held on the assistant chaplaincy issue. Pew rents were raised. Suggestions were heard about how brighter services could attract more subscriptions. Then the Samaritan appeared. Sir Catchick Paul Chater was an Armenian, baptised into the Armenian Church of Nazareth in Calcutta in 1846. He was a renowned entrepreneur in Hong Kong, a founder of Hong Kong Land with James Keswick and the Dairy Farm Company, a Justice of the Peace, an epic racehorse owner and member of the Executive Council.[10] He was not a regular attender or officeholder at St John's. He preferred St Andrew's, but at this stage of his life, his view of his adopted city was almost statesmanlike and the cathedral was a prominent part of its fabric.

The cathedral was informed that Sir Paul would take round a subscription list for an assistant chaplain. He came back with $12,100, almost all of which he probably gave himself. Eventually, the governor, Sir Henry May, who had a personal Christian involvement in the church, doubled the amount. The money was moved from what had been an Assistant Chaplain Fund into the Endowment Fund.

Henry May's involvement was active and political. He believed in democratic government of the church, and he showed more personal interest in it than any other governor did. On 4 January, the Church of England Men's Society branch in Hong Kong, an increasingly influential 'think tank', offered to raise the income balance required for a chaplain of $114 per month. May objected to there having been no circulated notice of this resolution. He demanded and, unsurprisingly, got postponement for more thought.[11] The scheme was printed and circulated, and the governor was satisfied. The Reverend H. G. H. Griffith was appointed in February 1915, and Chaplain Copley-Moyle got his first assistant. For the purposes of parish visiting, which was as vital an element of pastoral work in Hong Kong as it would be in High Wycombe, the two priests came up with an interesting division of labour. Griffiths took the island east of Garden Road, while the chaplain took it from the west.

Henry May's procedural objection was not the last of the governor's interventions for a more broadly based governance. He fully supported a later push from the seatholders and subscribers, whose quietness over Copley-Moyle's appointment had been misleading. In April 1918, they petitioned the bishop to call a special meeting of the Church Body to discuss amending the ordinance to give more popular control over clergy appointments.

Their proposal was that six fully communicant seatholders and subscribers should join the six Church Body members on a special appointments committee and that no further appointments or re-engagements of clergy should take place without the sanction of a subscribers and seatholders meeting.

It would be a mistake to regard the seatholders as a detached group of unruly radicals. The largest of them in 1918 were the Hong Kong Bank, the Hong Kong Dispensary, Jardine Matheson, Kelly and Walsh, Sir Henry May, Reiss and Company, Shewan Tomes and Company, Butterfield and Swire, and Chinese Maritime Customs. Amongst them too were Mrs. Earle, Mrs. Knight and Mrs. White (wives of Church Body members), Mrs. Lander (wife of the bishop), Mrs. Dowbiggin (wife of Colonel Dowbiggin), Lady Pollock (wife of Sir Henry Pollock K. C.) and Lady Jackson (wife of the chairman of the Hong Kong Bank), all three men pillars of the church and frequently Church Body members.[12] If this was revolution, it was Presbyterian, in petticoats and rolling downwards. May would have put through an amendment along the lines demanded, but ill health forced his departure from office, apparently taking the steam out of the initiative.[13] The Church Body remained in control.

Griffiths left in 1918, and still in October 1919, the Bishops' Commissary in London, the Reverend W. R. S. Holland, was saying that no candidates were available. St John's cast its net over the empire and came up with Holman Taylor Hunt in Canada, who accepted a two-year contract of $250 per month plus a $70 war bonus. Hunt, genial and helpful, was bookishly inclined and fell easily into a job as acting registrar at Hong Kong University. On 29 January 1924, we find the Church Body holding that perennial, cover-all social, an 'at home' in the church hall for the Reverend T. B. Powell, Hunt's successor, F. Mason, the new organist, and N. K. Peel, the new Chaplain to St Peter's.[14]

Thomas Bertram Powell, out of Pembroke College Oxford and a Sheffield curacy, had served in the ranks in the Great War. He was a perceptive, passionate young man, and in his words you read the franker spirituality and sharper-edged aversion to hypocrisy gusting through with young men who had survived the trenches. He was popular but refused a second term. He said he felt unappreciated, which was understandable since it was discovered that, through some administrative confusion, he had been underpaid. He did enjoy one new perk of office. Early in 1924, it was thought 'desirable' for the assistant chaplain to be a member of the Hong Kong Club. Trustee Airey stepped in with a whip-round amongst his fellows and raised $105 for the $100 entrance fee. The $5 surplus was given to the Waifs and Strays Society, a neat counterpoint to the exercise, which one imagines the socially principled Powell bit his tongue over.

He was followed by the Reverend H. V. Koop in 1928, after the Reverend W. H. Cammell had served for the interim. The last time the question was raised, somewhat rhetorically, of an assistant chaplain being needed as against the incumbent going it alone, was by Alfred Swann to the Finance Committee of the new Church Council in 1931. The committee replied unanimously that Copley-Moyle did not really manage by himself for all that long and that those days were gone. The principal and practice of having an assistant chaplain was fully established.

Well established, well before the chaplains and costing a lot less, were the cathedral's lay employees. There were, as we have seen in the scandal of the stolen *punkah* wheels, church 'coolies' or 'boys', at least two of them, and *amahs* of indeterminate number. Set above them would be a European, invariably drawn from the bottom drawer of the colony's social chest. The first mention of one in surviving cathedral documents comes in 1877, concerning Sexton G. Saunders, who was described in the trustees' minutes as being a verger too. The *Oxford English Dictionary* will tell you that a verger is a caretaker who carries a staff in processions, whilst the lowlier sexton 'looks after the church', rings the bells and digs graves. Since no burials are permitted in St John's, and there was only one bell till 1870, the distinction at the cathedral was probably a thin one.

Sexton Saunders obviously was not keen on the verger side of the job. He did not want to attend military services. Whether this was out of pacifism or idleness we do not know, but he had stopped wearing his gown too. For this he was reprimanded. In explanation, he said it had been stolen so, for this, the head coolie was also reprimanded.

Saunders had complaints about his pay, which was increased from $14.86 to $15 per month. When he quit, the trustees wouldn't assist his passage home, but they bought him a church Bible for $10, and the police magistrate recommended a successor.[15] How perilously close to destitution this income alone would have been for a European is shown by how near it was to the more senior ranks of the Chinese labouring class. At the end of the century, the head coolie was paid $10 a month after twenty-three years' service. In fact the coolies complained that they had to pawn their clothes every month to make ends meet. It is not surprising that two of them had to be dismissed over some minor exercise in 'squeeze' in 1892.

If the Church Body was not overgenerous in its payments, it was not heartless in its treatment of its local staff. The widow of Head Coolie Ah Yee was given a gratuity in 1916. They showed some indulgence towards Ah Yun, the Number 2 Coolie who replaced him. The chaplain encouraged this:

> ... be patient with him. He is new ... He doesn't understand the dignity of an English cathedral. Nor does he understand that we rank cleanliness next to godliness. He is keen ... He rushes over to some coolie and forcibly removes his hat. His zeal needs curbing and directing along right lines.

In 1925, Copley-Moyle had sacked Ah Ling, a man of seventeen years' service, and his wife asked the Church Body to rescind that. Claud Severn, honorary secretary of the Church Body, must have felt obliged to support the action but said it should have been brought to the Church Body. They awarded Ah Ling $80 in compensation, a not inconsiderable sum, and to do further penance and probably not before time, they installed flushing water in the coolie quarters.

One touchingly naive moment came that year when someone described as an 'old watchman' donated one share certificate from a defunct company called My San, in case there might be some dividend from its estate. The Church Body, moved by the old man's helpless piety, gave him a gratuity of $75.[16]

However much Sexton Saunders had to struggle on his pay, it seems that later vergers, as they became known, were part-time and had other, more sustaining employment, usually at some junior level of government service. Verger H. J. White is an example. He lived in 'White Dell' on Queen's Road East, a detail provided in the forepage of *Church Notes*. This tags Mr. White's social status against the honorary officeholders of the Church Body who were listed as residing on the Peak, May Road and Queen's Gardens.

Mr. White worked in government service but at what we do not know. He earned himself a promotion to a level which would not permit him the spare time to attend to his cathedral duties, so he resigned. Very shortly afterwards, according to the *Church Notes* of June 1905, he died 'under very distressing circumstances leaving a widow and six children'.

Mr. White was succeeded by James Vanstone, of whom we know rather more.[17] He presents us with an interesting curriculum vitae for a working-class white man in a Victorian colony. He came to Hong Kong in 1874. The reason is not told, but military service would be a predictable guess, since one of his jobs was as a police sergeant in the naval yard. He also worked as head watchman at Kowloon Docks and, hard though it is to credit, a tramway brakeman.

He may well have been a full-time verger at St John's eventually, because his 1921 obituary described him as a 'retired verger', and the cathedral gave him a $500 retirement bonus after seventeen years. His last address is given as the Masonic Hall in Zetland Street. This is currently the site of an electricity substation at the top of the path from Ice House Street down to On Lan Street. He was a Freemason with the title of District Grand Tyler, a rank bestowed on brothers of more modest means and a rather grand way of saying 'district maintenance man'. In its reflection of the Hong Kong establishment of the time, the cathedral was a raft of Freemasons, and Vanstone could have been easily recommended from one job to the other.

He is described in the newspaper obituary as having been of 'the most cheery disposition and greatly liked by all'. In that case, he was so against many odds. His first wife, Lizzie, died in 1907, and he was sick for weeks afterwards. Amidst the sonorous testimonies to benefactors and heroes and those who could well afford it, a plaque was placed in her memory on the wall of St John's nave in 1909. A year later, their daughter, age 18 and a bride of a few months, died of pneumonia. He married again and carried on being greatly liked. In a foreign land where work could be dangerous and disease stalked, to let misery linger and not push on could be fatal to men like James Vanstone.

St John's looked for a successor. If they failed to find a suitable European, the Church Body was considering promoting the 'Number 1 Boy'. Army Sergeant Everett, a member of the Church of England Men's Society (CEMS), stepped up to the job for the two years left of his posting, to be followed by Charles Dodson but only for a year.

By 1920, the annual cost of the verger and coolies was $887. Night-time watch of the compound was not included even though the coolies lived on the premises. In fact, security in the cathedral's early years was appalling. An English soldier stationed in Hong in 1849 recalls, 'On one occasion the Cathedral was robbed and the thief was caught as he was leaving a side door. A Chinese Policeman caught him and the thief cut the Policeman very much with a Knife.'[18]

In June 1865, it was realised that there was no key to the west door, which might have explained a lot. Not surprisingly, the silver plate was kept in Government House. By 1900, a night watchman—perhaps the share certificate donor—was employed but to little effect. On one occasion he did manage to stall a robbery, but neither he nor five others roused from their slumbers, nor three policemen who responded to their calls, could catch the culprit.

Staffing, both clerical and lay, was largely unaffected by the First World War. In 1915, the choir bade 'Godspeed' to two members off to join the war, and men were reported missing from choir practice because of war work, but what that could have been, so far from the conflict, was not explained. There was a shortage of sidesmen, but the system had only been introduced in 1913 and was not catching on well. Endacott believes that the war made little impact on the cathedral at all. It raged too far away to touch the colony. This frustrated some. Commodore Sanderson RN (retd.) is reported to have asked the Church Body to recommend steps to promote greater self-sacrifice among British residents of the colony.[19]

The cathedral did its best to promote greater self-awareness amongst its parishioners and a great deal more prayer over the slaughter that was going on. Intercessions were held daily at 10.15 a.m. for those fighting, but attendances were very small. Chaplain Copley-Moyle attempted exhortation. 'Ladies passing the cathedral might spare 20 minutes for prayer in this great crisis,' he said. 'War should be a call to women to be more earnest and frequent in their prayers.' He pressed on with the gender distinction. 'Men living on the Peak pass the cathedral every day on the way to business. Ten minutes makes all the difference to a day's work.'[20]

Holy Communion on Thursday mornings was taken with the war in mind, but not by many. When special prayers were held in 'home' churches, these were mirrored by St John's. The service marking the second anniversary of the war was attended by the governor, but unlike the first one, there were no parades. By the third anniversary, attendances and the offertory were down by half.

On 6 January 1918, when war news would have been more than usually depressing, a day of prayer received a fulsome response, and a record $1,238 was collected for providing the navy with minesweepers. On 29 December, a service of thanksgiving attended by the governor and addressed by the bishop was well attended. The United States national anthem was played as the recessional hymn.

It is unlikely that the St John's congregation was indifferent to the war. It is probable that clergy and laity saw it through a different lens. Priests would see public prayer as an urgency to widen the sense of consciousness over death and loss. The layman going down Garden Road to the office wanted to narrow that vision of hell down so that life remained bearable as the truth went out of control.

Copley-Moyle may not have heartened everyone by publishing what reads today as religious jingoism in *Church Notes* from time to time. A 'General's Letter' in March 1915 told readers they were fighting for world progress and the furtherance of the Kingdom. 'War is a great blessing for our Empire. It is bringing out the best of our national character … and many millions to a knowledge of the truth,' he said. He had never seen such religious feeling amongst men in the ranks, which one can imagine. All had an 'allotted part to play for Empire, king and King of Kings'.

The chaplain himself joined in with '… till, with God's good hand upon us, the purpose of Germany is utterly defeated'. But the biscuit was taken by the Bishop of Oxford, Charles Gore, an aristocratic Anglo-Catholic who was otherwise a progressive priest and theologian. Out he came with, 'Many of us who cannot be soldiers find ourselves envying them a road so direct and simple into the divine kingdom.'

An urgent post-war task was to build a war memorial. The Church Body, consisting of Messrs. Severn, Earle, Hogg, Compton, Knight, Moorhead and the chaplain, discussed this in January 1919. The annual meeting of that year asked them to decide on a scheme. Three were considered: a memorial side chapel in the north transept, a rood beam across the chancel arch, a memorial cross in the Iona style. The second proposal had certain striking qualities, but the third, outdoor, option was chosen. Mr. Leask of Leigh and Orange had a tough time coming up with a satisfying design. One was too expensive, followed by another which was too indistinct. As the construction of the cenotaph in Statue Square was already in view, a question was put in a Church Body meeting as to why St John's needed a separate war memorial. Because we have indivertible funds for it, came the ineluctable reply. A bronze tablet recording the names of the dead was set in the south wall of the porch with a shelf for brass flower vases given by the Mothers' Union. So exposed, it disappeared during the Second World War.

On Sunday, 30 January 1921, the cross was unveiled by the governor, Sir Reginald Stubbs, at 10.30 a.m. Vice Admiral Sir A. L. Duff KCB, Major General Sir G. M. Kirkpatrick KCB, KCSI and H. H. L. Gompertz KC, acting chief justice were in attendance. Claud Severn was there repeating that tricky combination of roles, colonial secretary and cathedral secretary. They sang 'For All the Saints', and a roll of seventy-four names was read. It was, briefly, to be the centre of remembrance of the war dead until the cenotaph in Statue Square was completed in 1923.

A spiritual spin-off from war was a fast-growing healing ministry. By early 1922, intercessions were being made in the Lady chapel at midday on the fourth Sunday, and a 7.45 a.m. Holy Communion on the second Thursday was for the sick with the laying on of hands. Prayer circles for healing were formed and met in a union in the cathedral hall on Fridays.[21]

On Sunday, 30 May 1920, Governor Stubbs had laid mortar on the foundation stone of that brand new hall. The day after he unveiled the war memorial, he was back to open the completed building. Discussion about providing a Sunday school room was started in 1918. When it was found that there was a 75-pound balance in the Testimonial Fund for the departed Assistant Chaplain, H. G. H. Griffith. It was sent on to him, but he returned it to seed the fundraising for a room. Sir Paul Chater, entering a high season of generosity to the Church, gave $5,000, and a donor, anonymous at the time, gave $20,000. History unveiled him as M. J. D. Stephens, a barrister. The rest was raised by subscriptions although, a promise being sometimes easier than its fulfilment, there was a shortfall of $1,500 on commitments.

Protracted discussions were held on plans and features. There was a Plan A, no longer to be seen, which was rejected. The Church Body went for the Perpendicular Gothic in a collegiate chapel style, one also popular with libraries and mental institutions at the time. Although it is a later fussier Gothic, they thought it more dignified and in keeping with the church's style.[22] That itself was momentarily in peril when a later suggestion was made in the January 1923 meeting that the cathedral be stripped of its stucco and replaced with Shanghai stone in emulation of the new Hong Kong Bank building.

The ACM was held inside the new hall as soon as it had been opened. Portraits of bishops had been hung on the walls, on the suggestion of the governor. A further anonymous donation had come as a $10,000 fund for the annual maintenance of the hall, any surplus to be spent on musical equipment for use within it. The Chaplain, Copley-Moyle, reported that they were no longer threatened with the closure of the church, and evacuation into the new hall because roof repair against the white ants, which had struck again, could be done in stages.

The hall was reported to be in regular use immediately afterwards by the Diocesan Conference, the Victoria Diocesan Association Working Group and the CEMS. However, after a short while and an incident with the Philharmonic Society, the Church Body decided that it could not be loaned free of charge to those considered friends of the cathedral, without Church Body's approval.[23] The Philharmonic Society came to be charged $250 for using the hall for 'practices'. During one season, they asked for a discount because their concert was cancelled for lack of support.

The hall had not been built without incident. Two coolies had been killed on the site during construction, and a collection was made for their families. The cathedral congregation raised $340. It does not seem much today, but in a time when there were no workers compensation schemes and the threat of legal action was not one available to the lower classes, it was a generous and helpful conclusion.

One more addition to the church's fabric which has abided was made at this time. In 1919, Mrs. Anne Bowdler donated the reredos for the high altar at the east end, in memory of her husband, Edward, who had been assistant surveyor general for twenty-four years and had donated 1,000 pounds to both the cathedral and the Peak Church. The Bowdlers lived in one of the earliest houses built on the Peak and named 'Fung Shui'.[24]

The reredos was a screen of panels in marble and Derbyshire alabaster by William Morris and Co., featuring statuettes of the Virgin and St John, sculpted by Henry Pegram RA. It is a striking and an unusual feature for a church in Asia. In considering the work at their meeting in April 1920, the Church Body had wanted to replace the cross and statuettes with mosaic panels. They may have considered the look to be too Roman. Mrs. Bowdler stuck to her ornate guns. 'After much consideration'—you can hear the discomfort—they accepted the design as executed. A year later it was resolved that the 'squares at the back of the cross be permanently blacked' and the statuette bases gilded.

All this could be seen rather better since electric lighting had been installed in St John's in 1907. Vision was still impaired by the use of *punkahs* in the summer months. Claud Severn, with his usual passion, undertook to raise money to replace *punkahs* with fans. This he achieved for $4,000 by 1923. 'The view of the beautiful East Window is no longer blocked by ugly punkahs', he declared with satisfaction when the task was complete. Press publicity surrounding the event suggested that, to keep cool, you should come to the cathedral. In the years after air conditioning became commonplace, opinion was to the contrary. Some of those same fans still rotate above the congregation, occasionally groaning at their joints in the middle of a sermon as though to indicate that they have heard the point often and long ago.

Recalling when he first joined St John's in 1921, 'Bunny' Abbott remembers what he described as 'the gentry at Matins'. The men were dressed from Savile Row, with nosegay, gloves and silver-topped cane and the ladies in taffeta and lace, with feather boa and parasol. The church did not look so smart. The organ pipes on the south side of chancel were dirty green. There was a tray a half-inch full of water under the wooden pipes to prevent contraction but which attracted mosquitos. The pews were three inches off the ground, hosting rats. There was a label with the renter's name on it and an IOU book with pencil for putting credit chits into the alms bag, the cathedral shroff having to chase around town afterwards to collect on them.[25]

In 1920, Bishop Lander resigned. An inscribed silver salver and $2,000 cash was presented to him at an 'at home' in the Helena May Institute. Lander had been particularly involved with the organisation of the Chinese diocese and the setting-up of the Chinese Anglican Province, the Chung Hua Sheng Kung Hui. Synods were set up in every diocese but for the Victoria Diocese, which involved the English-speaking churches which still looked to the Church of England, and a distinct Diocesan Conference structure had to be organised.

Lander did not like this separation. In his enthronement sermon at St John's he had quoted the conviction held by some that 'you can neither Europeanise the Asiatic nor orientalise the European'. There is no need to try, said the bishop. With Christ as the foundation, a church superstructure could be built, Chinese and European in perfect harmony.[26] He expressed his disappointment that this had been fallen short of at the conference's first meeting. 'Personally I would much have preferred to have one organisation ... but unfortunately Church of England members who sojourn here do not learn to speak Chinese.'[27] For the cathedral, he had hoped to create a chapter of Chinese and European canons, but that did not even see a beginning.

That first Victoria Diocesan Conference on 24 February 1920 entitled St John's to send two representatives for every one hundred communicants. Its deliberations came up with some proposals as sweeping as they were inoperable. One was that Hong Kong should be one large parish under the cathedral. Another, from Copley-Moyle, attempted to neatly package away the Oxford Movement by making St Stephen's 'more ornate' and having sung Eucharist every Sunday for those 'often described as Anglo-Catholics'.[28]

Succeeding Bishop Lander on 5 November 1920 was Charles Ridley Duppuy, freshly consecrated a bishop in St Paul's in June, where he had an African and an Indian bishop lay hands on him and believed it was the first time a European bishop had had that experience.[29] The 1920s were to be a decade in which Bishop Duppuy moved the diocese and the cathedral forward in a manner not spectacular but substantial. According to Endacott's history, 'His passion and genius were for order and administration.' He was keen to develop the triennial synods of the Chinese Church and to move the Church of England, the 'colonial' side of the diocese, closer to it. He was determined on a greater diocesan role for the cathedral. His collaboration with the future Dean Alfred Swann and the more progressive lights on the Church Body was crucial to the pivotal 1930 reform of St John's governance.

Duppuy's reception and first few days in Hong Kong are a rather apt summary of a bishop's world there at the time. He was met off the SS *Somali* by Archdeacon Barnett, Chaplain Copley-Moyle, the Reverends Lindsay, Vicar of St Andrews and Waldegrave of St Peter's, the Reverend Featherstone, headmaster of the Diocesan Boys' School, and the Reverend A. D. Stewart, headmaster of St Paul's College and his brother Evan, who was to succeed him. They all took the Seamen's Mission launch the *Dayspring* from Kowloon and chairs up to Bishop's House.

Duppuy met the staff and the boys, took lunch with the governor and had tea with CMS missionaries. In his welcome from the governor, he was told by Sir Reginald Stubbs that he was sorry to say that, in the past, the Church had not been properly supported. He spoke frankly, 'so that the bishop might know that he had not come into a field of roses'.[30]

There was a public welcome at the Helena May followed by his enthronement on 5 November. He was preceded down the cathedral nave by the choir, the St Andrew's Church Body, the Chinese Church Body, the Cathedral Church Body, the clergy, the Archdeacon of Hong Kong and the chaplain. He knelt at a fald stool in the chancel, which survives there still, and presented to the archdeacon and the chaplain Letters Commendatory from the Archbishop of Canterbury, requesting that they 'acknowledge, install and enthrone' him.

The congregation sang 'The Church's One Foundation', 'God of Abram', 'Come Holy Ghost Our Souls Inspire', 'Alleluia, Sing to Jesus' and 'For All the Saints'. The Blessing from Copley-Moyle moved Duppuy most. 'Be thou worthy, just, patient, sincere, as an angel and messenger of Christ'.

'Nearly all the seats were occupied ... hardly a seat vacant,' reported the *South China Morning Post*, trying hard to make the best of the fact that the cathedral was not completely full. The reporter had a good eye for a quote. He pulled out of the sermon an interesting light on Duppuy's faith. 'Christian life in the world today is not a survival of the past, it is a fragment of the future, it is eternity breaking into the world of time and it is here by the creative act of God.'[31]

There was a garden party at Government House on the Saturday, and on Sunday, he preached in the cathedral and in St Andrew's. They took him to Kowloon City, where he remarked on the 'many smells', and to visit one 80-year-old Pastor Fong. The public welcome by the Chinese church was at the YMCA, which made him 'desire very keenly to know the language'. He was never to become good at it. He visited Fairlea School and St Stephen's College and went to a St George's Society smoking concert. He watched a game of inter-port cricket with Shanghai and attended a CEMS social. Then he left for Canton for a welcome dinner by the Chinese vestry.

On Armistice Day 1920, just a few days after the enthronement, the *South China Morning Post* could report with satisfaction that St John's Cathedral was filled to overflowing with standing room only. Governor Stubbs was present with the General Officer Commanding, General Ventris and the navy commander, Commodore Bowden-Smith RN. They sang 'Fight the Good fight' and the 'Te Deum' to Oakley's 'Quadruple Chant'. They all processed over to the new memorial cross to the 'Dead March' from 'Saul' and laid wreaths. Guns on Murray Parade Ground fired to signal the two-minute silence. Business was suspended; trams, ferries, motor cars came to a halt.[32]

World war had been succeeded by financial instability. The high exchange rate, which had come with the weakening of sterling at that time, reduced the effectiveness of the bishop's salary from 10,000 pounds to 7,800 pounds. This had 'affected Bishop Lander keenly', according to Stubbs in his welcoming address to Duppuy. Claud Severn, rashly loyal, had wanted the bishop to be paid as though there were still two shillings to the Hong Kong dollar and for the cathedral to make up the difference, but other trustees baulked. The Church Body decided to give $100, or around 10 pounds a month, towards the shortfall. The cathedral had financial concerns of its own. As the 1920s were to be the decade of Duppuy for church organisation, it was to be the make-or-break era for cathedral finances.

On 20 April 1921, the Good Samaritan lifted the church up from the roadside. Sir Paul Chater made a donation of 25,000 pounds towards an endowment fund. His intention was that the money could go ultimately towards making all seats free and pay for more clergy. There was a distinct intent, on the part of the donor, to see the end of pew rents. It is a signpost moment in the church's physical survival. It turned the fiscal fortunes of the cathedral around, but not all at once. Endowment funds are meant for deeper planting, not for quick and easy disbursement. The cathedral's cash flow was still shallow and anaemic.

In January 1920, annual expenditure consisted of chaplains' salaries, $5,000; housing, $1,800; organist, $2,400; vergers and coolies, $887; *punkahs* and *wallahs*, $235. Income was from collections at $4,396, sittings at $2,966 and subscriptions at $3,382. The Assistant Chaplain's Fund stood at $16,900, and the Church Hall Fund had $31,445, which was about to be expended.[33]

Pew rents were $15. Jardines' sittings bill was $105, the Hong Kong Bank's, $150. Individual's bills were led by Major General Ventris, the Honourable Mrs. E. V. D. Parr and Mr. C. G. Alabaster CBE. Mr. Alabaster's career in Hong Kong is archetypical of the Christian Englishman of the time who worked for colony and cathedral. He was the son of Sir Chaloner Alabaster, for many years a British consul to China. He was a barrister called to the Hong Kong Bar in 1909 and made a Silk in 1922. Five times a Legislative Council member, he was Acting Attorney General, 1911–1912, and made an MBE for his services to the censorship of cables during the war. In 1917, he became a member of the Sanitary Board, the first if rather elemental body in Hong Kong to be elected.

In December 1920, finances at St John's were in such a poor state that an offertory donation to the Diocesan Boys' School was cancelled. In 1922 there was a $5,000 debit. The Assistant Chaplain's Fund had to be raided. The Church Body was in no mood to illuminate the tower to mark the Prince of Wales's visit that year when they were quoted $700 for the job. There is no record of the prince setting foot in St John's anyway.

The Assistant Chaplain's Fund was raided again in 1923, to repair the house of the chaplain, Kellet Crest, at 66, the Peak, probably the unhappiest purchase the cathedral ever made. Copley-Moyle said he needed a house because of the 'system of boxes'. This referred to the habit of quoting merely a GPO box number as an address, which made pastoral visitations difficult to arrange. He needed a house which he could ask people round to for a meal or 'a game of tennis'.

Out of the sort of regard that the chaplain earned from people, M. J. D. Stephens, who had donated anonymously to the church hall, gave $30,000, also anonymously, for the purchase of a house for him. The Church Body asked rather sardonically if he would care to donate another $15,000. The cost of building a new house on the Peak was $45,000 and a new build was what they believed was soundest. Copley-Moyle, however, wanted Kellett Crest, owned by Mr. Steeple-Smith. Initially the Church Body rejected this, but Copley-Moyle strong-armed it into rescinding the decision and buying the house, not least because it has shared access to a tennis court.

Almost immediately a typhoon hit it, and $10,000 was needed for repairs. In addition, the original donor now found himself being asked to pay for an extra room because the house was not really big enough. The steep drive made it inconvenient and was later to prove bad for Dean Swann's weak heart. Unabashed, the chaplain declared himself uncomfortable at losing his $150 rent allowance, because the house was sparsely furnished and equipped. So, it was replaced by a $100 'maintenance' allowance and $1,000 payment for expensive essentials, which apparently included cutlery.

By 1924, the Church Body found themselves with a deficit of $9,000 and nothing to cover it. This situation was partly due to an encouraging expansion of activities and to the devaluation of sterling. Now they were forced to raid the treasure chest. They sold their investment in Central Estate Debentures, which involved Prince's Building and the Hong Kong Land Company. This they credited to the current account. The Assistant Chaplain's Fund was empty and was closed.

At this point, Sir Paul Chater weighed in again with $9,000 to cover the original shortfall, which now left the Church Body with $10,450 in its current account. In March 1925, as moved by Claud Severn, the Church Body resolved to transfer the Chater Endowment Fund from London to Hong Kong and into Hong Kong currency. That was a small but noticeable decline of empire and severance of the link with 'home'. Chater came up with a further $31,000 to round the transferred sum back up to the originally intended $250,000.

How must the congregation of St John's have felt having to depend on the charity of an Armenian Indian to uphold the Church of England in the empire? Tellingly, apart from the fund itself, there was nothing material inside or around St John's to carry Chater's name. What must Chater have thought of these British businessmen and administrators who could not even support their own church fully? Perhaps he considered himself one of them. One of Chater's stated purposes of the original cathedral endowment was so that 'more spiritual help can be given to British people here'.[34] On 29 June 1925, perhaps a little disproportionately, he established another endowment trust fund of an equal $250,000 for St Andrew's, making that a very wealthy little church for its day. The comparative generosity may have reflected the fact that Chater attended St Andrew's, not St John's.

One pivotal source of income for St John's also carried with it constitutional consequences and a rumbling social problem. 'Sittings', also known as pew renting, yielded $3,000 per annum in 1919. By that time, reserved seating in church for the wealthy was falling out of accord with the shifting social feelings of the post-war period. An incident involving the military had begun the glacial erosion of the system. In 1915, the Territorial Battalion of the King's Shropshire Light Infantry took up garrison duties. They needed space, and seatholders were asked to make room. It was suggested that all seats should be free from three minutes to 11 a.m., the beginning of the principle service of Sunday morning.

It has to be appreciated that many seatholders did not come to church every Sunday. Worship would begin with empty seats in rows at the front of the nave. The objective was to provide a last-minute opportunity for those further back to fill them up before the service started. The grim prospect for some seatholders under this arrangement was that, if they arrived fractionally before the start or a few moments late, they would have to sit at the back with persons of a lower social class, possibly people they employed or, conceivably, Chinese.

At the 1917 ACM, outright abolition was proposed. The motion called upon each seatholder to give an equal sum in lieu of the rent. This was withdrawn in favour of a motion that all seats should be free five minutes before the beginning of the service. As usual, the turnout had been small, and alarmed seatholders called a special general meeting which overturned the resolution. However, as a compromise of sorts, all seats were made free at evensong. This was a service perpetually unfashionable with the social set but popular with young men from the armed forces. In 1918, there was further wearing away of the institution when the regulations changed to allow free seats at 11 a.m. matins after the bell stopped. You would have had to move quickly.

The influential CEMS—which had a Hong Kong branch that met in St John's—weighed in by publishing arguments against pew rents and, in 1919, the Archbishop of Canterbury's Select Committee of Enquiry findings led to the phasing out of pew rents in England, enabled by the Assembly Powers Act of that year.

St Andrew's abolished its pew rents in 1924. Nothing was done at the cathedral until 1927, when the wind of reform began to gust more briskly through St John's compound. The ACM of 1927 revisited the proposal that all seats should be free. It reviewed the various schemes concerning the ringing of the bells and the time of the clock. Previously, it had been felt that complete abolition could not be achieved for financial reasons, but now that the Chater endowment existed, they could think again.

Responses to a recent postcard vote had been 29 for and 23 against abolition. The poll was small but the size of the hostile minority was significant. Sir Henry Pollock K. C. of the Church Body suggested that 10.53 a.m. be the deadline for freeing up the seats. Another member, W. L. Pattenden, liked abolition but favoured starting that way. T. L. King asked the chaplain how evening services were affected when seating was free. 'Better congregations,' he replied '… and we get people up to the front row.'[35]

This turned King into favouring abolition and resorting instead to special collections. P. S. Cassidy worried that companies that had the security of seats through rents might stop making donations if they lost that. There was overall a cautious new feeling in favour of abolition, but the vote was for referral to the Church Body.

The Church Body commissioned another survey, and 58 out of the 107 seatholders replied and reported on 19 April 1927. Eleven seatholders, representing $540 of income, opposed abolition. Seven, representing $210 of income, were uncertain, and thirty-nine were in favour and undertook to make annual donations to the church. This was finally enough for the Church Body. Abolition was recommended to the 1928 church meeting and accepted. The Dean, Alfred Swann, was memorable at this point for recalling to that meeting the words of a clerical colleague in England: 'All kneelings in this church are free.'

The abolition of pew rents was the trigger for an organisational and inevitably spiritual reform towards which some more enlightened souls were striving and the cathedral in general struggling from the war years on. The question at the root of reform was a simple one: If you abolish seatholders, who or what is the ACM? The eventual answer was in the Church of England Trust Ordinance of 1930, which gave St John's its current form. It is worth taking a snapshot of a point in the middle of the preceding decade to see how far perception of this had come.

The time is January 1926, the frame of the picture is the Li Hall, now five years old, and in it, the Annual General Meeting of the Seatholders and Subscribers was taking place. Facing the seatholders were the Church Body, made up of the Bishop of Victoria, Charles Duppuy, the Assistant Chaplain, the Reverend T. B. Powell and the elected lay members, Sir Henry Pollock, Lieutenant Colonel T. R. Robertson, Professor L. Forster and Messrs. Compton, Pattenden and Owen-Hughes. The Senior Chaplain, Vyvian Copley-Moyle, was on leave, 'back home'. Home leaves were months long, and one did not steam back specially for anything, not even the ACM.

The assistant chaplain who had felt so unappreciated was about to be compensated by a first-class cabin for his own voyage home. He spoke of an *annus miribalis* for the cathedral although life on the streets that year had been less than wonderful, there having been a general strike and violent protests which were the tense political hallmark of the early 1920s. Services had improved, he reported, with an increase in congregations. Congregational singing practices, hard to imagine now as then, had been met with some surprise, he said, chiefly because there was no Old Testament authority for them. One imagines Mr. Powell is being waggish here. Not so about the Women's Guild, whose efforts, led by Lady Pollock, in keeping the church spick and span, he praised fully. The guild had been recently formed at the suggestion of the bishop who, somewhat frustrated by St John's weak finances, thought it might be about time that women were brought in to help. Powell believed the guild useful in saving British women from the 'endless strain of enforced leisure'. Its inaugural meeting was held on 11 November 1924.

The guild's main activities were supervision of the cleaning of the cathedral, care of altars, church plate, brasses, linen and furniture, and supervision of Sunday schools. Lady Pollock with the bit between her teeth went on to form the 'Women Church Workers Committee', with a misleadingly proletarian ring having her and Lady Severn and Mesdames Foster, Black, Witchell and Airey as members. Mostly these were wives of Church Body members, and one can imagine many initiatives through pillow talk. The guild itself was succeeded by the St John's Cathedral Women's Fellowship in 1938.

Points of wonder were that there was a Chinese sidesman and that two Chinese now sat on the Church Council. Talk of an advisory council had led to a report from the combative Reverend Powell, who had found the need for more lay involvement and less secrecy in the cathedral's government. This council which came about is not to be confused with the one that governs the cathedral today. In 1925, that was still firmly in the hands of the Church Body, which would not be reformed until the ordinance of 1930. The council was an imitation of the recently established parochial church councils in England. It was a gathering of well-meaning volunteers acting as 'watchdogs', in an early attempt to spread more responsibility into the laity. However, lacking a budget or specific authority, all it had was gums.

There was a hope that Chinese language services would be introduced, but that was still a long way from becoming an expectation. The Women's Guild and the CEMS had started a lending library, the ancestor of the present Kenneth Tyson Library, and the cathedral now hosted a Scouts and a Guides troop. Mr. Powell hoped that the coming year would see an end of pew rents. He was short of the mark but not far.

The treasurer, Mr. Owen-Hughes, reported on how the deficit of $9,000 had been wiped away by a donation from Sir Paul Chater. Without the monies that Chater repeatedly injected into the system, the cathedral could have been a wreck and St Andrew's and Christ Church possibly not there at all. That more modest but still munificent donor, Mrs. Bowdler, who had given the reredos, died that year. She left 2,000 pounds to the cathedral, which, thanks to the weakness of sterling, went into the books as $17,872. Sir Paul Chater found a safe investment for it to rest in. Collections were down $50 and donations were down by $12 over 1924. Wedding fees yielded $147 less, but just to string out financial doubt about their abolition, pew rents brought in $187 more. There had been a successful special collection for renewing the hassocks.

Bishop Duppuy announced that the Church Body had decided to give a gift of furnishings to the newly built cathedral in Foochow. One form of outreach which the cathedral has excelled at from the beginning has been to give assistance to smaller churches struggling to make a beginning. This was often at a time when, such as on this occasion, St John's itself did not have that much for its own needs. As we have seen, support was given to St Peter's and St Andrew's. After the Second World War, the cathedral was to have a policy for a while of donating to new or reviving Chinese parishes in Hong Kong. As recently as 2010, it gave HK$900,000 for stained glass in the re-opening of the former Cathedral of the Holy Trinity in Shanghai.

Bishop Duppuy had clear visions of a cathedral as a mother church of a diocese, a spiritual centre, a source of nurture for the parishes, a headquarters from which men and women went forth to help. A determined man, ready to make a decision that could upset, he was doing what he could to push that new age in.

The meeting was told that a new organ, 'second to none East of Suez', was almost complete in what is now the St Michael's chapel. Sudden changes in temperature had precipitated a crisis in the old instrument. The blowing systems were, to use an expression, 'blown'.

The boards of the three manuals were in 'a deplorable condition'. Currently, pipes were held together by wire and were virtually impossible to tune. Proposed was a two-level scheme with options, one at $4,000 restricted to the present organ box, and the higher at $14,000, which would involve bringing the organ forward so that its pipes in a new and more impressive casing faced onto the chancel.

The Church Body decided to go for a full renewal at $14,000. The organ builder was a Mr. Blackett, an 'elderly, bearded gentleman', recalls future organist Lindsay Lafford. He had been a member of an organ-building firm in England named Blackett & Howden, and had come to the colony to install one of their organs in a church. Finding the climate congenial, he had decided to stay, and set up a small organ factory in the city. He recruited a group of Chinese and taught them the trade.

Blackett's design for a new organ casing and side chapel screen was preferred over that of the honorary architect, Mr. Clemens' which was thought too elaborate and expensive, especially in the matter of certain stars embellishing the screen overhang. Carved woodwork was felt to be acceptable if it was kept below the line of the pipes. His was not. Mr. Clemens had always been that bit less favoured for his flourish, but he had successfully designed the flooring of Phoebe May's Lady chapel.

Bishop Duppuy reported to the meeting that $6,000 had already been raised against the costs and the healthy prospect of more to come. Fundraising had been suspended because of what was politically 'troublous times'. He was referring to the strike and anti-British boycott which gripped Hong Kong and Canton in 1925. It was inspired by a deadly shooting in a strike in Shanghai and fuelled to fever pitch[36] by a major shooting incident involving British and French guards killing demonstrators in the Shamian Island concession area of Canton.

Organised by the Kuomintang and the Chinese Communist Party, pickets stopped food and essentials from being shipped to Hong Kong, which was paralysed by early June 1925. The draconian reactions of the governor, Sir Henry Stubbs, only served to exacerbate the problem. Servants withdrew their labour. Upper-class expatriates and wealthy Chinese had to do their own housework and dispose of their own night soil. A surprisingly indomitable spirit and sense of volunteerism was shown by both groups before the boycott ended in October 1926.[37] Little mention is made of the boycott in cathedral records, but it would have made a considerable impact on the congregation. During the earlier labour upheaval of the Seamen's Strike in 1922, Chaplain Copley-Moyle had preached against the exploitation of labour and the risks of 'class war'.[38] By 1925, the people of St John's would have been sensitive to the accumulating challenge to British imperialism and a shift from social docility in the workers around them.

None of this compromised the organ, though. Photographs published in *The Outpost* in September 1927 show it to be of grand proportions and a magnificent sight set over the carved canopy of the bishop's throne. Services were first broadcast on ZBW Radio in 1927 from a transmitter on the Peak, and the organ would have been played to listeners over crackling radio sets and earphones. They had the advantage over us. Only a handful of people are left alive who can remember hearing it.

Musically, these were busy years. Choirboy scholarships to Central British School Kowloon were begun. Boys made progress through grades A, B and C, assessed on ability and good work by the cathedral organist. Mr. Mason offered $50 to increase the awards to $350 in 1930. A generous $30 was given to senior choirboy Herbert Smith on leaving the colony. Mason's predecessor, Fuller, had been an inspiring man, but his health had not kept pace. In December 1921, his salary was stopped because he should have been back from leave in October, but nothing was heard from him. In March, he returned but went straight into hospital. The Church Body felt 'sympathetic' and restored half his salary from the time he was due back until resumption of duties but 'withheld that for the time being' from him.

In 1923, he resigned after seventeen years in the post. His concluding effort was a concert featuring Wesley's 'Choral Song and Fugue', Stoughton's 'Garden of Iram', Widor's 'Toccata', Arthur Barclays's 'Allegro Appassionato' and Fuller's own recessional. Remarkably, in aid of the Organ Fund, Denman Fuller had raised $20,000 over the years. A great fuss was made of him at the ACM. They put a plaque to William Gould Bennett Denman Fuller FRCO LRAM on the organ casing, which also recalled his donation of a rotary blower, and they sent him a commemorative plate. To replace him, the Church Body looked for a school that needed a master who could double as an organist. This tradition lives on. Trustee Dowbiggin thought they did not need a first-class musician. Bishop Duppuy strongly disagreed. The Diocesan Boys' School agreed to guarantee a $150 salary for a 'priest-organist'. A Reverend Evers in India was found whom Duppuy knew and said would 'probably do' if his preaching was adequate and he could intone properly. Mr. Evers was offered the job but declined.

Frederick Mason succeeded Fuller on 22 November, not as a priest-organist but as a layman teaching music at Diocesan Boys' School and leading it at St John's. Relations with the Diocesan Boys' School were closer than they were to become after it moved from Hong Kong Island over to Kowloon. The school was a principal source of choir-boys, and the bulk of the school attended the cathedral on Sundays. In early 1925, the headmaster, the Reverend W. T. Featherstone, was asked to also put a senior boy at the end of each row of boys attending evensong because they were so badly behaved.

That they might be fractious at the end of the day is hardly surprising. DBS was a puritanical place, according to the account of one alumnus, W. J. Howard, who attended it between 1911 and 1919.[39] On Sundays, the senior boys had to walk from Bonham Road to St John's for the 6.50 a.m. Communion service. After walking back, all boys marched down to St Peter's church for 11 a.m. matins. After two hours memorising the collect and the gospel for the day, they had to walk back to the cathedral for evensong. It is a wonder they had the energy for mischief.

The boys were always impressed by Denman Fuller's skill on the organ, which drowned out their chatter. Howard recalls the volume of the great pipe organ as 'a Niagara compared to the new electronic organ's trickling stream'. He also recalls Sir Claud Severn's strong bass voice in St John's choir and how, as officer administering the government, Severn would send the governor's Crown car to fetch boys from DBS to join the choir. Gossip had it that Sir Claud almost married Miss Goggin, the school matron, a socially unusual prospect only ended by her death in January 1920. The Chaplain, Copley-Moyle, taught scripture to the matriculation class and laced it entertainingly with Roman history. Howard recalls that his sermons were 'refined' and 'fully prepared with copious notes'.

Ministry to young people was expanding during this period. Apart from the Sunday school at the cathedral, one was established at the Peak Church. There was also a weekly children's service, which was run on the novel theme of all the roles such as readers, intercessors and sidesmen, which were normally taken up by adults, being performed by children. When Alfred Swann took over as dean in 1928, he was reporting to the ACM that these services were a great success.

At the adult level the garrison connection was beginning to loosen. Church parade services, which required the full use of chapel, chancel and baptistery, were now to be held bimonthly instead of once a week, partly because different and disparate barracks sites had developed chapels of their own. Since broadcasting from the cathedral had begun, the early morning parade services that were still held there had become popular listening. Unlike at the lay civilian services, the church was filled with the voices of hearty young men singing hymns deliberately chosen for familiarity and simplicity and accompanied by a military band.

The Mothers' Union was strengthening its links to St John's. They held quarterly services in the cathedral and knitted woollen clothing for the Tsan Yuk Hospital and the Waifs and Strays Society. Could they keep and disburse collections from their quarterly services, asked Mrs. Duppuy of the Church Body? Of course they could. Who was going to argue with the bishop's wife?

The year 1924 saw some requests for a 'laying on of hands' service although support for it had run thin. The chaplain appreciated it, though, and lamented that 'members of the Church are far from recognising the importance of a healing ministry', which showed how quickly the post-war interest in this had waned. For the Advent season of 1925, a shortened evensong on Wednesday evenings at 6.30 was with organ music and a discussion meeting in the hall to follow. A 'teaching evensong' it was called.

On the second Sunday, the chaplain preached on 'Declension— and Ourselves'. He was not talking about grammar but in the sense of moral decline. From the 1925 Lent pew sheet,[40] we learn that the bishop and the chaplain split the season's preaching at matins into three Sundays each. At evensong, there was a series including 'Life's Helps' from G. E. S. Upsdell, 'Life's Hopes' and 'Life's Ideals' from A. D. Stewart, 'Life's Burdens' from E. W. Martin and 'Life's Triumphs' from G. T. Waldegrave.

The cathedral's natural role as a civic centre for memorial and celebration continued and extended itself. The loss of His Majesty's Submarine *M1*, which sank in the English Channel on 12 November 1925 with all hands, must have had an unusual impact on the British public conscience, because the crew were memorialised in a service at faraway St John's on the 21st. Attending were the governor, Sir Cecil Clementi, former governor Sir Matthew Nathan, who may well have been on his way home from his last posting as governor of

Queensland, and Vice Admiral Sir Edwyn Sinclair Scott, Royal Navy Commander-in-Chief, China Station. The service was conducted by naval chaplains, principally, the Reverend W. F. Scott RN of HMS *Hawkins*. The bishop preached. Six days later, most of them would have to be back again for the memorial service for Queen Alexandra, widow of Edward VII. We are told 'Prince George' was present. This was George, Duke of Kent, who was in Hong Kong serving on HMS *Hawkins*.[41] The dear old deaf Danish queen consort was mourned in Hong Kong by a grandson.

Freemasonry began to look to the cathedral for its public worship. The first annual service of the South China District Grand Lodge was held at St John's in January 1926. Officers of various lodges assembled in the hall, dressed in their masonic regalia, and processed across to the church. The bishop was District Grand Chaplain. The Honourable P. Holyoake, cathedral honorary secretary, was District Grand Master. J. Owen Hughes, treasurer, was Deputy Grand Master. The Reverends Scott (naval) Waldegrave and Upsdell were Masons and assisting. The bishop wanted this to be first of a series. The offertory went to the building of Foochow Cathedral.

Percy Holyoake, that prominent figure of English freemasonry, was not to see another masonic service at St John's. Within weeks, he was to be the subject of his own memorial service. 'A fountain of force and a shelter … of big spirit and big kindly constant heart', he died at home in England on a trip charged with 'business of high importance to transact for the colony'.[42] As well as being a member of both Legislative and Executive Councils, the Church Body and the committees of the Alice Memorial Hospital, the Boy Scouts and the YMCA, Holyoake was chairman of the General Chamber of Commerce and as such was known to have anxieties over the anti-foreigner boycott being waged by Chinese nationalist groups against foreign goods and outlets.

Perhaps this was the business of importance he was in England to discuss. As such, he was the classical and the best of the Hong Kong colonialist, embodying business, government, church and charity all in one and dying in their service. It showed very clearly at his memorial. The governor attended with the chief justice and all members of the councils. Ushers officiating were Colonel Robertson, P. S. Cassidy, W. L. Pattenden and W. Jackson of the Church Body. The building was packed with Freemasons, which meant most colonials of substance in Hong Kong.

Another quite different stalwart of the cathedral, Paul Chater, had died on 27 March 1926, only the day before Holyoake. The Grand Old Man, as he came to be known, came of the tradition in which burials rapidly follow death. Telephone calls were made between clergy and Church Body members, and suppliers began shortly after his death at 5 a.m. to prepare for the funeral service. It was held in the cathedral at 11 a.m., and Sir Paul was buried at 5 p.m.[43] Perhaps because of the unaccustomed rush, the local English journalists did not shift themselves in time to attend. There are precious few details of the service although it is fair to assume that the establishment as described for Holyoake's memorial would have been in a hurry to attend.

St John's could be a busy place in that it was a crossroads for Christians journeying into China in a way that was lost in 1949 and is only just, tentatively, re-establishing itself. The year 1924 was a notable year for this. The Church of England Victoria Diocesan Conference, which Bishop Lander had been so reserved about establishing, was held in the hall at the cathedral, beginning on 10 March, at the same time as the General Synod, from which language and self-perception separated it, was assembling in Canton. Bishops on the way to Canton were staying over in Hong Kong and mingling with bishops attending the conference. The formalisation of this natural fellowship was not to come for fifty more years.

The Diocesan Conference held two discussion sessions in the hall between 2.30 and 6.45 p.m. Topics were 'Where is Church Failing?' and 'What is meant by a Mission of Help? Do we need one in the Far East?' It was decided they did, because one showed up to indeterminate success some time later. Probably one of the most notable visits of the era was from the Bishop of London, Arthur Winnington-Ingram, in 1926. He was the leading Anglo-Catholic intellectual of the period and quite a wit. He must have been a relaxed prelate and a pleasure to host. He managed to play a round of golf in the morning before getting back to the cathedral to celebrate Holy Communion.

The end of an era also coincides with the peculiar ending of the Reverend Vyvian Henry Copley-Moyle's employment as chaplain. He is often referred to as Vyvian Copley-Moyle, but from the way he signed articles and letters he seems to have thought of himself as Henry. In October 1919, he had been employed on a permanent basis with six months' notice of termination from either side. At the Church Body meeting of April 1925, it was said that, 'in the natural course of events, the time was coming to write to the chaplain exercising the option to terminate his employment'. This was when he had only left on leave to England some three weeks before. The offer made to him was to end his employment two years after his return, or by 31 December 1927, whichever came sooner. This was thought to give him 'ample time if he so desires to obtain preferment or some other suitable employment at Home'.

The blow, because that is how it was taken by the senior chaplain, was softened with an annuity of 300 pounds for five years after retirement.[44] So ready were the Church Body to foresee him not coming back at all that, if he got a job while on this furlough and his return passage to Hong Kong was saved, he would be granted 500 pounds on top. Bishop Duppuy approved this decision on 29 April without demur.

An upset Copley-Moyle initially replied on 8 June asking that his services be kept to the end of 1930. Pollock, Severn, Owen-Hughes and Pattenden of the Church Body met on 27 July 1925. Were these the men set on ending the Copley-Moyle years? Could they have been acting for a bishop whose ambitions for the cathedral no longer chimed in with the chaplain's? They were unmoved and sent the chaplain a telegram. 'Church Body cannot reconsider as to two years and strongly advise you make every endeavour obtain preferment at Home now.' This did not have the tenor of a normal replacement process.

Copley-Moyle accepted these terms but wanted a separate agreement embodying them. He was told he could have that but was refused referral of the matter to the seatholders and subscribers, where, doubtless, the whole issue would have had a breezy airing. It seems likely that the view of the Church Body members and of the bishop on this matter would not have been easily shared by the wider congregation.

By 26 January, no further news had been heard from Copley-Moyle. Perhaps he was earnestly job hunting. A telegram was sent keenly extending his leave by a month in this interest. The bishop was actively seeking replacements for the chaplain in a far-from-provisional spirit. The Reverend Northcott of CMS was a hot favourite, followed by A. B. Thornhill, who might be persuaded to come back again from Holy Trinity Southport, or a C. G. Mannering from St Matthew's Brixton.

These moves were thwarted by Copley-Moyle's return on 2 March to serve to the end. His first meeting with the Church Body must have been uncomfortable, particularly for the laity who had perhaps hoped not to see him again. The chaplain reported that he had resented the tone of the correspondence he was having with the honorary secretary, 'particularly over matters of legal opinion'. The two sides had clearly been threatening lawyers. His house, Kellett Crest, had been let to a Mr. Dixon of Liverpool and London Insurance Co. during his leave. Now the Church Body had put a clause into the new agreement with Copley-Moyle, which provided for the continuing letting of Kellett Crest whilst telling the chaplain to go and find his own lodgings, again for $150 per month. He objected vigorously. The Church Body came up with a rather vapid excuse about it only being an option and relented.

A last-ditch plea from Copley-Moyle in 1927 to extend for a further two years was turned down, but an additional grant of 125 pounds for the years 1928 and 1929 was made to him. Was this compassion, lest he was poor, or unease over the treatment he was receiving? Whatever the reasoning, these payments were to become a considerable burden to St John's.

It is interesting to note that, on 13 September 1927, the Advisory Church Council expressed to the Church Body 'dissatisfaction in the decision not to extend Copley-Moyle's "contract" to the Church Body', and 'considerable discussion' took place at a subsequent meeting at which Church Body members attended to explain.[45] We do not know what the explanation for the termination of Copley-Moyle was or whether the Church Council was given a thorough one. One possibility was divorce. On 12 October 1928, Copley-Moyle petitioned for the dissolution of his marriage to his wife, Mary, in the Divorce Division of the High Court in London. The grounds were adultery with a Doctor Percival Sandys Connelan at the Haymarket Hotel London.[46] In the days before divorce by simple separation, this would have been one of those tawdry set-ups whereby a private detective would have made a pre-arranged 'discovery'.

The Singapore newspaper report—which shows how widely publicised around the empire the event would have been—tells us that they were married in 1912 and had three children. We do not know how frequently Mary Copley-Moyle was in Hong Kong or how well-known she was to the parish, but it is possible that the marriage was foundering for some while before it ended. For a clergyman of that period, even as the innocent party, the circumstances surrounding adultery and the need for divorce would have been painfully embarrassing. If the Church Body had got wind of this in 1925, this may explain the haste with which they acted and the avoidance of confrontation.

At his last ACM in January 1927, the chaplain registered no rancour. He was happy to detail his achievements during his office as he saw them. When he arrived, there was no room to meet except the vestry, and now there was a magnificent hall. The east end was ugly, and now there was the Bowlder reredos. The unsightly rodent-ridden seating platforms in the nave were gone. The services were now aided by a Guild of Sidesmen, the Women's Guild looked after the church, and the CEMS made the Church's voice heard on social matters through its local branch. Copley-Moyle was particularly proud that it was a 1919 sermon of his on the evils of the *mui tsai* system of indentured child domestic labour that had been heard by Commander and Mrs. Hazelwood and which had sparked them to begin the campaign which was working for its abolition through the Anti-Mui Tsai Society, 'a society which every Christian in the Colony ought to join,' he had said in a subsequent sermon on 5 February 1922.

Then there was, of course, the overarching benefit of the Chater endowment, which now brought in $21,000 per annum, when the cathedral's running expenses were $9,700. There was one small legacy of his term which had long-standing consequences. If tourists ever wonder why they have to labour two-thirds of the way up Garden Road to make contact with the Peak Tram, they have St John's to thank for that. When proposals were made to extend the tram right down to Central on trestles, it was the Church Body's objection to the disturbance it would cause to services as it passed by which put a stop to it.

It is unlikely that Copley-Moyle's successor, Alfred Swann, would agree to labouring up the hill for the tram. Despite his rowing blue from Oxford, he had a weak heart. In every other sense he was persistent: for reform, for the sacraments and for aesthetic standards. For the first time in St John's history, the coming of a new chaplain is a clear cause of change.

Chapter 5
The Making of a Cathedral, 1927–1941

A thinly veiled scrap was going on between the Cathedral Body and the bishop in late 1927. Flying between them were topics as varied as the management of St John's itself to the use of 'at home' cards. The issues at stake represented, on one hand, the guardianship of colonial distinctions which ultimately had nowhere to go but never quite went away and, on the other, the promotion of corporate and diocesan responsibility which had much of the future to address but never triumphed entirely.

Bishop Duppuy, on leave in England, had completed the recruitment of the Reverend Alfred Swann, Vicar of Liversedge in the Diocese of Wakefield. From his home in Harrogate, on 17 September, the bishop announced the appointment to the Victoria Diocesan Association, the foundation of which had been one of his first initiatives as Bishop of Victoria. He told them, 'After consultation with the Archbishop of Canterbury and others, I have decided that the Senior Chaplain of the cathedral shall have the title of Dean.' He pointed out that the title 'dean' was given at Holy Trinity, Shanghai. In Singapore, the clergyman was an archdeacon and in Cairo a 'sub-dean'. He went on, 'I am also asking Mr. Swann to be Archdeacon for English work in the diocese. Other diocesan arrangements, I hope to make on my return.'[1]

He had written too about how much he would miss Mr. Copley-Moyle, who would have gone by his return. On a personal level, that was doubtless sincere, but there is every sign that the chaplain's departure was what the bishop needed for a clean sweep in the cathedral. The Church Body did not exactly share his perspective. On 6 December 1927, they went on record saying that the bishop should have consulted them on the naming and status of a dean and archdeacon. They also noted that it was too late. He had publicised it.

Nevertheless, they set about a rearguard action. Swann would have to be inducted as a 'chaplain' not a 'dean', to be in accordance with the ordinance. In their traditional anxiety over anything that might divert the chaplain from his cathedral duties to them, the Church Body objected to the description of the dean having 'oversight of English work in the diocese'. Duppuy, realising probably that something would have to give and that the vision he had for the office would not suffer from the loss of this loose description, agreed to withdraw it.[2]

Annoyance was not quite done with. By 19 December, the Church Body had entered into an argument with the bishop over the reception arrangements for the new dean. It would not be privately catered for in the Helena May Institute, as the bishop had suggested. It would be held in the cathedral hall, organised by the Women's Guild, and no cards were needed. To rub it in a little, His Excellency the Governor would be informed of the changes.

Duppuy returned on 6 January 1928 with Alfred Swann, his wife and their two children, Timothy, aged 3, and Julia, aged 3 months. He counterattacked with a printed statement. St John's was the mother church of the diocese and the title 'dean' more accurately described this role. He quoted from Cathedrals Commission of the Church Assembly in support of this view.[3]

He explained that the dean was to be an archdeacon because the bishop needed a chief lieutenant. 'This is not primarily to provide me with relief,' explained Duppuy. It was to give the chief clergyman of the cathedral an appropriate stature with which to deputise for the bishop. It was all part of giving a strong lead from the centre and promoting 'general efficiency and the corporate spirit'.

Dean Swann could adequately fill both roles, which would not be distorted by responsibility for Canton. In harness with Swann's appointment as Archdeacon of Hong Kong, the bishop had announced the appointment of the Reverend Mok Shau Tsang as Archdeacon of Canton, an office which had fallen silent since the departure of the last occupant, John Gray. Mok could manage Canton and the Chinese church. Swann, who had more experience of the wider world, could handle English affairs from Hong Kong.

Duppuy's vision for a cathedral was clear and encompassing. It should be a busy centre of the diocese. It was the convector of the wider church and world, and it should send men out to the parishes. The Church Body persisted in worrying the bone. At their 8 January meeting they again responded with an explicit statement. Regarding the office of dean, 'it should be placed on record that the first regard should be had to the duties which are due to the Cathedral.'

In accepting the appointment of Alfred Swann, they had taken on board a man of spirituality, conviction and some tenacity. He was one of England's flowers who was not cut down by the war. Educated at Rugby School and Trinity Hall Cambridge, he took a first degree in medicine. During the First World War, he served in the Royal Navy, first as an ordinary seaman and then as an officer. He was awarded the Distinguished Service Cross—the second highest award for gallantry—for his part in the raid on Zeebrugge.

After the war, he felt a vocation for the ministry and went to Westcott House, Cambridge. He became president of the University Boat Club and earned a Half Blue as a runner. He painted landscapes in pastels and particularly delicate wildflowers and was keen on maintaining his own car. Swann was what they called an 'all-rounder'.

The disputed reception, held in the hall, seems to have passed in harmony. The bishop declared that Swann's titles were now threefold: Chaplain of the Cathedral, Dean of the Mother Church and Archdeacon. The middle one survived. The honorary secretary of the Church Body, J. Owen-Hughes, assured the Swanns that they could count on the spirit of tolerance and goodwill among the community. Swann himself seemed to fire a warning shot across the bows of the community's social sensitivities in his reply. 'Prestige and dignity unless acquired of the Spirit are useless,' he informed them.

The installation service which followed is described as 'amongst the most impressive as well as the most reverent and beautiful that the cathedral has ever witnessed'. The choir and sixteen clergy processed to the chancel singing 'All People That On Earth Do Dwell'. For his institution, Dean Swann knelt at the altar steps to receive his licence and benediction for Bishop Duppuy. He was inducted with Archdeacon Mok. The fair English rowing Blue and the diminutive, spectacled Cantonese priest stood together at the sanctuary steps while the 'Veni Creator' was sung in invocation. It must have been a moment when the church must have felt in its fullest sense catholic. The bishop then led them in turn, by the hand, to their stalls. Duppuy ended the service by leading the congregation in responsive prayers from the chancel steps.[4]

Dean Swann's arrival was just in time for the Annual Church Meeting, and to this gathering he delivered something of an opening manifesto for his term. There to hear it were the Church Body members, some of whom who had been so upset by the bishop's presumption: Lieutenant Colonel F. Hayley Bell DSO, of the Chinese Maritime Customs, T. G. Weall of Dodwells, T. L. King, W. Jackson, P. S. Cassidy of Hutchisons and C. Blake.

Swann was an aesthete. He stated that services should be beautiful, orderly, stately and not stiff. The music should be 'as good as we know how to make it'. The choir needed to be larger, giving a strong lead but without always being at full blast. He moved on to what was probably for him the most consuming issue of his incumbency. He was worried about Holy Communion attendances. If Holy Communion is allowed to fall from its true place, the life of the church becomes weak. 'The position of the service in people's minds determines the spiritual level of public worship', was his conclusion. He hoped to encourage people to attend the early Communions by laying on breakfast. This was the optimism of the new boy.

He conceded that matins enjoyed good attendance and that there was an interestingly large crowd of men at evensong. These were servicemen, mostly. The Peak Sunday school under Mrs. Stark was doing well, he thought, but the practice at the cathedral of alternating between Sunday school and a children's service was ineffectual. There should be one or the other. He told the meeting that, essentially, the cathedral needed to be more of a house of prayer. There needed to be more services and people praying there every day.

There also needed to be another clergyman. Apart from interim help, there had been no assistant chaplain since the departure of Powell in 1926. The gap was now filled by the arrival of H. V. Koop and his wife from St Helen's, Lancashire. He was a tall man and a very good rugby player, which was an interesting counterpoint to his sensitivity to good design, which he shared with his wife and would complement the dean's when it came to improving the look of the church.

Koop could also write. He launched *St John's Review* in 1929 to be a more ambitious and commercially successful successor to *Church Notes*, which nobody was actually paying for. The 'Review' took advertising and was charged with paying for itself, but why it should command a circulation when the 'Notes did not is not clear. There was a continued reluctance to subscribe. By 1932, *St John's Review* had three hundred readers but only ninety contributed to the cost. The magazine struggled. So did Koop in finding somewhere to live.

They started him on a $100 a month housing allowance, but he had a very difficult time finding anywhere suitable.

The project which the dean walked right into and helped carry through was the reformation of the cathedral's government. By the time of the church body's meeting of December 1928, a draft ordinance was ready for the next Annual Church Meeting's approval. Work on it had been extensive. A subcommittee of Swann, and trustees T. W. Ainsworth and W. L. Pattenden had dedicated themselves to it with the cooperation of Mr. Justice Jacks to help with the legal technicalities. Bishop Duppuy took some of the strain, which was not to help with his weakening health.

The only Church Body member to vote against reform was Colonel Hailey-Bell. On 27 May 1928, he unveiled a memorial tablet in the Lady chapel with the inscription, 'Erected by all ranks 1st Battalion The Queen's Royal Regiment while serving in China 1927–28 in memory of the two officers and 25 Other Ranks of the 1st Battalion who were killed on Active Service in China in 1860.' Colonel Bell had once commanded the regiment. Four hundred fifty of its troops were on parade. He left the Church Body shortly afterwards but not before offering the view that undergrowth outside the transept wall was affecting the organ.

Pew rents, or 'sittings', were abolished, and a new electorate was formed from those registered on the church roll. The Annual Church Meeting became the Church Body proper. It elected a Cathedral Council to which it delegated its executive authority. The ex-officio chairman of the Cathedral Council was the dean. There continued to be an honorary secretary and an honorary treasurer, and the council was to meet not less than quarterly. It could set up committees, and it did, initially with gusto. There were committees for arts, publications and publicity, finance, evangelism and children, and most of them found, eventually, that they had very little to do. The Advisory Church Council, which had the distinction of an army sergeant and two Chinese as members and concerned itself mostly with the problems facing single British women in the colony, was abolished.

An 1899 ordinance, strengthened by a further ordinance of 1904, had vested cathedral lands and leases in the trustees. Now, with these changes came the creation of the Church of England Trustees in whom the fabric and the finances of all Church of England places of worship in the colony were to be legally vested. The trustees were, initially, the bishop, the dean, the Vicar of St Andrew's and two members of the laity from each of those churches, this pattern to be repeated for any new churches added. This was all framed in Ordinance No. 2 of 1930 and signed into law by the governor, Sir Cecil Clementi. The Church of England trustees were to meet once a year as a body corporate and could acquire property and leases. St John's Cathedral was and remains vested in the trustees. If services cease and its purpose is no longer fulfilled, the property reverts to the state.

In effect, the trustees delegate to the Church Council the care and maintenance of the cathedral and provision for its administration. Bishop Duppuy devised this scheme of vesting and delegating, and it forms the present government of St John's. At last, the issue of who had authority over services was no longer filtered through stained glass but made plain and clear. Services are under the management of the clergy, subject to the bishop's approval to any major changes to customary pattern. Neither can changes in the customary patterns be made without the council's consent. The bishop has the right of visitation—to the layman, an inspection—and he can use the cathedral for special services of his choosing.

The council frames the budget, raises the money and allocates it. Jointly with the incumbent, it appoints and dismisses chaplains, the organist and all employed officials under the bishop's signature. The appointment and termination of clergy is handled in a particular way. A Board of Patronage involving the bishop, the dean as archdeacon, one lay trustee and four council members, makes a recommendation to the trustees who in turn seek the approval of the bishop. The appointees' salary is fixed by the Finance and General Purposes Committee of the council, its standing committee. To appoint a dean, the Board of Patronage consists of the bishop, the two cathedral trustees, two lay members of the council and one trustee from each of the other churches.

The first meeting of the new church council was held on 28 January 1930. At a meeting three weeks before, the Legislative Council had breezed through the legislation just after considering amendments to the Opium Ordinance. The two trustees under the new system were Mr. Justice Jacks and W. L. Pattenden. The dean's view was that the council's first and foremost duty was the development of primary and spiritual functions. It should have representation from the Victoria Diocesan Association, the Women's Guild, the

Mothers' Union, Sunday school teachers and music makers.[5] Swann persistently urged the laity to learn how to take executive roles and govern by committee.

So that it might hold this and staff an ambitious spread of committees, the council was a large one and remains so. Other members were H. J. Best, Lieutenant Colonel W. F. Christiansen, Professor L. Forster, Dr. G. A. C. Herklots (hon. sec.), F. Mason, J. Owen-Hughes (hon. treas.), E. G. Stewart, Lieutenant Colonel F. I. Wyatt, G. C. Archbutt, B. F. Frelder, Professor J. L. Shellshear and—as they were listed—the Medames, Black, Brindley, Evans, Forster, Grimble, Savage and Strachan and the Misses Acheson and Griffin.

On 5 February 1930, the council received its letters of delegation from the trustees and got busy on the housework that had to be done to meet the ordinance. Yet within six months, Lieutenant Colonel Wyatt, who had championed the Goodwill Offerings scheme to replace pew rents had gone back to England. So had Miss Acheson and W. L. Pattenden, one of the trustees. Such were the discontinuities that long leave furloughs and retirements back to England caused in organisation.

W. L. Pattenden's departure was particularly poignant. He wanted to return home to his wife and daughter and mother, who was getting old, but he regretted having to leave a place where he had spent so many years and lifelong friends some of whom he would not see again.[6] Such was the regard in which he was held that a farewell party was held on 19 March 1930 in the hall, presided over by the bishop, and the dean and stalwarts like P. S. Cassidy and Sir Henry Pollock present and praising him.

They spoke of his feeling for harmony and unity and his sense of kindliness and dignity. No specific act was attributed to him. Pattenden was a presence, a spirit, an aura of peace rather than a commander or leader. The dean said Pattenden's phone number had never failed him. He was a stalwart of the Cheero social club for servicemen at the YMCA, and those men subscribed to a present of framed cathedral photographs. He was given a cheque and gave it back as a donation for a new set of altar rails.

He recalled the cathedral he first came to at the beginning of the century as 'a dull and dreary place'. He hoped it would become 'a centre of work in the colony, a gathering place of all Anglicans irrespective of race and nationality and real force for what the people were striving for in becoming God's kingdom here on earth'. Testimony from such a frank and ingenuous source shows how far in spirit and activity St John's must have moved in those thirty years.

He was right about not seeing lifelong friends again. He died in England from a heart attack in his garden in December 1932, aged 68. In an obituary written for *The Outpost*, it was remembered that, in the evening, straight after a cathedral meeting, he would not go directly home or to dinner but could be found down at the Cheero club at the YMCA, 'moving among the men, quietly talking'.

Not everybody could match Walter Pattenden's calibre in selflessness. Dean Swann discovered early the disinclination to church work which colonial living encouraged. In an early letter in the 1929 *St John's Review* he observed rather quickly that the British 'who come out to Hong Kong stray from the habits of church going because old customs and connections which send them to church are missing and other newer distractions keep them away'. He soon felt for himself what he had been talking about. At the 1931 church meeting there were fewer present than had to be elected. He found he was doing everything himself, including making all the nominations. Swann pressed hard the concept of corporate responsibility.

> The church is you and I and all baptised persons. It is here to set a standard of mental and spiritual outlook. We hold an incomplete view of it. The Cathedral Council is in its infancy … it is useful but just arouses interest in two dozen people. Every member of the roll is of a band … we lack the idea of responsibility.[7]

'The congregations are quite good,' Swann told the 1932 church meeting, 'but the fans blow us away rather easily.'

The goodwill offerings, which Lieutenant Colonel Wyatt as treasurer so keenly pursued, had a choppy start. By August 1931, Dean Swann was reminding his congregation that the scheme was not a volunteers' bazaar, not some flash in the pan. A regular income was needed. Nine hundred people had been approached, naturally not all of them on the electoral roll, and $31,000 a year was needed, he estimated.[8]

Swann considered a hypothesis in which twenty-four firms gave $4 a week; one hundred individuals, $2 a week and four hundred individuals, $1 a week, which would yield a little over $35,000 a year. 'Am I optimistic enough to believe that that this is not too high?' he asked. Apparently, he was. Collections at services were wholly inadequate, he said. It was giving without self-examination.

'Ask "What does God think?"' he put to his readers. 'An honest churchman will reckon up and assess himself. If you give by weekly envelope and you don't come one week, bring two next time. When you make out a banker's order, think carefully what you could give each week and multiply it by four.' Annual cheque givers were the weakest self-examiners. At the 1932 church meeting, the honorary treasurer, J. H. Sutcliffe, said, 'Decide as early in the year as possible how much you can give,' in an attempt to stop donors underestimating their wealth to the cathedral as though it was the tax inspector.

The year 1932 proved to be testing for St John's new system. Expenditure was $49,200, but offerings, though up $3,000, stood only at $22,600 when $35,000 was needed. The Finance Committee was very concerned. It was now that closing St Peter's Church at West Point was suggested openly for the first time.

The 1933 Annual Church Meeting was told that goodwill offerings were indeed good at $24,000 even though income was $10,000 under expenditure and there was an overdraft of $3,000 causing additional discomfort. A proposed rough cast plastering of the cathedral exterior would have to be postponed. By the next year, however, there was an 'odd' surplus of $4,700 because there had been no assistant chaplain to pay after Mr. Koop's departure, and the ruinous annuities being paid Copley-Moyle had ended. The cathedral had looked rather desperately for help with the Copley-Moyle payments to supporters in England. The returned Walter Pattenden, acting on its behalf, was offered a paltry 3 pounds and $25, all crying poverty and economic depression. An additional if transient addition to the books in 1933 was the $4,000 anonymous donation to refurbish the rough cast on the entire exterior of St John's. This work was carried out in the autumn of 1934.

The new assistant chaplain, Harry Baines, was about to arrive, and by the same time in 1935, St John's was back in debt by $5,731. Swann, not too fond of bazaars and gimmicks, one imagines, said to the Annual Church Meeting of 1935 that he 'won't descend to undignified methods to raise money' and wanted 'straight giving'. Death is straightforward enough. In March 1935, Lady Maria Chater died, leaving $50,000 on trust for care of her grave and that of her husband, and the balance of income for the trustees to spend as they saw fit. Ah Sing, the hall coolie, may have got wind of this and asked for a raise but in vain. In fact, the money was eventually put towards the purchase of the On Lee property in Pok Fu Lam, originally for clergy accommodation.

Intermittent references to the cathedral's own subscriptions to others at this time reveal why it was less well off than it might have been. The Finance Committee report to the 1934 church meeting reveals a commitment of $42,000 to the Kowloon Tong church that was to become Christ Church, and that this would have to be paid in stages; $2,250 was being paid per year at that time to the diocese as the cathedral's quota.

A generous scattering of missionary commitments for 1932 indicate a kind ear easily caught rather than a well-considered plan. St John's Church Yunnan Fu had borrowed $10,000 at some point and was being paid $500. The CMS Mission in Lim Chow was getting $1,960. A scheme at Tsan Tsing got $250, a catechist, Lam Pak, was helped with $100 and St Hilda's Canton, $150. 'Bible women' in Canton got $100 and in Hong Kong, $170. CMS day schools in Hong Kong were given $100.[9] The cathedral supported a student at Hong Kong University with $100, and six orphans at the Victoria Home. It is fair to say that, around that time, $10,000 to $12,000 a year was being disbursed by St John's to aid other churches, missionary work and needy individuals.

This does not take into account money simply lost through bad judgement, which any organisation can make, but which St John's seems to have wallowed in over Kellett Crest, the chaplain's house bought for Copley-Moyle. The purchase price was $30,000. It had been a continual strain on St John's finances and on Dean Swann's weak heart, a two-coolie chair being needed to carry him up the drive. In 1936 it was valued at $26,000. Honorary Treasurer P. S. Cassidy thought letting it go for that was 'a breach of trust'.[10] The economic depression in Hong Kong at the time was no respecter of trust. It had to be sold in middle of 1937 for $13,000, having had $4,000 more spent on it to make it buyable at all.

Dean Swann's other struggle was one he considered of much greater importance than funding. He pressed hard upon his ebbing and flowing flock the importance of worship and, in particular, the taking of the sacraments. Special weekday services he noted had been seemingly impossible for people to attend. As the St John patronal festival approached in 1930, he stressed how important attendance was for the 'sense of corporate fellowship'.

'With changing personnel, it is so difficult to be like England,' he wrote, almost plaintively, 'to know what it is like to look to the parish church for inspiration, guidance and renewal. We long to see this here.' At the Annual Church Meeting of 1929, the new dean noted that the average Sunday attendance at Holy Communion was twenty-five. 'These numbers give pain to those who love Holy Communion,' declared Swann. Out of the new council, he set up an 'active service committee' for 'renewal of depth and power through the sacraments'.[11] With the approval of Bishop Duppuy, whose feeling on the priority of Holy Communion was very much in harmony with Swann's, an experiment was begun. On the second Sundays in Lent, Choral Holy Communion would be held at 11 a.m. instead of matins, which was to be sung instead at the 9.15 a.m. military parade service. Episcopal permission was given for the 1928 Communion service to be used at all celebrations.

This did not become a permanent feature. Matins returned to its 11 a.m. position. By 1936, there was one Sung Eucharist a month and a 12.15 p.m. Holy Communion on Sundays. The congregation needed longer acclimatisation, and parade services had to disappear before the Eucharist could take a central position. Nevertheless, it marked the beginning of a campaign by Swann and his successors over three decades to bring the sacraments into prominence. 'We only rarely use this great sacrament. We are missing something … it should not belong only to a few,' wrote Swann. 'It is the common spiritual meal of the Christian family. It is impossible to make good use if we only come to it occasionally.'[12] The breeze from the Oxford Movement had arrived in Hong Kong.

His quieter but likely deeper legacy was the nurturing of a 7.45 a.m. Holy Communion on the third Sunday of each month, something he asked Church Council members to go out of their way to support. As is the way with services that become beloved, a small fellowship grew out of it, centred in the breakfast that was always organised afterwards.

Mass followed by breakfast is a mysteriously powerful mover of men and minds, and the numbers attending this service became impressive. It impressed Bishop Duppuy's successor, R. O. Hall, on his first Sunday in early 1933. 'I was fortunate in striking the Third Sunday Fellowship Communion and breakfast in the cathedral. This was started two years ago by Alfred Swann. 80 to 100 cathedral members meet together for Communion and adjourn afterwards to

the Hall for breakfast together.'[13] The newcomer Hall could not resist
a light-hearted swipe at colonial manners. 'Old Hong Kong hands will,
I hope, not feel that British prestige is lowered by the fact that we are
not waited on by Chinese "boys" but by our own dairy maids.' By
current mores, points the bishop scored against racism were probably
lost for sexism.

Swann achieved a growth in use of 'that great sacrament' within his
own short time at St John's. One Sunday in December 1934 records
eighty-seven communicants and forty-seven staying behind for breakfast, which was being paid for by M. J. D. Stephens, the unsuccessfully
anonymous donor to the hall. It was Bishop Hall, again, who noted it
in his February 1935 letter to the Victoria Diocesan Association, 'The
best tribute to his [Swann's] work was the Easter Communion service
less than a fortnight after he had left. There were at the cathedral and
the Peak Church 438 communicants. In other words, in the seven
years of the Dean's work, the number of Easter communicants has
been doubled.' In August 1935, the Communion Fellowship which
had grown out of Holy Communion attendances and the breakfasts
was listed as 110 strong.[14]

It would be a mistake to see the progress towards more communicants as a steady one. Only four years later, at the church meeting
of 1940, the report was that matins and evensong attendances were
up but those at Communion were decreasing. They were down two-
thirds at the third Sunday celebration, and there were fewer at the
choral service as well. It was suggested that some worshippers were
transferring to the Peak Church but, given that the overall attendances up there were small anyway, this was thin reasoning.

In the face of entrenched habits, Dean Swann learned to brace
himself for disappointments. An interesting example of his approach
was connected to Bishop Hall's arrival. The bishop wanted a family
Communion followed by breakfast the morning after his enthronement on 30 December 1932. This meant a part-Choral Holy
Communion at 7.45 a.m. on New Year's Eve. Anticipating resistance,
Swann wrote in *St John's Review*, 'I know it's unusual. I know there
will be difficulties but if the desire is present to meet the Bishop then
no difficulties will stop us.'

As a place of worship for the English community, St John's was
increasingly busy and important through the 1930s. Most events
involving the Royal Family in Britain were marked under its roof. A
service of 'Thanksgiving for the Recovery of the King' was held on 7

July 1929, to celebrate George V's recovery from septicaemia. The governor was met at the west door. His Majesty's message was read. Psalms 21, 23 and the 'Te Deum' were sung and, before the blessing, a 'Peace version' of the national anthem was sung. Approved by the Privy Council in 1919 and published in 'Songs of Praise' in 1925, its sentiments seemed tilted towards the League of Nations and it is unknown today.

The *South China Morning Post* the following day was quite lyrical over the event. 'Rarely has such fervour been expressed by any one congregation ...,' it claimed, most improbably. This passion was 'expressed in respectful prayer and ... the timbre of the voice of the preacher. Dim light brought into relief the khaki and white drill of the navy and military.' Listed as present representing St Peter's Church was Miss Ruby Mow Fung. She was of a notable Chinese family which had returned from Australia. Along with Andrew Cheng, who was a member of the early Cathedral Councils, she was one of a handful of Chinese who were prominent in the cathedral before the war.

The records are silent on the abdication of King George's son, Edward VIII, but on the day of the coronation of his successor, George VI, early Communion 'with special intention for Their Majesties' was held followed by breakfast in the hall. The Chaplain, Harry Baines, had held lectures on the meaning of the coronation, which Edward VIII had done much to subvert, and the 11.15 service to mark the coronation itself was 'non-liturgical', to attract the widest possible attendance from the city. A choral celebration followed on the Sunday. Royal services were not restricted to the British monarchy. A memorial was held, jointly with the Lutherans, for the life of Queen Maud of Norway on her death in November 1938 although that she was a granddaughter of Queen Victoria and had died of a heart attack in London doubtless strengthened the sentiment. On the imperial theme, Empire Day on 24 May always saw the cathedral packed, albeit with children. Few adults made it, but for church schools, attendance was compulsory. Dean Swann took the 1934 celebration as an opportunity to take his steely pin to the imperial conscience. Of it, he wrote, 'The Church stands for responsibility and service not privilege and aggrandisement.'

The 21 October 1934 saw the first service attended by the entire judiciary to mark the opening of the Legal Year. Bishop R. O. Hall preached a sermon on justice of such passion that one wishes the stones of the church could utter it again. Although St John's retained no formal connection to the Crown, this event was an indication of the strong informal link. Interestingly, the judiciary still attends this service at the cathedral even though the Crown has gone entirely and the Special Administrative Region can in no sense be considered officially Christian. Quite simply, the cathedral has always had a natural appeal to organisations which wish to give thanks to heaven or seek its mercy.

The Mothers' Union in Hong Kong, run by Mrs. Strachan of 366 The Peak, had become joined at the hip to the cathedral by holding its meetings there and was in cheerful alliance with the Women's Guild, whose unlikely motto was 'Charity without chatter' and was run by Mrs. Handley Pegge of 12 Leighton Hill. In April 1930, they decided to hold jointly their quarterly corporate Communion service. This could sound grander than it actually turned out. In 1934, seven people showed up for it.[15]

A place which had a brief experience of small attendances was the Colonial Cemetery Chapel in Happy Valley. Anglicans were said to find it inconvenient to get from Happy Valley and Causeway Bay to Garden Road. Given that these two districts were some of the best connected on Hong Kong Island, this was an odd conclusion. Admittedly, the Colonial Cemetery Chapel in Happy Valley was sitting there, underused, in what was called the most beautiful cemetery in the world. Special permission was obtained from the government to hold evensong services each Sunday. The cathedral donated the old altar from the Lady chapel, where it had been recently been replaced, and the government raised the marble floor a foot for the step up to it. The first service, one of Holy Communion, was held on All Souls' Day, 2 November 1931, and there were eighteen communicants, which was prescient of the attendances to come.

In the following year, on 29 March, the chapel was dedicated under the name of 'The Chapel of the Resurrection'. The dean officiated in place of Bishop Duppuy, who was confined to his room with illness. Also present was the Reverend E. C. H. Tribbeck of the Wesleyans and the Reverend E. G. Powell of the Union Church. Other congregations used the chapel for burial services. The principal service was Sunday evensong, held at 5.15 p.m. because the cemetery closed at 6. Eventually, Holy Communion was held on the first Sunday of every month. The capacity of the chapel was forty, but attendances ranged from five to ten. In the last few months of services, 'no congregation' was entered in the service book more frequently. Other rare comments made there had a suitably mournful tone for a cemetery setting. 'Very cold' and 'Time wrongly advertised' can be found along with 'Diphtheria outbreak on increase', on 27 December 1931. The last recorded service at the chapel, in its sultry tropical graveyard, was held on 9 February 1936.

The Church Council had more success with new ideas for community services. In their meeting of September 1936, they discussed holding a seafarers service on 25 October, at which the cathedral would be presented with local merchant marine company flags and then display them. China Navigation, Indo China Steam Navigation, Douglas Steamship and Hong Kong, Canton and Macau Steamboat all offered theirs. At the beginning of the service, their representatives were received at the west door by the two trustees and escorted to the chancel steps, where the presentation was made. The flags were hung in the nave. Such was the good feeling generated by this that plans were made for a similar 'aviation service' for 15 November. Given the limits of air travel, the only two flags that could be summoned were the Civil Aviation Department flag and the house flag of Imperial Airways.

Later that month, there was less harmony. The sermon at matins on 30 November was disturbed by bagpipers of the Scottish branch of the Hong Kong Volunteer Defence Corps. Apologies were received, and to conciliate further, the general officer commanding promised that there would be no War Department blasting during divine service. What was being blown up so close to the centre of Victoria is not mentioned.

One service that was 'tremendously moving in itself but significant far beyond itself', according to Bishop R. O. Hall, was the consecration of Bishop Mok on 25 January 1935.[16] The cathedral was crowded. Many people had to stand. The laying on of hands was performed by Bishops Norris, Curtis, Hall, Ding and Nichols. A Chinese choir led the music. English and Cantonese were used, the Cantonese for the Litany and, remarkably, for the sermon, which was given by the Reverend P. Jenkins, who was about to retire after thirty years in the diocese and had a fluid grasp of the dialect. Bishop Hall saw in it a deeply touching promise for the church.

> The little old figure (Mok's smallness was one source of his impact) so moved and yet so unaffectedly simple, kneeling there, as before the Master Himself, to receive his Apostolic commission, joins all the richness and costliness with the future of infinite possibility.

At this time, evensong had become a service of alteration and experimentation, all with the intention of getting people to actually come out to it on a Sunday evening. In 1929, it was decided to sing the service up to the third collect as usual, after which there would be a hymn, a sermon and prayers, followed by discussion in the hall with the preacher present. 'Strangers to the church may find guidance in clearing their minds on subjects of vital importance,' said Bishop Duppuy of the change; 'it allows teaching the best possible chance of being accepted ...' This was a clear attempt to attract service personnel, who tended towards this service when their duty day was done.

Efforts to increase the civilian congregation were more utilitarian. In October, it was announced that the time of the service would be altered to 6.30 p.m. from 6 p.m. to accommodate bathers and tennis players and catch the golfers. Sport was essential to socialising on the one truly free day of the week, and in summer, taking to the water in one way or another was a compelling draw among the 22,000 Europeans living in Hong Kong, without air conditioning. This compromise was not the petty indulgence it appears to be. From as late as the 1960s, Muriel Clayton recalls it.

> Sunday evensong we would arrive straight from the beach to quickly don our cassocks and head into church, herded along under the supervision of a patient, and anxious, [Dean] John Foster, who had waited for his flock to rush through the door looking sunburnt and healthy. If only the congregation could have seen below the cassocks to the assortment of shorts and sandals we still wore, and grains of sand falling from our feet.

The time change did not work. People with less commitment still dawdled at the beach or by the pool. Bishop Hall proposed leapfrogging over the problem by holding the service at 9 p.m. In June 1938, it was moved to as late as 8.30, which only shifted the problem to the timing of dinner. Dean Wilson suggested a break in the tradition that nobody goes to church in the evening and that people had a lighter meal before or afterwards. It would be less work for them, he reasoned, forgetting, perhaps, that his congregation had servants anyway. They managed a maximum of fifty on one evening, but by winter, it was back to 6.30. In playing dinner off against bathing, evensong came out the loser.

It is difficult to assess how much preachers did for attendances. Some effort was put into seeking variety from a limited English-language pool. In August 1931, sermons were given by G.K. Carpenter, headmaster of St Stephen's College, C. B. Shann, warden of St John's Hall and J. Pratt of the CMS, visiting from Hingwa (Hinghua). A different note was probably struck by Father Walter Bentley, a former Shakespearian actor who was founder of the Episcopal Church's Actors' Church Union. He must have made an impression, because St John's showed a peculiar fondness for this institution and made several donations to it in subsequent years.

On 2 September 1937,[17] a typhoon struck Hong Kong and St John's. Part of the roof over the high altar blew off, the stained glass in the north transept was damaged and the wooded compound was torn about. It did not fare as badly as the Taipo Orphanage to which it contributed. That was destroyed. The cathedral coolies went into the church in at 2 a.m., rolled up the carpets and removed the frontals and linens which had been ruined when water flowed in over the altar. The floor was inches deep in sand and leaves, but they were ready for afternoon weddings.

The Church Council took a cavalier attitude when reviewing the situation. They calculated that the cathedral was damaged on average once every four years. The insurance premium necessary for that period would have exceeded the money spent on repairs. Having arrived at a conclusion that would make an insurer's toes curl, they went on to inform Leigh and Orange, the cathedral's official architects, that they were to take out no typhoon insurance unless they foresaw major damage. Leaving the firm in the role of oracle, the matter was closed.[18]

The deteriorating finances of late 1934 led to a suggestion in the last edition of St John's Review for that year that a Victorian-style Day of Humiliation be held to draw attention to the plight and 'to the inevitable condition which will arrive if we continue neglect of the financial side'. Here, the dean, who had spoken to his first trustees meeting of the importance of 'Art and Beauty', may have let his own aesthetic fears loose. It was imagined how the organ would break down at a critical moment, torn old prayer books would lie on seats without rattan, choir surplices would go unwashed and unmended, the lectern would be unpolished and the cathedral unkempt. In fact, photographs of the period show the church looking very kempt and gracefully equipped both inside and out. There had been some thoughtful purchases and contributions to the fabrics and furnishings from the beginning of Swann's period.

In 1930, larger altar tables were placed at the high altar and in the Lady chapel. With this in mind, Dean Swann went on a voyage of decorative discovery during his leave trip to England that year. Seeing, on his way, the fourteen-foot altar at the cathedral in Victoria, British Columbia, he felt justified in having extended St John's own to eleven feet. That table did not survive the Japanese Occupation. It was replaced in 1949 by one donated by the Royal Navy, also eleven feet long, with an anchor motif on it.

Swann visited as many cathedrals as he could on that trip, looking for inspiration. He got it from Chester Cathedral, where he saw a pattern he liked for the new altar frontals that would be needed for both tables. He bought the materials in England, and they were made up back in Hong Kong by the Women's Guild. Whether the design of the present frontal is of direct descent from these has not been established.[19] At Liverpool Cathedral, which he was being shown over by Sir William Furse, a golfing chum of the architect Sir Giles Gilbert Scott, a fald stool caught his eye. Scott donated the woodwork design on the stool, and this became the decorative base of the altar rails being funded by W. L. Pattenden.[20] Dedicated on Trinity Sunday, 1931, they were carved by Chow Fook of the Hong Kong Furniture Company. Sir Gilbert Scott was sent pictures of Pattenden's rails and wrote to Swann, 'I really think that your Chinese carpenter has been most successful.'

The rails were lost to a bomb during the Second World War, dropped on the Catholic convent and orphanage in Causeway Bay where they were stored, but it was a fald stool in the same design, yet again, which survived as an inspiration for replacements. These were donated by a trustee, David Margarett, and his wife, in 1950, and were placed originally in the east end and then moved with the altar to its present western position in the chancel. The old fald stool sits, nowadays, quietly to the right of the altar in the St Michael's chapel. The sanctuary of the 1931 high altar was finished off with the artistic flair of Mrs. Koop, wife of the chaplain. She designed rails with a grapes and wheat motif in the *art nouveau* style, which completed the enclosure. They were also placed at the altar in what was the Lady chapel, now the St Michael's chapel, where they still are today.[21]

Munificent members of the congregation gave items of value. Albert 'Bunny' Abbott of Kelly and Walsh Bookshops, who gave us the account of the choir ladies, was an indefatigable if opinionated giver. In February 1930, in the early stages of his generosity, he offered the council a brass altar cross and candlesticks. Interestingly, this was rejected, and it was suggested that he might give a sanctuary carpet instead. Mrs. Black, more in tune with the spirit of Medieval Gothic than her colleagues were, said that she liked the sanctuary tiles exposed and suggested that Mr. Abbott give new offertory bags.[22] This was a drop down the value scale too far for 'Bunny', so the sanctuary got a Peking carpet by Fette. In 1934, he donated a dean's stall in for the north sanctuary in the tones of a strong man correcting error. The present stall was not worthy, he declared, because it was more of a litany desk which should be next to chancel steps. In 1938, Mr. Abbott came up with a new flag for St John's, which had been designed in conjunction with advice from the College of Heralds and, for reasons which satisfied Mr. Abbott, the full approval of the Earl Marshal of England. Only war halted Abbott's giving, which resumed at the peace.

Rather more quietly, Colonel W. F. Christiansen gave a finely wrought silver chalice and paten in memory of his daughter, Dulcie, who had died in 1929. There was a touching sequel to this. Shortly after the liberation of Hong Kong, Colonel Christiansen wrote from England asking the then Dean, Alaric Rose, if the chalice had survived. Rose was able to tell him that it had. His wife and Miss Betty Bicheno had taken some of the altarware across to the French Mission building for safekeeping in a brief interim between the surrender and internment. The chalice was back in use.[23] Christiansen's letter of response describes the deep relief and happiness felt in his family, knowing that this vessel should have survived to keep the memory of his child alive in their beloved cathedral.

In 1928, P. S. Cassidy had stated a need for a wall tablet listing the cathedral chaplains. He got a response from an interesting source. The Reverend Holman T. Holman OBE, the Canadian who had been assistant chaplain from 1920 to 1922, was now the Chaplain to the British Legation in Peking. He donated a teak name board which was lost during the war but found again and hangs by the west door. Donated too by Holman, then lost but sadly not found, was a splendid free-standing copper ewer to serve the font. He also gave to the diocese the silver bishop's crozier, which fared better and can be seen in its stand by the throne in St John's today.

Cassidy, at that same 1928 meeting of the Church Body, one interesting for its resolution to throw beggars out of the compound, made public his awareness that the cathedral had no memorial to Sir

Paul Chater. Could not the restored organ be named after him?[24] The last notable restoration had taken place in 1925. It may have been visually spectacular, but it was technically flawed. Cassidy's reference to the organ doubtless came out of what Colonel Johnston's history calls its 'growing eccentricities'. Frederick Mason, who came from St Mary's Parish Church, Woburn, replaced Denman Fuller in 1923 and tackled the organ and taught music at Diocesan Boys' School. Lindsay Lafford, who took over in February 1935, concluded that the organ needed rebuilding.

He foresaw an all-electric and not a pneumatic organ because of the climate, with a console over the north vestry. This was almost prophetic of him. In the meantime, a more conventional repair had to be waited for. An appeal for the estimated cost of $3,500 was raised and a bridge and mah-jong drive was held at the Hong Kong Hotel roof garden on 27 April 1936. In October 1936, 'no organs in town are working because of a dry spell. Mr. Blackett is run off his feet,' reported *St John's Review*. Mr. Blackett, the remarkably skilled and adaptable organ builder, was 78 by now and the only one in the entire Far East. The council took to consulting the Tsang Fook Piano Company, which had been operating in Hong Kong since 1916, and Moutrie and Anderson in England. The St John's instrument was ready enough to be played in a limited way on Christmas that year and was rededicated in June 1937. Paul Chater's name was never attached to it.

Lindsay Lafford was quite right about the climate, of course. By December 1939, the organ was reported as malfunctioning again. So, for a while, was Lafford. He was a hardworking man, teaching in schools and broadcasting on Radio ZBW, but in June 1937 he came down with malaria. Illness took its toll in high places. Bishop Duppuy's health had been declining steadily over two years and, by 1933, his departure from Hong Kong had become compelling. Mrs. Duppuy was also suffering from illness to the extent that she could not even attend a farewell tea party for the couple at Government House.

P. S. Cassidy, on behalf of the council, paid tribute to the Bishop's Foundation of the Victoria Diocesan Association. Dean Swann touched on the reality of life as a missionary bishop when he spoke of the difficulties and weariness involved making long journeys by small river steamers, and he paid tribute to the bishop's intellectual labours in framing the Church of England Ordinance. He was presented with a gift of a sterling draft of 109 pounds 18 shillings and

6 pence with a little joke from Cassidy about this being the easiest item to get through British Customs. His Chaplain, Victor Halward, later an Assistant Bishop in Victoria and Canton, writing an appreciation of Bishop Duppuy for the Victoria Diocesan Association after the war, says he discovered in the bishop '... a deep personal devotion to our Lord, an amazingly broad and loving affection for his fellow men, a wise counsellor and a most sincere friend'.[25] The bishop returned to England and Worcester Cathedral as a Canon, where he died in 1943.

Duppuy's successor, R. O. Hall, was probably the most striking of all the occupants of the Victoria throne. Much has been written about him, and the overdue beginnings of a full biography are being made at this time. He has been described as brilliant, saintly, impetuous, frugal and even 'red'. He once called the Hong Kong colonial administration of the 1930s 'a comic opera government'. That faintly alliterative expression 'a legend in his own lifetime' might fairly apply to him.

His enthronement took place in St John's on Friday, 30 December 1932. Dean Swann and Archdeacon Mok led Hall to his chair. Prayers and the sermon were in English and Cantonese. The epistle was 1 Thessalonians 5:8–14 ending '... admonish the idlers, encourage the fainthearted, help the weak, be patient with them all'. A forging feature of Hall's spirit had been that he had lost his three best and closest friends in the Great War and had only been coaxed out of his emotional withdrawal by friendship with a Chinese, T. Z. Koo, a prominent Anglican layman in the Christian Youth Movement, about whom Hall eventually wrote a book. He opened his sermon with a poignant summary of that.

> Jesus of Nazareth wept over Jerusalem. My heart is still sore for my beloved Tyneside, for my fellow townsmen, for the pits and shipyards and heather hills of the north country. In a strange way God has tied my life to China ... I am proud and grateful to God that I am allowed to serve you here in this vigorous and beautiful colony, and also the great Chinese people, through whom God opened my heart again to friendship after the bereavement of the war.

The new bishop was always to have his patience strained by his English-speaking listeners. In his sermon that day, he also described St John's as 'the Mother church of our communion in the Far East, the Mother church in the growing family of God which we call this diocese'. He was to observe later that the English-speaking parts of the diocese—especially the cathedral—thought of the bishop as a sort of grand chaplain and resented his time and absence in the diocese.[26]

Humbler curates came and went too with some rapidity up to 1940. The Reverend Neville Watkins, who had been chaplain in charge of the ailing St Peter's, left in 1932 to take up a post in Christchurch, New Zealand. He married in the cathedral in 1930 and gave up teaching twenty hours a week for twenty dollars at St Paul's College because he 'could find better things to do'. He returned to Hong Kong on a visit in February 1971 and shared some recollections with *St John's Review*.

> I was measured for a Palm Beach-style suit in Wellington Street. St Peter's was 150 yards inland by then but davits for long boats were still attached. The congregation at the time was Chinese, Eurasians, White Russians, Hong Kong police and Hong Kong University staff.

He visited a gaol, took Holy Communion at the Peak Church, founded Toc H (Talbot House) in Hong Kong, joined the volunteers regiment and acted in a 'nigger minstrel group' entertaining troops at the border. What was not mentioned at the time was that he stood in occasionally as organist for Frederick Mason. 'It was a fine 3-manual instrument … the humidity made it "cipher" … a nightmare.' Watkins's strongest impression on his return was the 'integration of the Chinese into the whole life of the cathedral … a new feel in racial relationships is evidenced everywhere. Now, European women do their own shopping.'

After the departure, also in 1932, of the Reverend H. V. Koop to become Vicar of St Paul's, Princess Park in Liverpool, there was a hiatus until 1934, when Dean Swann, on leave, recruited Henry Baines as chaplain or as Bishop Hall put it, 'unstuck Harry Baines from St Mary's Oxford'. Swann was keen on this appointment. Baines was a tall, imposing man with charm and an 'Oxford accent', according to Lindsay Lafford.[27] This was not surprising. He was educated at Repton and Balliol. He was as affable on the sports field and over a pint of beer as he was as straightforward in his faith. 'Harry Baines and I will be in the cathedral every day to pray for you,' said Swann to his *St John's Review* readers, but his time was soon to be up.

In February 1935, the dean's doctors told him that he would not survive another summer in Hong Kong. His heart would give out. He left in April. Bishop Hall called him a 'sporting parson'. 'He has shown us religion as a sportsman shows on the sports field where a man must play hard and play the game.'[28] At his last meeting with the Cathedral Council, Swann left them with priorities. They must nurture the communicants' fellowship, for the Sacrament was the cathedral's most important activity; they must promote the training group, his initiative for ministry amongst laypeople and encourage the children's services and kindergarten.

Swann went away for eight months' rest in England, reimbursed by the cathedral for a Kelvinator, a Gestetner copier and a $1,160 extension to his garage. As often was the case when clergy were withdrawn from the deadly climate of southern China, Swann's heart revived remarkably for a while, though in health he was destined to suffer. Later he contracted cancer but, even in remission from that, he held down the acting deanery of another St John's Cathedral, this time in brisk Newfoundland. In an address on his death in April 1962, Swann's former chaplain, H. V. Koop, gave a steely glimpse of Swann's beginning in Hong Kong.

> There was opposition; of course, there always is. There were those who cannot endure the quality of the wholly dedicated man, who found his honesty too much for them; but that is the lot of God's elect.

Bishop Hall took over as dean in the interregnum and worked merrily with Harry Baines, who also came from Tyneside in the industrial north-east of England. They were about to become a trio of Tynesiders. The Board of Patronage, consisting of Sir Henry Pollock, Professor Forster, Mr. Barton and Mr. Cassidy, were paying close attention to the Reverend Leonard Wilson, Vicar of St Andrews, Roker, Sunderland. Wilson had been curate to a bishop and an incumbent in some of the most depressed mining communities of County Durham, where he had filled previously empty churches. P. S. Cassidy, on leave, interviewed him in comparatively balmy Brighton, and in February 1937, the board recommended him to the trustees as dean. Bishop Hall later described him as 'the man I most wanted …'[29]

Looking forward to the early 1960s, there were four Anglican clerics who were quite well known to the agnostic classes in England: the Archbishop of Canterbury, Michael Ramsey, for his bushy eyebrows; David Shepherd, Bishop of Liverpool, for once having been England's cricket captain; Bishop Trevor Huddleston, for his furious opposition to apartheid; and Leonard Wilson, Bishop of Birmingham, for being courageous and holy. In those days, British veterans of the war in the Far East still filled the Albert Hall every year for their Burma Star Association gathering. The BBC televised it; Bishop Wilson was there as their chaplain and simply everybody knew his story. He had been the Bishop of Singapore when it fell to the Japanese in 1942.

Imprisoned in Changi Prison, he had helped with escapes and resistance, been tortured for it and survived. When his tormentors asked him why his God was not saving him, he told them that he was, by helping him take the pain. After the liberation of Singapore, he found himself confirming a Japanese man, a former torturer who had seen Christ in Wilson's faith. Back in 1937, Mr. Cassidy and his colleagues had given the nod to a man who was to become probably St John's best-known dean.

Harry Baines said that Wilson had taken no easy decision in coming to Hong Kong and outlined its essence: 'An unfamiliar parish in a much disturbed part of the world compared to a northern English church sensitive and loyal to his leadership in a district clamouring for the power of Christ which only attracts a man of rare spirit.'[30] Interestingly, his chaplain at Roker, David Rosenthal, volunteered to follow him. Harry Baines had made it clear that he did not want to continue as chaplain for another contract. The council was again chewing on the issue of how to afford a dean and one if not two assistant chaplains. There was an Assistant Chaplains' Fund once again, now standing art $13,000, but it was in no condition yet to have allocations made from it.

Cassidy had empowered Wilson to find a chaplain before he sailed. Rosenthal, it was imagined, could work between the cathedral, St Andrew's and the new Kowloon Tong church of Christ Church. Long-distance planning was again rendered fictitious. After he arrived in September 1937, Rosenthal found himself with his hands full as Priest-in-Charge of Christ Church. Harry Baines was extended to April 1938, to bridge the gap in Garden Road. He left after a farewell tea party at which no one could guess, let alone Baines himself, that he would follow Leonard Wilson as Bishop of Singapore, after the war, or end his ministry as a rather radical Bishop of Wellington, New Zealand.

It was not until December 1938 that his direct replacement, the Reverend Alaric Rose, arrived from a curacy at Gateshead Parish Church, another north-east England location. Rose was the son of an Anglican missionary in China, educated at St Edward's Hall, Oxford, and Ripon Hall and ordained in 1933. No one could guess either that this young man would be tested with the leadership of the cathedral for a decade under the most extraordinary circumstances.

Dean Wilson was instituted and installed by Bishop Hall on 20 February 1937. The congregation was large and included the governor, Sir Geoffrey Northcote; his *aide-de-camp*, Captain Batty-Smith; Major General A. W. Bartholomew and his wife; Sir Atholl MacGregor, the chief justice, and Lady MacGregor; Royal Navy Commodore E. B. C. Dicken; and Mok Shau Tsang, now Bishop of Canton. The Reverend J R Higgs and cathedral trustees P. S. Cassidy and J. R. C. Hance presented Wilson to Bishop Hall. The new dean's salary was $750 a month, the dollar now standing at one shilling and three pence to the pound. A subcommittee was formed to find him a house. The subject of finding the dean a deanery has been neither resolved nor quite dropped until recent years, since when, modestly, any suitable lodging has sufficed.[31]

Wilson was a keen gardener, and so Ava Mansions on May Road was thought suitable for a moment or two. Mr. Eldon Potter offered a furnished place at Mt Cameron for $375 per month, and 112 The Peak was offered at $112. It was decided that building a deanery cost too much, given the war conditions across the frontier and the consequent costs. In January 1940, the council wondered about buying an old house for a deanery and modernising it. Events were soon to put an end to that conversation. Since then, deans have lived in Upper Albert Road, Bishop's House, the Cathedral Lodge, Mount Davis Road and even Mountain Lodge, the long-demolished Peak getaway of the governor, which was where Northcote let Leonard Wilson stay until he was accommodated.

The dean was slightly taken aback at his new congregation's relaxed attitude to religious observance. In his *Review* letter of Lent 1938, he chided them with a little irony over their absence for any weekday Communions and the Wednesday Lenten service. These figures could not be a true reading of the situation, he said. 'Some of you must be giving more attention to your prayer life. It is not a good idea to pull up plants to see how they are growing so I will be patient.' The Maundy Thursday service got 40 attending which, out of an electoral roll at that time of 407, was considered 'not bad'.

Other features of St John's congregational habits were still confounding Leonard Wilson a year later.[32] There were 8 o'clock regulars who were not seen again the rest of week, and tireless volunteers who never went to services. People, he said, did not understand the concept 'missionary church'. Nevertheless, this still habitually exclusive band of eccentric colonial worshippers did what they could in the years before the Second World War to improve and do good wherever they could. 'Outreach' was a term which was to come later into the vocabulary of organised Christian charity, but the cathedral congregation had a sense of it.

Contributions to the Victoria Home and the Waifs and Strays Society were consistent. In the year 1936, for example, St John's supported the Hong Kong Society for the Protection of Children, the CMS Leper Colony Hospital Pak Hoi, the Bible Churchman's Missionary Society and the Tai Po Chinese Boys' Orphanage. When the 1937 typhoon destroyed that, there was generous giving to restore it. There was organised lay visiting to Queen Mary Hospital, and every year, the girls of the Blind Home, Pok Fu Lam, were taken on their annual picnic.

In that same year, there was little the cathedral could do for the outbreak of cholera that occurred, but assistance was being provided in helping feed and shelter war evacuees from Shanghai and Hankow (Hankou). That ill wind brought some good. American church volunteers came into Hong Kong to help, among them the Reverend Michael Bruce of the Episcopal Church, who was secretary of the Chinese YMCA and became almost an unpaid member of staff at St John's.

The most elementary and earthed act of compassion in which the cathedral was a moving force was the Street Sleepers' Shelters Society, to which the St Peter's Church building was lent as a shelter until it was demolished. The Reverend N. V. Halward was the chairman of a strong British and Chinese committee. Sir Henry and Lady Pollock were prominent in a group of cathedral people who went along to help. Their aim was to provide a night's lodging for the homeless, including a bunk, hot water, soap and hot tea. From December 1933 to April 1934, for example, 16,372 street sleepers were accommodated.[33]

The democratisation of the cathedral, the growing awareness that there had to be more to the sense of community than attendances at matins and the dogged encouragement of a succession of clergymen who had fought in war which lost you your faith or grew you in it, was slowly building the habit of fellowship within the life of St John's. By 1936, most of the hopefully titled committees of the council set up in 1930 had blown away from lack of substance. Only the Finance and General Purposes Committee and the *St John's Review* committee were left, the latter being renamed from Press and Publicity because dealing with the magazine was all it did. However, there were some busy group activities which were run under the council.

Interesting and not repeated in less colonial times was the Cathedral Messengers programme, in which representatives from the parish working in government departments, businesses and schools reported to the clergy on newcomers to Hong Kong and others they worked with who were ill or were thought to be in need.[34] Eventually, it was discovered that this work was being duplicated by the Mothers' Union, and so the programme organisation was split into men's and women's groups. As organisation increased, effectiveness seems to have diminished.

There was the Training Group preparing adults for confirmation and the Communion Fellowship, both anchored by the chaplain. The Training Group had the recurring disadvantage of being either too small or too large. It was last heard of before the Japanese invasion and had twelve members. In 1938, though, there was an increase in adult baptisms, there were thirty-eight confirmations and it was claimed that the Chinese congregation was growing steadily.[35] The Bible Reading Fellowship was in an amazingly healthy state, having a declared membership of 113 under the leadership of Miss A. J. Bennett.

There was a considerable regiment of women. Apart from the Mothers' Union under Mrs. F. Archer, there was a Women's Catering Committee under Mrs. W. C. Clarke which, one feels sure, must have paid some obeisance to the Women's Guild under the redoubtable Lady Pollock. Organist Lindsay Lafford remembers her as radiating 'an impressive sense of power that was hard to escape. Whenever she hove into sight I had the mental impression of a galleon under full sail.' She was the wife of Sir Henry Pollock K. C., who was frequently a Cathedral Council member, often Attorney General and a founder of Hong Kong University. An example of Lady Pollock's style was her complaint to the council in 1937 that the coolie quarters were overcrowded and that something must be done about it. She managed to couple this with a 'demand' to be told what Christian instruction the coolies received. She accepted as adequate the information that the coolies' spiritual welfare was provided by 'the Reverend Lee'.

Lafford once witnessed her displeasure at the disappearance of the bananas from the Harvest Festival display:

> Ignoring me and bearing down on Ah Kau (the cathedral 'coolie')
> with all cannon at the ready, she unleashed a salvo at full decibel,

'Where are the bananas?' Almost taking a pull at his forelock, he ventured a feeble question/answer: 'I think lat live in organ?' he ventured. 'Yes,' agreed the Lady. 'A two-legged lat!'[36]

Although the Pollocks were in obvious ways colonial buttresses, and Pauline Pollock had all the resonances of a *memsahib*, they were compassionate if old school liberals. She was awarded an OBE for her efforts in setting up camps for Chinese refugees in 1940, and he persistently presented the British government with reasons why Hong Kong should have constitutional reform.

There was a Servers' Guild under Mr. A. Flynn and, after a false start in 1912, doubts about what they were supposed to do and difficulties in getting anyone to turn up on time, there was a functioning Sidesmen's Guild under David Kwok. An inaugural meeting of the Scout troop was held on 3 November 1938. Four boys attended although 'you really need 24 to play scouting properly' as the *Review* put it in its report. There was a weekly troop meeting and a Saturday outing. The khaki uniform cost $14, and the weekly sub was 10 cents.

There was also a Cathedral Club although precisely how it functioned as one is not clear. Membership was open to electoral roll members for $8, and it incorporated the Badminton Club, the Photographic Club, the Sketching Club and the Drama Club. The first reference to drama comes in the first 1932 edition of the *Review,* which reported on the Christmas play of 1931, *The Next Door House,* which ran for two nights and was a moral tale about a better-off family coming round to helping the worse-off one next door. The Naval Chaplain, F. Darrel Bunt of HMS *Berwick,* helped with the production. The Cathedral Club element in St John's life seems to have had its limitations in Dean Wilson's view. He put together a whole 'cathedral fellowship' as it was called, in which communicants, women's groups and these social fellowships became one and which he hoped would 'socially express itself beyond badminton'.

One very clear expression of fellowship beyond badminton was the beginning and takeoff of the Michaelmas Fair in 1937. It began as a 'sale of work' in the cathedral compound. It had been intended as a garden fete on a larger scale, possibly borrowing Government House grounds, but the state of war in China, cholera, typhoon and economic depression meant that the congregation had other things on their minds. The event was held on 2 December and earned a very creditable $1,529.25. It was resolved that the proceeds should not go to a specific fund but in aid of the cathedral funds, a policy decision which was to have a profound and unexpected impact on the cathedral's books in the years to come.

The Michaelmas Fair proper and so titled was opened the following year on Saturday, 15 October, by Lady Northcote at the Volunteers Headquarters, at the time just south of the church where the east wing of the Government Central Offices now stands. Patrons were the governor, the general officer commanding, the bishop, the colonial secretary and the commodore RN, who made a signal to ships in port advertising it. The cathedral had a consistent contact with ships in port. Service cards were sent round to them every week. Stalls included white elephants, curios and the provision of mineral waters. There was no bar, but there was a fun fair featuring 'multi clock golf', a 'swinging bottle' and euphonious 'balls in a bucket'. The 2nd Battalion, Royal Scots Band played, and tea was in the drill hall. The organising secretary was Colonel Geake, borrowed from Christ Church, Kowloon.[37]

The fair raised a very satisfactory $3,000. The *Review* noted that it was obvious some people regarded the fair with distaste ... that it had a 'church bazaar' dullness. To begin with at least, Bishop R. O. Hall was one of them. 'I must confess to disliking bazaars,' he wrote in *The Outpost*. 'They can be causes of disputes and a spiritual setback in the life of a congregation.' Dean Wilson had talked him round. 'I am convinced he is right and the cathedral will be better spiritually from the experience.' He did attend, of course. Those who did not 'missed out'. Children specially enjoyed themselves with clowns on the slide, which sounded both cumbersome and exciting for little ones.

Leonard Wilson certainly excited some of his parishioners, one way or another. Lindsay Lafford remembers him as a 'bluff, genial, hearty, outgoing, down-to-earth sort of character'. There was also a disinclination to compromise and a preference for rigour, shown in his handling of the Sunday schools of which, by now, there were several, in St John's itself, at the Peak Church and even one attached to the anomalous Chapel of the Resurrection Church in the middle of Happy Valley Cemetery.

The dean said that it was better to have no Sunday school teachers at all than bad ones. Children should not have to junk in later life what they learned at Sunday school. Six teachers had left and had not been replaced. The implication was abrupt. They appear to have been rapidly 'let go'.[38]

In another fit of searing frankness over their attitudes, Wilson told his flock in 1939 that 'Jesus did not die upon the Cross in order that a British community might have its Mattins at 11 and give catholic privileges to a chosen few'.[39] This statement straight in the face of his parish is part of the evidence of highly charged views on faith, colonialism and society that were about at the time, some radical and angry, others trenchantly conservative and, occasionally, hilariously obtuse.

Lady Bella Southorn, wife of the colonial secretary, after whom the Wan Chai playground is named, led the Girl Guides in Hong Kong and lamented the difficulties a Girl Guide on the Peak had to go through to visit a guide in Kowloon, in a *St John's Review* edition of 1932. 'If a Peak guide wants to meet a Kowloon guide, it takes her as long as to get from London to Brighton. She must take a rickshaw or chair to the Peak Tram, then a chair to Star Ferry, then a rickshaw or a taxi.' No awareness is registered of the adult labour and sweat devoted to carrying this little lady on her epic trip.

One of the issues social which the church concerned itself with was to be part of the pressure on the government to abolish licensed brothels for the suppression of vice and disease. These days, secular authorities often move in the opposite direction to achieve the latter, but in 1932, abolition was meeting with success, which the *Review* reported in an article, 'An Evil to be Checked'. Brothels operated by foreigners, in the Lyndhurst Terrace area, were to be abolished straightaway. Those operated by locals catering to foreigners, typically in Ship Street, Wan Chai, had six months' notice from 1 January 1932, and those which were Chinese for Chinese were to be more gradually reduced. Writing a vigorous letter of response in the July edition of the *Review* from No. 5 The Peak, Mr. G. H. Forster gives us a vivid and unselfconscious observation: 'I myself have been in brothels where the girls rush to the door in scant attire to shriek for customers ...' The best we can make of that for him is that he was a police officer.

Professor Forster of the council and Hong Kong University contributed 'Searchlight', a firm if gloomily predictive analyses of current affairs, for the *Review* right up to the Japanese invasion. The Japanese Occupation in China provoked a quite heated argument in the magazine's pages. An article entitled 'Christ in an Occupied Area', which generally questioned the validity of violent resistance, was answered by an aggressive piece, 'Advice to a Peacemonger', and a remarkable article on Hong Kong's colonial divide came from an anonymous writer titled 'Ajax'.[40]

Ajax liked the Chinese. He found them 'pleasant, naturally polite and ready to laugh at a joke'. The men looked 'boyish', and he asks us to even 'consider the beauty of the woman selling newspapers in the street'. Yet he felt sorry for the British, 'close to paradise, yet vilely discontented'. He saw theirs as a life of boredom, 'entertaining and being entertained and keeping fit so to be more entertained ... a social life that must astonish the Chinese'. Of Chinese social life in the backstreets, 'laughing, talking, joking', he thought they knew how to live. 'We call it childish, yet our religion stamps sophistication as a deadly sin. Except ye become little children ...' he adds.

That this should have appeared in the *Review* must reflect at least the consent of Dean Wilson. Its style, fresh amazement and infusion suggest its author may even have been one of the recently arrived Tyneside clergy if not Wilson himself. Ajax goes on: 'We make no attempt to study their culture ... we segregate clubs ... we haggle over 50 cents ... we show indifference to the burdens of coolie labour.'

Dean Wilson left to become Bishop of Singapore in 1941. On St. Mary Magdalene's Day of that year, 22 July, he was consecrated a bishop in St John's. Although a colonial bishop would normally have been consecrated at Canterbury, the war made travelling a risky arrangement, and Hong Kong was, at the time, the only place where the necessary three bishops for the purpose could be assembled. Hong Kong's own Bishop, R. O. Hall, was already here. Bishop T. C. Song managed to make it from West Szechuan Diocese. He was expected to take the lead in the ceremony until Bishop N. S. Binstead, an American, arrived from the Philippines church and turned out to have a year's seniority.

As the *Review's* correspondent wrote, 'We had to attribute even what we had to war which also made it possible for the service to be held in Hong Kong Cathedral.'

Before the service, Bishop-elect Wilson took an oath of allegiance to the King, in the cathedral hall, administered by the chief justice, Sir Atholl McGregor, and witnessed by the governor, Sir Geoffrey Northcote. This was nothing if not a state occasion. The master of music was J. R. M. Smith, and anthems by Wesley, Elgar and Byrd were sung. The communion service was set to Merbecke. 'Reverence, dignity and spiritual values prevailed,' reports the correspondent.

There was a 'brotherhood of nations with British, American and Chinese bishops present'.

The service was completed in two hours with 'no mishap' and 'before the black-out'. Japan's expansion had not quite burst in on the British Empire that July day though the Japanese were massing up the road in Sham Chun, and the atmosphere was tense. Leonard Wilson was about to leave on a ship for Singapore. He was to enjoy seven months as bishop before Singapore fell and his famous and fearful incarceration began.

In the farewell gathering for Wilson, cathedral trustee P. S. Cassidy was frank about the gulf in temperament between him and the dean. After years of experience in Hong Kong, he said that his instinctive response to Wilson's initiatives had been to say 'for heaven's sake, leave it alone'. But the problems with Wilson had run deeper. In a letter to Bishop Hall in June 1941, Cassidy had asked that he allow the appointment of the popular and hardworking Reverend N. V. Halward as the new dean.[41] Cassidy felt that Halward was a necessary antidote to a dean who had been abrasive with the congregation. Cassidy had admired Wilson and stood by him but said that his sharpness and impetuosity had meant that others had found admiration far harder to come by. He quoted the instance in 1940 when expatriate wives and children had been evacuated by ship to Australia and Wilson had gone with them to minister and as a holiday, 'without so much as a by your leave,' says Cassidy.

Hall refused Cassidy's request. He said that he must have at St John's a man with strong and recent preaching experience from England. Hall had always admired Wilson's own preaching, 'a freshness and directness, a real touch of the Gospels', he said about it. In the meantime Rose would stand in but, if he had not found the right man within a year, Cassidy could have his Halward. Sadly, no such year was to be left to them.

In 1941, for the Hong Kong British, the prospect of the Japanese taking on the British Empire was emotionally indigestible. Yet wives and children had been evacuated in the stark face of Japanese forces massed across the Sham Chun River, and the cathedral was certainly feeling the loss of womanpower. The Michaelmas Fair, which had truly got under way in 1938, could not be held in 1941. There was a Prayer and Gifts Day instead. Volunteers manned the cathedral on 4 December 1940, to receive gifts from 8 a.m. to 7 p.m. Just forty people showed up and twenty-nine sent in items. By the lights of those days, an impressive $4,500 was raised by just a few.[42]

Sunday school was all but lost, as were boys from the choir and practically everything requiring volunteer women. One small band that kept going was the Communion Fellowship. It was a reduced band by now. The breakfast helpers left just before the invasion were Misses Basto, Bicheno and Souza and Evan Stewart and Peter Wilson. Miss Bicheno, the choir mistress, was interned and helped provide the music for united church worship in Stanley Internment Camp, practising keyboard sometimes in the teeth of irritation amongst the Japanese guards. Colonel Stewart was wounded in the First World War and was about to be wounded again in this. He survived was interned and later awarded the Distinguished Service Order. Peter Wilson fought with the Volunteers. He was killed in battle. Like many, they did not foresee the swiftness of what was to come. The fellowship was concerned that the Volunteers had no provision for Holy Communion during training camps. These only lasted a week, they noted, but what would happen if they were mobilised? In the event, mobilisation endured for just two Sundays.

It was the centenary of the colony's foundation but needless to say not a festive one. Leonard Wilson's view was that a colony that counted only its wealth was a vulgar one. He made the point that Hong Kong 1941 had 'extravagant displays of wealth, cabarets, cinemas, racing, gambling and luxurious cars' at the same time as 'degrading poverty, slums and street sleeping'. It had few schools, no civic centre, art gallery, museum or library.

In those last months of freedom, the Church was most vigorous outside its walls. In February there was a joint effort to set up a church relief centre staffed by locals who knew who to help with a dollar here and forty cents there. The Hong Kong Society for the Prevention of Cruelty to Children was formed dealing with 14,000 cases of which only 1,800 were to do with actual cruelty; the rest concerned poverty and disease. In a battle against sublet slums, a Christian group actually took over three flats in Wai Ching Street, Wan Chai, and set them up properly for poor families. 'A candle in the dark' is how that was described. A boys' club was started for shoe-shine boys and street urchins. The Hong Kong Refugee and Social Welfare Council, set up in 1938 with strong backing from Bishop R. O. Hall, was coordinating these efforts. Almost all these organisations breathed again after the war.

The Bishop ordained Li Tim Oi as a deaconess on Ascension Day 1941 in the cathedral. This humble lady, thrust into controversy, was to light a path for women in the church universally, but she herself was inspired by one who went before. On 31 December 1931, a momentous event took place in St John's Cathedral. Janet Lucy Vincent was ordained as the first woman deacon in the Anglican Church. The congregation was a packed one, and a large proportion was Chinese. Bishop Duppuy officiated, and Bishop Mok, Dean Swann and the Reverends Blanchett, Shann, Lee, Stewart, Carpenter, Tsang So, Lee, Watkins and Martin were in attendance. There was an augmented choir with singers from St Stephen's, St Paul's and All Saints, Ho Man Tin. The lesson was Romans 16:1–2, commending Phoebe.

Li Tim Oi was present for this and it inspired her. A decade later, when she was deaconed, Bishop Mok preached. The Reverends Wong, Wittenbach, Brown, T'so, Strong, Myhill, Lei Kau Yan, Tsang, Chung, Martin, Halward and Deaconess Jane Vincent herself were present. Li went on to serve in Macau, and it was for that isolated congregation, deprived of the sacraments, that Bishop Hall was to take the momentous step in 1944 of ordaining her as a priest. In September, he ordained John Cheung as a deacon, preached his last sermon in the cathedral for what was to be a long time and left for a trip to the United States. The new Acting Dean, Alaric Rose, came out of seventeen days in hospital and finished his sick leave with a short holiday in Sha Tin, probably in the bishop's farmhouse home up there.

The Cathedral Council held its regular meeting on 24 November 1941. A $100 donation was approved towards the building of the parsonage for David Rosenthal at Christ Church. The Acting Dean, Alaric Rose, was teaching part-time at the university, so he returned an equivalent part of his stipend. The verger on the other hand had his wage increased from $24 to $25. A rather heftier $800 was needed to send Bishop Song back to Chengdu after Leonard Wilson's consecration. It was noted that there were no plans for compulsory primary education. Neither would there be for some time.

With stolid normality, the November 1941 edition of *St John's Review* printed the list of the month's servers, which included John Pau, George Ladd, Arthur White, George Budden, John Huang, James Reedie, David Parsons, Norman Smith and Luke Lim. You stare at the names and wonder about them a month hence. The magazine's last article is a book review of *The Nature and Destiny of Man* by Reinhold Niebuhr. Then there is silence.

Chapter 6
Out of Darkness, 1941–1953

Major General Christopher Maltby, general officer commanding, had only just sat down in his pew from reading the lesson on the morning of 7 December 1941, when a messenger slipped down the nave and handed him a note. He read it, stood and left the cathedral quickly, his party following. The Japanese were not yet invading. The Sunday morning attack on Pearl Harbour was still to come on the other side of the international dateline, but the 52,000 men of their 38th division were making ominous moves along the Sham Chun River. They invaded Hong Kong at 8 a.m. the following day.

Maltby's hurried exit was the first of the events that altered St John's irrevocably through the fall and revival of Hong Kong in the years to follow. The cathedral saw no battling or bloodshed. There was damage though, a collapse of all that was familiar, and decay and anxiety. The light of worship flickered within it for a while and then went out. Prayer continued elsewhere in the internment camps and in the Bishop's chapel, which the Japanese mercifully neglected.

Then darkness receded suddenly and thin, drawn men and women made their way back to St John's. A new light streamed in, literally, through plain glass windows, onto a church stripped bare of ornament as they were of fat. Many welcomed the austerity and simplicity of the place as an opportunity for a fresh start and, in many ways, that was taken. The decade of death and resurrection from Christmas 1941, also described by the tenure of Alaric Rose, was a catharsis in the congregation's history.

Attitudes did not change completely, nor did direction alter entirely. Colonial distinctions were not yet dead, but the superiority of the white man certainly was. An awareness of a world in which they were simply a part rather than controller was dawning in the core of the congregation. A new humility was being born.

During the battle for Hong Kong itself, services in the cathedral were conducted by Alaric Rose as priest-in-charge and the Reverend Charles Higgins of the American Episcopal Church, who had been seconded as a temporary assistant chaplain. He could have left earlier in the year but chose to stay with his wife and 2-year-old son. They were repatriated from Stanley Camp to the United States under a swap deal with the Japanese, and he submitted a detailed account to Bishop Hall of how matters stood in Hong Kong as he left it in August 1942.[1]

In the fighting, between eighty and one hundred people attended St John's on Sundays. They sat quietly as shells fell around the cathedral. The church attracted so much fire because of its proximity to the barracks and the Volunteers' Headquarters which stood right next door. Altogether, it received around fifteen direct hits from medium shells, including one in the north transept, which passed through the organ loft. David Leigh, son of the first Chinese archdeacon of Hong Kong, a music student and later an honorary canon of St John's himself, was due to play the organ that day, probably because the organist was fighting with his unit. His mother forbad him to go because of the dangers. Had she not, he would have been sitting there at the moment of impact.

The fighting touched the cathedral in poignant ways. Alaric Rose remembers 'a bunch of Indian soldiers who had been shelled and nerve shaken and wanted sleep'. They found it in the tunnel under the sanctuary. This is one of the rare references to any use being made of that feature. They slept there with their rifles and left cheerfully. 'I hoped they fared well,' he says.[2]

On the last fateful Christmas Day, Higgins reports that he drove, as usual, with his wife, Mary, to celebrate Holy Communion at the Peak Church. Nobody came. He carried on nonetheless and restored the Communion vessels to a cupboard from which they were ultimately rescued by Jesuits. He drove down to the cathedral under sporadic shellfire, to be stopped only by a futilely officious soldier who threatened to report him for unauthorised use of petrol.

He was robing for matins when the most damaging shell hit the cathedral tower. It left a gaping hole in the arches of the top section and broke the beam supporting the bells. As the congregation was leaving to an uncertain future, a resolution was moving among them to install a clock in the hole when the opportunity arose. To add to a

Figure 1   The trowel from the foundation stone laying

Figure 2   View of the cathedral looking north, 1897 (Wattis Fine Art)

THE NEW CHURCH, VICTORIA TOWN, HONG KONG.
The first Christian Church erected in the Chinese Empire.

Figure 3 St John's Cathedral. Early artist's rendering from the *Pictorial Times*, London, before the church was built

Vincent John Stanton

Figure 4

Three prominent clergymen from St John's history. Chaplain Vincent Stanton, 1843–1851, Dean Alfred Swann, 1928–1935 and Bishop George Smith, 1849–1865

Alfred Swann

George Smith

Figure 5   First known colour photograph of the cathedral from a postcard, 1899

Figure 6 The nave decorated for Easter with Mr. White, verger and 'Number 1 Boy', 1897

Figure 7 The choir with Dean R. F. Cobbold (third row, fifth from left), c. 1900 (The Cobbold Trust)

Figure 8 Foundation stone for the chancel extension, 1869 (Public Records Office)

Figure 9 Unveiling the Memorial Cross, January 1921 (Public Records Office)

Figure 10

Thanksgiving Service for The King's Recovery, January 1929. Dignitaries entering St John's, the congregation dispersing and Dean Alfred Swann conferring with Governor Sir Cecil Clementi (*South China Morning Post* / Public Records Office)

Figure 11 Bishop Duppuy and some Hong Kong clergy

Figure 12 The cathedral looking east, c. 1930

Figure 13   View towards the Peak from the Hongkong Club, c. 1912

Figure 14   The 'Jelly Mould', The Peak Church, 1929

Figure 15 The nave looking east, c. 1934

Figure 16 Ordination of C. B. R Sargent, 1934. Front left is Archdeacon Mok. Back row includes second right, assistant chaplain H. W. Baines, later a bishop, and A. S. Abbott as crucifer.

Figure 17

Font and cover in former baptistery

Figure 18

A 1930s wedding with Reverend Nigel Bates

Figure 19 Procession for Bishop Wilson's consecration

Figure 20 The Tower after wartime shelling, 1946 (Public Records Office)

Figure 21

The Lady chapel in south
transept before the war

Figure 22

The Organ and the Bishop's
throne

Figure 23 Former Dean, Leonard Wilson after his consecration as a bishop at St John's, 1941

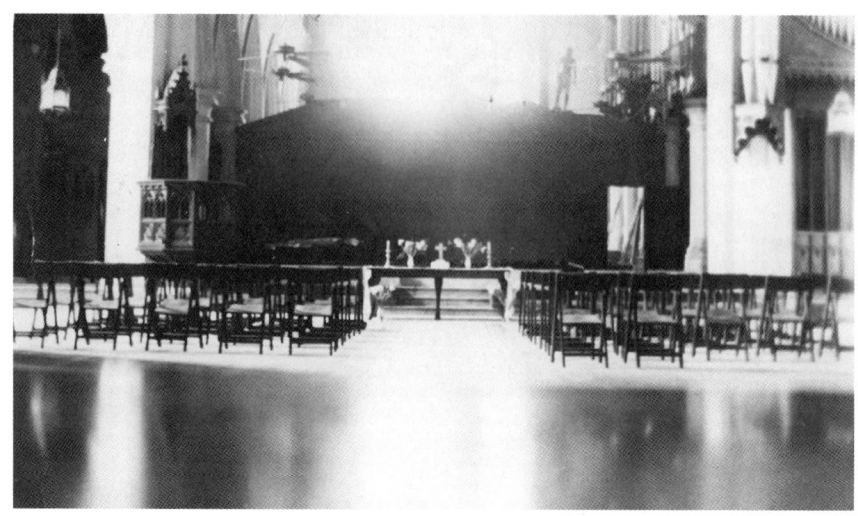

Figure 24 Makeshift altar in front of Japanese-built wall across the chancel, 1945

Figure 25 Ordination service with Bishop R. O. Hall and Dean Rose flanking Michael Goulder, 1950

Figure 26   Mrs. G. E. Marden opens the Michaelmas Fair, 1951

Figure 27   Bishop R. O. Hall and Michael Goulder at the Michaelmas Fair

Figure 28   East window with plain glass at Easter, 1954

Figure 29   Cathedral choir with Alaric Rose, Dean Temple, Donald Fraser, Cynthia Kwok and George She, 1954

Figure 30 The new hall, 1956

Figure 31 The Duke of Edinburgh greeted by (left to right) Bishop R. O. Hall, Dean Temple, former Dean Alaric Rose and Chaplain John Foster

Figure 32
The Captain Bate memorial
before its demolition, 1953

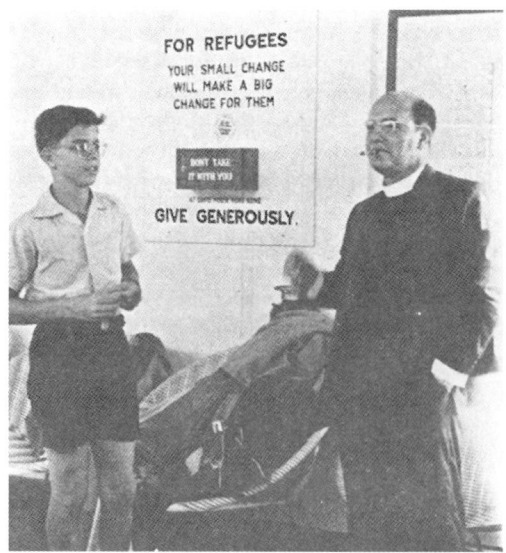

Figure 33
Alaric Rose and son at Kai
Tak airport departing Hong
Kong, 1961

Figure 34   Colonel Harry Owen-Hughes says farewell to Mrs. Rose at Kai Tak with Dean Barry Till behind.

Figure 35   The Reverend Frank Roe

Figure 36 From left to right: Bishop R. O. Hall, unidentified man, Dean Barry Till and Mrs. Shirley Till

Figure 37 Governor Sir Murray MacLehose and Lady MacLehose talk to Dean John Foster at a St John's Ambulance Brigade annual service

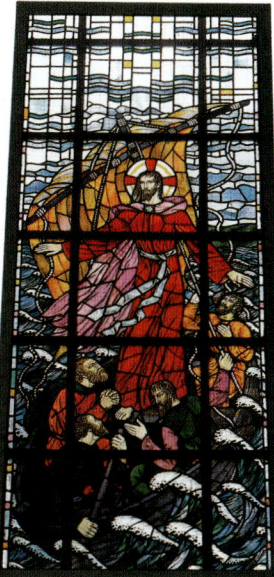

Figure 38   The east window and the north window central panel by Joseph Nuttgens

Figure 39   Princess Alexandra with (left to right) Cardinal John Baptist Wu, Bishop Gilbert Baker, Reverend Hugh Stevenson and Dean Stephen Sidebotham

Figure 40　The nave looking west, 1954

Figure 41 An overview of St John's, 1987

Figure 42 The cathedral looking south, 2012

peculiar sense of normality, the following morning, after the British surrender had been taken, the *South China Morning Post* published Charles Higgins's sermon, as usual.

Death came to the congregation over those seventeen days of fighting. J. R. M. Smith, the organist, had telephoned Alaric Rose on Christmas Eve to give him some details about an insurance policy, prior to going into action. It is interesting how attention to procedure can occupy men's minds on the brink of certain disaster. Nothing was heard of John Smith again. He died in the fierce fighting which ended the defence. Maurice Barton, secretary of the Communicants Fellowship and a candidate for ordination, was mortally wounded in his armoured car when the Japanese landed at North Point, and died after thirty-six hours of semi-consciousness in Bowen Road Hospital. Lindsay Lafford, who 'messed' with Barton in Bishop's House, recalls him as 'many talented and a close friend of Harry Baines'.[3]

Luke Lim, who was included in that last sidesman's list, a regular server, was killed by a direct hit on his first-aid post. He was a Borneo Diocesan medical student, chairman of the University Christian Association and an ordination candidate. Perhaps the youngest to die in the fighting was Peter Wilson, the senior choirboy. He too was a server and, as Bishop Hall described him in his inimitable style, 'the only layman actually in the sanctuary at Dean Wilson's consecration because he was faithful above all others, a devout worshipper and bursting with common sense'.[4]

The only combatant to be buried in the cathedral precincts was not an Anglican, and he was buried in a hurry, against regulations. Ronald (Roy) Maxwell was a Roman Catholic Eurasian, a former student of La Salle College belonging to No. 3 Company of the Hong Kong Volunteers. He was shot in the head by a sniper at his post in Wan Chai. It was known that Roy would have wanted to be buried in church ground, and three of his comrades managed to carry him in their retreat to the closest one at St John's.

Denominational distinctions were ceasing to matter under such fire. So were regulations. The 1847 ordinance stated that the cathedral precincts were not to be used for interments. A copy was obviously not to hand. The soldiers deepened a foxhole that was already under the tree at the west end and laid Maxwell's body in it. By strange and poignant chance, an Irish Jesuit priest, Father Ryan, was hurrying out of the then French Mission building at the top of Battery

Path. He was called over and said the words of the burial service. The three soldiers covered their bayonets in case reflections off them were spotted by Japanese planes flying overhead.[5]

So an Irish Jesuit came to bury a Roman Catholic Eurasian boy in Anglican ground. Such is a glimpse of the Kingdom that war can afford but peacetime finds expensive. Despite all the anomalies, the grave remains as a cathedral treasure. An offer was made to move the body to a war cemetery, but Maxwell's family preferred him to stay where he was. In 2010, a Commonwealth War Graves Commission headstone was formally placed over it in a ceremony attended by the British consul general and Private Maxwell's sister, Nancy.

Before the invasion, both Higgins and Rose had refused to be lay superintendents of hospitals, which was expected of clergy, preferring to be free to go about the island in their pastoral capacities. During the Japanese attack, the Church Guest House was a refuge for many who were able to get out of Kowloon before it was abandoned. The guest house had been set up in 1937 to receive missionaries and others fleeing the Sino-Japanese War. At first it was in Kennedy Road, and now it was part of Bishop's House. Rose commandeered rooms in St Paul's College and put boys from the Diocesan Boys' School on Kowloon side in the cathedral hall. He struggled hard to provide provisions for all of them. Higgins described his example of Christian patience in this as 'beautiful'.[6]

On 4 January after the surrender, enemy nationals were gathered by the Japanese and imprisoned first, in discomfort, in cheap hotels catering to the poorer classes or lesser instincts. After some days with little food or water but often sickness, they were moved to the internment camps. All the Anglican clergy with the exceptions of the army and navy chaplains were interned at Stanley. Two-thirds of the Cathedral Council was there, including the trustees, P. S. Cassidy and Professor L. Forster, and roughly half the congregation.[7]

However, the congregation could not simply continue as St John's at one uncomfortable remove. Facilities for public worship were so restricted that circumstances forced the clergy into an unprecedented ecumenism. A programme of union services had to be devised. This was conducted by a committee of clergy elected from the fifty-one British and American clergy who found themselves in Stanley. The Roman Catholics managed to maintain separation.

Alaric Rose was the secretary of the committee and, on him, most of the work fell. Higgins observed, for the time he was there, that 'the committee spent more time trying to prevent schism than it has in its constructive efforts to meet the religious needs of the internees'. However, he left early, and the union approach lasted until the end in 1945.

It would be misleading to speak of a United Church of Stanley. This was rather a series of united services of the type that had been held by the different denominations before the war but now of a greater and more regular frequency. This we are told by a remarkable document called 'The Church Review', bearing rough similarities to *St John's Review* and published within Stanley Camp in August 1942. How many editions there were is not clear, but of this one there were only five copies printed, and so a copy could be kept for only two days before being returned to the block librarian.[8]

There was a sermon, articles on camp life, including one titled 'Rumours', which concluded that they were as entertaining as they were harmful, and a lengthy piece on evangelism. There was a page from a letter home, waspish poetry, a short story and an outline of how the services were to be distributed among the denominations. Easter Day was given as a specimen.

It began with an open-air sunrise service conducted by Mr. Gates, an American Presbyterian. At 8.15 a.m. there was an all-Anglican Holy Communion with the Reverends Wittenbach, Myhill, Richards and Brown. At 9 a.m., Alaric Rose and E. W. Martin (Anglican), F. Short (Congregational) and R. P. Beaver (Evangelical and Reformed Church of America) celebrated Communion. At 10 a.m., it was an all-Anglican Communion again with Rose, Brown, G. E. S. Upsdell and Charles Higgins. At midday, J. E. Sandbach (Methodist) and K. Mackenzie Dow (Presbyterian) offered morning worship followed by the Sacrament of the Lord's Supper. The day ended at 4 p.m. with evensong and sermon from Anglicans Rose and Higgins and Congregationalist Short.

Whatever its flaws and fractures, the 'united programme' was a powerful development, perhaps too much so to be handled in peacetime. In a 1947 edition of *St John's Review*, Alaric Rose looked back on it as 'strengthening and enriching', making them realise 'we are united closely as fellow workers not rivals'. But unification was not to be embraced. He went on to write that now 'differing needs … diverse patterns of worship … serve God's purpose at the time'.[9]

In the absence, the regular clergy and the bulk of the congregation who fell into the category of enemy nationals, worship continued at St John's. The imperial Japanese attitude towards Christianity at this point, and in Hong Kong at least, seems to have been one of indifference. That its British and American followers were locked up seemed to be enough. An example of this distinction was when prayer books were sent into Stanley Camp by Dr. Charles Harth, the Austrian Jewish convert who became a secretary to Bishop Hall and who remained at liberty. The Japanese sole but vigorous objection was that they contained prayers for the King. 'God save the King' was replaced by 'God save the world'.

Dr. Harth was made a proxy trustee of the cathedral by Cassidy and Forster from their confinement in Stanley. He made a report on the wartime workings of the cathedral to the Victoria Diocesan Association after the war.[10]

From New Year of 1942, services at St John's itself were patchily, nervously ecumenical and international. That they were attended at all in the atmosphere of vicarious violence created by the Japanese military was still remarkable and courageous. A file of Japanese soldiers had appeared a few days after the surrender, looking for quarters to acquire and saw the letter of protection pinned on to the west door. They looked in and grew angry when they recognised the Union flag in quarters of the regimental flags still hanging. They made scissor-like signs that they would be cut out.[11]

The mainstay of English services were the Norwegian Lutheran pastors of the Tao Fong Shan Monastery at Sha Tin, Pastor Thelle, his son Gerhard, Pastor Reichelt, its founder and, from the Norwegian Seamen's Mission, Pastor Nielsen, who had never conducted a service in English before.

Karl Ludwig Reichelt, originally of the Norwegian Missionary Society, became looked upon as radical in his openness to Buddhism and his seeking for 'points of light and connection points' in Buddhism brought about by the Holy Spirit. He founded the Nordic Christian Buddhist Mission, which provoked a split with the society. He had to flee Shanghai and, in 1929, with Thelle, Reichelt came to Hong Kong and was given permission to build Tao Fong Shan ('the mountain where the wind blows') in Sha Tin. In 1931, Dean Swann laid the foundation stone.[12] This institute has since become the seat of Buddhist Mission's work in China.

Reichelt and his pastors from Sha Tin are said to have walked to the cathedral on Sunday mornings during the occupation to conduct the services when no other means were available. The relationship between the cathedral and Tao Fong Shan has remained warm ever after. Reichelt died in Hong Kong in March 1952. After his death, the relationship with Buddhism at Tao Fong Shan faded, but the monastery prospers as a Christian study centre, frequently used by St John's.

The Chinese clergy also gave support to the cathedral which, in itself, was not without risks. Association with Europeans, even neutrals, could lead to arrest by the Japanese. George She, barrister and later priest and stalwart of the post-war cathedral, spent three months in prison because of his friendly attitude to the British. Alaric Rose said that he raised morale in the local congregation and wrath in the occupiers by preaching in Cantonese, 'Don't you worry about what is going on; God still rules the world and he will not let this present regime of oppression and unrighteousness go on for long. One day not too far ahead, you will wake up and find your oppressors vanished.'[13]

The Reverend E. E. Low conducted services at St John's, as did the Reverend Lei Yin Pui, who then became Vicar of St Mary's. The Reverend Chung Yan Lap, Vicar of St Stephen's Church, which never closed during the war, agreed to be presented to the Japanese as pastor in charge of the cathedral when no one else dared put his name down, according to Dr. Harth's account.

Those outside the camp attempted to set up an interim cathedral council. It met once at Bishop's House on 21 January 1943. Its chairman was George She, the vice chairman, Katie Woo, and the secretary, Miss E. Westergaard. The treasurer and warden was Dr. Harth. The organists, Ruby Mow Fung and Mrs. P. G. Wong, were, for as long as it worked, the last people to have played a pipe organ in St John's. The ladies convener was Mrs. R. Souza. Other members were George Ladd, Dr. M. Klein, H. A. Keller, Dr. S. Yung and Mr. D. Javez.

The caretaker and verger was Ah Kau, who had been with the cathedral for many years up to the war and was baptised with his family in 1938, following a coincidentally advantageous accommodation swap with the single coolies the year before. He was to stay on, doing his best to guard the cathedral, throughout the war.

The cathedral's assets totalled 78 military yen. Collections averaged 8 yen. Thirty yen were required by the diocese, which, under Bishop Mok, was being run by an emergency executive committee, and 20 yen went to the Hong Kong Churches Union, a Japanese concoction under their government's Education Department. With this the

Reverend Chung Yan Lap would have nothing whatever to do. The two necessary delegates to it were named as She and Harth. Letters of thanks for their support were sent to Reverends Nielsen, Thelle and Lei Yin Pui.

Gatherings of any kind, particularly involving Europeans, were so easily open to misinterpretation by the Japanese. Harth says that they were simply 'advised not to meet again'.

In his report, Harth takes time to mention the Japanese Christians involved in the story. He was full of praise for them and, like Reverend J. H. Ogilvie, Vicar of St Andrew's, who gives account of Japanese Christians worshipping alongside Chinese there after the occupation, he seems to describe men and women who acted not against but somehow apart from their own people.

'That I have survived,' writes Harth, 'I have to thank ... also a Japanese pastor. Samejima is his name. I know for certain that he saved me twice from being arrested.' Samejima, a US-educated Methodist, was a professor and chaplain at the Christian University at Kobe. He was sent by the Japanese government as chief advisor to the Hong Kong Churches Union. On Easter Day 1945, Samejima baptised a young Japanese Cambridge University graduate in the chapel in Bishop's House. He persistently supported Harth's legal objections to any takeover of the house by the military government.

A Lutheran Japanese minister, Reverend Watanabe, was attached to the camp authorities. According to Harth, he took great risks to help the internees and prisoners of war. Samejima continued to send Christmas cards to the cathedral for many years after the war.

At some point, the Japanese took over the cathedral as a 'social club'. Harth, in his report to the Victoria Diocesan Association, says it was September 1942. Alaric Rose, in a similar document, tells us that it was 'autumn, 1943'. The *Hong Kong News* of 5 July 1944 records a celebration to mark the official opening of the 'former cathedral' as headquarters of the Yamato-Kai, which means, essentially, a society for Japanese culture. 'Those present included Lt-Col. Nagao, ADC to the Governor, Lt-Col. Masuhisa, Chief of the Information Bureau, high officials of the Governor's Office, members of the Japanese community and a number of women and children. A number of newsreels were shown during the afternoon.'

It is likely that the church was being used as a Japanese public hall before this official ceremony was organised but, whatever the date of the handover, it was clear that the Japanese wanted the place stripped of its Christian imagery and its furniture. Harth must have been as persuasive as he was courageous. He says that the Japanese lent him a truck for three days. With a friend, Mr. Owen Hughes, 'a fellow member of the F.A.U.', possibly the Friends Ambulance Unit, and Preston Wong Shiu Poon, a senior master of St Paul's College, they moved 'everything that was moveable'.

We do not know what notice of this Harth was given by the Japanese before they lent him the truck, but it was likely to have been inconsiderately short. There would have been an awful lot to move in three days. The heavy stained glass window parts had to be pulled out in a particular hurry without finesse. Those that did survive the war suffered from this, and it was one of the reasons why they were never to be reinstalled.

There is the belief that the cathedral was used for stabling horses. There are no clear references to this, and it is difficult to see how, in the change from church to social club, the Japanese would have been inclined to put it to such a lowly use. However, that is the fate that befell Christ Church Kowloon Tong and the Catholic cathedral in Canton.

A brightening feature of this gloomy time was the spirit of cooperation shown by the Roman Catholics. Bishop Voltara, an Italian, was having a hard time himself getting a glimmer of respect out of the Japanese, who insisted on calling him 'Mr. Voltara'. He had sent a strong letter of protest to the authorities when, at some point, there seems to have been a proposal that Japanese Buddhists take over St John's.

Now that the cathedral had to be evacuated, Bishop Voltara arranged for all the furniture and the stained glass to be received at St Paul de Chartres Convent and Hospital in Causeway Bay and to St Mary's Church there also. Later, Bishop Hall was under the impression that the windows had been stored in the cellars of Bishop's House, and it is possible that some should have been, except that there is no reference to this having been done. The French Fathers kept the cathedral's Communion vessels, the vestments and some brasses in the French Mission. The Irish superior of the Jesuits—a neutral national—retrieved the Communion vessels which Charles Higgins had used that Christmas morning in the Peak Church.

Services were transferred to the Bishop's chapel in Bishop's House. The Japanese military, out of quirkiness rather than kindness, had inspected the Church Guest House there, noticed the mix of nationalities and decided, initially at least, that it was an international settlement of some sort, best left alone. Worship went on there, relatively unscathed. The 'cathedra' itself, the old bishop's chair, was moved there, as witness that Victoria was still the See city. It seems likely that only the seat of the throne—that which survives—was moved and that the tall and elaborate canopy was detached, stored and lost.[14]

Bishop's House itself was seriously damaged in an air raid of 21 January 1945. Bishop Hall is cheerfully ironic about it in his 10 December letter to the Victoria Diocesan Association.[15] 'Poor Mrs. Duppuy! I remember with what care she told me that the Drawing Room curtains needed 72 yards of material and with what care we—in consequence—remained curtainless. And now a good Allied bomb has blown even the glass out of the doors ...'

The Sunday school, of all the church's activities, soldiered on in the house throughout the war. Betty Primrose, then Betty Wong, remembers how, as a teenage girl, she attended with ten to fifteen others every Sunday. They became starved of material until the very end of the occupation, when the former Dean Swann's son, now in the RAF, brought through some reading books from India. Betty was briefly in charge of the choir and accompanied them on the piano when services resumed after the occupation. In 1947, she married in St John's, as her parents had done before her.

Betty was the daughter of Preston Wong Shiu Poon. He was not only a schoolmaster, devout Christian and member of St John's but also a resistance worker against the Japanese. He was rounded up as one of the 'Thirty-Two', as they were called, who were executed by the Japanese on the beach at Stanley on 29 October 1943. They had operated a covert wireless, planned breakouts and had connections with the British Army Aid Group. They were military men, administrators—including the Deputy Attorney General—businessmen teachers and policemen. There were Chinese, British, Portuguese, Indians and Americans among them, all on the same charge, facing a common death. One of the Chinese was a woman.

Before they were shot, the senior officer in the group, describing Wong as the bravest man he had ever met, asked him to lead them all in prayer.[16] Under persecution and in death, a new polity was coming into being.

St John's Cathedral came back into its own with some speed at the end of the occupation. Canon Wittenbach, himself just out of internment, reported to the Victoria Diocesan Association that a service of

Holy Communion was held on 7 October, the first Sunday of freedom from the camps, in the Bishop's chapel, celebrated by Alaric Rose. It was attended by many from the camps who got a sense of the conditions of worship for those cathedral people who had been left to different perils outside.[17]

Much had to be done to clear away the detritus of the Japanese presence and restore St John's itself to its elemental state. During the church's brief and ill-fitting role as a Japanese social and cultural club, walls had been built to split it into three parts. The sanctuary was used for fencing and *ju-jitsu*, the chancel had been turned into a movie house and the nave was a canteen. In a room formed between the sanctuary and the choir, there were dozens of treadle sewing machines. A guess was that this had been the meeting area of the Japanese equivalent of the Women's Auxiliary, who also met, chatted and drank tea.

Concrete had been laid over the chancel floor, raising it by two feet. According to A. S. Abbott's account,[18] the stone font had been 'desecrated', but the manner of this was not described, leaving generations of imagination to follow on. Interestingly, the pulpit was neither removed nor damaged. The Japanese may have found a use for it.

There is a small photograph taken days after the cathedral was reclaimed, of workers tearing down a dark, high wall dividing the nave from the chancel, a shaft of brilliant light from the east bolting through where they had demolished the first corner. Beneath, at the foot of the chancel steps, stands a small innocuous table with a cross and flowers upon it, acting as the very first altar after liberation. On the back of the photograph, in an anonymous hand, is written the comment that the Japanese had kept the ashes of their war dead behind that wall. There is no other confirmation of this. It would have been ironic if a usurper observing the Shinto rite had kept his dead, unwittingly perhaps, in a Christian sanctuary.

There was a brief interim period of bizarrely liberating functions in and round the church. British government was set up again in the French Mission building, described by Alaric Rose as government 'with a walking stick and two typewriters and the faith that we were doing the right thing'. A police officer had the brilliant idea of establishing a traffic office in the cathedral porch. For a while there were three or four desks, telephone wires, cars with flashing lights and messengers running in and out.

A school of Chinese shadow boxing had been started in the compound during the occupation. Passers-by said it was an obstruction, and some feared the worship of unknown gods was going on. Getting rid of it was hard because clients had paid a lump sum for a course and 'were disinclined to allow the liberation to cancel the unexpired remainder', observed the dean.[19]

With a loan from the Hong Kong and Shanghai Bank, without need for security and with no conditions attached, St John's resumed services a few days after reoccupation. On 14 October 1945, Rose was celebrating the Eucharist in the church itself. 'The place was full of light and there were flowers everywhere,' reports Canon Henry Wittenbach to the Victoria Diocesan Association.

There are several references to the brightness of the church by returnees. 'The Cathedral is so light, spacious and peaceful,' records visiting missionary Margaret C. Knight.[20] The stained glass was gone.

Bishop Hall's impression of it was a succinct summary of the cathedral's aesthetic virtue. '… the clear light of the windows and the wide, deep chancel shows now the essential grace and beauty of the design of the cathedral and makes us daily grateful for the inspiration of the colony surveyor who designed it.' Cleverly must have blushed in heaven.

The newly returned Bishop Hall preached at the 11 a.m. service that day. There was Communion at 8, a union service with the Church of Scotland at 10, another service at 5 and evensong at 6. Members of the Union Church, whose building had been destroyed, led by Lieutenant Colonel Dr. Lindsay Ride, were also worshipping at St John's. The cathedral was packed at all the services, largely with contingents from the armed forces who were in Hong Kong in some numbers under the interim military government.

The cathedral was thick with uniforms of all colours. Even men who had been prominent as civilians in the church before the war came back to it in uniform on a Sunday morning. Harry Owen-Hughes, so dressed, must have seemed a big man because, by slip of the tongue of a Chinese member, he became 'Lieutenant Colonel Huge'. 'The truth will out,' said the bishop.[21]

In that same month of October 1945 there was the first confirmation service after the war. Candidates from the Sham Shui Po and Stanley Camps put their names forward. Hall described the sight as that of 'Nehemiah returning from captivity to Jerusalem. The yellow pallor of long starvation was still visible on all faces.'

By December 1945, the Sunday timetable included four services of Holy Communion, matins and evensong. Alaric Rose had been sent to England for a period of recuperation. Bishop Hall took over as dean for ten months. Because no official Board of Patronage could be assembled, Hall, on his own authority and with a characteristic flourish of justness, appointed Rose Dean of St John's, dated to Christmas Day 1941.

Marjorie Bray, a former council member whose marriage Rose conducted, remembers him as 'sincere and dead serious'. His wife, Mary, 'a sweet woman', was a Quaker by background. Rose was also an intellectual. According to Michael Goulder, in those early repairing days in Hong Kong, some of the brightest and the best, resident or passing through, could be found around the dean's simple dinner table, some nights up to twenty strong.[22]

In the first diocesan service after the war, George She was made a deacon, rapidly priested thereafter on St John the Evangelist Day, and appointed part-time chaplain. The cross-bearer at that diocesan service was Kenneth Wong, only son of the executed Wong Shui Poon, who had led the prayers for the condemned 'Thirty-Two'.[23]

Amazingly, Vyvian Copley-Moyle made the sea journey back to Hong Kong at 76, quite unbidden, to assist with the revival of the cathedral. This extravagant act of selflessness and surprise was a late insight into the dedication, self-assurance and showmanship which seemed to be characteristics of Copley-Moyle. The Chinese press caught on to the event and dubbed him 'the Aged Priest'. Hall made him a canon *emeritus* of the cathedral along with four new honorary canons, Paul T'so, Lei Kau Yan, H. Wittenbach and E. W. L. Martin, whose beloved wife had died in Stanley just before the end of internment.

The laity were fielding a strong team at this point. P. S. Cassidy was treasurer. Brian Crozier was secretary, and H. S. Margarett joined Cassidy as a trustee. He was the managing director of General Electric, who had been interned with his wife, and she became an inspiration to amateur dramatics in Stanley Camp. Mrs. Bicheno was the choir mistress, notable for roaring up to the vestry door in her small black sports car. Mr. Dickens was in charge of cathedral music, interim, and Mr. Wilby restarted *St John's Review*. Mrs. Wilby handled the altar linen, and Mrs. Rose, the flowers. David Kwok was head sidesman and Henry Kwok, head server.

O. W. Skinner took charge of reviving the Goodwill Offertory scheme and was reaping HK$1,000 a month by 1946. To repair the depredations from neglect and abuse and refill the church with basic furniture and fittings went beyond the scope of an offertory scheme.

Restoration plans called for $300,000 total expenditure, and trustees Cassidy and Margarett brought their connections and influence to bear amongst the British business community to come up with pledges of support for a 1947 Cathedral Centenary Appeal. Such was the scale of the works, including repairs to the roof and the tower, that promises of $100,000 were needed before it could start.[24]

The high cost of the roof repairs and the 11,000 square feet of tiling needed brought 'considerable disappointment' to the dean. Yet, by June 1947, it had been completely stripped. Tiles had been replaced or renewed, and the beams were scraped and replaced where necessary and left with a natural wood colour. The floors of the tower were replaced by ferro concrete. The old floor had positively sagged under the crowd at the consecration of Bishop Mok. Three thousand square feet of plaster was stripped, pounds of rust came off the cast iron window frames and the woodwork was bleached of dark varnish, followed by painting, colour washing and waxing.[25]

Direct gifts to the restoration fund by the business community provided the bulk of donations and meant that the congregation did not have to dedicate all its own efforts to bricks-and-mortar issues. On Sunday, 28 September 1947, a service was held to give thanks for donations of $130,000, all of which had been spent.[26]

Then came a lacuna. The financial year 1947–48 was 'not propitious' for fundraising because of civil war in China and freezing austerity in Britain. Sir Mark Young, the governor, restored from his captivity, and patron of the appeal, declined to sign any fundraising material directed at Britain, because he could imagine the unfavourable reaction.

On 19 July 1947, the bishop, the dean and a mix of clergy and council members gave a dinner in the cathedral hall for ninety-six Chinese men—and women who carried the earth—who were working on the cathedral. It was an appreciative and talkative gathering. Among the leaders of the workers was Mr. Cheng of Hung Yu, the main contractor working under the cathedral architects, Leigh and Orange, Mr. Leung from the Building Contractors' Association, Mr. Kam from Messrs. O Shun, the decorator, and Mr. Ma, secretary of the Carpenters' Trade Union.

The bishop gave an address, and Canon Martin explained what it was they were doing, that their Master was a carpenter and that it would be nice if the carpenters' union secretary might say a few words. Mr. Ma said not a few. For ten minutes he preached the Gospel from the platform with 'terrific zeal', according to Bishop Hall. It wasn't clear what Christian denomination, if any, he belonged to, but he told the bemused but delighted bishop in no uncertain terms why they ought to be Christians and what it meant.[27]

There were significant gifts of money or items from individual members of the congregation. Carpets and cathedrals might not readily suggest each other but they did in the minds of men back then. Carpets featured prominently in the generosity. The 9 a.m. service fellowship opened a special fund to provide them for the chancel and chapel. Fanny Li gave it $1,000. With the help of Dr. Ernest To, two green ones were provided for the high altar and the Lady chapel, at a cost of $2,700. L. E. Lammert of the auction house also gave a carpet.[28, 29]

The Royal Navy donated a new altar table of carved teak, through the offices of the Naval Chaplain, Clifford Davies, who had recently made it clear in the pages of St John's Review that he did not like the idea of ordained women.

One-half each of the two pairs of Communion rails created by Mrs. Koop—at the high altar and in the Lady chapel—had been lost. Using two halves together and shifting them from high altar to Lady chapel, Mrs. Koop's design was preserved in unity. They still stand in what is now the St Michael's chapel. Mr. and Mrs. Margarett donated the two replacements halves.[30]

Smaller items of need were almost put out to tender in St John's Review. The altar books needed rebinding at a cost of $100. Who would pay for that? There were three offers. Can someone supply a new chain for the sacristy lamp?

In the compound, thanks to council member Dr. Herklots, hawkers, food vendors and idlers were kept out by a four-strand wire fence between Battery Path and Murray Parade Ground. The result was, according to St John's Review, 'The North east corner cleared.' It had been 'used for all sorts of improper and disreputable purposes', it was reported, regretfully. Yet there was still a problem of the grass strip between path and parade ground and the low wall bounding it. Whether it was people practising tai chi or just sitting on the wall, they kept falling over it.[31]

Of Mr. Parry's original 1870 gift of bells, two remained intact and were rehung.

In 1949, it was thought timely to relaunch the Centenary Appeal to coincide with that of the diocese, and the decision was rewarded. To mark their 40th anniversary, Li Tse Fong and his wife give $5,000 for the bishop's throne. This was designed by Mr. Tebbut of Leigh and Orange. It was not the one wanted by Bishop Hall, but it was graciously accepted, even if the effect, anchored as it is, side on to the chancel wall, is of entering an old-fashioned first-class railway compartment.

Mrs. Marden, wife of George Marden of Wheelock Marden, who was later a member of the council, donated choir stalls, designed by D. Hindmarsh of Leigh and Orange, at a cost of $14,000, amounting to six rows. The choir then stood at 20 boys, 10 sopranos, 5 altos, 7 tenors and 7 basses. Prior to the socially aristocratic Mrs. Marden's generosity, they had been lodged in the gallery over the west door, which was a creative use of the location but far away from the locus of the service.[32]

There was an urgent need of furniture. The kindness of Bishop Voltara in having it stored in Causeway Bay when the Japanese took the cathedral over did not make it bomb proof. The Sisters of St Paul de Chartres Convent was a converted cotton factory compound which also accommodated an orphanage, school and hospital. Bombs from an Allied air raid rained on the compound on 4 April 1945, destroying buildings and killing seven sisters and many orphans and staff. Probably the least of the disaster was the loss of most of St John's furniture, including the choir stalls, the screen, chairs, stools and other bits and pieces. Talking of which, 850 yen was made from the sale of the remnants for firewood.

A further $100,000 was given for seating by the stewards of the Jockey Club. Six new benches were made and two hundred chairs, among which were distributed three hundred newly made hassocks.

As 'Bunny' Abbott got back into his pre-war stride as a generous donor of striking items, he made a gift of high altar decoration with riddle posts although, possibly from some shadow cast by their previous relations, he refused to contribute 19 pounds to altar decorations sent from England by former Dean Swann. Mr. and Mrs. Margarett gave a blue tapestry to the Lady chapel, now lost.

In 1949, the Japanese concrete overlay on the chancel and sanctuary floor was tackled without any certainty of what mess would be found underneath it. In fact, they had placed a layer of rubble under the concrete, which included chunks of the transept roof crosses. This had the effect of preserving the original. The tiles of the chancel and the marble of the sanctuary, so diligently funded and extended by Chaplain Cobbold, were found to be more or less intact.

At the suggestion of the new Verger-Clerk, H. L. Kwok, the same treatment was given to the Lady chapel, where the squares of original granite flooring were revealed. There had been a rocky period with vergers before the war. Mr. Shaw was fired for absence without leave, and his successor, Mr. Poye, got deeply into debt and the council did what it could to help him out of it. Mr. Kwok was not only a Chinese in the job, but he was a new level of verger with an interesting past. An employee of Gilman and Co., he was baptised and confirmed in the cathedral in 1941. At the beginning of the occupation, he toured the internment hotels with food, looking for European friends. When he moved to Canton, he was kidnapped for ransom and later became a lay reader—a remarkably uneven experience.

The memorial tablets which had congested the walls in the years before the war and hurriedly brought down in the middle of it were not restored. They still existed, piled up outside the church, some broken but some intact. The dean and his council decided that they were too ugly and too many to restore. A. S. Abbott described most of their inscriptions as 'doggerel'. Some were placed in the Happy Valley Cemetery Chapel. The rest were destroyed.

So too were the remnants of the stained glass windows. Evidence of their fate is patchy but conclusive. It has to be remembered that a disassembled stained glass window is a fragile collection of fragments. In the best of conditions—and these were nearly the worst—they are vulnerable. Wherever they were kept, be it in the convent or even Bishop's House, they survived the war but incompletely. They did not remain stored and then forgotten about, awaiting discovery. Mrs. Marjorie Bray, then a young parishioner about to wed her government cadet husband, Denis, recalls banging her shins on them regularly as she went into the cathedral. They had been reclaimed and lay piled up inside the west door.

The council took its time deciding what to do about stained glass. Perhaps people were enjoying the sunlight. In July 1947, the council installed 24-ounce plain glass windows in wooden frames in the east, because that which had been put in by the Japanese would have been blown out by the next decent typhoon.

A. S. Abbott, in combative mode, wrote to the dean about putting an end to 'the jigsaw puzzle games' with the surviving window fragments and commissioning a new one. There had even been a suggestion that surviving pieces of the Bishop Hoare memorial window from the south transept could be incorporated into the east somehow. On 8 August that year, Dean Rose wrote to James Parnell and Sons of London about making a stained glass east window. 'We still have the glass which was removed by unskilled workmen and stored badly. Can it be used again?' he asked. The answer was that it could not.[33] As Marjorie Bray believes, the pieces were thrown away.

Stockbroker and council member Noel Croucher, who became a noted if testy benefactor of many institutions in Hong Kong, offered the cathedral an east window. By 1950, the cathedral had not moved on this, and he felt they were being dilatory. The difficulty was that, although Croucher was prepared to pay 600 pounds, a window from England cost 2,000 pounds, and Croucher refused to share the donation. It was discovered that a window could be made in Florence for half the cost, but the dean didn't think that a Florentine window would satisfy the congregation, doing them the honour of believing that they would notice the difference.

By 1949, all that remained of the old organ were grimy sham pipes which had once made music and looked out with such authority over the chancel. They were taken down. The former organ box room was designated as a 'chapter house'. Bookcases were installed, and a library with five hundred books was begun. Alaric Rose had a traditional vision of the cathedral as a resource of knowledge.

The lost organ was the most spectacular St John's ever had. Lindsay Lafford, organist from 1935 to 1939, recalled it fifty years later.[34]

'It was a 3-manual J. W. Walker, probably one of the instruments the firm boasted as having been specially built to deal with the tropical conditions found in the Empire.' He was assisted in maintaining it by Mr. Blackett, the uniquely Hong Kong-based English organ builder. 'The humid, hot climate, while apparently to Mr. Blackett's liking, was extremely distressing for such objects as musical instruments,' observes Lafford. 'A sudden drop in humidity could be expected in the Autumn. When this came, an overnight drop would find wood shrinking and cracking with loud explosive noises. The organ wind trunks and windchests, mostly made of wood, would open cracks to the extent that the blower could not keep up with the leaks.'

To counter this, a concrete basin was placed under the main pipe work, and the Number 1 Boy had standing instructions to fill this with water whenever the humidity drop was expected. 'Since the drop could never be forecast with any accuracy, this was a kind of crap shoot,' says Lafford. 'The standing water under the organ in virtual undisturbed darkness was a heaven-sent breeding ground for mosquitoes, and an organist's ankles were constantly under attack.'

The organ was 'tubular pneumatic', whereby the pressing of a key on the console would open the valve under a remote pipe to permit air to flow into it and make it sound. Lafford explains the disadvantage in Hong Kong. 'This requires a large number of small pneumatic motors, miniature bellows, using calfskin for flexibility. But the severe climate affected the calfskin so that it quickly grew hard and cracked and useless. Replacements were not only difficult to come by but very expensive.'

Tubular pneumatic actions were becoming obsolete. 'During a very important service connected with the death of King George V, one of the loud pedal notes developed what is known as a cipher, that is, it stuck in the on position, only silenced when the blower was shut off. This was dramatic reinforcement of … my strong assertions that it was time for a major overhaul,' Lafford remembers. Blackett was charged with rebuilding the instrument, using a more modern style of action known as electro-pneumatic, allowing the console to be placed in a more remote location from the pipes.

This remoteness permitted the player a far better appreciation of the balance of sounds. Blackett set about devising his own version of electro-pneumatic action, involving a 12-volt generator from a car.

The organ was rebuilt and the console moved over to the north side of the chancel. Wires running through the sanctuary tunnel under the altar connected the two.

In 1949, to have replaced all that would have cost $100,000, and all the difficulties of maintaining a pipe organ in a tropical climate would have returned. A Compton electronic organ, which did not rely on glue or leather, cost $36,000. The organ fund already had $31,000, $10,000 of which had been given by the beneficent Mrs. Marden. The Hong Kong Singers held a concert in aid of the organ and the King's Theatre on Queen's Road Central and donated its Easter Monday takings to it.

Dr. Eric To, a council member and aficionado of the instrument, lent his own electric organ for a recital in St John's. His wife played it.

St John's Review said that they would be glad 'to obtain some impression of what our Compton will be like'. There was no report of what the impression was. The organ arrived in April 1949. Continuing the generosity of the business community, through sympathies both Christian and masonic, the instrument had been shipped out free by the Glen Line and was installed free by General Electric.

By May 1950, the new organ was already malfunctioning. The cathedral would not accept it as a going concern and demanded Messrs. Compton put it in order. The council refused to pay the technician's fares but would put him up. Comptons agreed, and the Roses paid the price of that economy by accommodating him. The nineteenth century was repeating itself.

The Royal Hong Kong Jockey Club had given $10,000 to the repair of the hall. Messrs. Cassidy and Duckworth split the memorial cross restoration cost of $2,400 between them. Duckworth had lost his brother at Vimy in the First World War.

There was still much to be done. Amplifying equipment was needed which would cost $6,300. Damp in the transept and baptistery walls would cost $6,000. The altar linen was worn out. The prayer books almost needed chaining, so great were the losses reported by the Lammerts' inventory. There were proposals to revive choir scholarships, because a shortage of regular choristers meant that weddings often went choirless.

Yet, the rolling urgency in which repair money was being spent immediately it had been collected, a feature of the previous two years, was slowing by 1950. In January, $48,000 of the centenary appeal had not been allocated. It was divided between restoration and clergy funds. It was decided to keep the appeal open till May but not to press it.[35]

No matter what repair was going on in the church itself, the cathedral was enjoying a renaissance as a centre of activity. In the October 1947 *Review*, the dean's report claimed that the cathedral was becoming more of an international centre for English speakers, 'a kind of Canterbury of the East', he thought. Like Cobbold, Swann, Lander and Duppuy before him, he urged readers to 'keep steadily in mind the idea of cathedral; prayer, worship, learning, study, music, beauty'.

It was a busy place for preaching. That year, Bishop Lyndon Tyson, Bishop of Hunan and Presiding Bishop of the Chung Hua Sheng Kung Hui, passed through Hong Kong and gave a sermon. He was one of many bishops of the Chinese and other Asian dioceses who attended meetings in Hong Kong or passed through to them elsewhere. For the most part, they would stay, modestly, in the Church Guest House.

This had moved out of Bishop's House to the former St Paul's Girls' School Hostel on Upper Albert Road, which had been reclaimed from the RAF. There were thirty-four double rooms, and it was usually packed out. Dr. C. J. Harth, who had been made a deacon of the church, was its warden. Mrs. E. Klein, who had been a member of that brief council of 1943, was its hostess, and its unofficial 'elder statesman' was Harold Smythe, a charming, generous and slightly eccentric businessman whose hallmark was to walk around the city in shorts and walking boots.

Communal worship picked up momentum in the post-war years. There was a memorial service for those killed in the Yangtze Incident on 29 April 1949, at which the band of the Royal Buffs played 'brilliantly'.[36]

On 8 May there was the funeral of Police Inspector R. F. C. Olivier, Sub-Inspector Haynes and Detective Corporal Wong Kam, killed by two of their locally employed seamen on the No. 1 Police Launch. This was a murderous mutiny which disturbed and puzzled the colonial community.

On a bigger and happier note was the diocesan centenary service of 29 May 1949, at which the congregation overflowed into matsheds from the west door and along the north wall. The churches processed in reverse order of their foundation. The bishop preached, the governor and Canon Paul T'so read the lessons, the Reverend Lee Kau Yan conducted part of the service in Cantonese and there was a combined churches choir of 160.

Ascension Day services were always regarded as worship in which schools must be prominent participants. The 1951 celebrations involved a 10 a.m. service for the Diocesan Boys' and St Paul's Schools, conducted by the Rev J. H. Ogilvie, the Diocesan Boys' School Chaplain, and George She preaching. At 7.30 p.m. there was a Chinese youth fellowship service. Schools were still shipped in for what were now 'Commonwealth Day' services. Attendance was 'good and representative', code probably for acceptable, although the end of this trailing imperial observance was in close sight.

Well-organised instances of collective worship should not mask the more ordinary Sunday evenings which still had attendance problems. During an evensong in 1953, four clergy walked in behind one choir member. A congregation of ten sat in the front four pews, and curtains drawn across rails on castors shut out the emptiness of the rest of cathedral.[37]

The choir itself, although falling short for weddings occasionally, was thriving in its vestry. Staunch member Zena Mansell married Jack Mitchell from Kowloon on 24 May 1947, forming a couple who were to be of invaluable service to both choir and council for the next thirty years. Betty Wong, who had been succeeded by Betty Bicheno, also married that year to become Mrs. Primrose.

Choir practice was on Wednesday, beginning with tea at 4.30, followed by practice for boys only, who were joined by the adults at 5.30. Mrs. Bicheno reported that one boy, Alan Barnes, had not missed a choir practice or matins for nine months. In 1949, Donald Fraser succeeded her as choir director and became the organist. Continuing the early tradition in 'multitasking', he also worked as a music teacher with the Education Department.

With Communion at 8 p.m., a growing Eucharist service at 9 a.m. and the main matins service at 11, the 10 a.m. service on Sunday was being given up for lack of support. The Sunday school, which had so pluckily stayed open throughout the occupation, was experiencing one of its periodic ebbs.

Dean Rose blamed parents for not imposing on children the same discipline over attendance that they would for day school. He chided them for their embrace of the modern notion that children might make up their own minds on religion. This was 'excessive toleration'. It placed 'on the shoulders of a child a heavy burden of strain'. 'Reasonable and sweet faith' in the mind of a child was being replaced by 'ugly and superstitious elements'.

As ever, cathedral income ebbed and flowed too. For 1947, it was $59,000 and over expenditure by a whisker of $29.60. By the beginning of 1949, the cathedral does not appear to have been awash with income or offerings. Expenditure in 1948 had been $69,000. Offertories, letting the On Lee property at Pok Fu Lam and $9,000 income from the Chater Endowment Fund had only come up with half of that. Goodwill Offerings had only seen 157 subscriptions, raising $28,000 of the $36,000 needed. The treasurer describes the response as 'surprising and distressing'.

Nevertheless, Bishop Hall could praise St John's generosity in paying $2,000 to the Victoria Diocesan Association—even though it had been deferred in 1947 out of penury—and for giving Sunday offerings to the diocese. Hall said that the cathedral had no record of such consistency of giving into the Chinese church or society before this.

The post-war years were to see an improvement in the record of giving to organisations outside the cathedral. A particular favourite of the bishop was the St James' Club and Settlement which St John's took to its heart. From its beginnings in a room in a Wan Chai temple, funds had been raised by 1951 for a new silver Nissen hut on Kennedy Road, the settlement's first permanent premises. Donations and fees raised $1,000 from a showing of the popular new release, *Passport to Pimlico*.

Traditional dedication to the unfortunate continued undisturbed. In early 1949, as the Communists were about to take over on the Mainland, ladies in the cathedral were busy knitting pullovers for the Taipo Orphanage and the Fanling Babies Home. They hoped to have as many pieces as possible finished before summer, 'which makes knitting unpleasant'.[38]

Certain changes in the cathedral's financial fortunes were making generosity more feasible. The Michaelmas Fair of 1951, held on Murray Parade Ground, raised $17,277, $10,000 of which went to the recently created Clergy Endowment Fund, and $7,000 to the General Fund and provision of a sound system in the church. The RAF, which had been compelled to hold its own rivalling fair on the same day, had gallantly announced the Michaelmas Fair over its own Kai Tak aerodrome speakers.[39]

Cannily begun again by Alaric Rose, the Clergy Endowment Fund, over years of steady growth, was promising an interest on capital which would take this burdensome element of clergy stipends off Goodwill Offerings from the congregation. In 1951, the goodwill scheme amounted to $43,000, or two-fifths of the cathedral's running expenses.

The objective was to leave the Clergy Endowment Fund untouched until it had reached a level of $200,000. By January of 1952, it had grown to a point where the bank advised it be split into two parts, one from which the clergy took their wages independently and the other from which the council could vote funds.

This caused a serious fracture in the council, setting the dean against some members. Opposition came from Mr. Skinner and Mr. Duckworth, who wanted the funds to be all one and the clergy to be financially bound to the cathedral as a whole. The dean wanted to be independent of congregation on matters of stipend, which happened in England through endowments managed by the Church Commissioners. Rose even threatened to set up his fund, independent of the council, if such a thing had been constitutional.[40]

The large and sensible figure of Harry Owen-Hughes crafted a compromise. Eventually, the matter was referred into oblivion, but it highlighted the fact that traditional debate over the status of the clergy still had life in it at St John's.

Alaric Rose stayed on for another contract after 1949. New to the cathedral was Michael Goulder, who was employed first as a lay reader in June 1950, at $10,000 a year, then made a deacon and finally ordained as a priest on Advent Sunday 1952 in the cathedral by Bishop Basil C. Roberts. He became an assistant chaplain along with George She in 1951.

Goulder was a bright and very special young man for Hong Kong. He was educated at Eton and Oxford and was in Hong Kong as a cadet with Jardines. He began his Christian experience with youthful evangelical movements but did not really fit that picture any more than he did Jardines. He attended St John's, became involved in youth work and was encouraged by Alaric Rose to come over to the church. This he did, and Bishop Hall 'gave thanks' for him being 'stolen' from Jardines' private office.

Hall was impressed by the spirituality of many of the cathedral clergy who served him. In July 1952, he rolled off a list of them whom he thought put his own to shame. It included Alfred Swann, Harry Baines, Leonard Wilson, Alaric Rose, George She and Michael Goulder. One he did not name he suspected 'had a direct line to God'.

George Samuel She went to Keble, Oxford, from 1933 to 1936 and was called to the Bar at Gray's Inn in 1934. He returned to Hong Kong as a barrister from 1934 to 1941, and he became a police magistrate from 1945 for two years. Yet She was a committed Christian who had been sent by the cathedral to study at St Augustine's Canterbury from 1928 to 1930. He was made a deacon and honorary chaplain in 1945, and a priest the following year.

For a while he was a heady combination of judge and priest. He worked part-time at the cathedral from 1947 and, after an initial refusal, consented to a full-time chaplaincy in December 1951. Though his tenure would be brief, his impact was to be considerable. As a Chinese priest, his position was not always easy. A bonus payment of $1,500 to him for shouldering much of the dean's work in Rose's absence in 1950 met some opposition on the Finance and General Purposes Committee for being money-grabbing and ungentlemanly.[41]

A far from original question arose about whether to have two part-time chaplains or one well-paid full-time one. By April 1952, the Finance and General Purposes Committee decided they needed a full-time third to replace Mr. Gould, who had worked well among young people. Finances were 'not pessimistic'. They resolved to cast about for a younger man who might encourage younger interests, which is where they needed more goodwill offerings from. It was carried that an 'about 24-year-old' chaplain was to be recruited for $1,200 per month on a four-year contract, with free quarters.

On Liberation Sunday, 1951, the governor, in an address, lamented 'how quickly the solid company of prisoners of war and internees has dispersed'. In the new colonial government posting system, the cathedral was losing stalwarts to other colonies. Herklots, Macdougall and Himsworth, who was described as 'a pillar' in Stanley, were transferred in quick succession.

A spirited, tragic and unrepeatable episode in the congregation's history was fading. Yet the story moved on. Lieutenant Colonel E. G. Hazelton, former trustee of Christ Church, was one of four ordinations that year. 'We are increasing the score of men coming from this small diocese,' observed a heartened Alaric Rose. Given the transitory nature of the congregation, he wondered if there was any 'really permanent building of unseen life and character here. We are not altogether idle, then.'

A look at the 1951 Cathedral Council gives us a glance at the leaders of that congregation and the cross-section of the professions if not of the society they were in. Three were from 'the Bank', Black Skinner and Slade. Five were educators, Stewart, Crozier, Endacott, and the Misses Bicheno and Grey. There were three lawyers, Kan, Kwok and Gould, and one policeman, Wilcox. Charter and Dark were architects, and Duckworth and Margarett were from utility companies. Beeching was from Jardines, Fielding from Hong Kong Land and Cassidy was from Hutchison. Dowbiggin was from Stewart Bros. and Harry Owen-Hughes from Harry Wicking and Co. There were two independent ladies, Mrs. Marden and Mrs. da Souza. Of the twenty-three laypeople, four were women and two were Chinese. Of that same number, sixty years on in 2011, seven were women, seven were Chinese and four of those were Chinese women.

Of course, those who were not Chinese were transitory. Rose himself was destined to depart in September 1952, with a canteen of cutlery and a carpet from a grateful congregation. He was not going far. He was taking up a teaching post at Hong Kong University and was still available for help at St John's.

Dean Rose had learned to take pride in his flock. Why had he been 'distracted to his wits end' to get any of his laity to do more for the church? Because, he realised, they were the ones up to their eyes already in communal work. It was in the post-war period, after some had died in service and others took the lead in internment, that he understood, he said, what a part they played in the life of Hong Kong. Much of the privately organised social service which forced the pace for the community was staffed by his church people. 'That has been the tradition of the congregation, I think … to carry into existing organisations of the colony the energy, faith, love and wisdom of Christian principles and ideas.'

Rose may have hit upon a truth which has a bearing upon times before and after him but which is difficult to fully illuminate. Unlike a conscientious parish church which sends organised activity out and about, St John's may act as more of a gathering place for worship, a centre of prayer and music and beauty which its deans have always yearned for and as a host to good works. Its parishioners, as individuals, do take back into their daily lives love and wisdom in Christ's name rather than, specifically, the cathedral's.

For Philip Cassidy, leaving the cathedral was of a more usual kind. After twenty-five years in Hong Kong, three-and-a-half of them in Stanley Camp, and the latter ones as *taipan* of Hutchison, he went home in June 1952. He was to visit Hong Kong again, but the rest of his life was spent in England, where he died in 1972. Alaric Rose summed him up with a lucidity and style: 'His life is large, transparent conscientious; although of many interests, yet of one piece, with one single-minded pattern going through it all whether in business, administration or the church to serve God in his generation.'

At his valedictory farewell, he noted that his last attendance at the cathedral was also for Michael Goulder's farewell sermon. Along with Copley-Moyle, Swann, Wilson, Rose and She, Cassidy said this young newcomer had impressed him.

Cassidy recalled his early experiences of the church. He said it had a shabby exterior, which would have been the case before the works of 1934. Interestingly, he observed that it 'lacked the light and the spaciousness of today'. In that, he may have been unconsciously enjoying the fact that the building had no stained glass. His conclusion went to demonstrate that, gradual though it may have seemed to some, change at St John's was visible to the long-stayer: 'The contrast between the Cathedral as I first knew it, when it was a parish church of the British element of the community with today when it draws its inspiration from the community as a whole is almost staggering.'

Looking back from 2011, the inclusiveness of the 1950s cathedral does seem rather nascent, but for one who arrived in the days of pew rents and *punkahs*, the shift in interaction between St John's and the Chinese world outside in Hong Kong must have seemed seismic.[42]

To the north of Hong Kong, the ground was quaking. A Communist state had taken over in the Mainland. For Anglican Chinese, there to be seen as attached to a Western colonial territory would compromise the church's effectiveness in China and pose potentially dangerous consequences for its members. The Diocese of Victoria and its bishop separated themselves from the Diocese of Kwangtung (Guangdong) and became the detached Diocese of Hong Kong in 1951. It asked for the Archbishop of Canterbury's oversight only a few years after having given it up. This time, however, the diocese welcomed him as 'chairman' of the worldwide communion. It was emphatically not reverting to the old colonial status.

A writer in the *Review*, tuned in early to the techniques of the 'non-aligned movement', went even further. The archbishop's oversight should be as a trustee. In future, Hong Kong should get a Chinese as bishop, and the archbishop should send an Indian bishop to consecrate him to convince the Beijing leadership that the church is international and not a handmaiden to the trading interests of Britain and America. There would be a thirty-one-year wait for a Chinese bishop, and an Indian consecrating in St John's has yet to be seen.

Dean Freddy Temple was installed there on 19 March 1953. He had been picked out to replace Alaric Rose by a patronage team of Bishop Hall, F. Duckworth and H. S. Margarett, now honorary treasurer. Governor Grantham, who had replaced Sir Mark Young, read a lesson at the service. Archdeacon Lee and the Reverend George She wore capes for the occasion. The shadows of war, that war at least, had receded.

Chapter 7
Shedding Colonialism, 1953–1976

Frederick Temple, always known as Freddy, had the most eminent clerical heritage of all the St John's deans and chaplains. His grandfather, Frederick, had been Archbishop of Canterbury from 1896 to 1902 and his uncle, William, was archbishop from 1942 to 1944 and regarded as one of the greatest primates England ever had. Freddy followed them in the family tradition of Rugby School and Balliol College Oxford. He never matched them in prestige, but he eventually became a very capable archdeacon and later a suffragan bishop. His gift was a pastoral one, and he bestowed it with considerable effect during his time at St John's. He was a very gentlemanly and popular dean, who was also a happy one, save, significantly, for the loss of his 6-year-old son, Michael, during a tonsillitis operation in 1954. One of the most moving sermons ever delivered from the pulpit in St John's came from Bishop Hall in memory of the little boy and support of his father and mother.[1]

The new dean's induction service was held on 4 March 1953, followed by a reception for all those on the electoral roll. At the service, the governor, Sir Alexander Grantham, read a lesson, and only three nave rows were reserved. Temple was sometimes bemused by the ceremonial which went with St John's being the unofficial state cathedral. He recalled his first conversation with the governor's *aide-de-camp*, prior to the governor's attendance. The officer asked that two seats be set aside for His Excellency. Temple asked him why two. 'The cocked hat, dear boy, the cocked hat,' was the reply.

Dean Temple had harmonious relations with most of his lay council members, who could range from the distinguished to the irascible. His first council included academic Dr. E. Todd, senior civil servant and Cantonese expert Ronald Holmes, *taipan* John Marden, Baronet Sir John Kinloch, historian George Endacott, business man and Volunteers Commander Colonel Henry 'Dow' Dowbiggin, and our keen and opinionated giver and chronicler, A. S. 'Bunny' Abbott.

It is a testimony to the balming qualities of Freddy Temple's approach that Abbott could say, at the 1953 church meeting, of the dean's first year, that it had been 'the happiest of my thirty-two years at St John's Cathedral'. Strangely, for a man so formal and yet understandably from one with passionate convictions, he could sign letters to the dean 'Love, Bunny'.

Relations with Bishop Hall, or at least his more experimental side, were not always that easy. His earlier idea that the dean might be housed in the old Peak police station had not come to a vote, but in May 1953, the council declined to lend him $50,000 to extend Bishop's House as premises for Chung Chi College. It was incautious and inappropriate, they thought. Perhaps more meanly but with equivalent sense of propriety, they also declined to fund a book of Alaric Rose's talks. Somehow, the bishop did that himself.

Temple faced a pastoral challenge almost straightaway. Assistant Chaplain George She left for the United Kingdom for further studies, and a man as yet unique in St John's history withdrew from the scene. He was to return a year later but then as headmaster of Diocesan Boys' School. She was a practical and spiritual comprador, a cross-cultural bilingual, witty Eurasian at home with Westerners, which the cathedral had never had before. He was 'an intellectual a professional, inexhaustible, guileful if need be in a Cantonese way, affable and open in an English way', according to the dean.

In particular, he was a pastor to the Chinese and the returned Chinese. From this position, he had achieved a remarkable breakthrough. He had begun and sustained a 9 a.m. Sung Eucharist with a hearty breakfast fellowship afterward. It was, in its way, a family group. She was 'Uncle George'. In no sense was it sectional, yet the origins and early mainstay of what is now the cathedral's principal Sunday service were Chinese.

Chinese Anglicans who preferred to worship in the English liturgy of the cathedral created this service. They had been educated in Anglican schools, so they were comfortable with English forms, and they found the Chinese prayer book too difficult to understand. They were a social elite or potentially so. Christianity in this form was an entrance door into the upper reaches of the English language and its society. It is a satisfying irony that all the efforts of previous British clergy among the Western congregation to improve the position of the sacraments in the cathedral's worship were carried through, just about, by a Cantonese priest with Chinese communicants.

Dean Temple was a deep fan of this development. He was also deeply concerned. He understood She's importance in making English-speaking Chinese feel that St John's could be a spiritual home along with the expatriate British. She's departure might see that effort crumble. 'I feel confident that our good Chinese and resident friends will remain loyal,' he wrote.[2] I find myself quite as much at home at the 9 o'clock breakfast on a Sunday as anywhere else in the colony.' Temple was busy with practical steps to sustain what She had left. He visited the Chinese laity. He held meetings in their homes. His confidence was borne out. Ten years later, when the proportion of Chinese in St John's overall was closing on 40 per cent, Dean John Foster had a pastoral committee of Chinese advising him on the relationship of Chinese laity to cathedral.

The quiet chapel, a bricked-off conversion from the old baptistery and a little musty from underuse, is supposed to be called 'the George She Chapel', but nobody remembers that. Soon he will be beyond recall, which is how it is for most of us. If you seek a more fluid memorial to She, be present in the nave at 9 a.m. on Sunday, hear the choir and the people strike up the introit hymn, see the cross hoisted and the procession begin, and you will find it.

George She was replaced by Jimmy Froud, one of four full-time chaplains appointed during Dean Temple's tenure, who included Timothy Beaumont, John Foster and Ernest Fisher. Froud was another novelty at St John's, a young man of little formal education, an ex-serviceman and formerly secretary of the Hong Kong branch of Toc H, the rest and recreational society founded in the First World War for service personnel. Bishop Hall had taken Froud on as a lay assistant to the dean. He was made a deacon and appointed as a chaplain for two years on $2,000 per year, and free accommodation and board in the Church Guest House. He was made a priest in October 1955. He was exceptionally good with service personnel but rather too much for Colonel Dowbiggin. When the time came for the council to discuss his extension for two more years from 1956, he and 'Bunny' Abbott went on record with their opinion 'that he was not the type of man fitted to hold the post of chaplain to a cathedral'.

You can almost feel Temple's pain over this outburst of class distinction as he tries to palliate the situation. Yes, he acknowledged that Froud was not educated at the 'right' schools or colleges or very much at all theologically, but he had other talents. At home they were ordaining people like this 'these days'. Come 1958, he would go home for theological training. He would only be a chaplain till then. He would not be coming back. The extension was approved with one abstention.[3]

The bishop, having wind of this, wrote to the council pointedly: 'I wonder if anyone has brought more people to church in the cathedral than Mr. Froud.' There was, between the bishop and these councillors, a variance in attitude over several issues, including the place of women in the ministry and relations with the Chinese church. In 1957, the bishop's jubilee year, Abbott wrote a furious letter to the editor of the *Review* about him putting Deaconess Jane Hwang in charge of St Thomas's church.

The Froud incident was a stark demonstration of how defensive elements of British society, especially colonial society, struggled as hard as they could to make the 1950s life in the 1930s by other means. Abbott was preoccupied with tradition and precedent, yet was, in any normal light, a bookshop manager. Dowbiggin was a businessman who began as a 'Mr.', took rank from his years with the Volunteers and became clerk of the course in the Royal Hong Kong Jockey Club. 'Irascible and disturbingly outspoken', according to the Reverend Frank Roe, who joined as a chaplain in 1960, and obviously concerned with status, 'Dow' also had a certain size and courage to him. In internment, the Japanese beat him for refusing to *kowtow*. He refused to call Governor Sir Robert Black 'Your Excellency' because they had shared night soil duties in Stanley Camp. Roe remembers that, when instructing his driver to take him to St John's, he would say, 'Right, Wong! Number One Joss House!'

When Jimmy Froud did go home, the congregation presented him with $3,000 in cash and a small silver salver. The 9 a.m. fellowship gave him a camera and projector, which must have delighted him. He had asked the council if they could fly him home so that he could 'see a bit of Europe'. In 1960, he married Mary Saull at Great Malvern, and Freddy Temple, then Chaplain to the Archbishop of Canterbury, officiated. He never went back to parochial life but founded an extensive social service organisation in East London which he ran for the rest of his working days.[4]

In 1955, for the first time formally, the cathedral had three full-time clergy. Timothy Beaumont came out from England with his wife to be an assistant chaplain, and a flat was found for them in 33

McDonnell Road. He was made a deacon in October in the cathedral as Jimmy Froud was priested. Beaumont was the social antithesis of Froud. From an aristocratic and conservative political background, he went to Eton and Christ Church Oxford. He was ordained just before he went to Hong Kong, and priested there in 1956.

In 1957, the bishop decided that he was the man for the vacancy at Christ Church, Kowloon Tong. Jimmy Froud was specifically barred by the trustees from applying because he needed more parochial training 'at home'. After two constructive years there, Beaumont came into a fortune and responsibilities upon the death of his father, which took him back to England. They flew back on a Comet jetliner. In London, he funded and ran church reform magazines and a political weekly. He went into Liberal politics but found being a millionaire radical vicar too contradictory, so he resigned his orders. He was given a new title, Lord Beaumont of Whitely, and became spokesperson for the Green Party in the House of Lords. When his political career faded and his money had run away into radical causes, he resumed his orders and became Priest-in-Charge of St Phillip's and All Saints, Kew.

By Christmas 1957, John Foster had stepped into the breach as chaplain, and he was to stay at the cathedral until he retired as dean in 1973. He was 'gentle and dedicated', according to Rosemary Inglis, wife of former treasurer Desmond Inglis and stalwart of the Michaelmas Fair. ('As soon as one was over, you started preparing the next one.') She recalls how Foster postponed his leave to give spiritual support to a congregation member, herself a nurse, who was going through a particularly difficult pregnancy.

The last appointment under Temple was not an entirely happy one. Ernest Fisher was 25 years old. He was ordained as a deacon at Worcester Cathedral on 2 September 1958, and flew out to Hong Kong 'tourist class' on 4 October with the promise of a four-year contract, $400 a month with board and lodging and the use of a Vespa scooter. Unfortunately, the speedy ordination followed by total immersion into parochial life seven thousand miles away, which had worked for the sophisticated Beaumont and the spiritually fascinated Goulder, did not serve Fisher well. By April 1960, with the agreement of the bishop, he resigned because was unsuitable. It ended happily, though. Fisher got a teaching job at Diocesan Boys' School, and he could buy the Vespa if he wanted to. The council resolved that any successor must have been ordained at least two years.[5]

The honorary secretary's report for 1953[6] described the year as a period of progress following consolidation in 1951 and transition in 1952. It is a fair overview of what was feeling like a fresh start in a new if not always brave world. Congregations were increasing, helped, it was noted, by the memorial service for Queen Mary followed with a speedy poignancy by the coronation of Queen Elizabeth II. On Monday, 1 June 1953, from 7.30 a.m. to 7.30 p.m., there were continuous intercessions for the Queen and Commonwealth.

Numbers were sustained, particularly in the precious matter of Holy Communion. In 1952, there were 8,000 Communions, 2,000 up on the previous year. On Easter Day 1953, 500 took the sacraments. By 1955, there were 14,000 Communions. The 9 a.m. service regularly saw over 100 communicants. The Lady chapel became too cramped for the regular 50 to 70 at the 8 a.m. Holy Communion. Matins collections were averaging close to HK$1,200 on Sundays. Thirty-two more seats were put into the nave and 100 in the aisles. Twelve additional sidesmen were recruited. 'Bunny' Abbott donated an additional 600 copies of *Hymns Ancient and Modern*. The dean was far from complacent. He thought the situation should be even more crowded. 'It is only a tiny fraction of the English-speaking population,' he noted, ambitiously.

Numbers at evensong during this time had risen from near nothing to a hundred. It was mostly a male congregation again, strengthened by men from the armed forces. It had its own choir of ten. A Miss Crossley did evening teas afterwards for the service personnel. They were obviously substantial because, for a while, she made Hong Kong famous in the homes of soldiers and sailors around Britain.

An Evensong Fellowship which really rolled its sleeves up was formed out of the choir. The Reverend Frank Roe, who arrived as assistant chaplain to replace Fisher in 1960, describes it as 'assisting in coolie work' building St Simon's School, Castle Peak. Roe had spent three proving years as a curate at Hayling Island, England, doing excellent work among holidaymakers. He was part of the newer classless Church of England which was spilling into Hong Kong. He had left school at 14, joined the Royal Navy as a rating and later studied at Braistead College and Westcott House. He was 'a good mixer and talked naturally', the council were told. Roe was a popular chaplain who was cheerfully direct. Rosemary Inglis believes that he was 'sidelined' for his frankness. When he moved over as Chaplain to the Seamen's Mission, he resigned in a disagreement with Bishop Baker over not being tough enough over the club manager's alleged racism.

The Evensong Fellowship visited the children at the St Christopher's Orphanage, and they began a Friday night youth club in the cathedral hall which attracted four hundred members. The Hilton Hotel hosted the youth club ball with sausages and mashed potatoes, and a band and a bow tie was whisked up for even the poorest Chinese boy. Those still remaining from the fellowship hold a reunion in England every three years, so memorable was the need they met and so strong was the bond that worshipping and volunteering together created.

The choir, led by Donald Fraser, was over seventy strong in 1954. By 1956, the total number had risen to eighty choristers in two choirs. The 9 a.m. choir numbered now fifty with just nine Westerners. Unfortunately, Mr. Fraser chose to stage one of his numerous and somewhat fluorescent resignations. This proved one too many for even the patient Dean Temple, and it was accepted. Cecilia Cheung, who had studied in England under the patronage of the bishop and was later to be married to head sidesman David Kwok, was serving as 'deputy acting organist' on $400 per month. Now she stood in as acting organist and choir mistress until someone else was found. No one was found. She served on for twenty-five years.

In April 1955, construction of the new hall and lodge was approved. In its early stages, it was often just called the Sunday school building, because the urgent purpose of any new structure was to properly house the growing numbers in Sunday school. By 1956, there were three hundred children in the school taught by sixty volunteer teachers who came in on alternate weeks. Much of this activity was the work of Mrs. Temple, who had an exceptional skill as not just as a Sunday school teacher but as a 'superintendent', a title of deceptively Dickensian forbiddance.

Designed for the neglected north-west corner of the compound, the building was developed to also include a wing for clergy accommodation, which went under the title of Cathedral Lodge. As well as illegal hawkers, two banyan trees and undergrowth which was said to conceal a multitude of mild sins, the Bate Memorial had been removed from the site. This edifice was to the death of a gallant Captain of Marines who was killed in the storming of the walls of Canton in the Arrow War. It was a pillar on a stone base, topped by a globe, and photographs suggest that its ugliness was almost inspired.

With no artistic merit to mitigate against its disposal, it was disassembled when Garden Road was widened and Battery Path reconstructed into its present form in 1954. The marble inscription tablet was set in the outer wall of the north transept, perpetuating a message of doubtful political tact but the memory of a man who was a regular worshipper at the cathedral and who dedicated much of his time to helping out there when he was in Hong Kong.

The cost of the new hall was estimated at HK$300,000. A fundraising subcommittee was formed, which included Noel Croucher, who was about to make a major donation of stained glass and was entering into the most active period of his service to the cathedral. The strategy was to raise money from income, from loans against investments and then by appeal. There was a congregational contrast in approaches to making an appeal. The 9 a.m. congregation, principally Chinese, decided to make approaches in person among their own people. The Europeans at matins thought that a letter to theirs would do very well.

The ever-reliable Leigh and Orange were architects for the new hall. On the council, it was a civil servant, C. R. Holmes, who taught his colleagues some basic truths about tendering procedures, including being very wary of the lowest bid. Sui Kin and Co. proposed by Messrs. Black and Crozier were the lowest and got only eight votes. Croucher and Dowbiggin proposed Lam S. Woo and Co. They were awarded it because they were known to some council members and were supporters of the church. A room in the new building to commemorate Harold Smythe was proposed and approved, but an illuminated statue of St John in the south wall was not. Mrs. Temple laid the foundation stone. Five thousand dollars was spent on tables and chairs and $10,000 on furniture for the clergy apartment, of which Tim Beaumont and his wife would be the first occupants. One thousand dollars was earmarked for books to go into a space which was to become the Kenneth Tyson Library, finally a home for the cathedral library which had lived everywhere from the west porch to the former organ box in the south transept.

In the building, gas was used for cooking, and electricity for heating the water. Servants were intended to cook their own food on kerosene stoves.

Sir John Kinloch was worried that pedestrians might use the new gate opened from Garden Road leading down the side of the building as access to Battery Path. In fact, it proved too obscure or intimidating to develop that traffic. In any event, the cathedral, in return for having donated small slivers of land to the government for the widening of Garden Road, clawed back the public right of way through the compound which had been ceded in 1892.

The compound was crowded enough anyway and particularly congested on Sunday through the attempt to pour a quart of cars into a pint pot of parking spaces. A particular objection was that cars could not get to the west porch to pick up and drop off, a complaint handed down from the days of the sedan chair and still heard today in defence of people with disabilities and overprotected children. An idea surviving brightly from the colonial spirit was that a police officer should be placed on the Garden Road gate to stop the traffic for cathedral children. This was never was arranged, as promised, with the Transport Department.

St John's Review reported a great response to the appeal for new hall funds. In nine months, $400,000 had been raised, which included enough to cover the furnishings. The new hall was used for the first time on Sunday, 28 October 1958, charging $50 a day thereafter for lettings. The magazine, understandably perhaps, gave rather less coverage to the 'Double Ten' riots in Kowloon by Nationalist against Communist sympathisers in which fifty-nine were killed and five hundred injured. 'It is not for a church newspaper to pronounce but for all Christian citizens to be actively concerned', was its calm, ambiguous advice.

One smaller expansion which was less easily achieved was the extension of the Lady chapel, which was still then in the south transept. In 1957, Mr. Abbott donated a rhodium-plated bronze cross and candlesticks to the high altar to mark Bishop Hall's jubilee. It is worth pausing here to tot up 'Bunny' Abbott's contributions over the five years to that point. He also contributed towards crosses and candlesticks in the two chapels, paid for furnishing in the St Michael's chapel, put up the diocesan plaques around the chancel and shipped in six hundred copies of *Hymns Ancient and Modern*. Spectacular but now long gone was his gift of four angel-topped riddel posts for the high altar. These, and the back altar hanging they supported, achieved a curious resemblance to a Roman campaign tent and totally obscured the cross and central panels of Anne Bowdler's William Morris reredos, perhaps deliberately so. After the angels were made redundant, they were used in 1972, as resting places for choir microphones in one of the succession of amplification systems the cathedral has struggled with.

Fresh from the rhodium-plated cross, and along with Colonel Dowbiggin, Abbott pushed the chapel extension proposal to a vote in council in July 1956. They found themselves the only two in favour. Years later, in his retirement speech, then treasurer Harry Owen Hughes recalled that he was so set against spending funds which he saw no prospect of replacing that 'I set my head and even my heart against them'. This was one such occasion. The impasse was breached the following year by an anonymous donation of $27,000 for the very purpose. The project also included the enlargement of the vestry and the installation of full-length cupboards down the south transept walls for altar frontals. The extended Lady chapel was dedicated on 12 October 1958. The first few rows of seating were pews. The rest were chairs. It meant goodbye to a space which offered the only chance of accommodating a pipe organ again, but since one would cost 13,000 pounds, it was hope too remote for consideration.

The replacement of the stained glass windows was much closer to reality. All that fresh, self-propelling sunlight was once again to be slowed and shaded through beautifully crafted glass. In a move that may or may not have been calculated to annoy stockbroker Noel Croucher, who had been trying to offer a permanent one, his per-ceived nemesis, *taipan* George Marden, offered a temporary stained glass window for the east end. The idea was rejected by the council, ostensibly because they did not like the lacquers on offer. Eventually, Croucher's vision prevailed. In September 1956, a new east window was dedicated to all those who suffered and died in Hong Kong during the Japanese Occupation. The five lancets grouped under the *Agnus Dei* symbol show Christ on the cross outside the walls of Jerusalem with Mary and the disciple John standing at a neat and tidy distance each side, the sun of the Resurrection rising behind.

Joseph Edward Nuttgens designed this window and subsequently those which went into the transepts. He was born in 1892 in Aachen, worked out of a studio in Buckinghamshire and was described as the last exponent of the stained glass movement stemming from William Morris. Over seventy years he designed windows for churches in all continents, and the St John's commission was one of his largest. In 1930, on his way home to England, Dean Swann would have seen his work in the nave of Christ Church Cathedral, British Columbia.[7]

Dedicated in October 1958, the south transept window, featuring scenes from the life of Christ, was donated by Mrs. John Liddell and a group of former worshippers at Holy Trinity, Shanghai.[8] European worshippers had left that cathedral, but it was still being used 'under great difficulty', according to *St John's Review*. Mrs. Liddell, widely known as 'Mrs. John', was June, the wife of John Liddell of Liddell Brothers and Company, which was of Hong Kong with branches in Shanghai and Tientsin. This window carries a bounty of freemasonic symbolism. Freemasonry and Anglicanism maintained their mutual attraction, if no longer in Shanghai, then without remit in Hong Kong.

The north transept window was donated anonymously in 1957 and dedicated on Whitsunday 1959, to all who lost their lives at sea. In the centre, a refreshingly windblown Christ stills a gusty storm. On each side are traditional and then contemporary, slightly self-conscious, seafaring images. Croucher is widely thought to have been the donor. The governor and the commodore read the lessons at the ceremony, which would have pleased him, but the design attracted criticism, which would not.

The north window came to preside over the most poignant chapel ever created in St John's. As early as 1950, Lieutenant Colonel A. W. Mann, commanding officer of the 1st Battalion of the Middlesex Regiment, which lost 105 men, indeed was obliterated, in the Japanese invasion in 1941, proposed a memorial chapel to the war dead. It began with a display of wartime memorabilia on tables, and ultimately, in April 1955, a chapel was established. It was rededicated in 1956 as the Chapel of St Michael and All Angels. This dedication of a war memorial chapel to the soldiering archangel was quite a common one in English churches, but it was also done to mark the death of Dean Temple's 6-year-old son, Michael, which was as ironic as it was sad.

Before going to Hong Kong, Freddy Temple had been Vicar of St Agnes, Rusholme, in Manchester. One of the reasons he took the St John's post was a doctor's recommendation that Michael needed warmer, cleaner air to combat the bronchitis which the dirty, damp atmosphere of South Lancashire was inflicting on him. The boy was responding well to his new surroundings. What no one could foresee was that his heart would succumb to the anaesthetic in a straight-forward tonsillitis operation. Temple's faith and commitment carried him through, but he did not always hide the pain. Before he went on leave in February 1957, he wrote a 'Profit and Loss' account for the previous four years. 'I will not call them happy,' he said. 'Far too much of us left this world with Michael.'[9]

The chapel was moved to the east of the south transept in 1968, when the chancel was rearranged and the Lady chapel moved to the east end. The wooden reredos made by Lieutenant R. Wood RN in the Sham Shui Po Prison Camp from box lids and a brass crucifix off a rubbish heap and inscribed with the prayer of St Richard of Chichester is mounted on the chapel screen wall. It was presented by the Reverend Charles Strong RN MBE, who had been chaplain in the camp. Even today, flowers under the reredos are always placed in an old jam jar, as they had been in the camp.

The colours of the British and colonial armed forces are laid up in this chapel. It is a commentary on the ways of post-colonial Hong Kong that there was neither pressure nor inclination to remove these direct emblems of the colonial power's previous military presence. Indeed, flags recalling the colonial power's civil authority have actually been added since. The flags include the Union Flag, the original colours of the Hong Kong Volunteer Defence Corps, which were dug up from their wartime hiding place during construction of the US consulate in 1958, and their replacement colours.

The colours of the Royal Military Police are there along with those of 28 Squadron of the RAF from Shek Kong, laid up in 1955, and the White Ensign of the Hong Kong Naval Reserve, laid up in 1967. There is also the plaque of HMS *Cornflower* which had been the Reserve training ship but was brought back into service in 1940 and sunk in Aberdeen Harbour in 1941. On 1 July 2011, the flag of the former Crown Colony of Hong Kong and the flag of the previously Royal Hong Kong Police Force were laid up in an early morning service. Everything suggests that this should be the last of these ceremonies, but such is the utility and flexibility of the cathedral in matters of remembrance that the possibility of suitable bodies that carry banners seeking a similar rest for them cannot be ruled out.

After much discussion back in the 1950s, illuminated display cases were decided for the Books of Remembrance. They line the south wall, and a page is turned in each book every day. Dean Alaric Rose put together a record of all the tablets which had been removed from the church walls, and that book lies there too.

The linen fold design wooden altar was carved by local artisans, and the striking teak and bronze altar crucifix and candlesticks were donated by the munificent Mr. Abbott along with Mrs. Todd and Mrs. Hart. The credence table came from Butterfield and Swire, in memory of Harold Swabey. The fald stool next to it is the sole survivor of the pieces bearing the original Gilbert Scott design motif and the post-war work was copied from from it. All this internal beautification could have been rendered close to naught in the interests of electricity consumption and economy. It was only with some difficulty that Professor Parsons persuaded the other council members not to install strip lighting.

The outsides of the cathedral were painted in April 1958, the first time since 1951. Two shades of grey were applied. A yellow-coloured tower was something that council resolved not to have again. As part of a renovation scheme, the tower was painted yellow again in 2009.

The church's activities were not of course all about embellishment. Congregation members volunteered their services in beauty and in scruff. There were four ladies on the council in 1957: Mrs. V. G. T. Davis, Miss B. M. Kotewall, Mrs. A. D. Scholes and Mrs. May Ho. Frank Wheeler was rated a great head server, reverent, orderly but not fussy. David Kwok continued as head sidesman—a job for life in a cathedral—and Major Doggett looked after the evensong sidesmen. Mrs. Hart was at the Sunday school. The scoutmaster was John Duthie. Up in the tower loft, Mr. Green and his team rang the bells. On the staff, Mr. Kwan continued as head verger, and Mrs. Remedios, the dean's secretary, had become indefatigable and indispensable.

Mrs. Swabey and Mrs. Washer, suitably named, took care of the robes. Mrs. Willcocks did the silver. Mrs. Sainsbury helped with Cecilia Cheung's choir practices. Cecilia, born in Hong Kong, a graduate of the Royal School of Church Music for which Bishop Hall had found her a scholarship, had come back to Hong Kong in 1951. She now ran a Eucharist and a matins choir. Because the organ console was now in the loft above the north vestry, she could neither hear the congregation nor see the choir at the east end. She had taken to putting a deputy at the console and conducting from the chancel. This she had been ticked off for doing as too theatrical. Her solution, she recalls, was to put ten choristers in her line of sight on the south side of the chancel. The effect was a new antiphony to the singing. It was lost after the 1968 chancel rearrangement had the entire choir facing the people. It was being sought again in new arrangements for the chancel put in place in 2011.

If the cathedral was seeing progress from 1953, it was not made without money. That year saw a $1,500 surplus in income over outgoings. Offerings had increased to $6,700. St John's could give away $5,000 to the St James' Club, $500 to the RAF Benevolent Fund,

$400 to the British Legion, $400 to the Sailors and Soldiers Home and $400 to the British and Foreign Bible Society.[10] By 1955, the overall surplus had become $7,400. Investments of $41,000 had become $91,000. The endowment fund stood at $386,000. Because John Marden and Noel Croucher were on the council keeping often-contesting eyes on the funds, this is not surprising. For a while, Croucher ran an anonymous one-man investment operation for the cathedral under the melodramatic acronym 'Z'.

At the March 1957 annual meeting, though, expenditure was reported as increasing and income was levelling off. Goodwill offerings were dropping among newcomers. This was put down to a new, less grateful generation. Still, at the end of the decade in the October 1960 council meeting, there is a record $19,000 surplus in the bank balance, which is looked on as low but cheerfully mitigated by $50,000 cash on fixed deposit.

The Michaelmas Fair, held on the parade ground, developed as a considerable force in the economics of the cathedral over this period. A working party to increase its impact had been started under Joan Temple. In 1953, the fair raised $23,000, of which $15,000 went to clergy salaries. In 1958, Lady Grantham, the governor's wife, opened it. The Royal Air Force promised to avoid holding a competing air display that day. Hopes were high. There was a target of $32,000 to help balance the budget. By 1960, it had gone beyond that and raised $53,000. Council member Mr. Fripp complained that it had become too commercial and was losing its character. Indeed, it should be discontinued. The Cathedral Council, obviously uncomfortable over the noise the golden goose was making but unwilling to throttle it, said that the fair should be reduced in scale to preserve its parish character. There is no evidence that this was done, and the fair remained a force in the working budget for over a decade to come.[11]

Another more mammon-like but thoroughly familiar Hong Kong source of income was the On Lee property in Mount Davis Road, bought with the funds bequeathed on the death of Lady Chater. The original idea behind the purchase was to provide clergy quarters. It never caught on. With occasional and brief exceptions, a succession of deans has shied away from moving in there. Though Bishop's House and grounds where they lived for $1,000 per month rent were ideal in many ways, there was a sense of insecurity about relying on the diocese to house the dean in an area that could be wanted any time. The deans were also a cause of overcrowding. In 1958, the bishop complained that Freddy Temple's servant, Ah Kai, and his family of eight made such a racket out the back that he could not work. Yet they could not steel themselves to Pok Fu Lam. It was regarded a simply too far out. Not everyone has a motor car, observed Dean Foster in 1968.

On Lee could be put to more fruitful purposes than housing clergy. By 1961, the Cathedral Council saw clear advantages to redevelopment and replacing the old structure with a block of flats. The plan was for fifteen flats and a penthouse in three low-rise units. Each should have servants' quarters capable of housing children, was the thinking at a time which did not foresee imported foreign domestic workers. The development cost was put at $1.4 million. A bank loan for it would take far too long to pay off, so it was resolved to sell some investments and release money on deposit. Over this development, Noel Croucher and John Marden held opposing views.

Croucher believed the design would reduce yield and saleability. He foresaw a glut in the large luxury flat market and advocated one taller block of twenty flats over 25 per cent of the area. Marden said that demand from firms for expatriate flats that size would increase. The council was worried about the government premium charge which a tall building would attract. They went with the Marden view. They attempted to mollify Croucher, crediting him with 'deep thinking' and 'thorough investigation' and saying that they were 'fortunate to have him'. That last remark has about it the sense that he might care to go at any time. It probably fuelled his apparently prolonged unease that he was not completely accepted in Hong Kong society.[12]

In May 1963, when rents were dropping, Croucher weighed in again, urging the sale of some units. This was thought to be difficult because, along with deans, the area was not popular with the Chinese. Europeans in those days rarely bought. Croucher's advice was again sidelined in favour of five- to seven-year leases.

Foreseeing the path of a congregation was no easier than predicting one for assets. At the 1959 Annual Church Meeting, Dean Temple stated how he saw the future of St John's as a worshipping community. Apart from the arrival of Tagalog with the Filipina domestic workers, and Mandarin with political change, neither of which he could foresee, his vision became the most optimistic identity of the cathedral for the following fifty years.

> We have amongst the Anglican churches the largest Chinese congregation. And it is right that that should be so and that there

should be no national or racial division in any way between the churches beyond one of language. There are some 12 different nationalities that worship in the cathedral every Sunday. The life and vitality of this English worshipping community should ever be increased.

The cathedral's other identity was that of a church of colonial ceremonial, and this did not diminish markedly till the colony's end. Memorial services were the hallmark of St John's, not least because they memorialised those of the great and the good who were precious to the full spread of nationalities in the community. Services were held for Gustav V of Sweden in November 1950, and Haakon VII of Norway in 1957. President Dwight Eisenhower was remembered in March 1969. Winston Churchill was obviously mourned and, less predictably perhaps, the Duke of Windsor, for whom a modified version of the Churchill service was used. The cathedral offered itself as a focus of grief after communal losses. In August 1971, a service was held to remember those killed by Typhoon Rose, and another in June 1972 for those lost in the torrential rains.

Ceremonial occasions were inevitably complemented by moments of mild amusement behind the formality. Rev. Frank Roe recalls that, minutes before the arrival of Princess Alexandra, the Queen's cousin, for matins, he was bent down under the high altar table where ashes are temporarily stored, in an urgent search for an urn needed for burial. He bobbed back up suddenly as head server Frank Wheeler was lighting the altar candles. Wheeler fainted and had to be carried, shoulders and feet, into the vestry, where Bishop Hall revived him, before the bishop scuttled round to the west door to greet the princess.

Council member Brian Hart had a warm and courtly moment with Princess Margaret, sister of the Queen, at another matins, in March 1966. It was a warm day and Her Royal Highness slid off her shoes. Then she lost them under the pew. Hart, sitting behind her, searched around down there and handed them back to the barefoot princess. 'She thanked me most graciously,' he remembers, loyally.

Freddy Temple had two stately visitors in what was to prove his last year in office. Prince Philip, Duke of Edinburgh, attended matins on Mothering Sunday 1959, at the altered time of 10.30 a.m. Extra seats were put in, but none was reserved. Frank Roe recalls that, on these visitations by VIPs, the church was filling up for the matins before the 9 a.m. Eucharist had barely finished.

The Archbishop of Canterbury arrived a month later, the very first time an English primate had ever visited Hong Kong. It was a semi-state affair. The dean and wife were woken early by a call from the governor's *aide-de-camp*. Harry Owen Hughes and Dr. Fok, as senior laypeople, accompanied them over to Kowloon where they were joined at Kai Tak Airport by the acting colonial secretary. Bishop and Mrs. Hall were already there, and mixing pomp perfectly with parsimony went off with Archbishop Fisher in a government car to eat at their 'farm' in Sha Tin.

On 5 April, the archbishop celebrated a diocesan communion in the cathedral and then preached at matins. Harry Owen-Hughes, as a cathedral trustee, arranged a tea reception and, as its president, hosted the affair at the Hong Kong Cricket Club. Sandwiches were from Dairy Farm at $1.50 a head, catering for two to three thousand people. This visit spelt the end of Freddy Temple's time in Hong Kong. Archbishop Fisher asked him to become his senior chaplain at Lambeth. He had resisted the proposal two years before, but now he complied. For his farewell, a pre-evensong presentation was made in the old hall, presided over by the bishop. The governor, Sir Robert Black, praised Temple on behalf of the whole colony, and Owen-Hughes did so, wittily, for the whole council. Sir Robert and Lady Black were regular attenders at St John's, but this was the last time that a governor in his official capacity felt disposed to bid farewell to a dean.[13]

Before he went, Temple wrote in *St John's Review* of what had pleased him about his tenure. The gift of a new peal of bells from the Hong Kong and Shanghai Bank had been dedicated for the coronation in 1953, and of the two surviving bells from 1870, one had gone to the St James' Settlement and the other to St Mary's, Causeway Bay. The year following, what Temple called the 'chill and despair' curtains behind which the once tiny evensong congregation huddled, could be taken away.

He had been delighted by the gathering of South-east Asian bishops in Hong Kong in 1955, who met in the old hall and which had included the return of Harry Baines as Bishop of Singapore. 'A Little Lambeth of East Asia', is how Temple described it. Brother Michael Fisher of the Franciscans, who had visited to investigate the prospects of a 'house' in Hong Kong, had made a great impact with his preaching, especially in St John's at Bishop Hall's 1957 jubilee celebrations. Temple was also impressed by Billy Graham's 'superb oratory, simplicity and unimpeachable biblical orthodoxy' when the evangelist came to Hong Kong in 1956. 'It is not the type of preaching which is popular in the Anglican church but have we become far too restrained ... forgotten direct evangelism?' he wrote in the *Review*.

Funds were raised throughout dioceses for Hall's silver jubilee as bishop. His intention was for them to be dedicated to the improvement of one particular church, but the Chinese churches did not much care for being so specific. The idea was broadened to a fund for general extensions, particular churches earmarked. The US Church gave to it US$50,000 which had originally been intended for China.

The dean clearly felt affection for former trustee and treasurer O. W. 'Ozzie' Skinner and his wife, Hazel, who were given a warm send-off 'home' in 1957. He had gratitude for the opinionated but passionately sincere A. S. Abbott for having given the altar cross and sticks and the crests of all the English cathedrals, arranged round the chancel in a frieze which, if you notice them, leave the momentary impression of a sports club lounge. 'Bunny' Abbott also left St John's that year. It was a quiet exit to a retirement in South Africa which obviously did not suit him. He returned to Hong Kong within the year and died in Tai Po in 1961. There is no reference to him having been back in the cathedral. Perhaps he could not cope with the changes wrought by Freddy Temple's successor.

Barry Till, Dean of Jesus College Cambridge and probably the most theologically charged of St John's deans, was installed at matins on 15 May 1960. He came with his wife, Shirley, and their two boys. He was, by too many removes to concern us, a cousin of the Queen. He had two men to assist him. The senior chaplain was John Foster, who was given the title of 'precentor', which made him the clergyman in charge of liturgy and worship. This office did not catch on at St John's. Till himself introduced such sweeping liturgical changes that Foster cannot have had much chance to lead. Foster did not pass on the office when he became dean although it was revived briefly for Stephen Sidebotham.

Till, interestingly, did much too to help establish the Church in the Philippines, but his greatest impact and his legacy at St John's was over liturgy and worship. The 1960s arrived at the cathedral with Barrie Till, bang on time. Dean Till introduced the ideas of the Church of England's Liturgical Commission by straightaway expressing his dislike of the font being at the north door and not the west and by rewriting the baptism service, which was now to be celebrated as part of matins. Bishop Hall may have been taken unawares. 'See how it wears,' he said, giving an uneasy nod to the change.

By May 1962, the new baptism service seems to have been accepted.[14] Now came the need to move the font to the west door. The council, cautious over the consequences of having this stone monolith in the doorway, wanted some form of 'mock-up' demonstration before the font was moved from the north transept. The move was never made. This was a pity, because Till had his keen artistic eye on the west door. A mosaic was created there in 1964, designed by Julia Baron, a local artist noted for this form. It is an octagon of Italian tiles to reflect the early baptisteries of Florence and Rome and was laid down by a local artisan, Luk Ah Yee. It incorporates symbols of the Trinity and a local white-bellied sea eagle as the symbol of St John. The cross at the centre of the octagon was copied from an approximately thirteenth-century one discovered in China, now at the University of Hong Kong's Fung Ping Shan Museum. Until recently, it was described as 'Nestorian', but historians regard this as a pejorative misnomer and now prefer to describe Yuan dynasty Christians as East Syrian or Church of the East.

The mosaic was dedicated to the memory of Dr. Arthur Woo. There was now the need of a font. Subsequently, Mrs. Arthur Woo, to celebrate her seventieth birthday in 1971, donated one. Designed by Eric Faber, a consulting engineer of many years in Shanghai and Hong Kong, it is designed around four Celtic crosses with a removable silver bowl, and it is on wheels. It is kept at the west door, where it holds holy water and is used for larger initiation ceremonies presided over by the bishop. For parish baptisms on a Sunday, it is often wheeled to the chancel steps.[15]

Till was struck by the disappointingly small impact that Lenten Sundays and Easter seemed to have on his flock in 1961. He announced liturgical changes for 1962 which he said were '... not going to be High Church. It's a silly label ... We should be past that.' Rather, they were special acts of worship to increase the drama.[16] He wanted to get away from the eighteenth-century form of matins, so he altered it. The litany was now sung, there were penitential psalms instead of canticles, and there were special antiphons at sung Communion. An antiphon or psalm replaced the gradual hymn, and a hymn was inserted between the sermon and the creed. *St John's Review* carried the intercessions rota for the month in tear-out pages for personal use. Till described the effect he was seeking as 'a mixture of Roman Catholic and Orthodox traditions and the "magic lantern" of the gospel hall'. You can see traditionalists wincing then and now. Not all of what he introduced survived, but a powerful body of it has.

In April 1962, he expanded the Easter liturgy, 'along the lines the Church has been observing for 1500 years'. He introduced the Vigil Mass and the striping of the altar on Maundy Thursday. He began the Easter Eve Eucharist with the lighting of the fire and the restatement of baptismal vows. *St John's Review* carried the additions to the services, set out in fourteen double-page spreads, the procedure on the right and commentary on it to the left. Till had a passion to explain. You can hear the commitment beating.[17]

Most strikingly and probably irrevocably, Dean Till moved the high altar and celebrated the 8 a.m. and 9 a.m. Eucharist facing the people. The permanent relocation of the altar from the east end to the top of the chancel steps was not achieved until 1968. However, Till proposed the concept to the council and it began it on a shuttling basis in April 1961. It was moved down for the two Communion services and back to the east afterwards. In November, the Cathedral Council discussed the new arrangement and rather liked it.[18] Mindful of the congregation, they asked, through a *Review* article, if anyone would like to revert to the old east-end arrangement for a month to at least think about it. By January 1962, there were only six responses to the piece wanting the east-facing celebration back, so the council declared the change permanent.

Even though the physical arrangement appeared transitory, some consequences were not. Two rows of choir stalls which had stood at the very western end of the chancel were now in the way and were moved to the back of the church on each side of the west door where they stand, strangely congruous and quite usefully, to this day. One other piece of staging introduced by the dean and with us still is the reading of the Gospel from the nave. Another, less frequent, one is placing the surviving seat of the old throne dedicated to Bishop Alford at the top of the chancel steps for installations, ordinations and confirmations, given that the bishop's throne proper defies leverage and is all but invisible to the congregation.

Barry Till's first year saw remarkable progress.[19] There was an increase in attendance, the biggest being at the 9 a.m. Eucharist, and an advance in finances. The balance sheet showed an increase of $350,000, which was mostly profit for the judicious sales of investments rather than a quantum leap in Goodwill Offerings. That profit allowed for greater giving, in particular to the Chinese Church. Till was delighted. St John's had given away 7 per cent of its income. Now it could give away 15 per cent.

A local initiative with which Dean Till was deeply concerned was the bringing together of the Chinese- and English-speaking Anglican churches. This was the last big colonial and incipiently segregationist hurdle to be leaped. A six-member working party, of which Till was chair up to his departure in November 1963, did not quite make it. By 1949, the diocesan bishop was still both a bishop of the 'Holy Catholic Church in China', a missionary legacy which included with its bounds the Chinese-language churches in Hong Kong, and 'Bishop of Victoria', who represented English-language Anglicanism. After the Communist victory in 1949, in order that the Church in southern China might not be compromised by colonial associations, Hong Kong's offer to withdraw in 1951 was accepted. The diocese was split into South China and Hong Kong and Macau. St John's became the cathedral of a rump.

The diocese came under the direction of the Archbishop of Canterbury, but this was anomalous. It was later placed under the oversight of the Council of Churches of South-east Asia, which included Episcopal Church in the United States. They had 'guardianship of the canons and constitution of the diocese'. Within the diocese was the Diocesan Synod of the Chinese Churches, which was what was left of the Diocese of South China and the Diocesan Conference of English-speaking Churches. Till's group was striving to amalgamate the three English parishes with the seventeen Chinese parishes. What had existed over the wider canvas of South China now survived on a postage stamp in Hong Kong. The only common point of governance between them was the bishop, and this in itself was a source of concern.

In January 1956, the Diocesan Conference meeting had reported discussion on the bishopric with the Chinese Synod. Financially, Bishop Hall was managing by his personal preference for living in Sha Tin and letting out Bishop's House, much of it to the cathedral for the dean. The Chinese Synod might not make the expected provision for a future expatriate bishop who chose not to live on a farm, and he was their right of election. An endowment fund was needed, they said, but that meant that most of the charge for it would fall to the cathedral. The cathedral disliked this as quite beyond its remit, and the matter was deferred, permanently.

In 1964, after Till had gone, the amalgamation discussion was sidelined too on the grounds that 'conduct of affairs was widely different'. The obstacle was presented as a pragmatic, financial one. The English churches had unusual expenses, including the provision of expatriate clergy, who were costly. Ironically, an increase in giving to the Chinese Synod, which had so delighted Till, was used in argument against amalgamation. How could that be maintained, along with compulsory dues, to the united diocese?

No dean made such an impression in so brief a period. Barry Till put faraway St John's in the vanguard of English liturgical reform, almost as far to the fore as it was in the ordination of women. It is remarkable that one of the most distant colonial cathedrals, with a predictably conservative pattern of behaviour when left to itself, should become associated with two radical changes when called upon, without demur or apparent stress. Of the introduction of the west-facing altar, the only criticism that Brian Hart can recall of it is was a characteristic English bashfulness over ritual: 'Why bother?'

As bright and inspiring as his presence had been, Till's departure was shaded and sad. In essence, his marriage collapsed. Shirley Till, a creative, hard-working woman with a feeling for innovation, worked hard on many projects, including the Michaelmas Fair and the St James' Settlement. A taste of Mrs. Till's approach was the 'Not So Ideal' stall she organised with cathedral members at the Ideal Home Exhibition to raise funds for the settlement. She re-created a makeshift squatter home for six. It grabbed headlines.[20] She became a founder of the CLARES, the Care Love Action Response Effort Service, in October 1962. By 1963, the CLARES, a re-formation of the Women's Guild, was providing the altar guild, making visits to the Sandy Bay Children's Home, sewing mattress covers for the St Christopher's babies, fundraising for St Simon's, Castle Peak and packing supplies for distribution by the Red Cross.

In the meantime, Mrs. Till had a relationship with another man. Fortunately, this did not grab headlines. She left Hong Kong, prematurely, in January 1963. The dean followed on leave later in the year, with the evident intention of returning with a patched-up marriage for his second contract. Infidelity within clergy marriages was not a part of the 1960s that St John's was ready for, it seemed. Bishop R. O. Hall wrote a letter to Barry Till, telling him not to return. This was plainly announced to the parish. A Board of Patronage rapidly appointed John Foster as dean, on a salary of $2,250 and an entertainment allowance of $750.

Till wrote a letter to A. T. Clarke, the honorary secretary to the council, expressing his dismay at his dismissal and unpleasant things that had been said in Hong Kong. Trevor Clark, described by Marjorie Bray as 'deep' and Rosemary Inglis as 'very clever', found himself in a rare but painful position that volunteer council members can suffer. He communicated sympathetically with Till. He must have navigated degrees of hostility towards the man's wife, of which no record remains.[21]

Till disputed his position no further. He had no job and he was hard up. The bishop told the council he hoped they could help out. They made him an *ex gratia* payment of $15,000. In the end, he received $20,000 and the anonymous gift of a car. The Tills ultimately divorced. He did not re-enter the parochial ministry. He put his strong aesthetic sense to great work as principal of Morley College for Adult Education in London, which specialises in courses in music, the visual arts and drama.

Barry Till remained well enough disposed to St John's to help find Stephen Sidebotham in England as their new 'third man'. The Tills remained together for long enough to have the Sidebothams for tea. He was in a curacy in Southampton. Till reported that he spoke with intelligence and a good sense of humour. His wife was 'very sensible'.[22] The bishop wanted somebody 'with better theology', but Sidebotham had other prospects and the Church Council did not want to dally.[23] Freddy Temple met him and approved, and a vigorous young man who was to be at St John's disposal for thirty-five years was taken on board.

In an attempt to maintain three men in its ministry and achieve a fourth, John Foster's incumbency saw a busy traffic of clergy moving through St John's. In 1962, Reverend Theodore 'Tad' Evans from the US Episcopalian Church had been seconded to St John's. He is remembered as being tall, handsome, great fun and good with young people.

In June 2011, Evans recalled a moment of his time at St John's.

> One of the most vivid memories I have … is that of my ordination to Priesthood. It was on the Sunday after Easter … on a steamy evening. In order to be there, I had to rise from a hospital bed where I was being prepared for major surgery on my lower back that week. In the ancient tradition when I knelt to have Bishop

> R.O. Hall lay his hands on my head, the several other priests present gathered around to add their hands. The sheer weight of all those extremities pressing down on my rather frail spine was both agonizing and, at the same time, strangely exhilarating.

He recalls the service as 'quite long as it was conducted both in Cantonese and English' and that Joyce Bennett, who was later to become the first woman ordained in the Anglican Church, was made a deacon at that same service.

His time was brief. He moved on to become Chaplain to the US embassy in Saigon in 1963 and ultimately a priest to the US military in Vietnam, where he ministered with distinction. As Rector of Stockbridge, Massachusetts, he was invited to preach the sermon in the National Cathedral Washington, DC, on Sunday, 14 November 1983, the day after the unveiling of the Vietnam Veterans Memorial in Constitution Gardens.

Foster, Roe and Sidebotham were joined in part by Reverend John Yates, who was, in fact, a diocesan appointment, shared with the cathedral and, as such, had the use of a Morris Minor Traveller. This, along with Stephen Sidebotham's second-hand Hillman, made them a two-car team. Till once responded to a letter criticising clergy using cars when so many Roman priests did not. He pointed out that the Roman Catholics placed less emphasis on visiting. St John's had three clergy to cover the island; they had 322 overall. Scooters were not an option. One could end up as a drowned rat. Buses might treble the time taken to make a visit.[24]

Office accommodation was now equally stretched, particularly since space had to be found for a bookshop called Challenge. The dean's office was elevated to a cockloft, constructed for $20,000 in the roof space of the old hall by its front door. It was a shoddy and palpably temporary measure which took on a semi-permanence, partly out of self-effacement on the part of deans and partly out of its appeal to honorary treasurers as an admirably economical use of space inside a structure which was remarkably wasteful of it.

John Yates, like Evans, acted as deputy to Michael Goulder, who had returned to Hong Kong at R. O. Hall's insistence, as principal of Union Theological College, a by-now misnamed and underpowered pre-war school which was shortly incorporated into Chung Chi College. Goulder described Yates as '... relaxed, fat and somewhat larger than life'[25] (see *Five Stones and a Sling: Memoir of a Biblical Scholar*), who infuriated the dean with his laid-back attitude. To Goulder, John

Foster was serious yet a *bon viveur*, a delightful preacher, a lover of books and a good manager of the cathedral bookshop.

Foster's seriousness took him into a lot of hard work which lay beyond the cathedral precincts and, in a way, he took the cathedral with him. He sat on an exhausting spread of committees, as a member and an officeholder, which were involved in the promotion of social welfare and reform in the wider community. He was involved in coop-eration with government and even setting a pace for it over social pro-grammes in a decade when the colonial administration realised that social control could only be kept through increased social welfare.

When Frank Roe arrived as assistant chaplain, Foster had so many commitments that he handed some, including the Discharged Prisoners' Aid Society, to Roe. Even before he became dean, he was on the executive of the Council of Social Service, of which he was to become chairman in 1967. He was a founder of Alcoholics Anonymous in Hong Kong, and he set up the first employment exchange. He became vice chairman of the Kowloon Christian Council, chairman of the Church Development Board and a new ecumenical library.

Barry Till picked up on what Dean Swann had perceived of his flock fourteen years before. In an address to the Victoria Diocesan Association in October 1963, which was to be his last as dean, he told them, 'What really warms my heart … is when I see our Cathedral or Church people are working for causes which may not be directly con-nected to the Church at all but which none the less are just as surely doing the work God wants done in Hong Kong.'[26]

The new dean came to spearhead this inclination. Foster appreci-ated ministry that went beyond parish boundaries. John Tyrell, a young Royal Navy chaplain who was to come into his service as an assistant chaplain in 1972, had a flair for working with children, which he took into the community, and Foster enjoyed this. Welfare organisations with no apparent religious connection were planned and brought into being within the bounds of St John's. By 1971, the dean had become concerned by the number of marriages he saw in trouble. He felt that the brief but generous two- to three-year expatriate contracts enjoyed by Western executives led to a lack of commitment, shallowness and instability which took their toll on marriages.

Dean Foster met Patricia Nicholl, who had recently arrived from England, where she had spent ten years with the Marriage Guidance Council. With the help of others, the two of them set up the Hong Kong Marriage Guidance Council in 1973. They only had the vaguest idea of what they were starting. Soon, such was the demand for the service from local Chinese too, that available time and space was rapidly filled. This bringing into being within the cathedral, this hosting and sponsoring role of wider initiatives, was to presage the current outreach ministries, including St John's own counselling service. It became a late-twentieth-century missionary model for a church so central and iconic in Hong Kong yet in such a minority in its faith.

The cathedral also hosted an event with impact far beyond its parochial concerns on an issue with which it will forever be associated. On Advent Sunday, 1971, in the cathedral, the Reverend Jane Hwang and the Reverend Joyce Bennett were ordained priests by Bishop Gilbert Baker. What was an issue of catholic importance and turned out to be a bone of contention among some in England was taken rather as a matter of course in Hong Kong. The synodical vote in favour had been overwhelming, because the issue had been discussed to exhaustion for over thirty years. The bishops of south-east Asia who were its guardians consented, and the usually cautious Bishop Baker went ahead.

The *South China Morning Post* tried to stir up a correspondence with an editorial and, apparently, not one letter was received. Indifference here might have been mistaken for calm. Just how far ahead of the curve the Diocese of Hong Kong and Macau was, though, is shown by the Church of England's refusal to accept the women as priests when they visited England. In 1982, when Joyce Bennett went to look after the Chinese congregation at St. Martin-in-the-Fields, the Bishop of London forbade her to act as a priest. In the Hong Kong Diocese in general and the cathedral in particular, women were being taken on board as paid or unpaid clergy well in advance of elsewhere. In busy, disrespectful Hong Kong, some traditions—or prejudices—could not maintain their hold.[27]

A ministry effort as perpetual as it was difficult to uphold was revived at the cathedral in 1969. In February, the dean initiated home fellowships. These were discussion groups of no more than twelve, to be located in different areas of the parish, involving no clergy. The aim was deeper involvement, a better understanding of one's own faith and the responsibility of the Christian in the community. They were not sustained. For the middle classes in Hong Kong, a sense of neighbourhood was too weak. For expatriates particularly, society was geographically fluid. If a sense of bonding was hard to achieve in the purposeful setting of a cathedral, how much harder it was in a block of flats.

In some ways, the cathedral's relationship with its own diocese, of which it was ostensibly the mother church, was more distant. In a May 1968 visitation by Bishop Gilbert Baker, who had succeeded Hall on his retirement in 1966, the main observations had been on the slimness of the relationship. Baker believed that St John's should have more of a diocesan focus. There should be more trust between the Chinese-speaking and English-speaking churches, of which the cathedral was obviously the leading force. St John's was regarded as one of the obstacles to the union of the two. It should increase its contributions to the diocese and the bishop's office, said Baker. This he believed should take the form of responsibilities for specific projects.[28]

In a council meeting of October 1966, Li Fook Hing, who was variously cathedral treasurer and treasurer of the Diocesan Finance Committee, had already stated that the council should support Bishop Baker, then new to office, if he wanted to see a closer tie-in between diocesan conference and synod. This was not to happen until 1975, but by March 1969, on giving at least, the cathedral made moves: $20,000 was given as part of $100,000 promised over five years to the rebuilding of a Chinese church, St Matthew's, Hollywood Road, including an elderly care centre and a kindergarten. This was the exercise in specifics that the bishop had in mind. Ten thousand dollars also went to the Diocesan Finance Committee to support diocesan expansion, and $45,000 went to the St James' Settlement. Toys and food were sent there at Christmas, as well as donations from the Harvest Festival.

The relationship between the cathedral and the settlement has always been likened to that of younger brother James to older brother John. A memoir by Robin Hutcheon, executive committee member from 1973 to 1986, entitled 'From the Very Beginning', described it as that of the 'poor, sponsored orphan of the well-to-do congregation', and in an area of pimps, prostitutes and poverty little visited by its members. Bishop R. O. Hall, its virtual founder, said of the effort in 1951 with typical vigour, 'St James' Settlement was founded by the Anglican Church and it is going to be Christian … We do not believe that the world's problems can be solved by cod liver oil and ping pong.'

Although there were other donors, St John's provided a core of volunteers. Michael Goulder dedicated himself to it. The St John's congregation's interest was gradually captured. Thousands of dollars came from the Michaelmas Fair. John Foster and his wife, Margaret, became closely involved with the settlement. Bishop Hall's quite audacious plan for a six-storey development bursting out of the Nissen Hut is one that truly soared.

Stephen Sidebotham later came to describe what lay behind the bishop's success as a fundraiser. 'R. O. got hold of people who weren't really Christians and got them to cough up. Remember he held the Military Cross from the First War. He had a lot of "street cred" with an older generation of Brits like Marden, Croucher and Lindsay Ride.' In the 1960s the old British *hong* congregation were still important at St John's. It was still a focal point of spirituality for the establishment. When people like that wanted to go to church, that was where they went. They gave help to the cathedral's causes because they had a vested interest in it which was, unusually, not fiscal.

The new settlement building was opened on St James' Day 1962 by the governor, Sir Robert Black. It held a church, day nursery, feeding centre, the boys' club, training shops and a primary school. Bishop Hall insisted that the governor should be introduced only to ordinary Wan Chai folk, whose place this truly was.

The cathedral was not averse to giving its own buildings over to needy causes. Between 1951 and 1954, the old hall and the north transept of the church itself were used as classroom by the students of Chung Chi College. Bishop Hall was the moving force behind the college and, since it had no premises, Alaric Rose had allowed it to hold classes in the hall. Lyon Y. Lee, one of those early alumni, recalls that when the hall was being used, students met in the church itself. Eventually, the college acquired a more permanent site in Caine Road, which was probably a more forward solution than extending Bishop's House as Hall had proposed. The cathedral had done what it does so well and quietly. It provided early foster care to an institution that went on to greater things. When you consider that Chung Chi became its founding college, it is not too fanciful to say that the Chinese University of Hong Kong began under the eaves of St John's.

Support was also given by St John's to smaller, nascent Chinese churches at Kei Oi Church in Sham Shui Po and St Thomas, Castle Peak, located close to the place Bishop Hoare was drowned. Indeed, the cathedral was doing what it saw as its best to meet need where it could reach it. Sometimes, during the mad post-war rushes of immigration, it reached where the government could not. For example,

$2,500 went to the Sandy Bay Home for Crippled Children, which would also become a St John's favourite, not least because of Noel Croucher's close involvement with it. Modestly but brightly, the Sunday school children's Lent project sponsored an ordinary working-class girl, Shar Suk Ling, with $360 towards her education. How she was selected is not clear, but she was in Primary 4 at Tanner Road Police Primary School, North Point. She lived with her mother, father, grandmother and four siblings in 245 square feet, comprising two cubicles and a sitting room. It would be nice to think that some of the St John's children visited the place and were evangelised, socially.[29]

Some of the Youth Club boys may have been, politically. In October 1967, a group of them were involved in a fight outside the Central Government Offices. Although *St John's Review* said it was not to do with 'the disturbances', it was bad enough for the club to be shut for a while.

Denial was also issued over a report that congregation members had been hailed as 'foreign devils' when leaving the church at the Garden Road gate. Given that Garden Road was the passage for Red Guard demonstrations up from the Hilton Hotel to Government House, it is difficult to see how persons so prominently Anglican emerging into a sea of *Little Red Books* could have avoided the attention. Brian Hart recalls in 2011, at age 94, that there was not too much trouble from that quarter. 'It was as well to keep away but if you became involved, a useful ploy was to wave your HSBC chequebook, if you had one, as it was the same colour as Chairman Mao's *Little Red Book*.'

Apart from the youth club there were Cubs and Scout packs, a day nursery and English conversation classes for poor children, in the old hall, by volunteers twice a week. The hall was lent out for pre-examination studies and as rehearsal space for three choirs and an orchestra. It had been refused to the Arts Festival as a venue, on the grounds that the audiences would be too disruptive.

The Sung Eucharist Choir Fellowship, led by Jean Yun and Eddie Ho, raised money for the Street Sleepers' Shelter Society, which was originally a cathedral initiative, and Holy Carpenter Church Hostel in Hung Hom, another outreach into the Chinese Church. In the earlier days of this choir fellowship, they organised a party for five hundred poor children. We have seen how their evensong equivalent had organised and run a spread of social activities for people beyond the cathedral. Choirs in previous decades had come up with similar autonomous initiatives. Choirs the size of a cathedral's can prove a considerable force for mission. They have a common passion, compulsory meetings and the discipline of performance. In the wider society of the parish they can be the equivalent of the military.

The Youth Club did not run purely on lay energy. In 1968, the Reverend Patrick Nicholas was appointed an assistant chaplain. The bishop's visitation of 2 May had concluded that the cathedral needed a Chinese priest. He would look to attach a young priest in training. St John's might sponsor the overseas training of that priest in return. That did not happen for a while longer and then not in the manner the bishop outlined. Instead, they got Nicholas He, who replaced Reverend Philip English, who arrived in 1966 and took over from Frank Roe, who had gone to the Mission to Seamen. English was not long for Hong Kong. He contracted tropical sprue, a disease of the small intestine involving malabsorption, usually afflicting expatriates. The only cure at that time was to leave the tropics.

Nicholas took to Asia well enough. He had a particular flair for inspiring interest in young people, and though there was no formal youth ministry at St John's, he came to define one. They put him in a flat in the diocese's new Upper Albert Road development, Ridley House, and added to the motor pool. The council found him a 1964 Volkswagen.

He was called on as a peacemaker in a critical dispute. There were now two choirs, the 9 a.m. Sung Eucharist and the matins, which was eventually to be given up. It was almost as though the memberships sensed that one would go. There were a total of eighty members, mostly young Chinese between the ages of 13 and 20, and the increasing rivalry between them bordered on the unpleasant. This was *esprit de corps* turned sour. Nicholas saw it and took a pastoral grip on it. He talked to the members, convened a conference of them in the summer of 1970 and took them on joint work camps. Peace was restored.

Nicholas produced an interesting report on youth work at St John's for the council meeting in April 1971. Two hundred children were registered for Sunday schools, meeting at 9 a.m. and 11 a.m. The expatriate teachers were always moving out, and attendances were irregular because parents had demands on the children too. His own service commitments meant Nicholas had inadequate clerical contact with kids. Most children were lost to the Church after the age of 11. There was no neighbourhood contact with young people around the cathedral.

He found that, in confirmation classes, Western children were more talkative in racially mixed classes, but the Chinese kids were more serious about confirmation. For Westerners it was more a social custom and a good behaviour 'bribe'. He concluded that there was a need to provide something to hook post-12-year-olds and to raise the standard of confirmation candidates.

In May 1969, after being made briefly precentor, Stephen Sidebotham was released to take over Christ Church, Kowloon Tong, to succeed the incumbent, Simon Ridley. Keeping three clergy in place at St John's was proving a slippery act. Bishop Baker promoted the appointment of Reverend J. L. Mitman from the Episcopal Church for his skills in mission preparation. The Finance and General Purposes Committee fretted over how this was to be funded and sent Mitman a holding letter, but by early 1971, he had arrived.

The cathedral had the prospect of three full-time clergy for eighteen months. It could afford this. The post-war endowment fund had foreseen it. Mitman was developing a programme for adult education and mission preparation rarely seen on a parish scale. Mitman's strength was in organising seminars, dialogues and study groups. He involved Brother Geoffrey, the Franciscan who was passing through Hong Kong in December 1971, and offered him a speaking engagement between March and April the following year. He actually operated a 'bar ministry' for six weeks, spending three to four nights in the Hilton Hotel and Mandarin Oriental bars, being available to people there. A lesser man in that setting would have ended up needing his own counsel.

Apart from asking for $125 to support this drinking ministry, Mitman was able to report that there was altogether more need of socialising to offset boredom and loneliness. Most particularly, it was needed after the 11 a.m. service, he said. The cathedral seems to have been going through a period of detachment. John Downes of Peak Mansions wrote to St John's Review complaining that no one at St John's knew if its members were sick or noticed if they stop coming. He and his wife had to almost cease attending for a period without anyone noticing—and he was a sidesman. He thought it a 'poor show'.

Then the clergy staffing picture dissolved again. John Mitman was diagnosed with a form of sclerosis and had to return to the United States. Fortunately, his condition improved enough for him to have a very impressive ministry, and he now holds the title of Special

Honorary Canon of Hartford Cathedral for work throughout the Episcopal Church.

At the Annual Church Meeting of 1970, John Foster looked back over the decade and announced,

> There is a limit to the amount of progress or change which an individual human being, family or community can absorb within a period. To press beyond that limit will see little true development, rather the likelihood of disintegration. I do not believe that this latter result is in accordance with God's will for his children.

You could see why Goulder described him as a serious man. He was also called a worrier, but the dean did have a point nonetheless. The 1960s had seen alteration to the point of eruption in the cathedral as well as the streets and society around.

In 1968, the whole of the chancel had been rearranged permanently. There had been a sequence of 'musical pews' as the Lady chapel made its third move up to what had been the high altar, and the St Michael's chapel crossed from the north to the south transept to take its place. An ingenious but ecclesiogically curious wooden chancel screen designed by Eric Faber and made of wood without any nails was erected to separate off the Lady chapel, when 'rood screens' had originally been meant to screen off the chancel from the nave.[30] It had the effect of a garden fence and was eventually removed and put up, in parts, as a screen for the St Michael's chapel. Enough had happened for Dean Foster. He planted his chair, Canute like, on the shoreline of 'disintegration'.

The year 1966 had not only seen the onset of the Cultural Revolution but two elections to the episcopal seat after the departure of R. O. Hall. Bishop Joost de Blank of Cape Town, an interesting external candidate, had been elected in a process in which the Diocesan Conference churches had taken part and to which the cathedral had submitted three names to the joint nominating committee: Bishop Daly, Archdeacon James Pong and Reverend Gilbert Baker. De Groot had been compelled to withdraw on doctor's advice, and the China-seasoned Baker succeeded in the second election.

In 1967, Dean Till's introduction of the moved altar and westward-facing celebration was to be fixed. The table was to stand at the steps permanently. A platform apron was to be extended from them to accommodate activity. The chancel seating and organ console was to be arranged, and the choir swung round as a body behind the altar to face the congregation. Bishop Baker, whose permission was needed, feared there would be less seating for diocesan services.

Still, these were Dean Foster's own proposals and the council approved them, in principle, in April 1967, urging the bishop to give his approval. Council member Miss Barker dissented from the proposal, but the bishop relented. The changes, completed in 1968, met with approval, or from Brian Hart's recollection, 'no particular objection', except that some disliked the placing of the bishop's throne.

There were quite a few particulars that could have been objected to. There was an element of modernist vandalism which can be found in many 1960s developments, even attached to this treatment of the chancel. To make this congregationalism work, the floor levels of the chancel were altered by layerings of plywood. Cobbold's precious sanctuary extension of 1898 disappeared. Oddly, the vestry doors half disappeared below the floor line. All sense of flow through the chancel was lost. Remaining was the reverberation of hollow floors and the clutter of a furniture auction room, which was tolerated for over forty years. One of the most refreshing moves the cathedral made for itself in 2011 was to pull the plywood up, rediscover the original floor, rearrange much of the furniture and restore the chancel to its authentic state.

At the 1967 Annual Church Meeting, Brian Hart, as honorary treasurer, made a summary of the endowment funds available to the cathedral. The Chater Endowment Fund of 1920 contained gilt-edged and fixed deposits, the annual income going to St John's. The Cathedral Endowment Fund, begun by Canon Rose in 1948, was for stipends, gratuities and pensions and came to be used for extensions to property ownership. The Cathedral Hall Endowment Fund of 1922 was given by M. J. D. Stephens for the running, insuring and upkeep of the hall. Anything in excess of $500 was to be spent on musical entertainment and the upkeep of the piano and other instruments in the Hall.

Forty years on, the picture has changed a little. Of the Chater Fund, there is no trace. It had been spent out. Newer to the assets are the Percy B. Dillon Fund, which began as $1.5 million created under the will of his widow, Cecile Norah Dillon, in his memory in 1982, for the upkeep of the church. The other is the Noel Croucher Endowment Fund. It represented at the outset the contribution of a portfolio of Hong Kong shares made by Noel Croucher.

Croucher was to live on until 1979, giving and serving generously and with sometimes insistent confidence, particularly when it came to stocks and shares. Other pillars of the laity at that time were M. W. Kwan, John Stokes and Dr. Eric To, whom Frank Roe describes as having the biggest sound system in the world and who donated a new Thomson electronic organ in 1966. Alastair Todd, who, sometimes honorary secretary, was director of social welfare in the government and later, on retirement, was ordained and took a parish in Eastbourne. Prominent too were G. L. Strickland, whose son John later became chairman of the Hongkong Bank; Li Fook Hing, educational philanthropist and later honorary canon; Li Fook Kow, distinguished public servant; and John Morley, barrister and judge and the cathedral's legal adviser. F. W. Stephens and W. E. L. Fletcher, both lay readers, were able to conduct evensong when called upon.

Up to 1969, evensong had been said every day until 'traffic congestion' reduced it to Wednesday and Saturdays in the week. It is the first and perhaps only record of services being altered for that reason. In the same year on Sunday, 15 February, the new Series 3 order for Holy Communion was introduced, on trial for a year, apparently to little fanfare or resistance. The order of service in 1969 was looking closer to what the cathedral has today, at least in respect of Sundays. Holy Communion was at 8 a.m. Sung Eucharist was at 9 a.m., matins and sermon were at 11 and evensong with sermon was at 6.30. There were two Sunday schools, one at 9 and one at 11. In the weekdays, Holy Communion was at 7.30 a.m. and said in Cantonese at 8.30 on Thursdays. There was a matins at 8 and the reduced evensong at 5.15. We can see that, on Sunday, matins carrying the sermon was still seen as the main morning service, but only just. Within a decade, the matins choir was gone.

The 23 January 1971 matins service became an unusual one. Francis Hsu, the Roman Catholic Bishop, preached in a swap with Bishop Baker, who did the same over at St Joseph's. It had never happened before, and the dean described it as 'a moment of grace'. Equally graceful but less elegant would have been the chaplain's 'chat-in' for young people, held in his flat in Ridley House two nights a week for two hours. Both in their ways were signs of those times.

There were ways in which the cathedral lagged behind the times in the tradition of the canny employer. In 1970, M. W. Kwan, the honourable treasurer, reported that the rising cost of living was making nonsense of the clergies' stipends. The dean was earning

$2,970 a month, John Mitman as senior chaplain, $2,100 and Patrick Nicholas was on $1,620. The assistant clergy were falling back on savings, which were nearly gone. One unnamed priest admitted to having to dip into savings at the rate of $600 a month. Another could not afford new clothes and was wearing those of a deceased friend. The dean had to pay three servants from his entertainment allowance, so no entertaining was done. An urgent review of salaries followed. The dean's was increased to $3,850, Mitman's to $2,850 and Nicholas's to $2,650. Perhaps it was holes in his soles that led Patrick Nicholas to move on and accept a chaplaincy to four schools in the diocese. John Tyrell, the Navy Chaplain, took over from him in January 1972.

Clergy were not the only cause for concern treasurer Kwan. He said of the retired verger pension of $600 'a shame' and that it should be trebled. He was also anxious about the living quarters of the minor staff. They live in 'pillboxes' outside the south door. He thought these unsanitary and unsightly. What about providing a small block of rooms by redeveloping the vergers' quarters next to the old hall? The chaplain could be put on the top floor and space in the new hall released for storage. The obligation to house the labouring staff on the premises was becoming redundant with the onset of public housing estates. For as long as it survived, it acted as one of the motives to restructure the old hall, which had a great deal of height but only one cockloft office. Varieties of plan for this ran through the 1970s and came to almost nothing.

John Foster left the deanship in January 1973. He said that he had taken to heart the advice of Freddy Temple's uncle, who said that no one should stay in an incumbency beyond ten years. He was not leaving for another job, he told trustee Li Fook Hing. To Bishop Baker he wrote, 'My special calling is to a personal ministry and those in special need. The time has come for someone here with more abilities as a teacher and an evangelist.' The cathedral's ministry needed reshaping to meet new needs, he believed.[31]

In a parting definition of his parish as he saw it, Foster said of St John's, 'We are not British or European or even westernized. We are an English-speaking Christian community in which no race may predominate by its own nature.' This was not exactly the case. Sixty per cent of the parish was still Caucasian and, although more Chinese influence was being felt through giving and fellowships, although 50 per cent of baptisms and confirmations were of Chinese, just a casual glance at the clergy, council and office-holding lists showed Western predominance.

Yet Foster's definition, incomplete though it was, had certainly become the vision of the cathedral for many of its membership as the post-war years rolled on. Although Hong Kong's territorial future was still muted, social change was increasingly voluble in the years after the 1967 riots. The increasing power of Chinese business, the localisation of the administration and the retreat of colonial trappings into tiny pockets of occasional ceremonial were irreversible. The cathedral's exclusiveness remained only in its language and perhaps its liturgy, and they were open to all who could handle them. What Foster described had not been reached. It was fanfare for the episode to come.

In appreciation of his ten years of service, the council voted John Foster a $100,000 gratuity. To balance generosity with self-denial, he waived his $40,000 leave pay. The parishioners collected $22,000 for him and presented him with a rose bowl as well.

In spite of the dean's wish to the contrary, things had carried on changing through the last few years of his incumbency. One innovation he led and which could well have been left aside was the alteration in the way the council did its business. It was decided that the council did not need to meet more than four times a year. It could save its full meetings for matters of substance. Committees would be given budgets, meet to their own cycles, be responsible for specific issues and be able to empower the dean. Finance and General Purposes Committee (F and GP) became the Standing Committee. Fabric and Furnishings Committee (F and F) had a lay chair. Thus three committees could get on with their routine within their funds and terms.

On paper, the deal looked sweet and utilitarian. In fact, it led to strife. The hotly defended financial authority of F and GP came into question. In particular F and F sought to exercise more autonomy than F and GP could accept. In June 1974, redevelopment of the new hall, just twenty years old and redundant in design, plus alterations to the old hall and the church itself, were again keenly contemplated. Architect J. Prescott was asked by the F and F for designs for buildings that would pleasingly offset the cathedral and maximise impact.

To those familiar with rushes of enthusiasm which burst out of general meetings and break on the rock of a finance committee, it will come as little surprise to learn that this initiative was criticised by F and GP under Li Fook Hing as a use of funds towards structural changes that were beyond its remit. It was withdrawn at the October meeting. Prescott was paid off. [32]

The Reverend Erik Kvan, an honorary chaplain of this period, capped all with the accurate observation that the council with its occasional meetings and agenda still heavy with reports, had become merely a rubber stamp. During the interregnum before the arrival of Rex Howe, Foster's successor, the bishop acted as dean, Tyrell as priest-in-charge and Erik Kvan was one of the three clergy along with Geoffrey Speake, headmaster of Island School and the architect of the English Schools Foundation, and Reverend P. T. Chan, executive director of Advancement of Christian Higher Education in Asia, who helped out.

Kvan himself was another of the highly accomplished clergy which the cathedral attracted to its service, free of charge. His work was in the fields of psychology and social science. He established the Psychology Department at the University of Hong Kong and later became head of the Social Sciences and Law Faculty. Shortly after he arrived in Hong Kong after the war, R. O. Hall encouraged him to be ordained. He acted as warden of St John's Hall, Master of St John's College and Master of Robert Black College. He pioneered physical rehabilitation in Hong Kong and for thirty years headed the Hong Kong Spastics Society.

The Reverend Rex Howe was 44 at the time of his appointment in 1973, and he arrived with his wife and four teenage children. He was a Cambridge graduate, trained at the Community of the Resurrection at Mirfield and had been Vicar of Redcar and Rural Dean of Guisborough. As the retiring dean was going on to a Yorkshire parish—Lythe near Whitby—so his successor was coming from one. In his inaugural remarks to the Church Council on 27 November 1973, the dean said that the upcoming 125th anniversary of St John's was a call to mission and that the gospel must be preached 'in and out of season'. Most immediately, he faced a human resources problem and the traditional difficulty in maintaining a full complement of clergy.

Rev. Barry J Simmons arrived to replace Patrick Nicholas. On the face of it, he was a good choice. He had done his military service in Hong Kong and fondly remembered the cathedral of 1956 with Temple, Froude and Beaumont. He had asked to come by sea, but by 1973, scheduling a sea voyage was not realistic. Neither, perhaps was Mr. Simmons. He came with his wife, and maybe it was she who recoiled from the climate or the company, but it was he who wrote a frank and regretful letter of resignation in November, saying that he could not make a go of it in Hong Kong and realised that his ministry should be in England.

Simmons proved not to be without courage. Later, back in the English parish of Shoreham, he attracted criticism and publicity for insisting that the names of soldiers shot for desertion should be included on the war memorial, because post-traumatic stress had not been understood at the time.[33] Prior to that, from 1980 to 1990, he was Chaplain of the Anglican Church of Luxembourg.

Manning fortunes swung back a bit. Patrick Nicholas had been helping out with the Sunday school, which was enthusiastic in staging 'walkathons' for charities. Now, while maintaining a chaplaincy at St Paul's Co-educational School, he came back onto the cathedral staff. Then they lurched the other way, sadly. Earlier in 1973, John Tyrell had married Veronica Kotewall. Veronica was diagnosed with a serious cardiac condition, the best treatment for which lay in Britain. They went back in June 1974. Reverend Hugh Stevenson arrived to take over from Tyrell and moved into Cathedral Lodge, bringing numbers back up to three with the dean in No. 1, Upper Albert Road and Patrick Nicholas in Ridley House.

March's new council that year saw Li Fook Hing giving up the treasurership to Desmond Inglis, citing pressure of work. Inglis recalls that, as treasurer, he bought shares in San Miguel Brewery, of which his father was a director. The council was flushed with disquiet at this and demanded that they be sold. This they were at a huge profit, Inglis remembers with satisfaction. Alan Lack, formerly of the Merchant Navy and Director of Marine, became honorary secretary. Hadland continued in F and F, and C. N. Harding took over the Pastoral Committee from the dean. Dr. B. M. Kotewall, teacher and daughter of the famed entrepreneur, patron and benefactor Sir Robert Kotewall, and J. D. Kit, for twenty-eight years director of the Hong Kong General Chamber of Commerce, were the trustees. Among the council members were Noel Croucher, L. M. (Bim) Davis, who was secretary for security, K. W. Farmer, Professor Frank King, D. B. Minns, Jack Mitchell, the Government Registrar who ran the Goodwill Scheme, A. D. A. G. Moseley, David Litchfield, Marjorie Bray, Mrs. S. Martin, R. F. May, D. M. Shea and D. E. Vessigault.

In the April 1974 meeting of the council, in the light of the Bishop's Working Party on Diocesan Reform, St John's role was discussed. F. H. Li believed Chinese-speaking churches should join in more at the cathedral, while R. F. May asked, one imagines rather plaintively, what it was the Chinese churches wanted of St John's.

In May, the council attended 6 p.m. evensong and met in the old hall to ponder whether they should increase the $20,000 annual donation to the diocese. Harding, in vigour, called for $60,000. Kotewall, with caution, said there were additional contributions being made that should be counted in. Harding, in compromise, said double and this was carried.

On the subject of replacements for Chaplains Tyrell and Nicholas, it was time for a Chinese, said the dean; but in fact, it was not. At the August meeting, Hugh Stevenson was chosen over an Australian expatriate Chinese but not without a countermotion by Messrs. Farmer and May. The Chinese of the priest in question was thought to be far from native, and employment on expatriate terms would dig an immediate gulf between him and the local clergy.

Of the cathedral's application to join the diocesan synod, David Litchfield asked why they should bother. Little interest was shown by Saint John's people in the Chinese churches, he said. That, for many expatriates in the congregation, was, sadly, telling it as it was. Nevertheless, the historic vote was taken at a special meeting in March 1975 of the Synod of the Chinese Churches to admit St John's, St Andrew's and Christ Church into their fold. They had been 'unequal yolk fellows', wrote Bishop Baker to the Victoria Diocesan Association, and now that was over. The vote that day was essentially to go forward with the union, and sort out the details at the first meeting of the combined synod on 2 November.

To the Victoria Diocesan Association newsletter, the bishop seemed to restrict his explanation for the merger and the disappearance of any obstacles to the miracle of simultaneous translation. Closed-circuit radio transmission and excellent translators meant everyone could understand each other. That the fifty years and more of separation and misunderstanding had all been down to a language problem was a nifty packaging of the tale. It may or may not have been bought by those members of that association who had lived and worked on the ground in Hong Kong.[34]

The 125th anniversary of the cathedral was taken without fireworks by the congregation. A dinner was held at the Hong Kong

Country Club, as any solid professional society might. The governor, Sir Murray MacLehose, and Lady MacLehose and four hundred people showed up to hear speeches by the dean and trustees J. B. Kite and F. H. Li.

In April 1975, the dean identified to *St John's Review* the high points of his ministry up to then. He attached importance to scripture and evangelism. There had been a course on John's gospel, an eight-week Bible study course and two lay study conferences attracting one hundred people. There had been 'ginger' Lent house meetings and a weekend retreat to Lan Tau. Canon Bryan Green, Rector of Birmingham and one of the most effective evangelists in the Church of England, had come on a mission.

If the choir had been quiet, it may be because Rex Howe was not very musical, according to choir mistress Cecilia Kwok. 'He wasn't very interested.' Dean Till was 'strict', she says. Dean Temple and, to come, Dean Phillips, chose the hymns. Dean Clasper played the cornet. Dean Sidebotham introduced contemporary hymns. Dean Howe restricted himself to telling her not to play the same voluntary more than twice a month.

The congregation, led by the CLARES, became laudably if unusually involved in one of the great overseas tragedies of the generation. In May of 1975, it organised twenty tons of light clothing to be sent to Vietnam although since Saigon had fallen on 30 April, it was difficult to know where that would be going. In June, rather more realistically, the cathedral acted as a transit reception area for Vietnamese orphans going to Canada and received the thanks of the High Commissioner of Canada.

The Queen came to Hong Kong in 1975 but not to church. The front south side nave pew with its coat of arms never did seat a reigning monarch. A week before the fall of Saigon, Bishop R. O. Hall died in England. It would not be true to say that this was the end of an era. Hall skipped through a few of those, and anyway his bishopric was already ten years past. It might be the moment to remember one of his more delightfully frank outbursts about the cathedral. On 12 September 1956, he wrote to his son Christopher,

> I was most acutely miserable for losing my temper with one of our most faithful 'Cathedralists' for calling the Chinese Diocesan Board of Finance 'a nondescript body'. I just despair of the English people here—so good and yet so smug and every time I try do things with them or for them—I get in then wrong. They

all assume the Bishop is some sort of ornament of the Crown of England. They do not realise, seem incapable of realising it, that there is a Chinese Church and my concern is to dig its roots down deep ...[35]

Even though his task in China itself had been put on lengthy hold, those 'Cathedralists' and their days were coming to a close.

Chapter 8
Towards an International Church,
1976–1992

In the first year of Stephen Sidebotham's deanship, Frederick Truman, who had been a choirboy at the cathedral during the First World War, revisited Hong Kong. Apart from recalling that Dean Copley-Moyle had been nicknamed 'Chocolate oil' by the boys in some connection with his hair lotion, and saying that soldiers had been needed to guard St John's one Sunday in a moment of more than usual anti-British sentiment, Mr. Truman remembered an incident involving Bishop Lander and a *punkah wallah*.

According to Truman, the *punkah* nearest Bishop Lander as he was preaching slowed almost to a stop as the youth operating it dozed off. The perspiring bishop stepped down to prod him with a swagger stick of sorts. Somehow, this action miscarried. Lander lost his grip on his stick; and his sermon notes, which were also in his hands, shot out all over the floor. The choir burst into laughter but were later fined for doing so.[1]

The cathedral that Sidebotham took charge of was certainly a less discriminatory and less pompous one than that of sixty years before, yet it was, in a sense, more parochial and less involved with China and matters Chinese than it had ever been. A reminder of this was another visitor, Canon Christopher Hall, son of Bishop R. O. Hall, who came back to preach in his father's pulpit in 1979. Christopher Hall was baptised in the baptistery of St John's Cathedral on 2 January 1936, by the Right Reverend Mok Shau Tsang, the formidable Bishop of Canton. One of his godfathers, Cheung Wing Kue, gave him the name 'Kei Do', 'Established in Christ'. Guests were a mixture of British and Chinese with a sprinkling of Norwegian Lutherans. That Anglo-Chinese sense of missionary purpose, the slow-burning fellowship of the long haul, had no resonance in late 1970s Hong Kong.

It was becoming a city of short contracts. Sidebotham chafed against it. 'Short timers can be stimulating but also disruptive and disappointing to belongers,' he wrote in *St John's Review* after a 'cathedral workshop evening' held in his home in June 1977 to identify cathedral priorities. The later twentieth-century Hong Kong church could be as socially insular as it was in the earlier years. The reasons were no longer so much an assured cultural supremacy of the Victorian merchant class as an uneasy ignorance from British suburbia, but the phenomenon was still there to a degree. Chris Phillips, who was dean from 1987 to 2003, recalls that, when he arrived in Hong Kong in 1977, 'the cathedral did serve as a parish church for English-speaking Anglicans. Its services were "C of E" and its worship very much in the style of a middle-of-the-road suburban parish church.' There is a flicker of insight into how 'C of E' the cathedral might have been at this point. At a 1979 fundraiser, 34,000 can ring pulls were collected and sent to a hospital towards a kidney machine. The hospital was in England.[2]

'It would seem from the priorities that we are solely concerned with ourselves. I would deny that we are an introverted cliquish body,' said the dean with resolute optimism. Nevertheless, he was concerned about the atmosphere at St John's at this time. Sidebotham noticed how people could be so easily and visibly left out, even inside the community and most particularly the Sunday morning parish breakfast. 'There are the standers and the sitters,'[3] he observed tellingly. Nearly ten years later, breakfast seating was still a problem, and it was rearranged in June 1987 to dispel the sense of an inner and outer circle.

In the *St John's Review* of June 1984, a member of the congregation, Mrs. June Powell, was allowed, on her farewell to Hong Kong, to give a frank account of her circumstances and her feelings about the cathedral. She spoke of her self-doubt and how she always compared herself poorly to others. Her husband had been interrogated by the ICAC (Independent Commission Against Corruption), which had made her very angry.

Low self-esteem and anxiety over a husband's position were not uncommon problems for expatriate women. In her worries, the clergy came out well. Rex Howe was 'a very gentle person'. John Tyrell, she felt moved to say, had 'good looks and a fine voice'. She straightforwardly dismisses the laity as 'an unfriendly congregation'. She gained some peace for herself from the healing service and the laying on of hands.

This slowness in fellowship, these shortcomings in the cathedral's view of itself, were tackled with an encompassing vigour. Influenced perhaps by the language of central planning just across the frontier, the dean came up with a five-year plan.[4] The idea was from Hugh Stevenson, the Chaplain at Stanley, who seemed to be the intellectual of the team with his thoughtful articles on social controversies in the *Review*. Sidebotham gave it body. Like all scheduled programmes which are intended to have the punctuality of a train, the plan was a long one.

One hundred adults were needed to commit to a training programme. Fellowship was to be developed through more and smaller groups. Churchmanship was to be nourished and the cathedral's organisation better structured. St John's needed to look out into the community. A study centre should be initiated. There should be a Christian counselling service with professionally trained laity, and a healing ministry. Ecumenism should be encouraged. Numbers needed bolstering by more attractive services and back-up visiting. Youth work needed to be developed among children who were church members and those who were not.

It would be invidious to identify what of that was achieved in any particular timeframe. One hundred people did not commit themselves to anything as a body. There had recently been a very successful 'family weekend' organised at the Salesian Monastery on Cheung Chau, involving one hundred parishioners. Perhaps that is how the figure made its appeal to the authors of the plan. Fellowship developed stubbornly in its own piecemeal way, and the cathedral's organisation followed developments rather than lead them, and looks remarkably similar now to what was unfolding around then.

Neighbourhood Caring Groups were wound down in April 1981 for a lack of leadership and likely a lack of neighbourhoods. It was not the first time that an effort in that direction had foundered. No study centre was created. In a society where the mercenary was vaunted, a notable weakness of St John's as a cathedral was in the intellectual.

However, a counselling service saw its beginnings, as did a healing ministry, on which Sidebotham was particularly keen.[5] By January 1981, an evensong service was being given over to it. Ecumenism got nowhere. The local Protestant churches were inclined to evangelicalism and suspicious of liberal Anglicans. The Roman Catholics, while amicable, were formally uninterested in any bonding. Service numbers grew, though, thanks to a quite unplanned influx of Filipinas and a widening desire for digestible liturgical worship in English, which the cathedral offered.

The cathedral did begin to strengthen its impact on society in the late 1970s and early 1980s, from small initiatives and early joint ventures often involving the dean, which took bigger shapes and unexpected directions in later years. What is now the St John's Counselling Service, the Citizens Advice Bureau (CAB) and the Mission for Migrants Workers (MFMW), which was having difficulties lodging in Holy Carpenter Church, were all invited under the cathedral's roof by Sidebotham and thrived there. In November 1978, Dean Sidebotham, as its chair, initiated the China Coast Community's search for a hostel.[6] As so often is the case, the cathedral was a benign foster agency rather than a missionary force marching as to war.

The Pastoral Committee made heartfelt and varied attempts to scale the walls of indifference. In October 1981, they resolved to split themselves up into six small 'functional' teams to simultaneously tackle the different items in their portfolio. This method left no legacy. In the same year, worried too about insularities, they called for the most diffident and possibly Anglican of solutions. They asked for 'suggestions for bringing people together in an unobtrusive way'.[7]

Dean Sidebotham, in one of his moments of frustration, spelt out a 'failure of church life' as being 'continual disappointment ... flashes of enthusiasm which fizzle because of inadequate leadership leaving you disillusioned and unwilling to try again'.[8] Sidebotham's vision for St John's was that it should move away from its English-speaking parish church function and more truly serve as the cathedral seat of a Chinese bishop, who appeared in the form of the Right Reverend Peter Kwong in April 1981. Sidebotham foresaw a Chinese dean with an English chaplain to look after the expatriates. Services might be bilingual, in English and Cantonese.

This foresight was still being mulled over in February 1988 at a council meeting over which Bishop Peter Kong Kit Kwong was presiding as acting dean. Bishop Kwong had been elected as the first Chinese bishop in 1980. There had still been a body of opinion which had held it was still too early to have a Chinese bishop. In fact, the timing could not have been better. Peter Kwong was able to build on his already considerable experience to help the Hong Kong Sheng Kung Hui to consolidate its identity and make strides into a period of quite rapid and political social change. The structure of the diocese, relations with the Mainland, even the place of the cathedral were all to feel his influence. Yet though he was the first Chinese bishop, he was far from keen to dismantle that of the Hong Kong church which was foreign.

The idea of a 'vicar' for the English congregation was put to Bishop Kwong. He stood reluctant to sideline English and turn St John's into a more Chinese church. He favoured a mixed church with an English-language base. The Mandarin service reflected that this was a basically Chinese diocese, he said. It redressed the perception that St John's was a solely English place. There were sufficient facilities elsewhere for Cantonese speakers.

This last observation by the bishop held a nugget of concern. St John's congregation was already large by local standards. To lure away worshippers from smaller Chinese parishes would be damaging. The integration of St John's was not a simple takeover exercise. The Chinese dean was to wait for another twenty years.

The laborious notion of bilingual services was not pursued and is only observed in small part on special occasions in the interests of correctness rather than comprehension. In worship there were one or two high points of change up to the early years of Chris Phillips's deanship. For the rest, it was cautious moves, a modest way up the churchmanship scale to include aspects of ritual and occasional experiments in the radical and the populist.

Dean Sidebotham, ever keen to get closer to the people in services, introduced the sedilia, which he likened to a bench of three judges, whereby the celebrant and the two deacons can more directly face the people.[9] He introduced the peace greeting, which still causes rumbles of embarrassed dissent. He could not find a method of overcoming the far separation of choir and congregation, which he disliked.

In the 1980 report to the Annual Church Meeting, a decision was announced to retain matins. That the abolition of this once central service was contemplated at all was amazing. It was described as an important part of the Anglican liturgy but 'vocally a very dull service'.

On a Sunday in February 1981, the matins congregation was invited to join in the HMS *Tamar* service. Those who will recall the size of that chapel will understand that the St John's congregation for matins could not have been large. In November 1984, the council was considering experiments to liven the service up. 'It puts newcomers off completely', was the worry.

The Eucharist was approached rather differently by the introduction by the dean of the *Alternative Service Book*—the ASB—in July

1981. Sidebotham had not acted 'like a dictator' in doing this he said to the *Review*. It had been passed by the General Synod of the Church of England and was being received around the Communion. The ASB was the latest in a series of attempts at liturgical reform that spread over the twentieth century. The 1928 reformed *Book of Common Prayer* had failed formal acceptance but had still been in common use. The Liturgical Commission recommendations led to a measure in 1965 which brought in Alternative Services 1, 2 and 3 which were a source of debate, variety and confusion for fifteen years. According to Sidebotham, Dean Foster had 'fought a stout rearguard action against series 2' until 1968. The ASB succeeded these as the first complete prayer book since 1662. Dean Phillips was still defending it in April 1991[10] as a source of language now common to other denominations and much the best for worshippers whose second language was English. It was superseded by Common Worship in 2000. Another innovation which stuck was a council decision of March 1982 to introduce a Saturday evening Eucharist as an anticipatory service. Today, it is the one service held entirely in Cantonese.

The Mandarin Eucharist at 10.30 a.m. on Sunday was begun in January 1987 under the Reverend Samuel Wu, a non-stipendiary priest. That was to anticipate political and social change and demonstrate what Bishop Kwong observed, that St John's was not entirely English on a Sunday. Samuel Wu was to be chaplain to the Mandarin worshippers for thirteen years. His immediate successor was Paul Kwong, now Archbishop; and the current Chaplain, Peter Koon, who is the provincial secretary, was preceded by Andrew Chan, who is also now a bishop. The congregation has stayed steady in numbers, at around one hundred, but fluid in components. There have always been worshippers from the Mainland, and these increasingly include students attending tertiary institutions in Hong Kong. Interestingly, some Filipina domestic workers show up. 'They enjoy the atmosphere,' says committee secretary Stephen Wu, son of the founding chaplain.

Dean Paul Clasper actually got laypeople up to preach on appropriate days. To his self-confessed surprise, Dr. Ronald Lo, an anaesthetist and sometime council member, found himself preaching for the first time in his life on Medical Sunday in October 1984. Clasper was the first non-British dean in the cathedral's history. He was a man of warm paradoxes. A senior lecturer in theology at Chung Chi

College, Chinese University, where he had made a firm friendship with the now Bishop Peter Kwong, he been ordained a Baptist in the United States and served as a pastor for ten years and as a missionary in Burma before turning to academic life. He made a brave move from Baptist minister to Anglican priest. He was attracted to Anglican spirituality and liturgy and served under the encouragement of Stephen Sidebotham as an assistant at Christ Church. He also represented a radical move by St John's in appointing its first non-British senior clergyman.

A former colleague said, 'I don't think he ever set out to be a radical reformer but under his leadership the cathedral began to feel more international and it was during his time that Eucharistic vestments began to be worn.' Another recalled that he could not bring himself to bow to visiting royalty and once called Princess Alexandra 'Mrs. Ogilvy'.

The Reverend Roger Holloway, a non-stipendiary minister at the time and, by paradox, a wine merchant, found Clasper's ministry 'pastoral and wholly unpompous'. Holloway, writing in the *Review* in the summer of 1989, wanted a window put up to him in the vestry showing him stocky and silver-haired as he was, puff-cheeked and blowing a trumpet, which he was skilled on and used to play in services occasionally. The idea found no takers. Clasper died on 29 October 2011 in Claremont, California, and the memory of him in Hong Kong was long enough for a well-attended memorial service in St John's Cathedral.

The departure of Stephen Sidebotham in 1983 saw the responsibilities of the cathedral towards organisations which operated outside its own walls greatly increasing. Sidebotham could be unnervingly humble over what he saw as failures. Writing in the *Review* in October 1982, he accused himself of being a 'butterfly', especially over church growth. He thought his had been a reactive ministry 'taking up what was asked but without goals'. He was observant of one feature over which he probably had little control. 'Membership of the Cathedral by local people was perhaps stronger in the Sixties, an area to which I paid insufficient attention.'

A longer perspective suggests that his period and that of Paul Clasper, who followed on up to 1986, contain the beginnings of two phenomena which distinguish the cathedral today from that of forty years ago: the daughter churches and the outreach ministries. The daughter churches were an entirely new development. St John's had taken on some responsibility for St Peter's, West Point, but only because it had been in decline from its seamen's missionary purpose. It successor church, Christ Church, was entirely self-sustaining, as St Andrew's in Kowloon had always been. The Peak Church and the Happy Valley Chapel had been purely chapels of ease without their own clergy. From the early stages of St Stephen's Chapel, Stanley, a commitment was made to give a significant portion of time of one of the cathedral chaplains to the congregation. This practice was followed afterwards at Emmanuel, Pok Fu Lam and Discovery Bay. The pull between acting as a cathedral chaplain from the centre and a priest in an outlying congregation became an interesting tension that is still there.

The strong connection with St Stephen's College made use of its chapel a comfortable arrangement to arrive at. It was built in 1950 and dedicated by Bishop R. O. Hall, to those who suffered in Stanley Camp during the war. The cross there is said to have been rescued from the Peak Church upon the Japanese invasion and used in Stanley Camp during the occupation. The Reverend Hugh Stevenson, who took up the Stanley challenge with enthusiasm, had a congregational nucleus of eight at the beginning, but in January 1978, he was reporting that it was growing in 'leaps and bounds'.[11] He had fifteen families coming regularly and hoped for a weekly 9.30 a.m. Eucharist before long. Within two years, they were experimenting with evensong too. The intent was not simply to make worship easier for south-side Anglicans who would otherwise have to face a long round trip to Garden Road. There was a whiff of evangelism in the foundation. In those days, 15,000 people lived between Shouson Hill and Tai Tam. There was the hope of attracting first-timers in the neighbourhood, or at least those expatriates who had attended church back home but were finding it all too difficult in Hong Kong. Enthusiasm was high. The St Stephen's Annual Church Meeting of April 1981 lasted a brisk five minutes and aimed to raise the $96,000 a year necessary to keep the chaplain.[12] A real sense of fellowship existed there. They used his fruit bowl as a font.

At its church meeting the following year, buoyancy was leading to thoughts of a long-term aim of independence.[13] Costs did not deter their enthusiasm. The bishop did somewhat. He objected. The congregation grew nonetheless under a succession of dedicated chaplains who took up the role of *de facto* priest-in-charge. Michael Simpson, who was later to become Vicar of Christ Church, succeeded Hugh

Stevenson in 1982. Before he left in 1984, he asked that a clearly designated priest-in-charge should succeed him at Stanley and registered disappointed because the bishop declined to do so.[14]

Hugh Stevenson had actually moved down to Stanley in 1981. His successors, Simpson, Michael Phillips and Peter Frowley, seemed to have spent almost as much time at St. Stephen's as any parish priest would have done. They lived, rent free, in a colonial-style bungalow in the college grounds. In October 1986, Michael Phillips hammered out with is congregation committee, chapel and housekeeping rules and guidelines on relations with the cathedral. It was a mini constitution of sorts though not officially one at all.[15]

The congregation developed a busy English-language prison-visiting ministry in nearby Stanley Prison. Peter Frowley, who had prison ministry experience before he arrived, expanded this. There were repeated but vain pleas to the bishop to supply Cantonese-speaking clergy visitors. In May 1991, Frowley went as far as to draft a synod motion on it.[16] Chinese clergy, at the time, did not see this as one of their roles. So complete was the daughter church's commitment to the chapel, that when St Stephen's College wanted to extend the chapel in 1987, the cathedral raised $650,000 of the cost out of gratitude for the arrangement.[17]

Even though the title 'priest-in-charge' was conceded to the daughter church chaplains, there was no concession over the issue of incumbency. They were, and remain in principle, cathedral chaplains. In April 1982, when a vacancy for Emmanuel, Pok Fu Lam, was advertised, the wording settled on was 'Chaplain on Cathedral staff whose principal responsibility is for a daughter church'. John Tyrell returned to Hong Kong in 1979 for a second bite at a cathedral chaplaincy. He took charge of the development of Emmanuel, Pok Fu Lam. Again, this was a church not entirely for the convenience of cathedral worshippers disinclined to catch the bus or compete for parking space in the cathedral close, as it was now officially called. The church had its eye on expatriates in the huge Baguio Villas development and the other residential blocks that had been built along Pok Fu Lam Road. The cathedral put Tyrell himself into one of these flats at Cape Mansion for $15,000 a month, because no flat in On Lee could be recovered. The congregation lodged in the chapel at St John's College, Hong Kong University's Anglican Hall of Residence, though not as comfortably as in Stanley. The college placed tight restrictions on its use.

Sunday, 19 October 1980, saw the first parish communion with a congregation of fifty. Three months on, there was a report of eighty-two committed members. 'Now we are in the second phase of growth with the usual relationship and personality clashes,' reported Tyrell to the council in March 1981. Liturgically, Emmanuel was going in a more evangelical direction from the more ceremonial St Stephen's. They were having free prayer during intercessions and 'spontaneous comment on new songs'. Sunday evening worship developed into fifteen minutes of worship and forty-five minutes of Bible exposition.

In January 1981, when Tyrell's contract and the flat were up for renewal, Emmanuel sent a memo to Cathedral Council members saying that Emmanuel was so orderly, did they want to continue a full-time clergyman? Tyrell left in June 1982, ultimately to become Dean of Nicosia, to be replaced by the Reverend Chris Butt, who stayed at Emmanuel for six years. During that period, in 1984, a constitution of sorts was also hammered out, but separatist tendencies were to become more pronounced in Emmanuel than in St. Stephen's.[18] The congregation showed considerable commitment to parish ministry, probably most notably in its dedication to street sleepers in Western. Penny Lawton and Peter Stobart from the Emmanuel congregation were devoted to this ministry. In 1988, they set up the St Barnabas Society with the cathedral's financial support.[19] The society exists to this day, working on the streets, very much Bible based and committed to evangelism. Its website says it was 'started by two people' but otherwise not a trace of Emmanuel or St John's remains on it.

The growth of the daughter church ministries was a response to the financial expansion of Hong Kong that had brought in a raft of expatriate English speakers, the 'short-timers' as Stephen Sidebotham would have them, to service it. The most recent daughter church grew up in one of the later and more unusual suburbs of Hong Kong Island, the Discovery Bay development. It is worth noting that the claimed figures for attendance or involvement in daughter churches—and indeed at St John's itself—were well above those who were willing to put their signature on a paper stating membership. At the cathedral's Annual Church Meeting in April 1983, the electoral rolls showed 361 enrolled members at St John's, 44 at St Stephen's and 26 at Emmanuel.

In January 1990, Bishop Kwong was asking the Cathedral Council if the establishment of a daughter church in Discovery Bay had their support. An interdenominational gathering there was already being served by a spread of non-Roman Catholic clergy, including those from St John's. Continuing organisation on this basis was likely proving difficult, and one of its leading lights, Neil Kraunsoe, was a devout Anglican and formerly of Christ Church. He lobbied for the cathedral to take it over.

It turned out well, especially given that its first chaplain-in-charge was the Reverend Robert Gillion, who joined the staff of St John's in June 1990. He held the various denominational groupings together with skill and understanding. Former Dean Chris Phillips recalls visits there with pleasure. '… a bit like going on an outing to the seaside. The congregation were very welcoming and people just got on and did things, no matter what their denominational background.' The congregation has met in classrooms and a school hall, where it presently worships. Gillion managed to persuade the Hong Kong government to give him some pastoral access to the Hei Ling Chau Vietnamese Detention Centre but had no luck in persuading the Discovery Bay developer to set up a church recreation centre. There was discussion about a church at Clearwater Bay. The cathedral earmarked $120,000 towards the project even though it was to be a diocesan church and not a 'daughter' of St John's. It must have been a suburb too far. It was never established as such. The money was joyfully released. A daughter church of St Andrew's, Kowloon, was later set up in that area. Within twelve years, three daughter churches of St John's were up and running. In mission and ministry, that was quite crisp. The outreach ministries took rather longer. Their development has been more of an evolution and could be considered still going on.

A considerable congregation of its own within the cathedral are the Filipinas. The growth of high-profit service industries such as design, marketing, and finance during the 1980s meant more Hong Kong women were drawn into employment. Families with two incomes sought help to manage their households, and this began the demand for domestic workers from the Philippines. Filipinas from the Philippines Independent Church gravitated to St John's, as well Roman Catholics, who found the liturgy of the cathedral sufficiently familiar.

Their working hours have always been long. In 1980, they told clergy that they did not wish to be organised, as they had so little time. This did not deter a Filipino Bible study course from beginning on Sunday morning in the Harold Smythe Room, led by the Reverend Eric Chong and Faye Hanson. Chong was a successor to Ian Lam and, in mild irony, one of the long-yearned-for Chinese-speaking chaplains who could appeal to a Cantonese congregation. Hanson, a parish worker for Filipinos, was an indirect lay successor to the Reverend Peggy Sheldon of the US Episcopal Church, who had come to Hong Kong with her husband, an executive of Dow Chemicals, and had been on the staff of the cathedral.

The Bible studies went well. Bishop de la Cruz from the Philippines visited. The following year, $20,000 was made available for priests of the Philippines Independent Church to come up to Hong Kong. By 1982, two Filipino missionaries, Cynthia and Juan Tellez from the National Council of Churches of the Philippines, were running a counselling service and were accommodated in the lodge. The council felt that it might need the lodge, unwanted as it was, and the suggestion was made that the pair should be assisted with living accommodation outside.[20] The understandable observation was made that 95 per cent of the Filipinos were Roman Catholic and that some contribution from that direction might be appropriate. That being unforthcoming, the Annual Church Meeting of 1982 announced its support of the rental of a flat from the Evangelical Reform Church in Kowloon Tong at $2,500 per month for Cynthia and Juan while the counselling went on from the cathedral.

This, should any be needed, is the point at which migrant worker outreach settles into St John's. In September 1983, the council noted that the 'Philipina Mission for Migrant Workers' was to supervise fellowship use of the new hall on Sundays. It received $42,000 in grants. In June 1988, the St John's Filipino Fellowship became regulated by appointment of a committee and enrolment of members. The fellowship was placed under the direction of a member of the cathedral staff. Whether they had time or not, the Filipinas had been organised.

Interestingly, at a council meeting of February 1989, a suggestion that there should be separate services for the Filipina congregation was 'totally rejected' by the Reverend Julie Leaves, a cathedral chaplain, who was involved at the time. Rejected too was an unnamed lady from Macau, who had been bringing in 'unusual tracts' and was told to go away. By May 1991, the council was recording that the MFMW was accommodated and assisted by St John's Cathedral but not part of St John's Cathedral. The separately registered status gave the mission more independence and placed a discreet firewall between the cathedral and some of the more radical social positions it sometimes adopted in support of its membership in the city.

Ultimately, after a brief extension in May 1987, Faye Hansen's contract had not been renewed. It was considered that an ordained priest was needed to meet the pastoral needs of the Filipinas. In September 1991, the Reverend Susan Hewitt came in as a non-stipendiary priest to give support. By April 1993, a priest from the Philippines was finally decided upon. Father Dwight de la Torre arrived on a three-year contract, stipulating that he spend three and a half days a week with the MFMW and two and a half days as a cathedral chaplain.[21] How, if at all, that division was monitored is not explained. Whatever the practice, the result was most satisfactory. Father de la Torre remains with St John's to this day.

Puzzlement over the distinction between the MFMW and the other cathedral outreach to migrants, Helpers for Domestic Helpers (HDH), is understandable. HDH's role is more specific. It was established by a group of lawyers in the congregation who were concerned about the legal vulnerability of individual workers. The organisation's work focuses mainly on employment and immigration problems. Terminated workers are assisted in making and pursuing labour claims. Much of its efforts are in persuading the Immigration Department to allow a terminated worker to take up new employment where permission has been refused.

In March 1991, solicitor James Collins produced a paper on the idea and made a proposal to the Cathedral Council in May 1991. He asked for a base office with a telephone. The dean found him the space. It was agreed to make available financial aid and other assistance and that the free services offered by the scheme need not be confined to members of the congregation. With lawyers at the helm, HDH was skilfully crafted into an unincorporated charitable society with constitutional affiliation to St John's Cathedral. It became an integral part of the cathedral's pastoral work.

Michael Corbett-Jones had left that work in the summer of 1980. His Australian Church Missionary Society sponsors were so stingy with his shipping allowance that there had to be a whip-round for him to send his books home. He had deserved it. He left behind the sound if small beginnings of a counselling service. The Reverend Ronald File was recruited into the chaplaincy to take up what Corbett had begun. Age 59 and described as 'deeply spiritual', he had worked as an industrial chemist and trained in clinical theology.[22] By 19 November 1981, File was reporting to the council that he personally was fully booked, seeing twenty clients a week. Importantly, ten lay people were qualified to counsel, and others were working their way through a three-part course. The council unanimously approved that the balcony in the new hall be enclosed to provide space for the service.

By May 1984, the counselling service had so grown that it needed a management committee, which was to include the dean and two council members. File returned to England in 1985 to fulfil an awkward caveat in the pension regulations whereby he had to be filling an active post in the Church of England or he would not get a pension. He was succeeded by the Reverend Gareth Jones in 1985. The Reverend Karlo Misso from Sri Lanka gave strength to the cathedral's international flavour by becoming director in December 1989.

An interesting meeting took place between the dean, the Pastoral Committee and the counselling service in the spring of 1993.[23] The dean found that many of the staff were both committed Christians and very professional. They did not impose values and provided something different from clergy counselling. They received referrals from other churches too. Mrs. Margaret Evans of the Pastoral Committee was firmly convinced that the service was not offering sufficiently Christian counselling. Mrs. Evans was also opposed to the sale of any items in the cathedral grounds on a Sunday. She is remembered for being moved, on occasion, to break into charismatic song at interesting moments during services, but she was not alone in sensing a possible compromise on doctrine over counselling.

A debate in the council over the name of the service in June 1990 preferred 'St John's Cathedral Counselling Service' over 'The Counselling Service, St John's Cathedral' on the grounds that the latter might be 'misleading' to Christians. The service's mission, 'to empower the human spirit towards greater awareness in making choices for growth and happiness', certainly meets its objective of being non-denominational. Today, its website has dropped the word 'cathedral' altogether. The cathedral accepted that psychological counselling of a spiritual value for all comers could not be professionally sound if it had to be avowedly religious at all turns. The counselling service has moved out from under the cathedral's crowded roof. The directorship has shifted from a clerical professional on the cathedral staff to a lay professional outside.

Initially, pastoral direction of the counselling service added to the swelling numbers in clergy ranks. An allowance had been made for a fourth man to cover time spent, overall, on the daughter churches. By the middle of 1981, Peggy Sheldon and Eric Chong, deaconed in St John's in September 1980, were full time at the cathedral. Michael Simpson was at Stanley, John Tyrell looked after Pok Fu Lam and Ron File ran the counselling service.

Over the following eleven years, fourteen chaplains served in the cathedral, each having fulfilled at least one three-year contract. At the beginning of the century, when to sustain one chaplain was hard enough and often not done, this would have been incomprehensible.

Accommodation was as haphazard as ever. The dean lived in St Martin's House on Upper Albert Road as a tenant of the diocese. Eric Chong had a flat there too. Michael Simpson lived in the St Stephen's College bungalow, Ron File was in another diocesan rental in Ridley House, John Tyrell was accommodated expensively in Cape Mansion and Peggy Sheldon lived, in admirable economy, with her husband.

In 1983, Tyrell was given a buffet supper farewell at the dean's house, and the dean himself said farewell at a $55-a-head dinner at the Hong Kong Country Club. His successor, Paul Clasper, moved into the lodge in the close because of mooted redevelopment plans for Upper Albert Road. Nothing was to come of the development till 2011, but Clasper spent three years in a gloomy, humid building, prey to lost souls, petitioners and petulant parishioners. It was part of his style that he did not seem to mind, but it was never lived in by clergy again.

The briefly serving Dean Smethurst rejected the lodge even before he had arrived, and his successor, Chris Phillips, as dean from 1987, did not have long to avoid it before it was sensibly converted into the administration office in 1991. Phillips had been a missionary school teacher in Zambia before taking a teaching job with the English Schools Foundation in Hong Kong. He was active in the congregation, chairing the Pastoral Committee, before becoming ordained at the 9 a.m. Eucharist on 22 June 1980, and joining the non-stipendiary support team. He became a full-time chaplain in December 1983, to replace Eric Chong.

At this time, the dean's and the chaplains' stipends were fixed to the government master pay scale. Chaplains were at point 27 and paid $5,115 a month, the same as the vicars of St Andrew's and Christ Church. The dean was at point 30. Eric Chong was on the 'Chinese scale' and paid $2,800 per month. Dignity over this point alone may have deterred Chinese clergy from taking up posts at St John's.

Phillips was the priest most available to carry out the duties of priest-in-charge during the interregnums following Paul Clasper and David Smethurst. In February 1988, following the sudden departure of David Smethurst, the Board of Patronage recommended that Phillips be made acting dean for a trial two years, because of his short time in the cathedral and holy orders. There was a gust of opposition to this. The honorary secretary and Reverend Chris Butt led a call for immediate permanent status. F. H. Li said it was people on the board, like Angela Smith, who were not St John's congregation members who were worried. These concerns were swept aside. D. Mace and S. Dobbing moved a motion to make Phillips permanent.[24] Both Frederick Johnson and John Foster had become deans directly from the chaplaincy, but Chris Phillips's evolution into the deanship from having been a layperson in the same cathedral only seven years before was peculiar in its speed. It bore testament to the management style of the trustees, his own talents and the quick-fire ethic of Hong Kong from which not even the Church was removed.

On the council there was change too. Alan Lack, the honorary treasurer and sometime trustee who had sat on it for twenty-three years, was the government director of marine leaving on retirement. He had been a characterful and energetic mainstay of the church, at the helm at demanding times. He was sometimes capable of proposals that were at once practical and indigestible. He wanted the west door shut during services in winter to keep out draughts. As treasurer he was succeeded by Peter Williams, another senior civil servant and formerly commissioner of the ICAC. In fact, the civil service predominance on the council was a thing of the past, but only just. Expatriate predominance remained, of course. At that point, it even had an African flavour.

One member, Laurence Stretton, a South African with still strong roots, was a juvenile court magistrate and was to die back there two years hence. Dr. Elizabeth Hynd, who was a science teacher, came from Lesotho; and Mike Sammes, like the other two, a devout evangelical, had previously been in Zambia, where he had been a lay reader and involved with the Church there. Other stalwarts of the council in 1986 were Michael Dennis, who had been with Hong Kong and Shanghai Banking Corporation since 1961, and Roger Kynaston, the operations manager of the MTR (Mass Transit Railway).

In October 1985, Canon Henry Wittenbach wrote to remind the dean that he was still an honorary canon of St John's. His name had been omitted from the list in the *Review*.[25] He was the last survivor of the four canons created by Bishop R. O. Hall in 1945, but survive he did. The recipient of the letter, Paul Clasper, was to become one of a new batch of four honorary canons, including David Leigh, who missed that shell in the organ loft in 1941, Jane Hwang, one of the cathedral's celebrated female ordinands, and Joe Gooch, a non-stipendiary priest who was catering manager of the Jockey Club. Cataloguer of his colleagues, Roger Holloway wrote of Gooch's almost exaggerated Cockney accent, his shiny cheeks, his bounce and his limitless generosity. Jim Gooch died two years after the honour was bestowed.

An interesting appointment in November 1988 was the Leaves couple, the Reverend Nigel and the Reverend Julie. They had met at theological college in England and had been recently married. Even though he had four chaplains on the cathedral roll, Dean Phillips had no one with him, full time, at the cathedral itself. The demands on the cathedral seemed to be growing. At the February meeting of the council there had been a call for the expansion of the clergy. The Leaves must have been an appealing prospect.

They were not exactly two for the price of one, but the economy in accommodation was not ignored. They were not, as individuals, well ahead of other candidates in their appeal. They were relatively inexperienced, Julie especially so. She was still a deacon. As an appointment, the duo were something of a risk. Yet it was one that the council took. It turned out to be quite inspired. Nigel was scholarly and good with young people. Julie joined an AIDS support group. In June 1991, she became involved with Comfort Care Concern, which was originally begun to help people cope with terminal illness. Julie took a special interest in AIDS victims, and by December, she had Comfort Care Concern meeting in the cathedral. Dean Phillips picked up on this with enthusiasm, and when the Leaves left for Perth in January 1992, he made it clear he wanted ministry on these lines continued. The ultimate result, the HIV Education Centre, a major outreach ministry, began in 1996. Julie Leaves is now known as Mother Julie, Rector of Sandgate-Northpoint Parish in the Diocese of Brisbane. Father Nigel, Associate Priest there with her, is also a Canon of Brisbane Cathedral. Julie might also make a claim as a mother of a St John's outreach ministry.

The non-stipendiary ministry supporting the cathedral expanded. Jenny Wong and Stephen Green were priested in 1989 in St John's.

John Chynchen was deaconed in Salisbury.[26] Chynchen was a chartered surveyor who had run a successful practice in South-east Asia for some years. He was later to join the full-time ministry of the cathedral. Wong was a schoolteacher who was to become principal of St Stephen's Girls' College. Green was an executive of the Hong Kong and Shanghai Bank who later went on to be its global chairman and then join the British coalition government in 2011 as minister of state for trade. In November 1990, Erik Larsen arrived on the team from the Episcopal Church. He described himself to John Chynchen, now playing reporter for the *Review*, as a Connecticut-born cradle Episcopalian who attended their divinity school in Boston.

The Leaves and Peter Frowley gone in one sweep, Dean Phillips travelled to England on a recruitment trip and returned empty-handed. He reported to the council, 'It is difficult to attract clergy to work here. Why that can be I am not quite certain.' It had always been difficult. In the past there were the distances involved and the threat of discomfort, disturbance and disease. These had been minimised by the 1980s but, to a younger priest in England, so had the prospects. Mission to China remained sealed off. Ministry would be to a floating parish of middle-class expatriates, and for that he would put himself dangerously out of the preferment loop back in England. Hong Kong may have been a shoppers' paradise, but towards that and the sort of recreation his parishioners could afford, the chaplain's salary would not go very far.

The cathedral's income did not go very far either in that decade. Replacement of the roof, which an appeal for had not entirely covered, had been an outstanding challenge at the beginning of the decade. Commitment to diocesan funds was significant and consistent. The generosity of the council, if not boundless, pushed resources to the limit. Many members saw Hong Kong as changing and needful both in the church and outside it. Where the cathedral was not establishing ministries of its own, it wanted to give to those that did. There was conflict in the council between the needs of the cathedral and the wider world. Sometimes it was dramatic, on occasion it was painful, inevitably it was formative.

In 1983, there was an overall budget deficit of $357,000. Hands went to the pumps. In January 1984, there was a reversal of policy on the disbursement of Michaelmas Fair Funds. After endowment funds had made the cathedral's income more stable, the fair's funds had been released for donation to outside charities. Now the

Michaelmas Fair Committee was asked to agree that $70,000 of the takings should be given to the General Fund. Some, including Dr. Michael Sammes, objected to money being diverted from charity to the deficit. The dean, using what seemed like a sleight of hand, said that the $70,000 could be allocated for use in the cathedral close. Since the close was open for the benefit of the general public, this could be regarded as charity.[27]

Council member Jack Mitchell, who was to become a temporary administrator of the cathedral in his retirement, had called the 1983 budget 'inward looking' and the congregation 'complacent'. John Yaxley said at the council meeting of April 1984 that the cathedral compound could hardly be called a charity and expressed disappointment that the cathedral's contribution to the diocese had also been reduced. Clearly disturbed, he was driven to blunt language, calling the cathedral, 'an inward-looking expatriate congregation cut off from the mainstream of the diocese'. Both these men were senior civil servants. Perhaps their working involvement with the majority of the population made them more acutely aware of what was needed for this expatriate congregation to integrate. They spoke about important instruments, the budget and the diocesan allocation. In its giving overall, the cathedral was much more praiseworthy.

Even allowing for the $70,000 shaved off for the close, the Michaelmas Fair raised $124,000, distributed amongst the CMS ($10,000), the Diocese of Sabah ($10,000), the Bible Society ($5,000), St Christopher's Home ($5,000), Holy Nativity Church ($5,000), St James' Settlement ($30,000), Hong Kong Sea School ($2,000), Kam Tin Church School ($5,000), Rotary Club School ($4,000), the Spastics Association ($15,000) and the Mission For Migrant Workers ($3,600).[28] The Cathedral Council was perfectly capable of giving $120,000 towards street sleepers or $650,000 to St Stephen's Chapel and, later in 1990, $500,000 for a Bishop Hoare memorial chapel to St Peter's Castle Peak, near the place that the bishop had drowned. At one point, the Pastoral Committee, which had a modest working budget of $30,000, blew the lot on a needy school in Papua New Guinea.

There was disparate giving from all directions. In 1984, for example, there was a retiring collection for the Busoga Trust Uganda and donations to the Kwun Tong Health project and the rebuilding of a Sri Lankan church. Let it be remembered too that the Sunday school raised money towards a horse for a Philippines priest.

In October of 1985, the council and the Michaelmas Fair Committee were in disagreement again over charity giving.[29] The council complained that too much was being given to the already well-funded St James' Settlement. They wanted to be more involved in making the list of recipients. In March 1986, they resolved to work towards a formula for giving. The solution they arrived at, opaque in its wisdom, was that there should be no formula. In the same year, the council allocated $60,000 to the Diocesan Finance Campaign and $60,000 to diocesan clergy stipends. This was only $10,000 more than was given in 1979, and the Pastoral Committee urged them to make it $150,000. By 1987, the budget had a deficit projection of $520,000. When Carrian Holdings imploded, $80,000 had been lost. Onto this scene of conflicting priorities came the Reverend David Smethurst.

Paul Clasper had resisted a mild clamour for him to serve a second term. He was 65 and wanted to see more of his grandchildren in the United States. He felt he had one more opportunity to practise a different kind of ministry and took up visiting professorships at Virginia Theological Seminary and the General Theological Seminary in New York. Alarm bells over David Smethurst's suitability as dean in succession to Clasper were pealing before he was appointed. He was not the first choice for the job. A more favoured candidate had dropped out. After he had visited Hong Kong, at least two council members expressed written reservations to the Board of Patronge.[30] A deputation of the clergy went to them with concerns. The board listened politely but was not swayed. One of the trustee members from St Andrew's was keen on Smethurst's evangelicalism. After the liberal road which he felt Paul Clasper had gone down, he told one of the cathedral clergy that it was necessary to 'redress the tendencies'.

Smethurst had considerable talents. He preached well. His ideas on stewardship were creative. Yet his evangelicalism and his fondness for the charismatic were not hidden. In an interview with the *Review*, shortly after his arrival, he happily admitted that he had once been called in by the Bishop of Manchester for unorthodox use of laypeople in Holy Communion. Nonetheless, clerical referees spoke warmly of him.[31]

For a priest who was so personable socially, it surprised many how quickly he alienated people. At the first staff meeting, he told the clergy, 'I know a dead church when I see one.' The Cathedral Council minutes, normally models of the calm in the passive voice, positively hum with tensions.

At the May 1987 council meeting, the dean criticised the council's forward planning. He ordered committees to submit plans for the following twelve months and to cap the session, he proposed comprehensive review of the Church of England Ordinance to reflect social change. In the June meeting, Dr. Hynd, a supporter of the dean, began with a proposal to put street sleepers on the upper floor of the lodge. The discussion was so protracted and divided that its length was complained about. There was disagreement over an art exhibition in Holy Week, and one clergy member asked to go on the record to disassociate himself from an invitation to a prominent American evangelist, Luis Palau. Increasingly, the dean found support from groups who favoured conservative evangelicalism and charismatic renewal. These were in a minority in a congregation which had recently enjoyed Clasper's more catholic liberalism.

The main point of difference between the dean and his council was radical. He believed that churches like St John's should give away much of their money. In the final volcanic council meeting he chaired on 15 October 1987, he said that they had nothing to fear about the church remaining an economic entity after giving, because God favours charity. What he failed to understand or refused to accept was that the cathedral was only just an economic entity, even with its endowments, which were carefully locked down against precisely the disbursing passions which were in the dean's chest.

The matter came to a speedy head when Canon David Bindon, commissary from the Church of Melanesia, arrived in Hong Kong on a fundraising tour. A hurricane had struck the Solomon Islands and destroyed an Anglican college. He needed $2 million. The dean wanted to help in a very significant way. He was advised that the college had assets in Auckland. Smethurst countered that they were tied up. The irony was that so were the cathedral's. Nevertheless, he instructed the Hong Kong and Shanghai Bank to liquidate the trust funds. This cannot be done with a dean's signature alone. Trustees Alan Lack and Li Fook Hing refused to add theirs.

The dean revealed this and a subsequent difficult session with the council in his sermon at the 9 a.m. Eucharist, which packed maximum exposure by being in front of the governor and broadcast that day on RTHK. The eruption over this came at the very end of that October meeting, the last official trace of Smethurst as dean. He was accused of revealing confidential matters, misrepresenting the church's wealth, circumventing the council and raising matters inappropriate to a worship service. The dean replied that his sermon was prophetic and that prophecy leads to discomfiture. The dean led the congregation, and the bishop supported his mandate. He could not be bound by the council. He was wrong on both points. The trustees got his resignation. The bishop revoked his licence in Hong Kong.

Smethurst had some considerable support in the congregation. There were those who saw a purity in disendowment for charity as deeply attractive. The congregation was not exactly divided but certainly fractured. Council minutes were leaked to the *South China Morning Post*. There was a brief slanging match in its letters column. The November 1987 council meeting was almost as painful as the October one. There were those on the council, like Michael Sammes and Elizabeth Hynd, who felt that the speed and confidentiality with which Smethurst had been removed was opaque and had circumvented them. The trustees were compelled by a vote to give the membership a confidential account, which was accepted. There was concern too for Smethurst's future. Lady Heath, wife of the government's director of protocol, asked if the Archbishop of Canterbury had been informed of what had happened to him. Indeed, the archbishop had.

In a letter sent out to the congregation on 18 December 1987, it was felt necessary to say, 'We realise that members of the congregation had received from David and Dorothy love friendship and spiritual counsel on a personal level and we extend our sympathy to those individuals in their loss.' Yet there was added an observation which found its way back to those earliest meetings of the trustees, in the long-vanished vestry, in the humid half-apse, at the east end of the original church, '... from time to time the trustees may be forced to make very painful decisions for what they believe to be the overall well-being of the cathedral'.

St John's steamed on through its crises. Though deans came and went, the 1980s to the early 1990s was a period of quite significant structural alteration, some of it very clear and some of it difficult to see. Nevertheless, what was done has left the church more viable as a building and more functional as a cathedral. The least visible but most enormous alteration was the replacement of the roof during 1981. The termites—the white ants—had taken their destruction to a new level. For only the second time in its history, St John's was having to take its top off and replace it. Man Sing and Co. were contracted to do the job for $2 million. The total cost turned out to be $3 million. Dean Sidebotham firmly believed the money would be forthcoming through donations and that there would be no need to launch an appeal. The predicament was publicised to the congregation, interested individuals and *hongs*. The dean pledged to sit outside the cathedral on All Saints' Day to receive gifts.

Vigers and Man Sing representatives met at the cathedral on a Tuesday evening to pray for the project and the safety of the workers. Work began, and what had threatened during major works in times past came to pass this time. All services, including the major Sunday celebrations, were moved into the old hall. The contractors moved with what despatch was possible in matters as weighty as roofs, to return the congregation from its exile. The church was re-roofed with Spanish tiles over Japanese plywood and Malaysian hardwood. Ventilation was improved, and the opportunity was taken to improve the lighting and install new organ speakers. For months, the building was a cavern of scaffolding, dust and plastic sheeting.

The congregation repossessed it on the first Sunday of October 1981. The physical exercise had been a success. The financing had not quite matched it. In March 1982, towards the total cost of $2,962,453, some $601,000 had come from cathedral funds, members and friends had given $1,003,000, and companies had donated $1,045,900. Over $300,000 was still needed. The one physical casualty of the restoration had been some of the pews. The work being done inside the church was too sweeping to allow the furniture to sit amongst it. There was no alternative but to move it outside, where it got caught in the February rains. The thought that it might have been stored in the old hall and the congregation worship in the rains must have been dismissed.

Weather was not the only threat to the pews. The council was looking at them stormily. They were, admittedly, in bad shape by the time the restoration work was beginning. Their long-term maintenance was in question. It was not just a question of replacing the rattan seats and backing, but whether the wooden joints of the framework would give up on being further tested by time. Chairs and benches were being considered as an alternative, the best of the old seating being moved to the north transept. It looked as if St John's signature seating might be usurped. At a meeting in September 1981, Li Fook Hing came down strongly on the side of retaining the rattan. A demonstration pew had been satisfactorily restored for $2,500.

To do them all would cost $125,000. Concerns about the joints had been magnified. They would last longer than ten years. To throw away these treasures in rosewood would be wrong and expensive, he thought. The idea of replacing them is still mooted today. They are notoriously heavy, and the difficulties in moving them reduce flexibility for alternative services and performances. However, the seats are unusually generous and well aerated for pews, and the nave would be duller without their uncomplicated colonial grace. Nobody can summon up enough ruthless utilitarianism to do the deed.

The organ was replaced at this period, too. It was the sixth the cathedral had had and the fourth in forty years. You can imagine the scepticism over the usefulness of electronic organs and the nostalgia for a return to pipes. However, in June 1987, it was realised that, even if the space had still been there, the only hope for the survival of a pipe organ was to air-condition the whole cathedral. There was obvious disappointment that the Allen Digital Computer organ 623–3 from 1979 had become something of a wreck in such a short time. It had no trade-in value either, and no one could work out why twenty-seven clothes pegs were found inside it. Yet Allen still stood high in reputation, and it was to them St John's took its business again. The Coxion Fund for Organs, set up in memory of his father by Dr. Eric Tso, who had done so much towards the 1966 Thomas organ, was so endowed that only the income from it and not its bulk could be used for purchase, so the very flexible and bountiful Percy Dillon Fund was used to buy the organ.

On 20 April 1989, the installation took place of the new Allen ADC8350A digital computer with eighty-three speaking stops using draw knobs. It had seventeen speaker channels feeding thirty-six separate speakers and 1,700 watts of power. Carlo Curley, virtuoso American organist, came out specially for a 12 May inaugural concert. He was described by the *Review* as, 'outrageous, eccentric and skilful', and admission to hear him was $75. Doreen King recalls of Curley that 'he was a very large man and one could only be amazed by the deftness of his feet'.

The most evident of the alterations undertaken at this time is also the most recent change to the layout within St John's. From spring 1990 to the end of 1991, the lodge, the new hall and the old hall were renovated. In June 1988, a working group made a preliminary report on the uses and possible alterations to these three locations, including an extension to the old hall. With what one suspects was a touch of weariness, Li Fook Hing summarised three previous schemes which had the same objectives and had come to nothing. In 1974, Dean Howe had been quite enthused over a rather advanced idea to redevelop the new hall, make alterations to the old hall and even integrate the church itself into the scheme by creating a walkway into the north transept. He saw this as assisting the flow of people and theological ideas. The council saw it as a vast expense and it did not happen. Neither, as Li pointed out, did a 1975 plan to extend and create three storeys out of it for staff quarters, a verger's flat, meeting hall and even a coffee bar and patio. A subsequent idea for a new office building on the north lawn proved to be impossible, because of the $2 million that would be needed for a retaining wall along Battery Path. So, the council had to be satisfied with minor alterations in the new hall and soundproofing of the extraordinary cockloft office arrangement which the dean had been hoisted into at the east end of the new hall.

The tentative plan of 1988 found more traction if not simply because a stage had been reached in the use of space where something had to be done. It began with the remaining loyalty to the idea that clergy should be accommodated in the close, not now in the lodge but in apartments that could be tacked onto the old hall. There was a clear pastoral appeal in having a priest on the premises, and because of the skyrocketing rental market, economy figured in the reckoning. Yet it was an extravagant use of working space to deliver what would have been cramped quarters. Along the way, this item disappeared from the plans. A building committee was appointed, and $150,000 was allocated to exploratory works. In February 1990, Alan Gilbert and Associates were appointed to start the renovations.

As matters stood, all the administration was conducted from the old hall. In that cockloft were three office spaces, including one for the dean and one for the CAB. Under the cockloft was the bookstore. All this was to go. At the east end were the kitchen, the lavatories and what had been the old verger's quarters being used by the CLARES Castaways for the charity sale of second-hand items. It was very much the arrangement you will find there today. The one-storey annex next to the entrance was where the dean's office used to be before he was usurped by the general office reception area and storage needs. There are small structures, brick huts which stand near the clergy vestry and the Castaways shop. Known as the 'pillboxes', which hints at their charm, they were actually used for minor staff quarters. As one long-serving priest recalled, 'Families lived in them. Children may have been born there.'

In the new hall the Harold Smythe Room had been subdivided to give office space to the CAB and MFMW. A meeting room with storeroom was behind it. Upstairs was a large room—now the Fanny Li Hall—which doubled as a theatre with stage and a dining room with kitchen and lavatories. Halfway up the stairs was the library. The balcony overlooking the first floor room was blocked off for the counselling service. *Amahs* lived in the basement. The lodge, now the administrative centre of the cathedral, had become two largely empty floors put to casual use.

In April 1990, the council approved Alan Gilbert and Associate's plan to reorganise the space and shift functions to the purpose which you see today. Dr. Mary Board resigned from the council because they passed the plan before she had chance to see it and because she was sure that it would interfere with facilities available for the Michaelmas Fair, for which she was responsible that year. For some, the fair was a loyalty above all. The project was finished in December 1991. The lodge became the main office and the dean's office. The new hall now housed the David Kwok Conference Room and the Kenneth Tyson Library. The old hall had cleared itself. The bookstore found a permanent home in the single-storey annex. Some of the organisations which it had been hoped to house did not find space. Most notably, the CAB had to move out. This is recalled with regret by some, because the CAB was an early port of call for many newly arrived expatriates who would become acquainted with St John's thereby.

At the July Annual Church Meeting in 1992, Dean Phillips paid tribute to the immense amount of volunteer work and expertise which had been put into the project, particularly from trustee Eric Bohm and the Reverend John Chynchen, who had all but sacrificed his practice as a chartered surveyor to be on site in the cathedral. Still, Phillips thought that this degree of volunteerism was neither fair nor easy, and he stated specifically that, in future, renovation projects needed a project manager.

New and reworked spaces were given particular names, some of which fell into immediate disuse. The office in the old lodge should have been 'Church House'. No such pomposity ever fell from a lip. It has always been called 'the Office'. The new hall building is supposed to be called 'The Tebbut Wing', and it is a pity this never caught on. It was named after an official cathedral architect who was responsible for much work round the cathedral in its more recent years. At a January 1990 meeting of the council, Mrs. June Li was concerned about where money was coming from for the renovation in conjunction with the costs of the newly adopted Discovery Bay daughter church and the recent donation to the Castle Peak Church. The answer seems to have been from the Lord through Mrs. Tebbut. At that point, the architect's wife, Daisy, gave $1 million in memory of her husband.

June Li and her husband, Fook Hing, were in the forefront of private donors to St John's. In honour of this, the building that had variously been referred to as the cathedral hall or the old hall was formally named the Li Hall. This was not for any particular gift to that recent project. The Lis gave prodigiously to the Church church in many directions over the years. It is fair to say that, if they had not brought their generosity to the replacing of the roof a decade before, the congregation would long ago have been sitting amidst fallen debris in puddles of rain.

June Li's prudence over money is laudable in a great church where worshippers are forever custodians for posterity. Yet she doubtless had an instinct for where the money was coming from. It was coming from successive generations of people like her, like Daisy Tebbut, Mrs. Percy Dillon, Noel Croucher, Sir Paul Chater and M. J. D. Stephens, who originally funded most of the old hall and had hoped to remain anonymous. Giving through faith runs strongly on anonymity. Because lips were sealed and records lost or never kept, there can be no account of the dollars that ran through St John's with no name attached to them.

The May 1985 edition of the *Review* carried a letter written to the Dean, Paul Clasper, from John Foster, in which he talks about the shortcomings of the still-unreformed new hall. 'I would like to have demolished the whole block and rebuilt,' he writes. Forty years hence, his successors would still like to do that. 'We even discussed the possibility of pulling down the whole of St John's Cathedral and building a skyscraper with a cathedral on the ground floor.' His successors think rather less of that. Then Foster recalled the words of an old friend and worshipper which drew him back from the fancy: 'Tread lightly on the stones which form the floor of St John's, for beneath them lies part of my heart.'

It is difficult to evince pomp or civic ceremony in the ground floor of a skyscraper. St John's continues to stage that. Bishops have continued to be consecrated and installed as bishops, in the case of Peter Kwong in 1981 and 1999, and Paul Kwong in 2000, with the great dignities of the English Church's tradition and to the sounds of trumpets. St John's has managed to remain a civic centre of thanksgiving and memorial worship for communities beyond the Anglican and, on occasion, Christian fold. People removed from England and with only the mistiest notions of Anglican values feel comfortable gathering in recognition of some fellowship under St John's Gothic roof.

Yet there was one grand and poignant moment when St John's Cathedral was a colonial church for the very last time. The British governor, Sir Edward Youde, died of a heart attack on 5 December 1987, on a visit to Beijing to negotiate the terms of the joint agreement under which the colony would be finally and irrevocably be returned to China. A courageous and erudite man who had worked exhaustingly and with diligence and could broadcast his Christmas messages in Chinese, he established a surprisingly deep respect among Hong Kong Chinese. He was granted what is described in the United Kingdom as a royal ceremonial funeral, a rare honour, approved by the sovereign and involving a procession and full military honours. His coffin, borne on a gun carriage, was escorted by a large contingent of the British garrison and high-ranking official mourners, to a slow march, down the hill from Government House to St John's. Within the church built by the governors who began the colony, to the strains of the 'Death March' from 'Saul' and Elgar's 'Enigma Variations', the governor who arranged its end was bidden farewell.

A plaque to Edward Youde from the Hong Kong Civil Service, a little too large, perhaps, but suitably unadorned, is on the wall in the south-west corner of the nave. It was supposed to have gone somewhere further up the church, but that was judged over-prominent. After one hundred years of the saintly, sad, great and good of the empire being up there, the only memorial tablet left on the walls is to a Welsh nonconformist who gave it away. For a church that has known surprises and professes selflessness, the irony and the purity in that are perfect.

Chapter 9
Into the 'Chinese Century'

The 1954 building, the Tebbut Wing, is the most recent structural addition to St John's but far from the last word on the compound's north-west corner. To the contrary, the council discussed the site's future in 2011, and a strong possibility was that Dean Foster's wish may be granted and the whole structure razed as part of an altogether more ambitious project. From that last point of the church's alteration, as colonial authority waned in favour of irresistible Chinese sovereignty, history shunts into the back of current affairs. The cathedral may still have been the spiritual refuge for economic transients and 'short-timers', but Hong Kong has developed new generations of 'belongers'. Many who worshipped and worked at St John's twenty years ago do so still. There are still living and competing memories of events.

The handover to Chinese rule in 1997 was a smooth passage for Christian denominations in Hong Kong. The newly formed Province of the Sheng Kung Hui treats the Mainland authorities with a certain deftness and achieves cooperative results. Representatives of the State Council's Bureau of Religious Affairs attended the installation of Paul Kwong as Bishop of Hong Kong Island on 15 January 2007. They continued attendances at ceremonies involving church leaders. At the consecration of the former Dean of St John's, Andrew Chan, as a bishop on 25 March 2012, there was a pew full of Mainland officials, including members of the Central Government Liaison Office, representatives of the Bureau of Religious Affairs and the Chinese Communist Party in Beijing. Also present were sixteen guests from the China Christian Council in Shanghai and Guangdong.

The cathedral felt barely a breeze from the handover. There was the briefest of conversations over the future of the fabled freehold and whether this might have to be converted to a lease with the new government. That would have been unaffordable for the Church and probably have caused its departure from the site, which was a result no one sought. In any event, the covenant under which the land was used had so many restrictions that a change in status did not become an issue.

The Church in Hong Kong did some nation-building of its own in harmony with the handover. The anomaly created by Hong Kong's withdrawal from the Chung Hua Sheng Kung Hui in 1951 was faced up to as the end of British rule neared. The wandering Diocese of Hong Kong decided to anchor itself as a province at a synodical meeting in December 1991.

The options before it were independence or joining up with Sabah, Taiwan and Singapore in a new joint province. Interestingly, most delegates were comfortable with the *status quo*, but they were persuaded by Bishop Peter Kwong that coming political change compelled the Church to keep pace. The appeal of a union with the other dioceses was a stimulus to internationalism and grew from the sense that Hong Kong was too small to go it alone and that the diocese lacked the experience and the time to put something together for itself.

On the other hand, there was little contact with the other dioceses, and to create it and maintain it would be expensive. The dioceses did not have much in common with one another, and the Hong Kong Diocese's independence and traditions would be compromised. This faintly chauvinistic reasoning was partly a cover for a political reality. The Anglican Church in a Hong Kong newly regained by the motherland should not appear, from the point of view of secular Chinese authority, to be under instruction from outside sovereignties. That reasoning won the day. Peter Kwong was to be installed as first Archbishop of the Hong Kong Sheng Kung Hui in 1998. This was achieved in the face of a scepticism on the part of Canterbury as strong as opposition from any other quarter. After a fact-finding visit to Hong Kong, which opened the eyes of the Anglican Consultative Council to the realities on the ground, the communion's bureaucracy was won over.

George Carey, Archbishop of Canterbury, had visited Hong Kong in September 1994, on his way to China, and preached in the cathedral on missionary faith in a pluralistic world. For his pains, he attracted vigorous criticism in an editorial in the *Eastern Express*. Undeterred, he came back for the inauguration of the new province and the enthronement of Peter Kwong on All Saints' Day 1998. This was one great ceremony that St John's stood silent for. So great were the numbers expected that it was held in the Convention and Exhibition Centre in Wan Chai. The starkly multipurpose hall, built blind to senses of occasion, was decorated by ecclesiastical motifs and back-lit by *faux* stained glass windows. The impression of a Hollywood lot was redeemed by the joy over what was being achieved.

Following his retirement in January 2007, the vindicated Peter Kwong became Archbishop *Emeritus*. Peter Kwong can be regarded as the principal architect of the Hong Kong Anglican Church's survival into the Chinese century. From 1984 to 1990, as Bishop of Hong Kong and Macao, he worked tirelessly as a member of the Basic Law Drafting Committee. He did a great deal to assure Hong Kong's religious freedoms, not least by making close connections with the Religious Affairs Bureau of the State Council of the PRC. He also forged closer and more forward-looking relationships with the leaders of the Chinese Christian Three-Self Patriotic Movement and the China Christian Council, the institutional embodiment of non-Roman Christianity in the Chinese mainland. He became especially close to Bishop K. H. Ting (Ding Guangxun), the last Sheng Kung Hui Bishop in China, who was then head of both bodies.

The cathedral's part in this movement to a province was not insignificant but on the sidelines nonetheless. The meetings from 1 to 5 December 1991, which set the scene, were held in the Li Hall, a convenience which underscored the symbolism and physical centrality of St John's. According to the former Dean, Chris Phillips, 'there was a great deal of goodwill towards the Sheng Kung Hui and a real desire to be part of the diocese. There were, however, issues involved in the relationship . . . It was far easier to let the "parallel universes" continue so long as relations were amicable.'

The expressed wish on the part of the clergy and leading laypeople to come closer to the newly forming province was sincere. At the Cathedral Council meeting on 8 January 1998, members were urged to attend a scheduled talk by the bishop on the new province. At the June meeting that year, the dean spoke of the importance of attendance at council meetings in the year ahead, because of issues that would affect St John's status and its place in the province. These issues did not arise, at least not in the council.

By the September meeting, a consultation document on the province 'In Christ We Move Forward' had been issued. The English-speaking churches had what appeared to be a small role. St John's set up a discussion group including the dean, Chaplain Peter Yeats, and council members Timon Shum, Justin Ko and Cindee Lee. On 14 October 1998, the council members of all three English parishes came together to air their views to the provincial secretary, the Reverend Paul Tong. At the council 'Away day' in September the following year, Dean Phillips still lamented the little involvement that St John's was having with the new Hong Kong Island Diocese. More must be done, he said, to 'be taken seriously' and get involved with the province's five-year plan.

Archbishop *Emeritus* Peter Kong, in conversation in April 2012, recalled that secular and lay committees set up to study the future and the choice of membership was based on suitability not representation. Any perceived exclusion of the English-speaking churches was not deliberate. He pointed out that it had been the habit of history before that time for both language sides of the church in Hong Kong to overlook each other.

Through goodwill and logic there was an attempt to integrate the cathedral physically into the new province, but for much the same reasons as secular government left the freehold alone, it did not get anywhere. The question of making a change of ownership from the trustees to the province was discussed in a council proposal in October 1995. This would involve relinquishing the freehold and making a re-grant by the state which would then have involved $170,000 a year in rates. Simply handing over the freehold was not an option. A proposal that the cathedral should issue a declaration that it held the freehold for the bishop and the province was considered well meaning but not meaningful. An article by Rowan Callick on the province in the 1998 spring edition of the *Review*[1] patiently outlined the circumstances. The Hong Kong Sheng Kung Hui had separate legal status from the English-speaking churches. The Hong Kong Anglican Church had not been a part of the Church of England since 1912, whereas the English churches were firmly established under the Church of England Trust Ordinance, and all their properties were held thereunder. Fraternal gifting or even gestures were impossible outside some profound and sensitive alterations. An extraordinary meeting of the trustees in February 1997 put the cap on it. Advised by the Diocesan Chancellor, Moses Cheng, it was agreed that there should be no substantive change in method of governance and therefore no change to freehold.

The parallel churches set themselves for a slow convergence in the appointment of the first Chinese dean. After Phillips left hastily in 2003, a move attributed to ill health through stress, Stephen Sidebotham was invited to return as an interregnum dean while bishop and council wrestled with what to do with the office. The Reverend Andrew Chan Au Ming, the provincial secretary, previously a local parish priest trained at Ming Hua and Salisbury Theological Colleges, was invited to become dean. He was installed in May 2005.

The Reverend Ian Lam, who had been the first Chinese chaplain since George She, said quite plainly in the November 1978 issue of the *Review*, as he left office and went to study theology, that, 'on reflection, it is not essential to have a Chinese chaplain'. When the time came for a Chinese dean, it was certainly not for him to be a dean for the Chinese. Andrew Chan's application of himself across all of the cathedral's congregations was thorough and inspiring. His difference from his Western predecessors was in his management style, founded in faith, which led to a courageous, trusting willingness to let others develop by developing tasks for themselves.

It will take time to realise what Andrew Chan's impact really was on St John's, but it may turn out that his ethnic value was in relations between the cathedral and the province where, for once, and literally, the two could speak the same language. Chan was elected to succeed as Bishop of West Kowloon in 2012. To have a Chinese diocesan bishop who was once a dean is likely to make the cathedral and the Church in Kowloon, at the very least, more aware of each other.

'We are ever more international, ever less "colonial", ever less "Church of England",' said Dean Phillips in a report to a parish conference on 2 November 1991.[2] Andrew Chan would still have been noticing that fifteen years later, because this lessening process is a gradual one. In 1991, the Reverend Donald Reeves, Rector of St James's Piccadilly, visited and spoke about the challenges of the new decade. Inspired by him, the congregation conducted a parish survey which reported in October of that year.[3]

One of its subgroups, under Ms. Sally Stewart, surveyed the congregation over the summer months. Out of a sample of 417, 23 per cent were visitors, 26 per cent had lived in Hong Kong for three years or less and 15 per cent were complete newcomers. This was a very transient population.

Of the sample, 61 per cent had English as their mother tongue, 19 per cent claimed Tagalog and 14 per cent spoke Cantonese. Anglicans or Episcopalians made up 65 per cent, and a striking 22 per cent were Roman Catholics, Filipinas who preferred to go to St John's and probably could not see much difference anyway. Ninety-five per cent of those who walked through the door were baptised and, of those who were not, most were Cantonese. Whatever the linguistic breakdown, the ethnic Chinese who attended were not so much 'locals' as 'repatriates'. They were emigrants from the 1950s onwards who had returned from overseas and found it either more familiar to worship in English or associate with expatriates. The one regular Cantonese service was and remains the 'anticipated' Communion on Saturday evening for those whose work does not allow them to attend on Sunday. The cathedral was chosen for this because of its central location. It was never meant to be the seedbed of a separate congregation, and originally, clergy from all around the province officiated in rotation to make the point. Even so, Archbishop Peter Kwong recalls that the more regular worshippers tried hard to make it so.

If Ms. Stewart's exercise had been repeated twenty years later, changes would have been noticed in the increase in the percentage of Filipinas, a reduction in English mother tongue and the appearance of Mandarin speakers from the Mainland. Denominational allegiances would be harder to speculate about. St John's liturgy 'liberalism', and standards of preaching and music mean that the 'open altar' policy has made the cathedral an attractive haven to an eclectic gathering of Christians.

From the debate in that province forming the 1991 synod, time was taken to say that St John's should 'continue its dual role as cathedral of the diocese and parish church to the international community'. As we have seen, this duality was a concept but not a practice. St John's role as a diocesan cathedral was symbolic more than working. Now that the former diocese was to be split into three smaller dioceses and there were no plans for cathedrals in East and West Kowloon, the role of St John's as the sole cathedral and purely for Hong Kong Island was drifting into anomaly.

Archbishop Peter Kwong recalls that the suggestion that St John's might become a provincial cathedral did not get very far. Expansion into that role threatened its international identity, among the clergy as much as the laity. A counter-idea took hold for a while. The Episcopalian Diocese in Los Angeles had sold its cathedral and resolved to do without one. Nothing in canon law stipulates that a diocese has to have a cathedral. At the Annual Church Meeting of 1995,[4] the dean noted that the status of the cathedral in a new province was still unsure and that maybe the Los Angeles-style should be adopted. Phillips was clearly uncomfortable with abandoning 'the dramatic statement' of a cathedral church in the middle of a city. Under this passing tension, 'St John's Cathedral Parish' was adopted as an official description, as though in readiness for the first half of that statement to fall away.

That did not happen. In a typically Anglican resort to patient passivity, the whole issue was left alone and affairs fell into place around it. East and West Kowloon eventually got cathedrals of their own. St John's is available to its diocese—its smallest in 163 years—as a gathering place without having to be particularly mothering. It is still a dramatic statement in the centre of the city and a parish church to repatriates as much as expatriates and foreigners of all Christian stripes. This is a twenty-first century distillation of what St John's was born with. The 'international community' of 1849 was small, precise and largely British. It was the ruling colonial community, and the cathedral was governed by some of its most influential members. Today, the British do not rule. Their numbers in the international community are diminishing.

Of the laity on the 2011 council, there were six Britons. Four members were Hong Kong Chinese, three were Americans, of whom one was ethnically Japanese and another Chinese, one was a Canadian, one a Malaysian Chinese, one a Singaporean, one a Filipino and two were Indians. Occupations were too diverse to summarise. They ranged from investment analysts and teachers to a wildlife preservation director and a pest controller. The Church Body of 1928 would have failed to comprehend it or would have believed that some advanced form of French Revolution had taken place among the colonies.

Another feature of the modern cathedral which would have surprised them in the 1920s is the prevalent misconception that St John's has a lot of money. Because it has endowments, and cash flows appear to be in seven figures, it is almost dismissed as a rich church. It is a common response from secular society keen to sniff hypocrisy and convinced that no religious institution should have any money at all, without bothering to consider how that might work. Like many cathedral churches, St John's struggles to maintain a financial position from which it can operate with a modest degree of confidence. Its assets might not be wiped out at a stroke exactly, but any church which is custodian of an antique building, has a very varied and sometimes courageous scope to its ministry and relies so much on giving, then funds could well be eliminated by two wing beats from one of global finance's 'black swan events'.

Against this background, finances at St John's in the 1990s experienced what might be called 'business as usual'. Good management and good fortune rather more than compensated for mistakes, over-stretching and ill luck. Where giving to the church was concerned, the 1994 stewardship campaign came close to its $3 million target, even though three-quarters of the congregation made no pledges. In November 1995, Dr. Eric To, stalwart of St John's, gave $820,000 in memory of his wife, a sad but illuminating example of how unforeseen donations came in as significant and repeated fillip to the cathedral's fortunes. When it came to giving its money away, there was usually a majority of St John's decision-makers doing that. At the January 1995 council meeting, all the Michaelmas Fair proceeds were voted to charity, and the old argument that they should go to cathedral funds was this time defeated. Thirty per cent went to Helpers for Domestic Helpers, which some were content to interpret as 'in house', 10 per cent then went each to the St James' Settlement, China Coast Community, the House of Shalom, Bethune House, the Children's Cancer Fund, the Society for Relief of Disabled Children and Heep Hong Handicapped Children.

Then, as usual, matters could suddenly go less than well. The October 1996 meeting of the council was being told of a deficit of $673,000 and a decline in stewardship of $340,000 in the first two quarters, put down to inflation, departures and a general 'decline in participation'. Eric Bohm, treasurer and a trustee until his retirement in 2012, was minuted, interestingly, as 'threatening to balance the budget to face realities'. Bohm recalls that, apart from him, there were only four treasurers who could even for once qualify as members of the 'Surplus Club'.

At the May 1997 council, to haul matters round, the three trustees—presumably including the dean—took on the role of treasurer jointly for three months. The scene lit up a little. By January 1998, there was a reported increase of $400,000 worth of pledges over the year 1996, and the cathedral administrator, Viola Ip, had 'tightened up' the cash flow.

The On Lee apartment building in Pok Fu Lam, bought long ago with funds from the late Lady Chater, and whose shape was fought over by Croucher and Marden, had become a crucial piece in the cathedral's financial game. In the late 1980s and early 1990s, Bohm and Roger Cole, chairman of the Furnishings and Fittings Committee, had upgraded each flat as it became vacant, to maximize rental value. By 1994, On Lee rents represented 34 per cent of revenue against 31 per cent from stewardship and 16 per cent from collections. It was vital to St John's income. However, at the Annual Church Meeting of 1995, that year's stewardship campaign, forcefully led by the just-departed Chaplain and Precentor Erik Larsen, had brought pledged income just past On Lee's rental income. The annual report for the following year observed that the costs of repairs and maintenance at an ageing On Lee would make it less likely to be 'the cash cow' it once was.[5] Today, the building plays a lesser role of being helpful but not crucial to cathedral income.

Some seek neatness and purpose in mission statements, but St John's mission refuses to be defined or bounded. Its ministries grow up without much premeditation and run without regimentation. An urge to define what St John's is or should really be all about is as strong in recent years as ever. It is thwarted as ever by a rambling spontaneity. The Holy Spirit does not seem to move men and women by pattern. There is a desire to help street sleepers, then orphans at the St Christopher's Home, then a hospice at Sha Tin, the people of Wan Chai at St James', then mistreated domestic workers, then families wracked by AIDS.

The cathedral works well, as most cathedrals should, as a city church and a centre of ministry and reflection for a weekday working community. Around St John's the number of offices is huge and grows. They have dwarfed the building and long ago blocked its view of the harbour. Yet their occupants approach in their scores before the day begins, through the lunch hours and their working weekends, to seek refuge from office politics, deals going bad, fears for their job, fatigue and worries over relationships and families. St John's has not been entirely passive in this ministry. Organised meditative prayer was introduced on Monday lunchtimes in 2009. The lunchtime concerts continue. Christians in Central hold a speaker lunch in the Li Hall once a month. Once a week too, there is a lunchtime Eucharist, and every weekday at 1 p.m. a priest says prayers in the nave.

The lunchtime ministry has grown up in recent years along with the MFMW, HDH, the counselling service and HIV/AIDS education.

Eventually, Reverend Julie Leaves's involvement with AIDS Comfort Care Concern and the library on AIDS-related topics she left behind developed into a fully fledged outreach programme. In September 1994, the Pastoral Committee looked for support for the AIDS ministry and set up a working party. It seems the widespread misconceptions about contagion from meeting people with HIV/AIDS had infected some in the cathedral. Hugh Phillipson of the Pastoral Committee, at its November meeting, said that St John's should be a source of strength and solace, not ignorance, and that the congregation needed educating about AIDS. In September 1995, the HIV Drop-In Centre was set up and opened by the governor's wife, Lavender Patten, in the new hall wing. The cathedral donated $100,000, and other funding came from the AIDS Trust and the Matilda Hospital Charity. Moral support came from the Diocesan Welfare Council, and in May 1995, Elijah Fung was appointed full-time manager with a small staff and a group of volunteers. As yet, it is the only faith-based organisation to take up an AIDS ministry in Hong Kong. Its principle purpose is still the prevention and education on HIV/AIDS among women and young people in particular, and to reduce the stigma attached to the disease. The impact of the centre and the success of its methods have made it a resource for other provinces of the Anglican Communion looking to provide the same ministry.

Among the outreach ministries is ranked the Cathedral Bookshop, which, apart from doing a brisk trade in theological works, cards and candles, is a stopping place for some of the thousands a week who pass through the close from Central to the Peak Tram. It is a first point of enquiry about the cathedral, and on occasion even about the church and Christianity itself. The CLARES, begun back in 1962 by the unhappy Mrs. Till, is in high spirits, and its Castaways Shop for second-hand clothes and books thrives next door, in no apparent competition to the bookshop next door.

In 2011, the Sunday school, at over 200, has reached the levels of attendance seen in the high days of Mesdames Swann and Temple and Sidebotham. The irresistible opportunity of a morning's free English conversation leads some parents, with no particular religious belief, to set their children on a course of contact with the Christian message. One hundred sixty years ago, the parents of boys at St Paul's College, bemused perhaps but ambitious for them, did the same thing. Today, though, when the child comes to the altar rail after the school it is to receive the Sacraments and not just a blessing. St John's has embraced child Communion, in common with other parishes in the Anglican Communion.

The choir developed a rigorous excellence under the direction of Raymond Fu, music master at St Paul's, who took over from the indefatigable Cecilia Kwok. Standards have met the considerable demands of the English Church choral repertoire. No complexity is shirked. Soprano voices had been supplied by St Stephen's Girls' College for a while. Now voices are recruited from men and women across a wide spread of the congregation and its contacts, so long as they can truly sing—and maintain an uncompromising practice programme.

The diversity of the cathedral and its worship is reflected in the sprouting of choirs. The main Choir remains at its core for the Sung Eucharist and a monthly choral matins. Apart from that, there exists now an Evensong Choir, the Children's Choir and the Filipino Choir. In 2011, the Main Choir returned delightedly to the past. A less satisfactory consequence of liturgical reform was reversed. The chancel was restored to much of its pre-1968 order and floor level. The original marble flooring was revealed, and the whole space regained its classic symmetry and openness whilst keeping the west-facing altar at the steps. The choir was put back into two parts, facing each other, north and south, in a way which is traditional and, they believe, makes better music.

Vyvian Copley-Moyle, who was commended for having handled the cathedral alone for periods at a time, would have been amazed and perhaps joshingly scornful over the seven stipendiary and seven non-stipendiary clergy available to the dean at St John's in 2012. Spreading what becomes a rich collection of temperaments and talents over the cathedral's four languages and eclectic involvements is a management challenge for the second decade of the twenty-first century. There is a view that we should not really count William Baxter in 1854, because he was never properly appointed as dean. However, if you do, and the Holman T. Hunt's teak board by the west door says we should, then Canon Matthias Der, who was installed in succession to Andrew Chan in October 2012, is the twenty-third Chaplain and Dean of the Cathedral Church of St John the Evangelist.

Vincent Stanton would not have been surprised to know that he had a successor of that number. He may have been a little shocked that that the Union flag was no longer flying over him, perhaps happy that he lived within the bounds of a reformed Chinese government but sad that it was atheist. What Stanton would have envied, if such a sin was open to him, is the gushing of educational opportunity which the diocese provided and the teaching that went on in the cathedral that could bring between one and two hundred people a year—mostly Chinese—to baptism and confirmation under its roof.

He would have applauded the opportunity which this church he had helped found had grown to. That it was surrounded by materialism and unbelief would have not surprised him. That, in essence, is how it was with his beginning. He would probably have said to Dean Der that his inestimable advantage was that St John's was there and it stood strong, no matter that the landscape was venal, corrupted and sceptical.

Beneath the east window, which miraculously dulls to near silence the downhill racket of the Garden Road traffic, a thousand pray every Sunday; uncounted hundreds kneel in solitude through the week. Couples who know little about God and nothing of the future take a leap of faith. Those who now know everything about their future lie in caskets. Judges pray for their judgements. Ambulance workers give thanks for their work, and Americans give thanks for being so in November. Welshmen, Filipinas and visiting English schoolchildren sing. Vespers is sung to jazz. The sick are prayed over. Babies are baptised, national reconciliations are rejoiced over. At midnight on Christmas Eve, the people are crammed in every nook, they spill out back through the west door, and they sit in rows on the lawn watching on a screen. How the engineer in Charles St George Cleverly would have marvelled at that.

The marvels can be in the smallest things in St John's. A home group of Kerala Indian members from the St. Thomas Christian churches, led by a member of the St John's Cathedral Council, attend a service of evensong in the cathedral. Prayers are said in Malayam. Nothing of this sort could have been imagined by Chaplain Stanton or even foreseen perhaps by Dean Sidebotham.

The cathedral has moved from imperial confidence, through Edwardian complacency, reform, innovation and bouts of parochialism, to synodical unity, Chinese sovereignty and being the biggest church in the smallest province. From that 163 years of growth and shift, St John's is finding the role that makes paramount pastoral sense for it as an English-language Anglican church in a great Chinese city; that is, to be open, working and praying for all who it can touch and all who touch it.

Appendix 1
List of Chaplains, Deans and Bishops

Colonial Chaplains

John Vincent Stanton 1843–1851
Samuel Watson Steedman 1852–1853
William Baxter 1854–1855
James John Irwin 1856–1865
William Robert Beach 1867–1870
Richard Hayward Kidd 1871–1879
William Jennings 1880–1891

Cathedral Chaplains

Rowland Francis Cobbold 1892–1902
Frederick Franch Johnson 1902–1912
Vyvian Henry Copley-Moyle 1912–1927

Deans

Alfred Swann 1928–1935
John Leonard Wilson 1938–1941
Alaric Pearson Rose 1941–1952
Frederick Stephen Temple 1953–1959
Barry Dorn Till 1960–1963
John William Foster 1963–1973
Rex Alan Howe 1973–1976
Stephen Francis Sidebotham 1976–1982
Paul Clasper 1982–1986
David A. Smethurst 1987
Christopher J. Phillips 1987–2003
Stephen Francis Sidebotham 2003–2005
Andrew Chan Au-Ming 2005–2012
Matthias Clement Tze-Wo Der 2012–

Bishops

George Smith 1849–1865
Charles Richard Alford 1867–1872
John Shaw Burdon 1874–1897
Joseph Charles Hoare 1898–1906
Gerrard Heath Lander 1907–1920
Charles Ridely Duppuy 1920–1932
Ronald Owen Hall 1932–1966
John Gilbert Hindley Baker 1966–1981
Peter Kwong Kong Kit 1981–2006
Paul Kwong 2007–

Archbishops of the Hong Kong Sheng Kung Hui

Peter Kwong Kong Kit 1998–2006
Paul Kwong 2007–

Appendix 2
List of Stipendiary Assistant Chaplains and Chaplains

Frederick T. Johnson 1899–1902
A. J. Stevens 1906
A. B. Thornhill 1908–19011
H. G. H. Griffith 1915–1918
Holman T. Hunt. 1920–1922
T. B. Powell 1923–1925
H. Koop 1928–1932
N. Watkins 1929–1932
H. W. Baines 1934–1938
Alaric P. Rose 1938–1941
George She 1951–1953
Michael Goulder 1951–1952
Jimmy Froude 1954–1958
Timothy Beaumont 1955–1957
John Foster 1957–1963
Ernest Fisher 1958–1960
Frank Roe 1961–1964
Tad Evans 1962–1963
Stephen Sidebotham 1964–1969
John Yates 1963
Philip English 1965
Patrick Nichols 1968–1971
J. L. Mitman 1969–1971
John P. H. Tyrell 1972–1974
Patrick Nicholas 1973–1974
Barry Simms 1973
Hugh Stevenson 1973–1980
Ian Lam 1974–1976
Michael Corbett-Jones 1977–1980
John P. H. Tyrell 1979–1982
Eric Chong 1980–1983

Ron File 1980–1985
Peggy Sheldon 1980–1982
Michael Simpson 1982–1984
Chris Butt 1982–1989
Chris Phillips 1983–1987
Michael Phillips 1985–1988
Steven Harrop 1989–1993
Nigel Leaves 1988–1992
Julia Leaves 1988–1982
Peter Frowley 1988–1992
Erik Larsen 1990–1994
Robert Gillion 1990–1998
Dwight dela Torre 1993–
Karol Misso 1993–1994
Chris Briggs 1993–1997
Martin Hollingworth 1993–1996
Peter Yeats 1994–2000

Jan Joustra 1997–2004
Chris Tweddell 1998–2000
Susan Hewitt 1993–1997
Frank Nelson 1999–2003
John Roundhill 2002–2006
Desmond Cox 2001–
Matthew Vernon 2003–2009
Will Newman 2004–
Sharon Constable 2004–2010
Peter Koon 2006–
John Chynchen 2007–
David Pickering 2009–2012
Mark Rogers 2010–
Nigel Gibson 2010–
Catherine Graham 2012–
Robert Martin 2012–

Notes

Chapter 1   Genesis, 1841–1850

1. *Friend of China and Hong Kong Gazette*, 12 March 1847.
2. Ernest John Eitel, *Europe in China* (London: Luzac and Co.; Hong Kong: Kelly and Walsh, 1895), 246.
3. John M. Carroll, *A Concise History of Hong Kong* (Lanham, MD: Rowman and Littlefield, 2007), 12.
4. *General Correspondence of the Trustees 1841–1880*. Public Records Office (PRO), Government Records Service, Hong Kong.
5. *General Correspondence*.
6. *UK Foreign Office Summary*, December 1845.
7. *General Correspondence*.
8. *General Correspondence*.
9. Carroll, *Concise History*, 20.
10. Eitel, *Europe in China*, 242.
11. British Army Education Corps, *A History of Victoria Barracks* (Headquarters, British Forces, 1979), 26.
12. V. Copley-Moyle, 'St John's Cathedral', *The Outpost*, July (Victoria Diocesan Association, 1927), 13. Victoria Diocesan Association, based in London, was founded by Bishop Duppuy. One of its principal functions was to link the diocese in Hong Kong with former members and supporters at 'home'.
13. George B. Endacott and Dorothy E. She, *The Diocese of Victoria, Hong Kong: A Hundred Years of Church History, 1849–1949* (Hong Kong: Kelly and Walsh, 1949), 11.
14. George Smith, *Exploratory Visit to the Consular Cities of China* (London: Seeley and Burnside, 1847), 506–508, 512–513.
15. Endacott and She, *Diocese of Victoria*, 9.
16. W. Travis Hanes and Frank Sanello, *The Opium Wars: The Addiction of One Empire and the Corruption of Another* (Naperville, IL: Sourcebooks Inc., 2002), 107–113.
17. Endacott and She, *Diocese of Victoria*, 10.

18. Endacott and She, *Diocese of Victoria*, 11.
19. *Record of Episcopate of Bishop Charles Richard Alford, 1867–1872*. Public Records Office (PRO), Government Records Service, Hong Kong.
20. Endacott and She, *Diocese of Victoria*, 13.
21. *UK Foreign Office Summary*, December 1845.
22. Carl T. Smith Collection. Hong Kong Central Library.
23. Erik Kvan, *St John's: Documentary Evidence*. St John's Cathedral Records Office.

    A sequence of correspondence between September 1843 and June 1851 which involves discussion between the Hong Kong government and the Colonial Office on the design, construction and payment for the cathedral was put together by the late Reverend Erik Kvan. It was researched from Colonial Office records to aid Doreen King in the writing of her own book, *St John's Cathedral Hong Kong: A Short History and Guide*, published in 1986. She passed Father Erik's typed work, 'St John's: Documentary Evidence', to this writer. It now rests with the Cathedral Office. The correspondence referred to is to be found in Great Britain, Colonial Office: Hong Kong: Original Correspondence: CO 129 (usually referred to as 'CO 129'), 1841–1951, microfilm copies of which are deposited in the Public Records Office, Hong Kong, and the University of Hong Kong Libraries.
24. *General Correspondence*.
25. *General Correspondence*.
26. Ah is a prefix placed before names, denoting familiarity amongst family and friends, or a servant or someone of lower status.
27. Mott Connell Ltd. and Lovell Chen Pty Ltd., *St John's Cathedral Hong Kong: Conservation Management Plan Volume 1*, 2007. St John's Cathedral Trustees, Hong Kong.
28. *General Correspondence*.
29. *General Correspondence*.
30. Bonham to Grey, 19 August 1850, CRO 129.
31. Mott Connell Ltd. and Lovell Chen Pty Ltd., *Conservation Management Plan Volume 1*.
32. Doreen King, *St John's Cathedral Hong Kong: A Short History and Guide* (Hong Kong: St John's Cathedral, 1986), 22.
33. *General Correspondence*.
34. *General Correspondence*.
35. *General Correspondence*.
36. Pulpit drawings. National Archives, Kew, UK, and Public Records Office (PRO), Government Records Service, Hong Kong.

Chapter 2   Imperial Parish, 1850–1873

1. *General Correspondence.*
2. 'Original Letters Patent creating Bishop of Victoria—1849', *Record of Episcopate of Bishop George Smith 1849–1864*, 4–6. Public Records Office (PRO), Government Records Service, Hong Kong.
3. Endacott and She, *Diocese of Victoria*, 17.
4. Rowan Strong, *Anglicanism and the British Empire, c.1700–1850* (Oxford: Oxford University Press, 2007), chapter 4.
5. Endacott and She, *Diocese of Victoria*, 17.
6. *Diary of Mr. John Fortunatus Evelyn Wright, June 1849–September 1853*, 30 March 1850, 102. Public Records Office (PRO), Government Records Service, Hong Kong.
7. Endacott and She, *Diocese of Victoria*, 17.
8. *Episcopate of Bishop Alford.*
9. *Diary of J. F. E. Wright*, 31 March 1850, 102.
10. Endacott and She, *Diocese of Victoria*, 18.
11. Bowring to Russell, 29 June 1855, CO 129.
12. *Episcopate of Bishop Smith.*
13. Caine to Grey, 21 August 1854, CO 129.
14. Carl T. Smith Collection.
15. *Journal of the Royal Asiatic Society*, Vol. 36 (1904).
16. *General Correspondence.*
17. Minutes of Meetings of the Trustees and Seatholders 1858–1935. Public Records Office (PRO), Government Records Service, Hong Kong.
18. *List of Pre-war Memorial Tablets, St John's Cathedral.* Public Records Office (PRO), Government Records Service, Hong Kong.
19. Christopher Munn, *Anglo-China: Chinese People and British Rule in Hong Kong, 1841–1880* (Hong Kong: Hong Kong University Press, 2008).
20. *General Correspondence.*
21. *General Correspondence.*
22. Minutes of the Trustees and Seatholders 1858–1935.
23. Carl T. Smith Collection.
24. Minutes of the Trustees and Seatholders 1858–1935.
25. Carl T. Smith Collection.
26. *Church Notes*, August 1924. Public Records Office (PRO), Government Records Service, Hong Kong.
27. Minutes of the Trustees and Seatholders 1858–1935.
28. Minutes of the Trustees and Seatholders 1858–1935.
29. Carl T. Smith Collection.
30. Minutes of the Trustees and Seatholders 1858–1935.
31. Minutes of the Trustees and Seatholders 1858–1935.
32. Carl T. Smith Collection.

33. *Musical Times*, May 1868, Hong Kong, 391–392.
34. *Record of Episcopate of Bishop Charles Ridley Duppuy, 1920–1932.* Public Records Office (PRO), Government Records Service, Hong Kong.
35. Minutes of the Trustees and Seatholders 1858–1935.
36. Endacott and She, *Diocese of Victoria*, 31.
37. Endacott and She, *Diocese of Victoria*, 32.
38. Carl T. Smith, *Christians, Elites, Middlemen and the Church in Hong Kong* (Hong Kong: Hong Kong University Press, 2005).
39. *Episcopate of Bishop Smith.*
40. Minutes of the Trustees and Seatholders 1858–1935, June 1868 to July 1871.
41. Kennedy to Kimberley, 11 September 1872, CO 129.
42. King, *St John's Cathedral*, 20.
43. Carl T. Smith Collection.
44. Minutes of the Trustees and Seatholders 1858–1935.
45. Alastair Montieth-Hodge (former organ scholar), in discussion with the author, October 2011.
46. Minutes of the Trustees and Seatholders 1858–1935.
47. Carl T. Smith Collection.
48. Patricia Lim, *Forgotten Souls: A Social History of the Hong Kong Cemetery* (Hong Kong: Hong Kong University Press, 2011), 488.
49. Minutes of the Trustees and Seatholders 1858–1935.
50. Endacott and She, *Diocese of Victoria*, 57.
51. A. S. Abbott, *St John's Cathedral Hong Kong: A Photographic Handbook with Reminiscences and Explanatory Text* (1955). Public Records Office (PRO), Government Records Service, Hong Kong.
52. Endacott and She, *Diocese of Victoria*, 33.
53. Endacott and She, *Diocese of Victoria*, 46.
54. *Journal of the Royal Asiatic Society*, Vol. 11 (1879).
55. Bowring to Lytton, 22 August 1858, CO 129.

Chapter 3   Quiescence and Struggle, 1873–1906

1. Minutes of the Trustees and Seatholders 1858–1935.
2. Endacott and She, *Diocese of Victoria*, 59.
3. Endacott and She, *Diocese of Victoria*, 59.
4. R. F. Johnston, *Manuscript History of St John's Cathedral*, 1937. St John's Cathedral Records.
5. Endacott and She, *Diocese of Victoria*, 91.
6. *Church Notes*, 1898.
7. *Church Notes*, January 1898.
8. *Church Notes*, September 1900, 4.

9.   Endacott and She, *Diocese of Victoria*, 76.
10. Endacott and She, *Diocese of Victoria*, 79.
11. *Church Notes*, January 1898, 5.
12. King, *St John's Cathedral*, 58.
13. *Church Notes*, November 1905, 7.
14. *Church Notes*, May 1919, 4.
15. Abbott, *St John's Cathedral*.
16. David M. Paton, *R. O.: The Life and Times of Bishop Ronald Hall of Hong Kong* (Gloucester: The Diocese of Hong Kong and Macao, 1985).
17. Peter Cunich, 'Alford, Charles Richard', in *Dictionary of Hong Kong Biography*, eds. May Holdsworth and Christopher Munn (Hong Kong: Hong Kong University Press, 2012), 3–4.
18. Bishop John Burdon. Correspondence. Church Missionary Society (CMS) Archive, Baptist University Hong Kong.
19. *China Mail*, 14 December 1847.
20. Endacott and She, *Diocese of Victoria*, 49.
21. Endacott and She, *Diocese of Victoria*, 50.
22. *Record of Episcopate of Bishop John Shaw Burdon 1874–1876*. Public Records Office (PRO), Government Records Service, Hong Kong.
23. Minutes of the Trustees and Seatholders 1858–1935.
24. Bishop John Burdon. Correspondence.
25. *Episcopate of Bishop Burdon*.
26. Robin D. Gill, *A Dolphin in the Woods* (Key Biscayne, FL: Paraverse Press, 2009), 213.
27. Carl T. Smith Collection.
28. Minutes of the Trustees and Seatholders 1858–1935.
29. Endacott and She, *Diocese of Victoria*, 68.
30. Endacott and She, *Diocese of Victoria*, 69.
31. Johnston, *Manuscript History*.
32. Minutes of the Trustees and Seatholders 1858–1935.
33. *Church Notes*, February 1897, 4.
34. *Church Notes*, July 1899, 5.
35. Minutes of the Trustees and Seatholders 1858–1935.
36. Carl T. Smith Collection.
37. Johnston, *Manuscript History*.
38. Carroll, *Concise History*, 64.
39. *Church Notes*, July 1899, 5.
40. Johnston, *Manuscript History*.
41. Endacott and She, *Diocese of Victoria*, 73.
42. Endacott and She, *Diocese of Victoria*, 79.
43. *Church Notes*, November 1902, 5.
44. *Church Notes*, September 1899, 5.
45. *Church Notes*, March 1897, 3.

46. *China Mail.*
47. *Church Notes*, May 1911.
48. *Church Notes*, March 1900, 7.
49. Johnston, *Manuscript History.*
50. *Church Notes*, May 1898, 5.
51. *Church Notes*, February 1899, 6.
52. Peak Church Minute Book 1882–1958. Public Records Office (PRO), Government Records Service, Hong Kong.
53. *Episcopate of Bishop Alford.*
54. *Church Notes*, March 1902, 9.
55. *Church Notes*, April 1902, 6.
56. *Church Notes*, October 1906, 5.
57. Banister, William. 'The Anglican Communion in China', in *Twentieth Century Impressions of Hong Kong, Shanghai, and Other Treaty Ports of China: Their History, People, Commerce and Resources*, eds. Wright, Arnold and H. A. Cartwright (London: Lloyd's Greater Britain Publishing Company, 1908), 326–332.

Chapter 4   The Search for Substance, 1902–1927

1. Endacott and She, *Diocese of Victoria*, 75.
2. Endacott and She, *Diocese of Victoria*, 74.
3. *Church Notes*, March 1906, 4.
4. *Church Notes*, January 1907, 4.
5. *Church Notes*, August 1911.
6. 'Letter from the Bishop', *The Outpost*, January (1928): 3.
7. 'P. S. Cassidy on the Cathedral', *The Outpost*, July (1952): 17.
8. Endacott and She, *Diocese of Victoria*, 81.
9. 'Extracts from a Diary of a Life Member of the VDA 1906–09', *The Outpost*, July (1953): 26.
10. Liz Chater, *A Prominent Armenian from Calcutta and the Grand Old Man of Hong Kong: Sir Catchick Paul Chater: A Brief Personal Biography* (Kolkata, India: The Armenian Church, 2005), 36.
11. Endacott and She, *Diocese of Victoria*, 78.
12. *Church Notes*, June 1918, 6.
13. Endacott and She, *Diocese of Victoria*, 85.
14. Johnston, *Manuscript History.*
15. Endacott and She, *Diocese of Victoria*, 61.
16. Minutes of St John's Cathedral Church Body, 1925 Public Records Office (PRO), Hong Kong.
17. Carl T. Smith Collection.
18. James Bodell, *A Soldier's View of Empire: The Reminiscences of James Bodell, 1831–92* (London: The Bodley Head, 1982).

19. Endacott and She, *Diocese of Victoria*, 83.
20. *Church Notes*, June 1915, 4.
21. *Church Notes*, January 1922, 6.
22. Church Body Minutes, 1919–20.
23. Church Body Minutes, 1921.
24. King, *St John's Cathedral*, 55.
25. Abbott, *St John's Cathedral*.
26. 'Extracts from a Diary kept by a Life Member of the Victoria Diocesan Association when attached to H.M. Naval Yard, Hong Kong, 1906–09', *The Outpost*, July (1953): 26.
27. Endacott and She, *Diocese of Victoria*, 136.
28. *South China Morning Post*, 25 February 1920.
29. *Episcopate of Bishop Duppuy*.
30. *Episcopate of Bishop Duppuy*.
31. *South China Morning Post*, 5 November 1920.
32. *South China Morning Post*, 12 November 1920.
33. Annual Church Meeting, 1920.
34. Chater, *Sir Chater*.
35. Annual Church Meeting, 1928.
36. Steven Tsang, *A Modern History of Hong Kong* (Hong Kong: Hong Kong University Press, 2004), 94.
37. Tsang, *A Modern History of Hong Kong*, 95.
38. *Hong Kong Daily Press*, 7 February 1922.
39. W. J. Howard, 'Diocesan Boys' School. Seventy Years Ago', *Journal of the Royal Asiatic Society Hong Kong Branch*, Vol. 24 (1984).
40. *Church Notes*, March 1925, 21.
41. *Hong Kong Daily Press*, 28 November 1925: 5.
42. *Episcopate of Bishop Duppuy*.
43. *Church Notes*, June 1926, 2.
44. Minutes of the Church Body, March 1926.
45. Minutes of Meetings of the Colonial Church Council 1925–28. Public Records Office (PRO), Government Records Service, Hong Kong.
46. *Straits Times*, 14 November 1928.

Chapter 5   The Making of a Cathedral, 1927–1941

1. 'The Bishop's Letter', *The Outpost*, October (1927): 3.
2. Minutes of the Church Body, December 1927.
3. Minutes of the Church Body, January 1929. Enclosure.
4. 'Service of Institution and Installation', *The Outpost*, July (1928): 6.
5. 'The New Electorate', *St John's Review*, Vol. 1, no. 8, December (1929): 20–21.
6. *Episcopate of Bishop Duppuy*.

7. Minutes of Meetings of the Cathedral Council. Annual Church Meeting, 1931. Public Records Office (PRO), Government Records Service, Hong Kong.
8. 'Cathedral Finance', *St John's Review*, Vol. 3, no. 4, August (1931): 87–90.
9. 'Our Missionary Commitments', *St John's Review*, Vol. 4, no. 5, May (1932): 167–169.
10. 'P. S. Cassidy on the Cathedral', *The Outpost*, July (1952): 17.
11. 'The Open Door Lent: 1930', *St John's Review*, Vol. 1, no. 11, March (1930): 8–12.
12. 'The Open Door Lent: 1930', *St John's Review*, Vol. 1, no. 11, March (1930): 8–12.
13. 'Letter from the Bishop', *The Outpost*, January–March (1937): 10.
14. 'Cathedral Letter', *St John's Review*, Vol. 7, no. 6, June (1935): 219–221.
15. 'Church Announcements', *St John's Review*, Vol. 6, no. 4, April (1934): 124.
16. 'Letter from the Bishop', *The Outpost*, April (1935): 2–7.
17. 'Cathedral Notes', *St John's Review*, Vol. 9, no. 10, October (1937): 373.
18. Cathedral Council, September 1937.
19. King, *St John's Cathedral*, 25.
20. King, *St John's Cathedral*, 25.
21. King, *St John's Cathedral*, 25.
22. Cathedral Council, February 1930.
23. Correspondence file, St John's Cathedral.
24. Annual Church Meeting 1929.
25. N. V. Halward, 'Ridley Duppuy', *The Outpost*, June (1946): 15.
26. Paton, *Bishop Hall*.
27. Lindsay Lafford, *Memoir of St John's Cathedral 1935–39* (Hong Kong: St John's Cathedral Records, 2011).
28. 'Letter from the Bishop', *The Outpost*, April (1935): 3.
29. 'Letter from the Bishop', *The Outpost*, July (1937): 3.
30. 'Cathedral Letter', *St John's Review*, Vol. 10, no. 2, February (1938): 41–42.
31. Cathedral Council, March 1937.
32. 'The Dean's Letter', *St John's Review*, Vol. 11, no. 2, February (1939): 35–37.
33. 'Letter from the Bishop', *The Outpost*, July (1934): 6.
34. Annual Church Meeting, 1938.
35. Annual Church Meeting, 1938.
36. Lafford, *Memoir of St John's Cathedral 1935–39*.
37. 'Cathedral Notes', *St John's Review*, Vol. 10, no. 10, October (1938): 363.
38. Annual Church Meeting, 1939.

39. 'The Dean's Letter', *St John's Review*, Vol. 11, no. 2, February (1939): 36.

40. 'First Impressions of Hong Kong', *St John's Review*, Vol. 10, no. 10, October (1938): 364–366.

41. Correspondence file, St John's Cathedral.

42. 'Cathedral Notes', St *John's Review*, Vol. 13, no. 1, January (1941): 3.

Chapter 6   Out of Darkness, 1941–1953

1. 'Extracts of a Letter from the Reverend Charles Higgins', *The Outpost*, July–December (1942): 3–12.

2. A. F. Rose, 'Old St John's', *The Outpost*, February (1957): 35–37.

3. Lindsay Lafford, *Memoir of St John's Cathedral 1935–39* (Hong Kong: St John's Cathedral Records, 2011).

4. 'Letter from the Bishop', *The Outpost*, July (1942): 3.

5. Thomas F. Ryan, *Jesuits under Fire in the Siege of Hong Kong, 1941* (London: Burns Oates and Washbourne, 1944).

6. 'Extracts of a Letter from the Reverend Charles Higgins', *The Outpost*, July–December (1942): 3.

7. St John's Cathedral, *Annual Church Meeting Report* (1946).

8. St John's Cathedral, *The Church Review*, August (1942).

9. 'Reunion at Victory House', *The Outpost*, August (1946): 16.

10. 'Address by Dr. Harth', *The Outpost*, June (1946): 11–14.

11. A. F. Rose, 'Old St John's', *The Outpost*, February (1957): 35–37.

12. Tao Fong Shang Service Unit, 'A Retrospect of the History of Tao Fong Shan', http://www.tfssu.org/pdf/ARetrospectoftheHistoryofTaoFong Shan.pdf.

13. 'Reunion at Victory House', *The Outpost*, August (1946): 17.

14. 'Letter from the Bishop', *The Outpost*, January (1946): 2.

15. 'Letter from the Bishop', *The Outpost*, January (1946): 3.

16. 'Cathedral Service', *The Outpost*, June (1946): 8.

17. 'Report by Canon H. A. Wittenbach', *The Outpost*, January (1946): 16.

18. A. S. Abbott, written account on St John's Cathedral, 1955, Public Records Office (PRO), Hong Kong.

19. 'Old St John's', *The Outpost*, February (1957): 36.

20. Margaret Knight, 'Journal', *The Outpost*, January (1950).

21. 'Letter from the Bishop', *The Outpost*, January (1946): 3.

22. Michael Goulder, *Five Stones and a Sling: Memoirs of a Biblical Scholar* (Sheffield: Sheffield Phoenix Press, 2009).

23. 'The Bishop's Letter', *The Outpost*, January (1946): 4.

24. St John's Cathedral Council, April 1947, Finance and General Purposes Committee.

25. 'Report by the Dean', *The Outpost*, July (1950): 20.

26. 'Notes and Notices', *St John's Review*, Vol. 14, no. 8, November (1947): 195.

27. 'Searchlights', *St John's Review*, Vol. 14, no. 6, September (1947): 135–136.

28. 'Notes and Notices', *St John's Review*, Vol. 15, no. 11, November (1948): 413–414.

29. 'Notes and Notices', *St John's Review*, Vol. 15, no. 12, December (1948): 461–462.

30. King, *St John's Cathedral*, 24.

31. 'Notes and Notices', *St John's Review*, Vol. 16, no. 4, April (1949): 110.

32. 'Notes and Notices', *St John's Review*, Vol. 16, no. 2, February (1949): 42–43.

33. Correspondence file, St John's Cathedral records.

34. Lafford, *Memoir of St John's*.

35. Cathedral Council, January 1950.

36. 'Notes and Notices', *St John's Review*, Vol. 16, no. 6, June (1949): 183.

37. 'The Dean's Letter', *St John's Review*, Vol. 24, no. 2, February (1957): 19.

38. 'Notes and Notices', *St John's Review*, Vol. 16, no. 2, February (1949): 40–41.

39. 'Michaelmas Fair', *St John's Review*, Vol. 18, no. 11, November (1951): 349–352.

40. Cathedral Council, January and February 1952.

41. Cathedral Council, May 1950, Finance and General Purposes Committee.

42. 'P. S. Cassidy on the Cathedral', *The Outpost*, July (1952): 16.

Chapter 7   Shedding Colonialism, 1953–1976

1. Paton, *Bishop Hall*.

2. 'The Dean's Letter', *St John's Review*, Vol. 21, no. 2, February (1954): 21.

3. Cathedral Council, 1956.

4. Aston-Mansfield, 'A Brief History of Aston Mansfield', http://www.aston-mansfield.org.uk.

5. Cathedral Council, May 1960.

6. Annual Church Meeting, 1963.

7. King, *St John's Cathedral*, 57.

8. King, *St John's Cathedral*, 38.

9. 'The Dean's Letter', *St John's Review*, Vol. 24, no. 2, February (1957): 19.

10. Annual Church Meeting, 1954.

11. Cathedral Council, November 1960.

12. Vaudine England, *The Quest of Noel Croucher: Hong Kong's Quiet Philanthropist* (Hong Kong: Hong Kong University Press, 1988).
13. 'Cathedral Farewell Tea Party and Presentation', *St John's Review*, Vol. 26, no. 7, July (1959): 200–205.
14. 'Editorial', *St John's Review*, Vol. 29, no. 5, May (1962): 89.
15. King, *St John's Cathedral*, 34.
16. 'Editorial', *St John's Review*, Vol. 29, no. 3, March (1962): 41.
17. 'Editorial', *St John's Review*, Vol. 29, no. 4, April (1962): 62–63.
18. Cathedral Council, November 1961.
19. 'Editorial', *St John's Review*, Vol. 29, no. 4, April (1962): 62–63.
20. 'The Cathedral CLARE', *St John's Review*, Vol. 29, no. 11, November (1962): 253–254.
21. Correspondence file, St John's Cathedral.
22. Correspondence file, St John's Cathedral.
23. Cathedral Council, June 1963.
24. *St John's Review*, April 1962.
25. Goulder, *Five Stones and a Sling*.
26. 'Church in the Front Line', *The Outpost*, October (1963): 21.
27. Stephen Sidebotham, 'Celebrated Women', http://www.womenandthe-church.org.
28. Annual Church Meeting, 1968.
29. Cathedral Council, May 1969.
30. King, *St John's Cathedral*, 28.
31. Correspondence file, St John's Cathedral.
32. Cathedral Council, October 1974.
33. *Daily Telegraph*, 4 February 2000.
34. 'Bishop's Letter', *The Outpost*, April (1975): 1.
35. Paton, *Bishop Hall*.

Chapter 8   Towards an International Church, 1976–1992

1. 'Around the Cathedral: Reminiscences', *St John's Review*, Vol. 44, no. 3, April (1977): 3.
2. 'St John's Children Help Kidney Patients', *St John's Review*, Vol. 66, no. 1, January (1979).
3. Annual Church Meeting, 1979.
4. 'The Dean's Letter', *St John's Review*, Vol. 44, no. 7, August (1977): 2.
5. Annual Church Meeting, 1981.
6. 'China Coast Community', *St John's Review*, Vol. 45, no. 11, November (1978).
7. St John's Cathedral Council Minutes of Pastoral Committee, October 1981. St John's Cathedral Office.
8. 'The Dean's Letter', *St John's Review*, Vol. 67, no. 11, November (1980).

9. 'The Dean's Letter', *St John's Review*, Vol. 44, no. 4, May (1977).
10. 'The Dean's Letter', *St John's Review*, Vol. 59, no. 4, April (1991).
11. 'Stanley Congregation', *St John's Review*, Vol. 45, no. 1, January (1979).
12. Cathedral Council, April 1981.
13. Cathedral Council, April 1982.
14. Cathedral Council, November 1984.
15. Cathedral Council, October 1986.
16. Cathedral Council, May 1991.
17. Cathedral Council, June 1987.
18. Cathedral Council, February 1984.
19. Cathedral Council, January 1988.
20. Annual Church Meeting, 1982.
21. Cathedral Council, April 1993.
22. Cathedral Council, April 1980.
23. Cathedral Council, April 1993.
24. Cathedral Council, February 1988.
25. 'Letter to the Dean', *St John's Review*, Vol. 52, no. 5, May (1985): 9.
26. Annual Church Meeting, 1990.
27. Cathedral Council, January 1984.
28. Cathedral Council, January 1984.
29. Cathedral Council, October 1985.
30. Correspondence file, St John's Cathedral.
31. Correspondence file, St John's Cathedral.

Chapter 9   Into the 'Chinese Century'

1. *St John's Review*, Vol. 60, no. 6, Spring (1998): 14.
2. 'A Report to the Parish Conference', *St John's Review*, Vol. 59, no. 11, November (1991): 5.
3. Cathedral Council, October 1991.
4. *St John's Review*, Vol. 60, no. 3, June (1995): 5.
5. *St John's Review*, Vol. 64, no. 4, June (1996): 5.

Bibliography

Primary Sources

Abbott, A. S. *St John's Cathedral Hong Kong: A Photographic Handbook with Reminiscences and Explanatory Text*. Hong Kong: Public Records Office (PRO), Government Records Service, 1955.

Carl T. Smith Collection. Central Library, Hong Kong.

Church Missionary Society (CMS) Archive. Baptist University Library, Hong Kong.

Colonial Church Council 1925–28. Public Records Office (PRO), Hong Kong.

CO 129 (1842–1951) Great Britain. Colonial Office Records. The University of Hong Kong University Libraries.

Johnston, R. F. *Manuscript History of St John's Cathedral*. St John's Cathedral Records, 1937.

Kvan, Erik Rev. St John's. Documentary Evidence. St John's Cathedral Records, 1986.

Lafford, Lindsay. *Memoir of St John's Cathedral 1935–39*. Hong Kong: St John's Cathedral Records, 2011.

Mott Connell Ltd./Lovell Chen Pty. Ltd. *St John's Cathedral Hong Kong: Conservation Management Plan Volume 1*. St John's Cathedral Trustees. Hong Kong, 2007.

Peak Church Minute Book 1882–1958. Public Records Office (PRO), Hong Kong.

Pre-war Memorial Tablets, St John's Cathedral. Public Records Office (PRO), Hong Kong.

Record of the Episcopate of Bishop George Smith, 1849–1864. Public Records Office (PRO), Hong Kong.

Record of the Episcopate of Bishop Charles Richard Alford, 1867–1872. Public Records Office (PRO), Hong Kong.

Record of the Episcopate of Bishop John Shaw Burdon, 1874–1876. Public Records Office (PRO), Hong Kong.

Record of the Episcopate of Bishop Charles Ridley Duppuy, 1920–1932. Public Records Office (PRO), Hong Kong.

St John's Cathedral. *Church Notes, 1897–1928.* Public Records Office (PRO), Hong Kong.

St John's Cathedral. *General Correspondence of the Trustees, 1841–1880.* Public Records Office (PRO), Hong Kong.

St John's Cathedral. Minutes of the Church Body, 1892–1930. Public Records Office (PRO), Hong Kong.

St John's Cathedral. Minutes of the Meetings of the Trustees and Seatholders, 1858–1935. Public Records Office (PRO), Hong Kong.

St John's Review, 1928–. St John's Cathedral Library.

Wright, J. F. E. *Diary, 1849–1853.* Public Records Office (PRO), Hong Kong.

Published Sources

Bodell, James. *A Soldier's View of Empire: The Reminiscences of James Bodell, 1831–92.* London: The Bodley Head, 1982.

British Army Education Corps. *A History of Victoria Barracks.* Headquarters, British Forces, 1979.

Carroll, John M. *A Concise History of Hong Kong.* Lanham, MD: Rowan and Littlefield, 2007.

Chater, Liz. *A Prominent Armenian from Calcutta and the Grand Old Man of Hong Kong: Sir Catchick Paul Chater: A Brief Personal Biography.* Kolkata, India: The Armenian Church, 2005.

China Mail, 1845–1870. Hong Kong.

Colonial Church Council, 1925–1928. Public Records Office (PRO), Hong Kong.

Cunich, Peter. 'Alford, Charles Richard', in *Dictionary of Hong Kong Biography,* edited by May Holdsworth and Christopher Munn, 3–4. Hong Kong: Hong Kong University Press, 2012.

Eitel, Ernest John. *Europe in China.* London: Luzac and Co.; Hong Kong: Kelly and Walsh, 1895.

Endacott, George B. and Dorothy E. She. *The Diocese of Victoria, Hong Kong: A Hundred Years of Church History, 1849–1949.* Hong Kong: Kelly and Walsh, 1949.

England, Vaudine. *The Quest of Noel Croucher: Hong Kong's Quiet Philanthropist.* Hong Kong: Hong Kong University Press, 1988.

Friend of China newspaper, 1842–1961. Hong Kong.

Gill, Robin D. *A Dolphin in the Woods.* Key Biscayne, FL: Paraverse Press, 2009.

Goulder, Michael. *Five Stones and a Sling: Memoirs of a Biblical Scholar.* Sheffield: Sheffield Phoenix Press, 2009.

Hanes, W. Travis and Frank Sanello. *The Opium Wars: The Addiction of One Empire and the Corruption of Another*. Naperville, IL: Sourcebooks Inc., 2002.

Hong Kong Register newspaper, 1843–1858. Hong Kong.

Howard W. J. Diocesan Boys' School: Seventy Years Ago. *Journal of the Royal Asiatic Society*, Vol. 24, 1984.

Journal of the Royal Asiatic Society, Hong Kong.

King, Doreen. *St John's Cathedral Hong Kong: A Short History and Guide*. Hong Kong: St John's Cathedral, 1986.

Legge, J. L. Rev. Lecture delivered November 1872, Colony of Hong Kong. *China Review*, Vol. III, 1874.

Lim, Patricia. *Forgotten Souls: A Social History of the Hong Kong Cemetery*. Hong Kong: Hong Kong University Press, 2011.

Munn, Christopher. *Anglo-China: Chinese People and British Rule in Hong Kong, 1841–1880*. Hong Kong: Hong Kong University Press, 2008.

The Outpost. Magazine of the Victoria Diocesan Association.

Paton, David M. *R. O.: The Life and Times of Bishop Ronald Hall of Hong Kong*. Gloucester: The Diocese of Hong Kong and Macao, 1985.

Ryan, Thomas F. *Jesuits under Fire in the Siege of Hong Kong, 1941*. London: Burns Oates and Washbourne, 1944.

Smith, Carl T. *Christians, Elites, Middlemen, and the Church in Hong Kong*. Hong Kong: Hong Kong University Press, 2005.

Smith, George. *Exploratory Visit to the Consular Cities of China*. London: Seeley and Burnside, 1847.

Snow, P. *The Fall of Hong Kong*. New Haven, CT: Yale University Press, 2004.

South China Morning Post (SCMP). Hong Kong.

Straits Times newspaper. Singapore.

Strong, Rowan. *Anglicanism and the British Empire, c.1700–1850*. Oxford: Oxford University Press, 2007.

Tsang, Steven. *A Modern History of Hong Kong*. Hong Kong: Hong Kong University Press, 2004.

Vines, Stephen. *The Story of St John's Cathedral*. Hong Kong: FormAsia Books, 2001.

Index

Where a subject entry comprises a number, for example '59th Regiment of Foot', it is placed in the alphabetical sequence as if it were written, viz: 'Fifty-ninth Regiment of Foot'. References to subject matter in captions to the photographs are given as 'Fig. 1' or, if more than one, 'Figs. 3, 18'. These are placed at the end of the sequence of page references.